FAITH ...

PHILOSOPHICAL ENQUIRIES

Series Editors:
Laurence Paul Hemming and Susan Frank Parsons

Contemplating Aquinas

Inspired by the challenge to consider anew the relation of faith and reason that has been posed by the papal Encyclical Letter of 1998 *Fides et ratio*, this series is dedicated to paying generous heed to the questions that lie within its scope. The series will comprise monographs by a wide range of international and ecumenical authors, edited collections, and translations of significant texts, with appeal both to an academic community and broadly to all those on whom the apologetic task impinges. The studies it encompasses are informed by desire for the mutual engagement of the disciplines of theology and philosophy in the problematic areas of current debate at the highest and most serious level of scholarship. These may serve to illuminate the foundations of faith in the contemporary cultural context and will thus constitute an ecumenical renewal of the work of philosophical theology. This series is promoted by the Society of St Catherine of Siena, in the spirit of its commitment to the renewal of the intellectual apostolate in the Catholic Church. http://www.caterinati.org.uk/

PUBLISHED

Restoring Faith in Reason

A new translation of the Encyclical Letter *Faith and Reason*
of Pope John Paul II together with a commentary and discussion
Laurence P. Hemming and Susan F. Parsons (editors)

FORTHCOMING

Devaluing God: Postmodernity's Overcoming
Laurence Paul Hemming

Contemplating Aquinas

On the Varieties of Interpretation

Edited by
Fergus Kerr OP

scm press

© The Editors 2003

British Library Cataloguing in Publication data

A catalogue record for this book is available
from the British Library

Because of the late withdrawal of a chapter by a
contributor, the main text starts on p. 27. *Series editors*

.

0 334 029922 8

First published in 2003 by SCM Press
9–17 St Albans Place, London N1 0NX

www.scm-canterburypress.co.uk
SCM Press is a division of
SCM-Canterbury Press Ltd

Printed and bound in Great Britain by
Biddles Ltd, www.biddles.co.uk

Contents

Contents

Contributors

David B. Burrell CSC is Theodore Hesburgh Professor in Philosophy and Theology at the University of Notre Dame. He is author of *Knowing the unknowable God: Ibn-Sina, Maimonides, Aquinas* (University of Notre Dame Press, 1986); *Freedom and Creation in the Abrahamic Traditions* (Georgetown University Press, 1995) and *Aquinas: God and Action* (University of Notre Dame Press, 1979).

Laurence Paul Hemming is Dean of Research Students at Heythrop College, University of London, a series editor of *Faith in Reason: Philosophical Enquiries* and author of *Radical Orthodoxy? A Catholic Enquiry* (Ashgate, 2000) and *Heidegger's Atheism* (Notre Dame University Press, 2002).

Mark D. Jordan is Asa Griggs Candler Professor of Religion at Emory University, Atlanta, and author of *Ad Litteram: Authoritative Texts and their Medieval Readers* (ed., with Kent Emery, University of Notre Dame Press, 1992); *The Alleged Aristotelianism of Thomas Aquinas* (Toronto, Pontifical Institute of Mediaeval Studies, 1992) and *Ordering Wisdom: The Hierarchy of Philosophical Discourses in Aquinas* (University of Notre Dame Press, 1986) as well as a number of other texts in medieval and contemporary theology, especially gender issues.

Fergus Kerr OP is Regent of Blackfriars, Oxford, and an honorary fellow of the Divinity Faculty of Edinburgh University. He is editor of *New Blackfriars*, and author of *Immortal Longings: Versions of Transcending Humanity* (University of Notre Dame Press, 1997); *Theology After Wittgenstein* (SPCK, 1997 [1986]) and *After Aquinas* (Blackwell, 2002).

Robert C. Miner is Assistant Professor of Philosophy at Baylor University, Texas, and is author of *Vico, Genealogist of Modernity* (University of Notre Dame Press, 2002).

Fran O'Rourke lectures in Philosophy at University College Dublin. He is author of *At the Heart of the Real* (Irish Academic Press, 1992) and *Pseudo-Dionysius and the Metaphysics of Aquinas* (Brill, 1992).

Susan F. Parsons is Fellow of the Margaret Beaufort Institute of Theology, University of Cambridge. She is a series editor of Faith in Reason: Philosophical Enquiries, author of *Feminism and Christian Ethics* (Cambridge, 1996) and *The Ethics of Gender* (Blackwell, 2002), editor of *Challenging Women's Orthodoxies in the Context of Faith* (Ashgate, 2000) and *The Cambridge Companion to Feminist Theology* (Cambridge University Press, 2002), and co-editor of *Restoring Faith in Reason* (SCM Press / University of Notre Dame Press, 2002).

Otto-Hermann Pesch is Professor Emeritus for Systematic Theology at the Evangelische Fakultät der Theologie of the University of Hamburg. He is the first Roman Catholic theologian in the Federal Republic of Germany to be a member of an evangelical-theological faculty. He is author of *Theologie der Rechtfertigung bei Martin Luther und Thomas von Aquin. Versuch eines systematischen-theologischen Dialogs* (Matthias Grünewald Verlag, 1985 [1967]); *Das Gesetz*, Aquinas *Gesammelte Werke*, vol. 13 (Graz, 1977); *Thomas von Aquin: Grenze und Grösse mittelalterlicher Theologie: Eine Einführung* (Matthias Grünewald Verlag 1995 [1988]) and *Christian Existence According to St Thomas Aquinas* (Toronto, Pontifical Institute of Mediaeval Studies, 1989).

Philip L. Reynolds is Associate Professor of Catholic Theology at the Candler School of Theology, Emory University, and author of *Food and the Body: Some Peculiar Questions in High Medieval Theology* (Brill, 2000) and *Marriage in the Western Church: The Christianization of Marriage During the Patristic and Early Medieval Periods* (Brill, 1994).

Herwi M. Rikhof is Professor in Systematic Theology at the Katholieke Theologische Universiteit te Utrecht and Director of the Thomas Instituut. He is author of *The Concept of Church: A Methodological Inquiry into the Use of Metaphors in Ecclesiology* (Sheed & Ward, 1981) and *Over God spreken: Een tekst van Thomas van Aquino uit de Summa Theologiae I, Q. 13* (Delft, 1988).

Rudi A. te Velde is a Professor of Theology at the Vrije Universiteit, Amsterdam, and author of *Participation and Substantiality in Thomas Aquinas* (Brill, 1995).

Preface

Recent years have seen the expansion of studies and contemporary readings of St Thomas Aquinas in what has been a lively renewal of scholarship amongst theologians and philosophers alike. Following the significant work of Étienne Gilson and the *nouvelle théologie*, and given further impetus by the widespread assessment of modernity that occupies all of the academic disciplines today, the study of Aquinas has become both a fruitful and a challenging undertaking. Typically much of this scholarship has been conducted by specialists whose own groundbreaking work in the interpretation of Aquinas is evidence that the way into this study demands the highest level of intellectual attention. That this study gives occasion for self-questioning of the assumptions of an age, and so affords the possibility for thinking anew the fundamental matters of faith and of reason, is one of its more disturbing promises. Something of this spirit characterises the work gathered into this collection.

The essays brought together here are indication of the great variety of approaches to Aquinas's thought that are being taken up primarily within the Anglophone world. Arising from a one-day conference in June 2001 under the same title, the collection is intended to provide an introduction and a way of access to this range of approaches for a general and scholarly readership. The reader will find here some widely differing and often starkly contrasting interpretations of Aquinas, which are not pressed into some coherent overall frame of reference, nor given a broad historical background against which they should be viewed. Rather it is expected that the reader will discover in each chapter an invitation to go deeper into the scholarship from which it emerges and so find for themselves a way into the reading of Aquinas.

Grateful acknowledgement is given to the Thomas Instituut te Utrecht for permission to reprint the text of 'Thomas Aquinas and Contemporary Theology' by Otto Hermann Pesch, translated from the German by Colin Berry, and originally published in 2002.[1] The other contributions have been prepared specifically for the conference and this volume.

---

[1] P. Van Geest and H. Goris, *Aquinas as Authority* (Utrecht: Thomas Instituut and Leuven: Peeters, 2002).

Thanks are due to Fr John McDade SJ, Principal of Heythrop College, and to the Society of St Catherine of Siena for co-sponsoring and organising the conference at the College; to Laurence Paul Hemming and Susan Parsons for their help in the editing of this collection; and especially to all of the authors whose new work undertaken here will be a significant contribution to the furtherance of Aquinas scholarship.

Fergus Kerr OP
Palm Sunday
13 April 2003

Abbreviations

The following abbreviations are used in the footnotes to refer to the works of St Thomas Aquinas:

CT	*Compendium Theologiae* (1269–73)
DSS	*De substantiis separatis* (1271–3)
In DDN	*Expositio super Dionysium De divinis Nominibus*
In Job	*Expositio super Job* (1261–4)
In BDT	*Expositio super librum Boethii De trinitate* (1258–9)
In DA	*Sententia super De anima*
In Joh	*Lectura super evangelium Johannis* (1269–72)
In LDC	*Expositio super librum De causis* (1271–2)
In Sent	*Scriptum super libros Sententiarum* (1252–6)
QDM	*Quaestiones disputatae de malo* (1266–7)
QDP	*Quaestiones disputatae de potentia* (1265–6)
QDSC	*Quaestiones disputatae de spiritualibus creaturis* (1267–8)
QDV	*Quaestiones disputatae de veritate* (1256–9)
QQ	*Quaestiones quodlibetales* (1256–9)
SCG	*Summa contra Gentiles* (1259–64)
ST	*Summa Theologiae* (1266–73)

The Varieties of Interpreting Aquinas

FERGUS KERR OP

Reception of Thomas Aquinas's work has been contentious from the beginning: as one recent study observes, 'There has never been one Thomism'.[1] In contrast, Alasdair MacIntyre asks whether there are just 'too many Thomisms?'[2]

One way of dealing with Thomas is to ignore him completely. The University of Oxford has one of the great faculties of theology in the Anglo-American world: a faculty from which one could graduate with a degree in theology without knowing anything of Aquinas. This ignorance might be better than the selective and partial version of Aquinas to which students would otherwise most likely be exposed. In the standard introductory courses in the philosophy of religion, for example, students will often hear of the Five Ways, taught as an early variety of natural theology. Again, until recently, if, for instance, in the University of Oxford one were to choose the paper on the history and theology of the Western Church from 1050 to 1350 (an option seldom taken), one would be expected to study 'on the theological side', issues of Aquinas's doctrine 'above all on transubstantiation and natural law', followed by 'Scotus's voluntarism as a reaction to Aquinas on intellect and will'. Third, in another optional paper, again seldom taken, one would work on Thomas, rather than on one of the other eight major theologians on offer from Origen to Tillich, but, as a glance at past examination papers would confirm, the questions would permit candidates to focus entirely on the Thomas whose work is interesting principally because of theistic proofs and natural law: his significance as a theologian could have been ignored.

Why is this interpretation of Thomas so prevalent? Is it because theology at Oxford is predominantly Anglican, and therefore sympathetic towards the use of reason in natural theology and Christian ethics? Or is it rather because theology in Oxford is affected by the presence of one of

---

[1] Thomas F. O'Meara, *Thomas Aquinas: Theologian* (London: University of Notre Dame Press, 1997), p. 155.

[2] Alasdair MacIntyre, *Three Rival Versions of Moral Enquiry* (London: Duckworth, 1990), p. 58.

the strongest philosophy faculties in the world, interested in philosophy of religion, if at all, then only from the perspective of the quality of the logical arguments in which it can engage?

Perhaps there are answers here. Anglican theologians are, anyway, famously sceptical about systematic theology – and so sceptical about the very idea of a theological system – and Aquinas's theology has long been widely supposed to be, if nothing else, then certainly a 'system'. Where did this idea come from? The assumption that Aquinas's theology is a system, articulated in terms of Aristotle's metaphysics of being, and laying emphasis on theistic proofs and the natural law basis of ethics, has been taken for granted in British universities and mirrors the variety of Thomism that has been propagated in Catholic circles since the 1870s. This view is exemplified in many of the textbooks of 'philosophia aristotelico-thomistica', from the late nineteenth century right into the 1960s: it was this version of Thomism that was wanted in the Catholic Church as a defence against 'modern thought', by which was meant Descartes, Kant, the German idealists, the British empiricists, the French positivists and the whole panoply of nineteenth-century philosophical positions. To this must be added the fact that Anglo-American philosophers, at least until very recently, have been suspicious of anything that smacked of 'metaphysics'. Here again, Thomas Aquinas has been widely assumed to be a (or indeed the) 'philosopher of being'. This does not commend itself to the most sympathetic interpreter of Aquinas in Oxford, Anthony Kenny, who concludes a chapter on 'Being' in these words:

> The theory of the real distinction between essence and existence, and the thesis that God is self-subsistent being, are often presented as the most profound and original contributions made by Aquinas to philosophy. If the argument of the last few pages has been correct, even the most sympathetic treatment of these doctrines cannot wholly succeed in acquitting them of the charge of sophistry and illusion.[3]

The divine simplicity and God as *ipsum esse subsistens* is reduced to being called 'sophistry and illusion'! Where Anglo-American philosophy got its contempt for philosophies of 'being' from would be a long story in the telling. Specifically, when one reads Kenny (who has done more than anyone to keep Aquinas on the Oxford philosophical agenda), it appears that what he most deeply dislikes is the interpretation of Aquinas, not so much in the seminary textbooks of Aristotelico-Thomistic philosophy nor in transcendental Thomism, but especially in the work of Étienne

---

[3] Anthony Kenny, *Aquinas* (Oxford: Oxford University Press, 1980), p. 80.

Gilson and Jacques Maritain – respectively 'the metaphysics of Exodus', and 'the degrees of being'.

Too many Thomisms? If the understanding of Aquinas still current in British universities is the mirror image of the Thomism of the Catholic seminary textbooks since the 1890s (such authors as Louis Billot, Josef Gredt, Thomas Maria Zigliara and so on),[4] this was already challenged in Catholic circles in the 1920s by what would come to be called Transcendental Thomism (Joseph Maréchal, Pierre Rousselot, Johannes Lotz, Karl Rahner, Bernard Lonergan); the work of Gilson and Maritain; and several different 'schools', such as the Dominicans of Le Saulchoir (Antonin Sertillanges, Ambroise Gardeil, Marie-Dominique Chenu); the Dominicans at Toulouse (Michel Labourdette, the brothers Nicolas) and at Louvain (Désiré Mercier, Fernand van Steenberghen) and many others.

Many years ago, Henri de Lubac argued that Thomas is not only notable for the 'robust but a little static mass of his synthesis' – a phrase that encapsulates the then standard view – but equally notable as 'a transitional writer': indeed, 'the ambivalence of his thought in unstable equilibrium, ransom of its very richness, explains how it could afterwards be interpreted in such opposed senses'.[5] The 'ambiguity of Thomism', as he goes on to call it, which concerns de Lubac, bears on a quite specific question: how to interpret what Thomas meant by 'natural desire for God', and how to assess the validity and significance of the many conflicting understandings of what he meant. In retrospect, the controversy set off by de Lubac did more than anything else to reveal how deeply readers of Thomas could differ. The controversy spilled over into accusations and counter accusations, indeed to professors being dismissed from teaching, in the light of Pope Pius XII's Encyclical Letter *Humani generis*.[6] The Pope's admonitions about not subverting Catholic doctrine by playing down the sheer gratuitousness of salvation were thought by many at the time, rightly or wrongly, to be inspired by Réginald Garrigou-Lagrange and others, defending the interpretation (standard since Thomas de Vio Cajetan and other Dominican comment-

---

[4] Cf. Louis Billot, *De Deo Uno et Trino: Commentarius in primam partem S. Thomae* (Rome, 1893); Josef Gredt, *Elementa Philosophiae Aristotelico-Thomisticae* (Freiburg im Breisgau: Herder, 1909); T. M. Zigliara, *Propaedeutica ad Sacram Theologiam in usum Scholarum seu Tractatus de Ordine Supernaturali* (Rome: Polyglot Press, 1903).

[5] Henri De Lubac, *Surnaturel: études historiques* (Paris: Aubier, 1946), pp. 435–6. 'la masse robuste mais un peu statique de sa synthèse . . . un auteur de transition . . . l'ambivalence de sa pensée en équilibre instable, rançon de sa richesse même, explique qu'on ait pu dans la suite l'interpréter en des senses si opposés'.

[6] Pius XII, Encyclical Letter *Humani generis*, in *Acta Apostolicae Sedis* 42 (Rome, 1950), pp. 561–79.

ators) according to which – for Aquinas – nature and grace were quite separate realities, with their distinctive teleologies, against de Lubac's supposed naturalisation of the order of grace by supernaturalising the order of nature. In fact Teilhard de Chardin, the Jesuit and friend of de Lubac, was more likely to have been the target.

The repercussions of the quarrel over the relation between nature and grace were never much heard or discussed outside specifically Catholic circles. It was here, however, where the ground began to shift, when it became unavoidable to choose between the Aquinas who inaugurates theistic proofs and the tradition of foundationalist apologetics that runs on into our own day, and the Aquinas who inherits, synthesises and transmits the patristic tradition of Augustine and Pseudo-Dionysius, and the legacy of Christian Hellenism.

We owe a great deal to pioneering studies by great scholars like Martin Grabmann and Franz Ehrle, as well as Gilson and many others. In the last sixty years, however, research on Thomas's sources, and on his interaction with his contemporaries, as well as a much wider familiarity with the whole range of his writings, has transformed our understanding of his work. The very idea of conceiving of his work as a 'system' rests on the assumption that the *Summa Theologiae* is all that matters. Nowadays we are more likely to speak of Thomas's theological vision or of his perspective, or to say that he made certain 'options' – rather than claiming that he left anything in his wake that is as rounded and coherent as a system. Readers who regard the *Summa* as a system, we might suspect, unwittingly allow themselves to be unduly impressed by the surface of relentless progress through objections, response, solutions to objections, and the like, instead of following the references to Scripture and patristic authorities that characterise the whole structure of Thomas's discussions.

Ironically, as the Thomism of the Roman universities and most Catholic seminaries lost its privileged status in the 1960s, the volume of research has expanded, exponentially it seems. Serge-Thomas Bonino speaks of a 'hermeneutic conflict, more or less hidden', in recent interpretations of Thomas's work: medievalists, philosophers and theologians focus on aspects of his work that give rise to somewhat divergent readings; a 'truly Thomist approach', he argues, ought to be 'catholic' (small c, of course, its being French), 'integrating these diverse approaches'.[7]

Whether or not the Dominicans at Toulouse – of whom Bonino is perhaps a representative voice – are anywhere near achieving or even envisaging the possibility of any such integration of approaches, we

---

[7] Serge-Thomas Bonino OP, 'Thomistica', *Revue thomiste* 97 (1997), pp. 563–603, p. 563.

surely have to say that in Britain we have yet to become fully aware of the diversity of approaches, and even fully to understand that there is a hermeneutic conflict.

The picture of Aquinas as of interest principally because of his episte-mology, theistic proofs, natural law ethics, and so forth, gains a great deal of its authority from a certain grand-narrative which is widely believed amongst English-speaking theologians. By considering the unity of the divine nature before considering God as revealed in three Persons, as happens in the *Summa Theologiae*, Thomas obscures the specifically Christian God and even initiates the way to Enlightenment deism and eventually to modern atheism, or so the story goes. For examples of this argument, see T. F. Torrance, Eberhard Jüngel, Colin Gunton, Catherine Mowry LaCugna, and countless others in widely read books.[8]

It is a story that can make an appeal to august authority: 'In Catholic dogmatics, which follow St Thomas, the life of God was identified with the notion of pure being'.[9] In other words, 'the idea of God was not determined by the doctrine of the Trinity, but . . . shaped by a general conception of God (that of ancient Stoicism and Neo-Platonism)'.[10] Thus Karl Barth has argued, as long ago as 1940, representing a view still widely assumed to be correct.

This account, generally taken for granted by Reformed theologians, has also gathered distinguished Roman Catholic support: you don't have to be Barthian to regard Aquinas's God as non-Christian; the Catholics themselves admit it! For example: 'According to Karl Rahner, the first decisive move in the isolation and subsequent sterilisation of the doctrine of the Trinity was the separation of the discussion of "the one God" from the discussion of "the triune God".' Indeed (as I believe has been said before), the deleterious effects of this separation have been classically illustrated in Karl Rahner.

These days, Hans urs von Balthasar rises higher than Rahner in the Roman Catholic theological galaxy. Much less frequently cited in this regard, for whatever reason, he too once claimed that Thomas has a defective doctrine of God. Bizarrely enough, he charges Karl Barth as

---

[8] Thomas F. Torrance, *The Christian Doctrine of God: One Being Three Persons* (Edinburgh: T&T Clark, 1996), pp. 9–10; Eberhard Jüngel, *God as the Mystery of the World: On the Foundation of the Theology of the Crucified One in the Dispute between Theism and Atheism* (Edinburgh: T&T Clark, 1983), p. 145; Colin Gunton, *The One, the Three and the Many: God, Creation and the Culture of Modernity* (Cambridge: Cambridge University Press, 1993), pp. 138–42; Catherine Mowry LaCugna, *God for Us: The Trinity and Christian Life* (New York: HarperCollins, 1991), pp. 145–50.

[9] Karl Barth, *Church Dogmatics*, II/1, trans. T. F. Torrance and G. W. Bromiley (Edinburgh: T&T Clark, 1957), p. 329.

[10] Barth, *Church Dogmatics*, II/1, p. 329.

well as Thomas Aquinas with favouring discussion of the one God, creation, conservation and providence, and especially ethics and eschatology, at the expense of the doctrines of the Trinity, Christology and the Church.[11]

Much as with his teacher and friend Henri de Lubac, Thomas is admitted by von Balthasar to be a 'transitional figure': 'Whoever does not realise how Thomas was open both to the past and to the future will misunderstand his position in the history of human thought.'[12] Yet, if de Lubac encouraged us to read Thomas as the inheritor of the patristic conception of natural desire for God, von Balthasar (here at least) preferred us to read Thomas more in terms of what was to come. The notion that philosophy and theology should divide and go their separate ways is the 'authentic spirit of Thomism'. In the event, the three treatises that did not interest Aquinas – God as Trinity (here Thomas demonstrates his excellent formal training but the doctrine has no shaping influence on the project of the *Summa Theologiae*), the doctrine of the nature of Christ (carefully done but with no influence on all that precedes), and the doctrine of the Church (simply absent from treatment or discussion) – are, von Balthasar contends, precisely what Christian theology is about. In other words, for von Balthasar here, Thomas's options already opened him to the modern account in terms of theistic proofs, natural law, and so forth. Von Balthasar's discussion of Thomas's options turns on the argument that Thomas's predominantly philosophical methodology prevents him from doing Christian theology properly. Von Balthasar reminds us above all else that, for Thomas, theology does not deal with singularities: the very particular historical events – these are to be interpreted as mere examples. So, in the end, von Balthasar chooses Barth over Aquinas, precisely because Barth's methodology means theology practised as a knowledge and science of singular events.[13]

Considered more widely, the story runs that Western Latin Catholic scholastic medieval rationalist philosophical Aristotelian essentialism (to categorise endlessly) is opposed to the properly biblical Christian Trinitarianism of the East, and of (especially Greek) Orthodox patristic theology – a story deriving from a misreading of the survey of Trinitarian doctrine conducted by the French Jesuit Théodore de Régnon, in the 1890s.[14] Michel René Barnes has started to break the grip that this myth has held on Anglo-American theology, though the news has not

---

[11] Cf. Hans urs von Balthasar, *The Theology of Karl Barth: Exposition and Interpretation* (San Francisco, CA: Ignatius Press, 1992), pp. 263–6.

[12] von Balthasar, *The Theology of Karl Barth,* p. 262.

[13] von Balthasar, *The Theology of Karl Barth,* p. 266.

[14] Théodore de Régnon, *Études de Théologie positive sur la Sainte Trinité* (Paris, 1892).

yet spread far into university course books and suchlike, so far as I can see.[15]

Thus, the standard British account of Thomas is backed by Barthian suspicions of the role of 'being', but also by Catholic claims such as are offered by Rahner and Balthasar, about there being in Thomas's work a defective doctrine of the Trinity; and, behind this, de Régnon's story supposedly setting a philosophically inspired essentialism against a biblical-patristic Trinitarianism. All of this is allowed to add up, confirming the inadequacy of Aquinas's contribution as a specifically Christian theologian. The result is that, with these various narratives in play, you cannot but approach Thomas as an exponent of natural theology and a philosopher.

An account like this may very well have a strong appeal to those who wish to defend Aquinas, as we will find with Norman Kretzmann. Those who dislike it may employ the story as a way of discounting Thomas, as Protestant theologians usually do; but it would be possible to take a different line altogether – interpreting Thomas, even in the *Summa Theologiae*, as starting not from God understood as Father (Rahner is surely right about that, albeit he thinks this a defect), nor simply from the God of the ancient philosophers either (certainly not from the God to whose existence modern apologetics might reason by means of theistic proofs). Rather, so this account might argue, Thomas has a phased or layered conception of the One God: that is to say, God as source and goal of the world, *principium et finis*, the God of whom the pre-Christian philosophers – 'wisdom-lovers' – had knowledge; second, that God understood as the Lord whom the people of the Law were commanded to obey; and third, the very same God as Trinity, of whom knowledge has been communicated by Christ to the Apostles and thus to Christian believers.

On this reading, one which would need to be supported by argumentation and quotations from his biblical commentaries, Thomas would not be a precursor of modern natural theology but more like a theologian engaging with diverse religious traditions: the already religious wisdom-loving of ancient pagan philosophers; the Law revealed on Mount Sinai to Moses and the Israelites; and the fulfilment of both in the revelation by Jesus of the Triune God in the Christian dispensation. This is to accept a certain reading of the philosophy of ancient Greece, as itself already religious and indeed theological.

Such a reading is also dependent on accepting a certain reading of Holy Scripture. In particular, when Aquinas cites Scripture he cites the Vulgate. This, in turn, means that Thomas's theology is rooted, not in the

---

[15] Michel R. Barnes, *The Power of God : Dunamis in Gregory of Nyssa's Trinitarian Theology* (Washington, DC: Catholic University of America Press, 1999); 'De Régnon Reconsidered', *Augustinian Studies* 26 (1995), pp. 51–79.

Hebrew scriptures, but in the Septuagint of which Jerome's Vulgate was a translation. If there is any understanding of God accessible solely in virtue of the originally Hebrew books of the Bible, it has to be said that, for Thomas, it would already be decisively modified by the Greek books (not in any way 'apocrypha' or supplemental for him) and by the Septuagint translation.

In short, centuries before Thomas Aquinas, Jewish philosophers such as Philo of Alexandria could envisage God as the metaphysical first principle of the universe, perfectly simple, unchangeable, and with many of the attributes of the Greek philosophical understanding of the divine. Thomas's One God may be approached, that is to say, not as the first step towards presenting God as 'the God of the philosophers', oblivious to Scripture; but as a significant moment in the long tradition of considering the God of the Septuagint in the light of a Platonising ontology that dates back at least to Philo and receives a strong Christianising influence in the person of Philoponus.[16]

If it is possible to read Aquinas like this, in addition we now also want to read Thomas in the more immediate context of his interaction with his Jewish and Muslim predecessors. In his recent work, for example, David Burrell shows how Thomas fashioned his doctrine of God and his doctrine of creation by drawing on the work of Ibn Sina and Rabbi Moses ben Maimon.[17]

It cannot be said that this work has yet percolated into the standard teaching and writing of the philosophy of religion. But what this interpretation demonstrates is that whatever others may feel free to do, the scholarly work of interpreting Aquinas should not be focused on some generic notion of deity. What Burrell questions is the point of ever attempting to treat of God whilst prescinding from the specific religious tradition in which the understanding of God arises. He prefers to acknowledge that human beings' primary relations with the divine occur in specific historical settings and that the major religious traditions have developed sophisticated ways of articulating and criticising their theologies. In this recent work, Burrell retraces the immense effort of conceptual clarification in the three traditions, Judaism, Christianity and Islam, particularly as it comes together in the Middle Ages. He offers 'the medieval crucible of exchange' as 'an object lesson for our understanding of the matter in hand', rather than simply as an historical inquiry on its

---

[16] Especially in his commentaries on the works of Aristotle and against the interpretations of Proclus. Cf. esp. the translation by C. Wildberg of Philoponus's *Against Aristotle: On The Eternity Of The World* (Ithaca, NY: Cornell University Press, 1987).

[17] Cf. David Burrell CSC, *Freedom and Creation in Three Traditions* (Notre Dame, IN: University of Notre Dame Press, 1993).

own. It would be misleading to say that he offers a distinctively new (or for that matter reheated) version of 'Thomism'.

On the other hand, Burrell clearly believes that the distinctions made by Thomas, as he learns from his great non-Christian precursors, come much closer to the truth about the matters in hand than a good deal of modern theology has been able to achieve. By exploring the 'interfaith' perspectives operative in thirteenth-century philosophical theology, Burrell certainly challenges the standard account of Aquinas as the precursor of post-Enlightenment apologetics.

A different, much more recent and successful approach is surveyed by Roger Pouivet under the heading of what he labels 'Wittgensteinian Thomism'. This was inaugurated by close friends of Wittgenstein in his last years: Elizabeth Anscombe, in her work *Intention*, can be seen demythologising modern notions of will,[18] and Peter Geach, in *Mental Acts*,[19] drawing more openly on Aquinas, and quite bluntly contemptuous of 'decadent Scholasticism' and the work of 'many of [Thomas's] professed followers', doing the same for notions of mental states.

Anscombe's pupil, Anthony Kenny, who had already studied philosophy at the Gregorian University, attended her classes on Wittgenstein in Oxford between1957 and 1958. He – 'like many others' – came to Wittgenstein's *Investigations* regarding the attack on the very idea of a private language 'with incomprehension mixed with hostility'.[20] He goes on to say:

> The seminar completely changed the way in which I looked at issues in philosophy of language and philosophy of mind: various lines of thought which until that time I had found seductive, and which many others still follow enthusiastically, lost all their attraction and were revealed as blind alleys and dead ends.[21]

Thus, in their approach to Aquinas, it was assumed that there were – are – two major issues: first, the 'Cartesian' conception of the self, involving privileged access by means of introspection of our interiority; and second, if we are to have knowledge, the need to posit intervening entities of some kind, sense data or whatever, that stand between our minds and the objects that exist in 'the external world'.

---

[18] G. E. M. Anscombe, *Intention* (Oxford: Basil Blackwell, 1957).

[19] Peter Geach, *Mental Acts: Their Contents and Objects*, Studies in Philosophical Psychology (London: Routledge & Kegan Paul, 1957).

[20] Anthony Kenny, 'The First Person', in C. Diamond and J. Teichman (eds.), *Intention and Intentionality: Essays in Honour of G. E. M. Anscombe* (Brighton: The Harvester Press, 1979), p. 3.

[21] Kenny, 'The First Person', p. 3.

In contrast, Aquinas thinks of the objects in the world as becoming intelligible through actualising our intellectual capacities – there is nothing intervening between the mind and the world ('intellectus in actu est intelligibile in actu').[22] This is a central plank in what John Haldane has recently labelled Analytical Thomism.[23] While it would be exaggeration to claim that this use of Aquinas is transforming current debates in analytical philosophy about the relationship between mind and world, there is a significant appeal to Aristotle which now often also includes reference to Thomas.

'We need to stand firm on the idea', John McDowell says, 'that the structure of elements that constitutes a thought, and the structure of elements that constitutes something that is the case, can be the very same thing',[24] a claim, as John Haldane says, that comes 'as close as makes no substantial difference to the old orthodoxy of Thomist metaphysical realism'.[25]

So, this way of engaging with the work of Thomas Aquinas is to explore (1) his non-Cartesian approach to self-knowledge and (2) his mind/world identity view of knowledge as possible ways of recovering from what are perceived as still deeply entrenched and widely influential modern philosophical myths about the self and about our cognitive situation in the world.

In Wittgensteinian Thomism (from about 1957 onwards) and Analytical Thomism (from about 1994) Thomas has been appealed to as a source of good philosophy. Not, therefore, as the source of the theism, natural theology, and so forth, that allegedly distorts and subverts Christian doctrine (as Barth, Rahner and others suggest), but as a resource in identifying, exposing, and overcoming Cartesian and empiri-

---

[22] Cf. *In II Sent*, Ds. 17, Q. 1, art. 1, resp. ad 4; *SCG*, Bk 1, Ch. 46, N. 3; *ST* Ia, Q. 12, art. 9, obj. 1 *et passim*.

[23] For a discussion of Analytical Thomism see *New Blackfriars* 80 (1999), *Thomism and the Future of Catholic Philosophy*, pp. 157–216, with bibliography. See also the recent collection by John Haldane, *Mind, Metaphysics, and Value in the Thomistic and Analytic Traditions* (Notre Dame, IN: University of Notre Dame Press, 2002).

[24] John McDowell, *Mind and World* (Cambridge, MA: Harvard University Press, 1994), p. 27.

[25] John Haldane, 'A Return to Form in the Philosophy of Mind', in D. S. Oderberg (ed.), *Forms and Matter: Themes in Contemporary Metaphysics* (Oxford: Blackwell, 1999), pp. 40–64; 'On Coming Home to (Metaphysical) Realism', *Philosophy* 71 (1996), pp. 287–96, here p. 293; cf. also John Haldane's wonderful essay 'The Life of Signs', *The Review of Metaphysics* 47 (1994), pp. 451–70, where (among much else, and perhaps mischievously) he compares McDowell's Wittgensteinian view of the mind's place in reality with the view attributed to Meister Eckhart: intellect as 'a deprivation of being – always ready to be filled by one thing or another and to be wholly informed by the nature of its object so long as this is present' (p. 462).

cist presuppositions about self and world that continue to drive much thinking – presuppositions (we might naughtily suggest) that are not too difficult to find at work in much modern Christian theology.

On the other hand, we need not write off natural theology. On the contrary, one of the major achievements in recent Anglo-American philosophical theology is the reading of Thomas's *Summa contra Gentiles* that is offered by Norman Kretzmann, in a set of lectures at the University of Oxford.[26] He argues that, in the *Summa contra Gentiles*, we have not just a monumental achievement of medieval philosophy, but a vast thought experiment that should be studied on its own, for itself (and so independently of the *Summa Theologiae*); but also a great work of philosophy that offers the best available natural theology in existence.

Kretzmann holds that, prescinding from appeals to divine revelation as evidence and justification, it remains possible, desirable, indeed inescapable, for a philosopher, with the appropriate skills and interest, to investigate by means of analysis and argument, the question of the existence and nature of God and the relation of everything else to God considered as reality's first principle. Not all, or even many, philosophers in the analytical tradition are likely to turn their attention to these issues; but, for Kretzmann and the 'school' he has built up round his work at Cornell University, there is nothing marginal, second-rate, out of date or vaguely shameful about dedicating philosophical energy and textual scholarship to the study of medieval philosophy and specifically of the work of Thomas Aquinas.[27]

From a theological point of view, given the pervasive 'Barthian' suspicions of natural theology, it is even more interesting that, for Kretzmann, there is nothing misguided or misleadingly inadequate about reasoning about God: on the contrary, it is now, as it was before the birth of Christianity, and quite independently of personal religious allegiances, a worthwhile and enjoyable intellectual endeavour. Interestingly, it is with Thomas's *Summa contra Gentiles* that Kretzmann was primarily concerned. Beginning in 1983 when he taught a graduate seminar at Cornell based on this text, he continued to work on it and to inspire a generation

---

26 See Norman Kretzmann, *The Metaphysics of Theism: Aquinas's Natural Theology in Summa Contra Gentiles I* (Oxford: Clarendon Press, 1997); and *The Metaphysics of Creation: Aquinas's Natural Theology in Summa Contra Gentiles II* (Oxford: Clarendon Press, 2001).

27 Something of Kretzmann's influence may be measured in the festschrift published in his honour, and entitled *Aquinas's Moral Theory: Essays in Honor of Norman Kretzmann*, ed. S. MacDonald and E. Stump (Ithaca, NY: Cornell University Press, 1999). This includes contributions by the editors and by Anthony Kenny, Gareth B. Matthews, Mark D. Jordan, Peter King, John Boler, E. Jennifer Ashworth, Jan A. Aertsen and Paul Vincent Spade.

of younger students to consider central philosophical topics in the light
of how they were treated in the Middle Ages.

If this is not extraordinary in itself, consider the remarkable revival
of interest in 'virtue ethics', increasingly engaging with Thomas. Here
again, the key intervention was Anscombe's famous attack in 1958 on
modern moral philosophy.[28] To summarise briefly, in the days when
philosophers were split between the attractions of utilitarianism (conse-
quentialism as Anscombe renamed it) and Kantian deontology (in the
form of R. M. Hare's prescriptivism), Anscombe dismissed the former as
barely worthy of being called moral philosophy at all, and concentrated
on exposing the latter as continuing surreptitiously to feed off biblical
theism. Her argument was that now that belief in divine law has
been abandoned, the deontological interest in such notions as duty, obligation, and the like had become senseless. She claimed that while
Protestants at the time of the Reformation did not deny the existence of
divine law, their most characteristic doctrine was that the law was given
by God, not to be obeyed, but to show sinful humankind's incapacity to
obey it, even by grace; this applied particularly to the requirements of
'natural law'. Anscombe's proposal, in this ground-breaking essay (much
cited since) was that the best course was to abandon any further attempt
to make sense of duty or obligation, and to return instead to Plato and
Aristotle. Should we do this, we would then find that 'philosophically
there is a huge gap, at present unfillable as far as we are concerned' – a
gap which needs to be filled, she contended, by 'an account of human
nature, human action, the type of characteristic a virtue is, and above all
of human "flourishing"'.[29]

While not explicitly mentioning Thomas Aquinas, Anscombe's
provocative sally signalled the return to Aristotle (rather than Plato, as it
turned out) and the massive expansion of interest in 'virtue ethics', particularly since the work of Alasdair MacIntyre. As he recognised, her
essay was the catalyst.[30]

Another preconception that colours interpretations of Aquinas has to
do with 'classical theism' and the impossible impassibility of God. When
Thomas identifies God as *ipsum esse subsistens*, 'being itself',[31] the
word 'being', for many people, connotes something static, empty, inert,
virtually dead. Barth, for example, says that if God is *actus purus sine*

[28] G. E. M. Anscombe, 'Modern Moral Philosophy', *Philosophy* 33 (1958),
pp. 1–18, and reprinted in *Collected Philosophical Papers III: Ethics, Religion and
Politics* (Minneapolis, MI: University of Minnesota Press, 1981), pp. 26–42.
[29] Anscombe, 'Modern Moral Philosophy', in *Collected Philosophical Papers III*,
p. 41.
[30] Alasdair MacIntyre, *After Virtue* (London: Duckworth, 1981), cf. esp. p. 51.
[31] Cf. *In I Sent*, Ds. 23, Q. 1, art. 1, resp. ad 4 *et passim*; *SCG*, Bk 3, Ch. 19, N. 3
et passim; *ST* Ia, Q. 4, art. 2, resp. *et passim*.

potentialitate,[32] that means God lacks all capacity for change, life, development; whereas we need God to be dynamic, and so understood as becoming, or being in process. To speak of God as the 'unmoved mover', students often suppose (incredible as this may seem), is to say that God never moves. Even worse, to say that God is impassible is to say that God doesn't suffer, and is thus incapable of love. To say, as Thomas does, that, while creatures are really related to God yet God has no real relationship with creatures, appears to have the effect of rendering God as something aloof and incapable of relationships, a being that is entirely self-sufficient.

Over against all this, we have Tom Weinandy's splendid book, *Does God suffer?*[33] For a vast number of modern theologians the patristic and medieval tradition of divine impassibility is regarded as utterly unacceptable, in the light of the immense record of suffering of the twentieth century. Think only of Jürgen Moltmann's statement: 'The doctrine of the essential impassibility of the divine nature now seems finally to be disappearing from the Christian doctrine of God.'[34] Once the doctrines of divine immutability and impassibility have been jettisoned, it is no wonder that the only way to read Aquinas is as unbiblical and unchristian, or as offering only the Aristotelian or Parmenidean God.

There is much else I could mention to illustrate the breadth and contradictions in the current plurality of readings of Aquinas; in particular the effect on reading Thomas of certain readings, and misreadings, of the Heideggerian story about the 'forgetting of being' (with its ambiguous objective and subjective genitive), *Seinsvergessenheit*. Here we can find some readers conceding that Thomas is yet one more instance of ontotheology, while others contend that Thomas is the unique exception, the one who got away from the Heideggerian history of being.[35]

But to understand this debate fully would require us to make a crossing of the English Channel into the European discussion which has hardly even begun to touch Anglo-American concerns, and would be to begin to explore many other varieties of understanding Thomas than

---

[32] Pure act without any potentiality. Cf. Aquinas's definition of God in *CT*, Bk 1, Ch. 11: 'deus est actus purus absque alicuius potentialitatis permixtione'.

[33] Thomas Weinandy OFM Cap., *Does God Suffer?* (Edinburgh: T & T Clark, 1999).

[34] Jürgen Moltmann, *History and the Triune God: Contributions to Trinitarian Theology*, trans. J. Bowden (London: SCM Press, 1991), p. xvi. Originally published as *In der Geschichte des dreieinigen Gottes: Beiträge zur trinitarischen Theologie* (Munich: Christian Kaiser Verlag, 1991).

[35] See in this regard the contrast between Jean-Luc Marion, *Dieu sans l'être* (Paris: Presses Universitaire de France, 1981) [ET: *God Without Being*, trans. Thomas A. Carlson (Chicago, IL: Chicago University Press, 1991)] and John Caputo, *Heidegger and Aquinas: An Essay on Overcoming Metaphysics* (New York: Fordham University Press, 1982), and the contribution by Laurence Paul Hemming in this volume.

those which have achieved even limited respectability in the United Kingdom or North America. The purpose of this collection of essays is to disclose something of the range of current interpretations – rival, conflicting, even incommensurable – the very many ways of contemplating Aquinas.

The *Summa*'s Reform of Moral Teaching – and Its Failures

MARK D. JORDAN

According to one census, there were 662 commentaries on the *Summa Theologiae* or its Parts by 1923.[1] They ranged from the restrained to the loquacious or even chatty, from the once influential to the ever desolate. Looking back to the census now, we can see that it omits many other commentaries, especially from the late European Middle Ages and from early modern Latin America. Then there are the commentators of the last 75 years. With only the most sober additions, we could now bring the total count well above a thousand.

Recent readers of Thomas's *Summa* occupy various positions with respect to this great mass of commentary. Most simply ignore it – indeed, they quite literally know nothing of it. Others engage some part of it. A few have lost themselves in it. Some of the best-known recent readers have taken the safer way of gesturing towards the commentaries as a grand 'Thomistic tradition' without ever moving too close in.[2]

My plan in this essay is not to categorise these readers' positions – much less to praise a fantastical tradition. I want instead to take the count of commentaries as a reminder that Thomas's *Summa* has from its

---

[1] Anton Michelitsch, *Kommentatoren zur Summa theologiae des hl. Thomas von Aquin*, Thomistenschriften 2.1 (Graz and Vienna: Styria, 1924).

[2] In saying this, I am not sure whether or not I disagree with Alasdair MacIntyre in *Three Rival Versions of Moral Inquiry: Encyclopaedia, Genealogy, and Tradition* (Notre Dame, IN: University of Notre Dame Press, 1990). On the one hand, MacIntyre will write that Thomas's texts were misread almost from the beginning (p. 135) or that the papal announcement of neo-Thomism could only 'lead in a variety of alternative and conflicting directions' (p. 73). On the other hand, he will speak of 'the tradition which Aquinas reconstituted' as the only site for accurate readings of the *Summa* (p. 135) and regularly uses the analogy with craft to argue for a continuous 'tradition' of Thomism (pp. 65, 128, and so on). MacIntyre nowhere identifies the historical community which has carried this tradition of Thomism, unless it is the 'historical scholars of the [modern] Thomistic movement', identified as 'Grabmann, Mandonnet, Gilson, Van Steenberghen, Weisheipl' (p. 77). The list is unhelpful, because the authors named have neither any strong institutional connections nor any deep agreement about the theological or philosophical implications of the historical reading of Thomas.

composition been in the play of institutional readings – that is, of institutional purposes. I will argue that these purposes mostly run counter to the *Summa*'s own project of curricular and community reform.[3] The failures in the *Summa*'s institutional reception help us as recent readers to see what Thomas wrote and how we still fail of reading it well.

The essay comes in three parts. In the first, I tell a suggestive story about what Thomas tried to accomplish in writing the *Summa* for his Dominican brothers. The story begins tentatively from historical circumstance, but ends more surely with textual comparisons. In the second part, I argue from a variety of genres that Thomas's accomplishment was missed or rejected by the medieval Dominicans. Then, third, I suggest that something analogous to the medieval fate of the *Summa* is replayed in many recent readings – though for contrary reasons. The three parts together may seem an odd mix of exegesis, institutional history and readerly self-examination. I intend precisely that odd mix – and I will try to show its necessity as I reach the conclusion.

The project in the *Summa*

What can be discovered about the origin of Thomas Aquinas's *Summa of Theology* suggests, as convincingly as circumstances ever can, that the book was a masterful improvisation in the face of very Dominican circumstances for the teaching of Christian theology. In June 1259, at the age of 34 or 35, Thomas left Paris to attend the general chapter meeting at Valenciennes, where he served as a member of a commission working on the promotion of studies within the order. In the months after that chapter meeting, and perhaps in response to it, Thomas returned to his ecclesiastical home, the 'Roman' or Italian province of the Dominican order.[4] He had behind him a brilliant if occasionally controversial career as a student and regent master of theology in the University of Paris, but his work in Italy would be within the houses of his order and not at a uni-

---

[3] When I speak of the 'project' or 'intention' of the *Summa*, I am personifying structural and rhetorical features of the text. These features will soon be described less metaphorically both by comparison with contemporary texts and by speculating about peculiarities in the *Summa*'s reception. When I speak of 'Thomas', I mean the author whose own 'intentions' can be reconstructed only through structures in the texts. What we think we know about Thomas's biography can sometimes suggest that we look at neglected textual structures, but it can never replace or overrule the reading of those structures.

[4] See the summary chronology in Jean-Pierre Torrell, *Initiation à saint Thomas d'Aquin* (Fribourg: Éditions universitaires Fribourg; Paris: Éditions du Cerf, 1993), p. 480. There are controversies over the exact date of Thomas's departure from Paris and his exact whereabouts in the surrounding months (Torrell, *Initiation*, pp. 145–8).

versity. After some five or six years of such service, in September 1265, Thomas was assigned to open a house of studies for Dominicans in Rome – perhaps as a result of his own lobbying.[5] There was no university in the city and no previous academic establishment for the order. Indeed, the new venture may have been the province's attempt to create a middle step between its conventual schools and the order's international *studia*. The Roman school looks to have been the first attempt anywhere for an intermediate Dominican school of theology. It was entirely centred on the theologian Thomas as *lector* or teacher. The way was open for his pedagogical invention. What he invented was a reform of Dominican theological education.

The prevailing theology curriculum in Dominican houses relied on Scripture and books of scriptural history, of course, but also on collections of texts for sacramental doctrine, manuals of the moral life, and some reference works of canon law and the Church Fathers. Thomas seems to have had other plans at Rome from the start. During his first year, he tried revising his earlier, Parisian commentary on the *Sentences* of Peter Lombard. He began not with the fourth Book, often used by Dominicans for teaching on the sacraments, but with the first Book, with its doctrine on God as unity and trinity. After revising and supplementing parts of the first Book, Thomas set the project aside.[6] He turned instead to what we call the *Summa*,[7] which begins much as the Lombard's *Sentences* does, but goes on to a more rigorously ordered consideration of the whole of theology. In short, the evidence we have from Thomas's writing at Rome suggests that his main effort was directed at expanding the pastoral and practical curriculum of Dominican houses by placing it within the frame of the whole of theology. The frame is the *Summa*. It is a frame meant to reform the Dominican tendency to separate moral manuals from theological or scriptural treatises.

To view the *Summa* as Thomas's remedy for a defect of Dominican education in no way reduces it. Thomas had a habit of conceiving

---

[5] See Leonard E. Boyle, *The Setting of the Summa Theologiae of Saint Thomas*, Etienne Gilson Series 5 (Toronto: Pontifical Institute of Mediaeval Studies, 1982), pp. 9–12; Torrell, *Initiation*, pp. 207–11; M. Michèle Mulchahey, *'First the Bow is Bent in Study . . .': Dominican Education before 1350* (Toronto: Pontifical Institute of Mediaeval Studies, 1998), pp. 278–306.

[6] Leonard Boyle, 'Alia lectura fratris Thome', *Mediaeval Studies* 45 (1983), pp. 418–29. Boyle's essay reconsiders and supplements the evidence adduced in H.-F. Dondaine, '"Alia lectura fratris Thome"? (Super I Sent.)', *Mediaeval Studies* 42 (1980), pp. 308–36. See also the recapitulation and sample of questions in Mulchahey, *'First the Bow'*, pp. 281–7.

[7] It is important to remember that this most familiar title may well not be Thomas's own. See the variety of early testimonies in Angelus Walz, 'De genuino titulo Summae theologiae', *Angelicum* 18 (1941), pp. 142–51. Nothing can be deduced about Thomas's work from speculations as to what a *summa* is supposed to be.

occasions for writing in the widest terms. The two best examples come from the period immediately before his assignment to Rome. Thomas was asked by the Pope to provide an expert opinion on the allegedly patristic citations in a compendium pertinent to negotiations between the Latin and Greek churches.[8] Thomas replied to the commission in the *Contra errores Graecorum* with a careful reflection on the presuppositions of theological exegesis under controversy. There is also a legend that Thomas wrote the so-called *Summa contra Gentiles* in response to a request by Raymond of Peñafort for a missionary's manual. If the legend is more than pious fiction, and I doubt that it is, then Thomas translated the request into a mandate for an exemplary ascent through wisdom to revelation. So if Thomas answered in Rome the needs of his Dominican students or the posting of his provincial chapter, that does not mean that he gave them what they expected – or that the work he wrote has no wider usefulness.

There are other complications in my story. I have so far interchanged Thomas's writing with Thomas's teaching. They need to be distinguished. In saying that the *Summa* was the centrepiece of Thomas's effort to counteract the neglect of studies often lamented by his provincial chapter, I do not mean to suggest that it was the script or the record of what Thomas actually taught in the Roman *studium*. It has been objected that if Thomas taught through the first 40-odd questions of the *Summa*, he would have covered much of the same ground during his second year that he had already covered in 'reading' the first book of the *Sentences*.[9] But there are other issues here, more interesting ones. What exactly would it mean to say that Thomas taught a text like the first Part of the *Summa* to his students in Rome, whether *in toto* or from Question 45 on? We cannot really imagine him conducting each article before the students as a separate *disputatio*. Thomas did conduct a number of disputes at Rome.[10] They look like his other disputed questions – and unlike the articles of the *Summa*, which are much simpler and more tightly connected. The *Summa*'s articles form part of a structure promised in its main lines from the beginning – and not in the terms used to justify the stringing together of disputed questions.

If Thomas did not dispute the articles of the first Part of the *Summa* at Rome, how might he have taught them? Do we imagine Thomas writing

---

[8] The anthology was Nicholas of Cotrone's *Libellus de fide ss. Trinitatis*. For Thomas's response to it, see Mark Jordan, 'Theological Exegesis and Aquinas's Treatise "against the Greeks"', *Church History* 56 (1987), pp. 445–56.

[9] Torrell, *Initiation*, pp. 233–4; compare Mulchahey, *'First the Bow'*, p. 294.

[10] Mulchahey, *'First the Bow'*, p. 303, provides a summary of her own conjectures about the debates. Everyone would agree at least to the disputation of the 83 articles *De potentia Dei*.

out sections and then reading them aloud? Or do we imagine Thomas giving an oral summary that was copied down by his assistants and then redacted into finished form? Absent direct archival or anecdotal evidence, we must reason from the texts. The articles of the *Summa* are unlike not only the questions Thomas disputed at Rome, but also both the notes of the Roman 'reading' of the *Sentences* or the first redaction of the expositions of Paul and the expositions of Pseudo-Dionysius that may also have been written in Rome. If we want a structural parallel to the *Summa*, we do better to go back a few years. The articles in the *Summa* most resemble those chapters of the so-called *Summa contra Gentiles* written as condensed disputes – only the *Summa*'s articles are more condensed still and more rigorously ordered. Now there is no evidence that Thomas taught the *contra Gentiles* verbatim. The resemblance suggests that he did not teach the *Summa* verbatim either. The *contra Gentiles* is, I continue to believe, an ideal pattern of persuasion to Christian wisdom. The *Summa* is, I propose, an *ideal* curriculum for Dominican education – and the last of five such curricula with which Thomas experimented.[11]

The *Summa* is not a transcript of Thomas's teaching nor is it a teacher's script for immediate classroom use. It is a single sequence of illustrative topics and typical arguments. It is not meant to 'prep' the student for higher study, but to lead the student from the beginning of theology to its end along a single inquiry. The sequence is ideal so far as it is exemplary – and in two senses. First, the *Summa* does not pretend to be comprehensive and, indeed, invites particular extensions or applications. Second, the *Summa*'s ordering of texts, terms and argument is non-exclusive in the way that Christian wisdom is. It offers itself with a kind of universality to all 'beginners' in the things of 'Christian religion'. Perhaps that is why Thomas chose not to be more explicitly Dominican in his prologue, his rhetoric and his acknowledged sources.

The *Summa* is not so much the report of Thomas's classroom performance or his script for future teachers as it is the pattern for an ideal pedagogy, a pedagogy for middle learners in a vowed community of preachers. When enriched by adaptation to a particular classroom, the pedagogy teaches the place within theology of its moral part in the only way anyone can (on Thomas's account of teaching). Learners are invited to moral teaching through a clarifying reminder of arguments about God as creator and governor; they are habituated into moral knowledge not only through practice with its disputative elements, but through dialectical narration of patterns for lived virtues and ways of life; and they are

---

[11] The four other patterns are the Lombard's *Sentences*, the structure of the Boethian corpus, the structure of the Dionysian corpus, and the so-called *Summa contra Gentiles*.

then shown, in the great disclosure at the turn from the second Part to the third, that the power moving their inquiry back to God has been the power of the incarnate Lord. When Thomas began to write the pro- gramme of the *Summa* at his Roman *studium*, and however exactly he adapted or amplified it in his own daily teaching, he invented it as a curricular ideal, not as a classroom script. It is a strictly unified curricu- lar ideal meant to guide moral teaching in various Dominican communi- ties or other Christian schools. The teaching is to be a single, continuous solicitation to acquire and exercise the habit of theology in all of its parts.

Failures in Dominican reception

If the *Summa* offers itself as an ideal curricular form for Dominican theology, its offer was refused from the beginning – and in various ways. I would like to survey some of the moments of that refusal and then to consider their causes. I select moments from the medieval Dominican reception, then comment much more briefly on the early modern redis- covery of Thomas's *Summa*.

Let me begin with what may seem the most trivial kind of failure in reception, a failure in textual transmission. From the beginning, the *Summa* is rarely copied as a whole. There are good material reasons: a codex large enough to hold the whole *Summa* would be a very unwieldy codex. The text is usually copied as individual units corresponding to the Parts, with the second Part divided between Prima Secundae and Secunda Secundae. So, for example, in the fourteenth-century Dominican library of the convent in Padua, there were two copies of each unit or eight codices; in the contemporary library at Mantua, one copy of each unit or four codices.[12] The numbers in these cases are equal, but across hundreds of manuscript collections the striking fact is that the units of the *Summa* are copied at very different rates. The most frequently copied unit is the Secunda Secundae, the detailed consideration of lived virtues and vices followed by states-of-life.[13] Indeed, the Secunda Secundae seems to be

---

[12] Luciano Gargan, *Lo studio teologico e la biblioteca dei domenicani a Padova nel tre e quattrocento* (Padua: Antenore, 1971), pp. 191–220, on the Paduan library inventory of 1390; Thomas Kaeppeli, 'Antiche biblioteche domenicane in Italia', *Archivum Fratrum Praedicatorum* 36 (1966), pp. 5–80, pp. 24–6, on the Mantuan inventory of 1417.

[13] Here I use the admittedly imperfect figures in James A. Weisheipl, *Friar Thomas d'Aquino* (augmented edn, Washington, DC: Catholic University of America Press, 1984), pp. 360–1: Prima Pars, 246 copies; Prima Secundae, 220; Secunda Secundae, 280; Tertia, 213. We will have much more exact figures when we have a completely indexed version of Dondaine and Shooner's catalogue of Thomas manuscripts.

the most frequently copied of any of Thomas's works.[14] The effort to integrate moral teaching within a unified theological curriculum was undone early on by market forces – by the demand for copies of the units that were judged most immediately useful.

The medieval Dominican reception provides more striking examples of the stripping out of the *Summa*'s moral teaching. As early as fifteen years after Thomas's death, John of Vercelli, master of the order, commissioned Galen of Orto to prepare an abridgement of the Secunda Secundae of the *Summa*. Here we have the moral matter not only extracted, but condensed.[15] A few years later, John of Fribourg would rewrite Thomas's teaching into a *Summa confessorum* (1298).[16] This confessors' *Summa* would itself be abridged, simplified and alphabetised – so that we have pieces of Thomas now twice or three times redacted. The redactions were popular: there are between two and three times as many copies of one alphabetised redaction, the *Summa Pisana*, as there are of the Secunda Secundae of Thomas's *Summa* itself.[17] In proposing a curricular ideal, Thomas would seem to have badly mistaken the wants of his brother Dominicans, who preferred and produced better moral manuals.

In some cases, medieval Dominicans wished not only that Thomas had written separate manuals, but that he had conformed to older models for their organisation. One of the deliberate structural accomplishments of Thomas's *Summa* is to reject an organisation according to the seven capital sins. Thomas treats the seven separately, but he explicitly sets them aside as an organising principle.[18] Yet we find not a few treatises on the seven capital sins made up of excerpts from Thomas. More grandly, we find in the great works of fifteenth-century Dominican morality both

---

[14] I leave aside the liturgical works, where questions of authorship and circulation are different. The only rival among the authentic writings is the booklet *De articulis fidei et ecclesiae sacramentis*, for which Weisheipl lists 277 MSS (p. 392). Of the major works, the nearest rivals would be the *Contra Gentiles* and the fourth book of the *Scriptum* on the *Sentences*, with 184 and 167 MSS respectively (Weisheipl, pp. 358–9).

[15] Martin Grabmann, 'De summae divi Thomae Aquinas theologicae studio', in *Miscellanea Dominicana in memoriam VII anni saecularis ab obitu sancti patris Dominici (1221–1921)* (Rome: F. Ferrari, 1923), pp. 151–61, at p. 157.

[16] Leonard E. Boyle, 'The *Summa confessorum* of John of Freiburg and the Popularization of the Moral Teaching of St. Thomas and of Some of His Contemporaries', in *Commemorative Studies* (Toronto: Pontifical Institute of Mediaeval Studies, 1974), 2, pp. 245–68.

[17] There are some 600 surviving copies of the *Summa pisana* as against about 280 copies of the *secunda secundae*. See Boyle, 'The *Summa confessorum*', p. 260, on the character of the text; Thomas Kaeppeli, *Scriptores ordinis praedicatorum medii aevi* (Rome: S. Sabina, 1970–93), 1, pp. 158–65, 'Bartholomaeus de S. Concordia', item no. 436, where the number of extant manuscripts is given as 602.

[18] See, for example, the important qualification in *Summa Theologiae* IaIIae, Q. 84, art. 4, ad 5, to which compare *De malo* 8.1 ad 1, ad 6, ad 8.

reference to Thomas and resistance to his programme for teaching. The *Summa Theologica* of Antoninus of Florence (completed around 1457) refers to Thomas ostentatiously for many of its definitions and a few of its arguments. But Antoninus rejects Thomas's programme in two ways. First, Antoninus's whole *Summa Theologica* is concerned only with moral matters. Antoninus makes moral teaching a species of theology rather than a part of theology – makes it an autonomous inquiry. Second, more importantly, Antoninus organises his *Summa* not according to the structure of Thomas's Secunda Pars or either of its sections, but according to a series of older schemata, including both the Ten Commandments and the principal sins.

The rejection of the structure of Thomas's *Summa* by the medieval Dominican tradition is not confined to moral matters, but it is most striking in moral matters – precisely because the *Summa* is most interested to organise moral matters rightly. Faced with so striking a misappropriation, we must be curious about its causes. Causes, I say, and not justifications. Someone might perfectly well argue that Thomas taught in Rome at the pleasure of the order and wrote at its behest. Certainly later generations of the order had a right to recombine, rewrite, or simply redo his teaching according to its changing circumstances. This could be a plausible claim, but it is beside my present point. I do not accuse the medieval Dominicans of injustice in their reception of Thomas. I am considering that reception for what it shows of failures in reading the *Summa* – and perhaps for failures in the writing of the *Summa*. If the main accomplishment of Thomas's *Summa* is precisely its structural unity, its continuous moral pedagogy, then taking it apart to use it in other structures suggests either an ignorance or a deliberate rejection of the work's principal purpose. Let me consider both possibilities, rejection first.

Thomas's Dominican successors may have been right to reject the *Summa* precisely on educational grounds. The work projects a hybrid genre that is fully suitable neither for university nor for pastoral use. University teachers took particular arguments from Thomas and incorporated them into disputed their questions or treatises – or their lists of condemnations. The first Thomist controversialists, the authors of the *correctoria* in the 1280s, stuck with the list of 118 passages singled out for attack by the Franciscan William de la Mare. Most of these passages were taken from the *Summa*, but they were then treated by critics and defenders as detached loci. Indeed, later defences of Thomas's views in the *Summa* often re-arrange the disputed loci according to the order of the *Sentences*.[19] Even so ardent a Thomist as John Capreolus composes

---

[19] Martin Grabmann, 'Eine ungedruckte Verteidigung der theologischen Summa des hl. Thomas von Aquin aus den ältesten Thomisten-schule (Cod. Vat. lat. 4287)', *Divus Thomas* [Fribourg] 2 (1924), pp. 270–6.

his *Defensiones divi Thomae* around currently controversial topics indexed to the order of Thomas's first commentary on the *Sentences*. Capreolus sometimes prefers the *Summa* to the *Sentences*-commentary so far as the older Thomas had better command of the authorities, but he scrambles the order of the *Summa* in order to fit it into a standard arrangement of theological topics.[20] In the same way, as I have suggested, moral manualists re-arranged bits of the *Summa* according to older or more popular pastoral forms. One might conclude that Thomas wrote the *Summa* for an audience that did not exist, that is, for a theological readership at once academic and pastoral.

It may also be that the *Summa* was judged too subtle in its connections or too slow in its teaching rhythms. Perhaps some medieval readers felt the anxiety of more recent readers over what appears the delayed appearance of Christ. Indeed, we might imagine that the text's teaching style was not obvious enough in several ways. The *Summa* offers the most important moral principles almost tacitly, more by quiet habituation than by loud assertion. Readers of the *Summa* are expected to learn the most important principles and their first complications by seeing them applied over and over again across a range of typical topics and select authorities. One might imagine that many medieval Dominican teachers found this pedagogy too demanding.

These imagined possibilities point to the other side of the question, how far the curricular reform in the *Summa* was simply missed or misunderstood. It is entirely possible that the growing advocacy of Thomas among the friars (from the chapter of 1278 on) went right along with a thorough misunderstanding of what Thomas actually achieved, especially in the *Summa*. Indeed, the intellectual reasons for Thomas's growing importance may have depended upon such misunderstanding – on the supposition, say, that he was offering clear doctrinal and moral formulae (rather than slow or subtle dialectical sequences). Thomas's clarity of style and simplified order of teaching could easily have been mistaken for unambiguous tenets and tight codification. Certainly they have been misunderstood in this way by various brands of neo-Thomism. The apparent rejection of Thomas's ideal curriculum could have been based on wishful or wilful misreadings that made him more useful to institutional purposes. This would be not so much Thomas's failure to match textual pedagogy with community needs as his inadvertent vulnerability to changing institutional programmes. Perhaps the *Summa* was exactly what many medieval Dominican teachers needed – and did not want to accept.

---

[20] See the notion of Thomas's growth in John Capreolus, *Defensiones* I d. 27, q. 2, sol. 1, ad 1 (ed. Paban and Pègues, 2, p. 256).

The failure of the *Summa* as theological reform may point to something wistful in the very project of its moral part – in the very hope that Dominican theology could become an enrichment and corrective to ancient moral philosophy. More emphatically and more coherently than his teacher Albert, Thomas Aquinas is committed to the notion that the moral part of theology fulfils and transmutes the best teaching of the Greek philosophic schools. But the Dominican manualist tradition both before and after Thomas suggests a rather different view of theological morals: they appear increasingly either as rather simple moral exhortation (in the model of William Peraldus) or as the application of canon law to confessional practice (as in Raymond of Peñafort). The *Summa* is neither simple exhortation nor applied law. It explicitly rejects Peraldus's hortatory organisation and it incorporates bits of Raymond's legal compendia into a work that is rather the opposite of a topically ordered code. Thomas's reforming proposal that moral teaching subsume Greek philosophy into a unified theological wisdom may, in this sense, be surprisingly un-Dominican.[21] It may propose a reform that in fact contradicted the felt urgencies of thirteenth and fourteenth-century pastoral practice – and so may have been rejected or ignored as curiously impertinent to actual Dominican purposes.

The apparent triumph of the curricular reform proposed in the *Summa* comes after the high medieval period, in the sixteenth-century Dominican reform movements. Detailed attention to the structure of the *Summa* comes with Köllin, Cajetan and Crockaert (the last of whom is traditionally credited with substituting the *Summa* for the *Sentences* in the classroom). Of course, for these early modern Dominican advocates, Thomas was rehabilitated not as a failed reformer, but as a Dominican founder – as a witness to the order's pristine intellect. Thomas appears in sixteenth-century Paris or Lombardy or Salamanca not as an author whose masterwork failed to persuade his confreres to change their teaching habits, but as someone who long ago laid down the lines of Dominican teaching. Then again, the sixteenth-century expositors of the *Summa* thoroughly distort its moral structures in other ways, not only by distending it, but by inter-cutting topics, procedures and epistemological expectations contrary to it. The topics are often those of the Scotists, Ockhamists or Albertists. The procedures are those of the new casuistry. The expectations are those of the early modern notions of 'science'. So that the structure of the *Summa* appears finally to triumph just when it cannot be read for its own manner of moral teaching.

---

[21] Here I may disagree with Boyle's ringing conclusion (*Setting*, p. 30), though in another sense probably not.

Failures in recent readings

Most recent readings of the *Summa* do not mistake its project in the way that medieval Dominicans did. This gives us no occasion for gloating. We do still ignore Thomas's project, if for opposite reasons. We do not carve it up into moral manuals, because we hardly see that it is about morals at all. We have cast out one devil to make room for seven.

The papal sponsorship of Thomas in the late nineteenth century was not a simple rediscovery of Thomas. Thomas had no need of rediscovery in Catholic theological schools, where he had remained a forceful inter-locutor. The papal sponsorship of Thomas meant rather to accomplish what were perceived as culturally urgent philosophic ends – the refutation of scepticism, for example, or the critique of modern science and modern historiography.[22] The polemical agenda of neo-Thomism dictated an interest in certain parts of the *Summa* at the expense of others. So the first Part was picked over for unassailable ontological, epistemological and physical principles, while the second Part was relatively neglected except for the argumentatively useful 'treatise on natural law'. This selective interest was powerfully reinforced by institutional separations of philosophy from theology or among the specialties within theology, including a moral theology subservient to canon law.

At the same time, but incidentally, papal sponsorship of neo-Thomism motivated prodigious achievements in the editing of critical texts and in the practice of those kinds of historical reading championed by Mandonnet and Chenu, by Ehrle and Grabmann, by Callus and Boyle. The expansion of medieval studies, in part under Catholic patronage, multiplied the contextual material that could be brought to bear at any point in the Thomist text. Of course, the historico-philological Thomas sustained uneasy relations with neo-Thomism, as illustrated most poignantly in the condemnation of Chenu.[23] After the Council, it seemed for a brief time that official Thomism had evaporated – as quickly and unexpectedly as official Marxism – and that simple exegetes would at last

---

[22] See, for example, Wayne J. Hankey, 'Pope Leo's Purposes and St. Thomas's Platonism', in *S. Tommaso nella storia del pensiero: Atti dell VIII Congresso Tomistico Internazionale*, vol. 8 = *Studi Tomistici* 17 (Vatican City: Libreria Editrice Vaticana, 1982), pp. 39–52, and Hankey, 'Making Theology Practical: Thomas Aquinas and the Nineteenth Century Religious Revival', *Dionysius* 9 (1985), pp. 85–127. The most comprehensive narrative in English of the speculative anxieties leading up to the promulgation of *Aeterni Patris* is Gerald A. McCool, *Nineteenth-Century Scholasticism: The Search for a Unitary Method* (New York: Fordham University Press, 1989).

[23] See Giuseppe Alberigo, Marie-Dominique Chenu, Étienne Fouilloux, Jean-Pierre Jossua and Jean Ladrière, *Une école de théologie: le Saulchoir* (Paris: Éditions du Cerf, 1985).

have an exiled Thomas to themselves. It is clear now, if not already 15 years ago, that official Thomism is hardly dead – and that it resists as ever the suggestions or critiques of historians and philologists.

I tell this fable – fabulous both in reductive simplicity and moral clarity – because I want to end by arguing that the modern regime of Thomistic authority is liable to produce more bizarre misreadings of the *Summa* than any of the medieval Dominican ones. The medieval Dominican manuals – and the most important early modern commentaries – had two virtues lacking in most recent readings. First, they understood that the *Summa* was written for the sake of its second Part, that is, for the sake of integrating moral teaching into a unified theological pedagogy. Second, the medieval Dominicans understood that the *Summa* was written for the sake of a community of moral formation – not for a public forum of philosophical disputation. To judge from its structure, the *Summa* was not written as a foundational encyclopaedia of Catholic philosophy and theology. It was written to provide an ideal curriculum of theological wisdom in which moral teaching found its necessary place – but only when the teaching was enacted by application to a community.

It is astonishing that many readings of the *Summa* continue to ignore the second Part and particularly the Secunda Secundae. The pedagogically decisive distinction of the two moral sections, Prima Secundae and Secunda Secundae, is not well explained by recent commentators. Sometimes it is collapsed into other distinctions, as that between *exitus* and *reditus*.[24] At other times the two sections of the Secunda Pars are likened to the premises of a syllogism, their connection being somehow a deduction.[25] Even book-length studies of the *Summa*'s organisation refuse to enter into the plan or position of the Secunda Secundae.[26] But worse than the omission of moral parts is the systematic misreading of whatever moral passages we happen to remember.

The most damaging effect of the authority presumed in neo-Thomism is that it treats Thomas's text as canonical for certain purposes. The text is canonical: it is fixed and then dismembered for quasi-legal citation. The text is canonical for certain purposes: it is meant to supply responses

---

[24] See Th.-André Audet, 'Approches historiques de la *Summa theologiae*', in *Études d'histoire littéraire et doctrinale* (Montreal: Institut d'études médiévales; and Paris: J. Vrin, 1962), pp. 7–29, at p. 15.

[25] See, for example, Martin Grabmann, *Einführung in die Summa theologiae des heiligen Thomas von Aquin*, 2nd edn (Freiburg: Herder, 1928), pp. 84–8; Francis Ruello, 'Les intentions pédagogiques et la méthode de saint Thomas d'Aquin dans la *Somme théologique*', *Revue du moyen âge latin* 1 (1945), pp. 188–90; Marie-Dominique Philippe, 'La lecture de la *Somme théologique*', *Seminarium* 29 (1977), pp. 898–915, at p. 904.

[26] For example, Ghislain Lafont, *Structures et méthode dans la Somme théologique de S. Thomas d'Aquin* (Paris: Desclée de Brouwer, 1961), p. 262.

to scepticism, relativism, nihilism, to chasten Modernists and to outwit Anarcho-Syndicalists – or 'liberals' and Liberationists, in the current Church controversies. To read the *Summa* under this regime of authority conceals all the ways in which the text is an exemplar for a single act of theological teaching. It is to miss the *Summa*'s immanent pedagogical programme.

Repeating this claim about the programme written into the *Summa*, I might seem to recommend that we gloat over the adversities of neo-Thomism and retreat into private re-readings of the *Summa* with full benefit of history and philology. I confess that I have sometimes hoped that the disruption of official Thomism after the Council would open spaces in which the *Summa* could be read afresh. I do believe, perhaps too piously, that an astute reader can go far in following the work's curriculum. She can practise its terms, divisions and argumentative sequences. She can become familiar with its disposition and reinterpretation of authorities. She might even be habituated in its principles to the point of making new terms, divisions and sequences. She might at last be able to enact the deep narrative of the *Summa* – its plot, its peripeties, its disclosures. But the dream of a marginalised, private reading leaves out important conditions that the book supposes for its own enactment.

The *Summa* was written as an ideal curriculum and so presumably for private study by teachers of theology. As an ideal curriculum it was hardly meant to end with private reading. It had to be completed by teaching for the sake of a community. The *Summa* was written to correct and rebuild certain sorts of community – to correct a community that segregated moral instruction as merely practical, to rebuild it as a community in which moral instruction was central to the whole of theology. An integral reading of the *Summa* cannot then be divorced from the making of community. The *Summa* is read whole when it is taught – taught to a community of beginners in the pursuit of an integral theology. It is taught by being enriched, qualified, applied, adapted to the circumstances of such learners. The *Summa* is read whole when it is enacted as a single theological teaching, with morals at its centre and the Passion of Christ as its driving force, before a community committed to sanctification through mission, with the consolations of sacraments and liturgy, in the illumination of contemplative prayer.

Many academic readings of the *Summa* are then necessarily partial in obvious ways. So are the readings of much neo-Thomism. The *Summa* is not read whole when it is made into the foundational encyclopaedia of anti-modernism. If the famous five ways to God do not persuade every atheist, it is not because they commit gross logical errors or invoke faulty principles of a discredited physics. They were never meant to function as free-standing demonstrations for non-believers. They are highly abbreviated reminders of philosophical lessons for religious students beginning theology. And so for Thomas's teachings on creation out-of-nothing, human freedom, virtues and vices, and the natural law – which has suffered perhaps the most curious fate in modern and recent readings. Indeed, recent misconstruals of the notion of natural law show very clearly the regime of authority that makes the *Summa* a canon in which everything is considered and resolved.

Reading the *Summa* whole means taking it as an ideal curriculum for a reformed community. I have repeated this – and I end with it, under three qualifications.

First qualification: The failures in medieval Dominican reception of the *Summa* ought to remind us forcefully that there is no easy rule by which to recognise communities that read the *Summa* well. Being a medieval Dominican was certainly no guarantee of full reading. So now there is no reason to suppose that the *Summa* is owned by mendicants – or by members of Catholic religious orders or possessors of a *mandatum*. The *Summa* may build its communities elsewhere.

Second qualification: As an ideal for teaching in community, the *Summa* calls for application, enrichment and perhaps even contradiction. For this text, successful teaching is not teaching that replicates itself verbatim in its students. Thomas, its author, did not intend to produce Thomisms of the strict observance. He meant to invite his students to acquire active habits of dialectical inquiry, not to memorise invariant formulae – except perhaps as rhetorical topics, that is, as starting-points for producing new arguments. So there is no reason to suppose that we can identify attentive readers of the *Summa* by counting the Thomistic formulae they repeat. Learning theology is more active and more unpredictable than that – as Thomas tells us at several places in the *Summa* and shows throughout.

Third qualification – and the last: I have described what it might be to read the whole project in the *Summa*. Is it also worthwhile to read the *Summa* partially and even badly? Of course it is. We can learn many things from it by reading it incompletely, ineptly, under obedience, in solitude or even in a graduate seminar for a secularised programme of Religious Studies. But we ought not to proclaim that we are reading it whole when we are reading it very partially – or well when we are reading it badly.

Understanding the *Scientia* of Faith: Reason and Faith in Aquinas's *Summa Theologiae*

RUDI A. TE VELDE

Introduction

From the perspective of the modern separation of faith and reason, the project of the *Summa Theologiae* may appear to the reader as a rather confusing hybrid of a faithful exposition of Christian doctrine, and a genuine philosophical search for understanding the ultimate nature of reality. In its overall vision of the universe, of God and of human life, the *Summa* represents an inextricable unity of philosophy, that is, rational inquiry into the truth of things, and theology, conceived of as a thought-ful listening to the message of biblical revelation, as it is handed down in the Christian tradition. As a consequence, Aquinas's masterwork of scholastic theology contains, to the taste of some, too much philosophy and rational speculation to the detriment of the mysteries of faith, while others, mainly philosophers, are inclined to deplore the fact that rational thought remains bound by the limits of faith and the authoritative theo-logical tradition. Philosophers may feel attracted by the claim made by Aquinas that theology is a science and will use rational argument where it is possible. They have focused traditionally on those parts of the *Summa*, such as the proofs of the existence of God, which provide the building blocks for a natural theology, conceived of as a purely rational enterprise independent of religious faith and historical revelation. Theologians, in contrast, hasten to emphasise the specific character of 'science' in this connection, and the subordinate role of reason in the *Summa*: it is not a science in the normal sense of the word, a product of rational investigation and reflection, but it stands for a 'body of know-ledge', received from God by revelation. The *Summa* deals with a science of faith, which should be distinguished sharply from any philosophical science, even if philosophical argument plays a role in it.

The subtle balance and interplay between reason and faith, philosophy and theology, in the *Summa* undoubtedly constitutes one of the main challenges for any serious interpretation of Aquinas's thought. Many

interpretations, approaches and presentations of Aquinas run the danger
of emphasising one pole of this relationship at the cost of the other. Most
of the recent interpretations are dominated by the tendency to stress the
theological nature of Aquinas's thought. In contrast to the traditional
Thomistic approach, which was characterised by the distinction between
natural theology, conceived of as a foundationalist enterprise on the
basis of pure reason, and a sacred theology, which deals with the contents of biblical revelation and the positive doctrine of the Church, the
'new Aquinas' is sometimes portrayed with distinctively Wittgensteinian traits in repudiating philosophical proof and rational foundations.

Aquinas's *Summa* presents one notorious stumbling-block for those
approaches to his thought which tend to contrast reason and faith in a
specifically modern way, according to which reason is considered to be
the source of objective, universal and necessary knowledge, while faith is
delegated to the factual beliefs which are shared by a particular religious
tradition and which are only accessible to those who believe. The
stumbling-block I have in mind concerns the meaning and the necessity
of the Five Ways in the beginning of the *Summa Theologiae*, where
Thomas argues for the existence of God. One might think that to start a
systematic and comprehensive treatment of theology with a demonstration of the existence of God is the logical thing to do. Especially if
theology is conceived to be a science about God, treating everything that
is true of God, the first thing one should do is to demonstrate that God,
as the subject matter of this science, exists. Thus one might think that the
point of the proofs of God's existence in the beginning of the *Summa* is
to ensure the objective reference to reality of the theological propositions.

In the light of this – commonly accepted – view one will be greatly
surprised by a small footnote in a recent book of Norman Kretzmann's,
in which he contends that the Five Ways are not essential to Aquinas's
theological project of the *Summa* and could therefore, in principle, be
dismissed.[1] The project of the theological *Summa* can do without philosophical arguments for the existence of God. According to Kretzmann,
the *Summa* is an introductory textbook of revealed theology. In contrast
to natural theology, of which the *Summa contra Gentiles* is an example
(at least as far as the first three books are concerned), revealed theology
starts with premises that are taken from revelation. Even if Aquinas
argues that the revealed doctrine of Christian faith (*sacra doctrina*) can

---

[1] Norman Kretzmann, *The Metaphysics of Theism: Aquinas's Natural Theology
in Summa contra Gentiles I* (Oxford: Clarendon Press, 1997), p. 56, n. 5: 'Theoretic-
ally, the inclusion of the famous Five Ways near the beginning of [the *Summa*] should
constitute a digression from the project Aquinas is undertaking there.'

be treated in the manner of a science, it is definitely not a science based on human reason, in which propositions must be justified by providing sufficient rational evidence. It is a science, as explained by Aquinas himself, which proceeds from principles received through divine revelation. In Kretzmann's view, it is a science dependent upon data of revelation, which are taken to be true on faith, not unlike the way an empirical science may choose its starting-points in empirical data. The suggestion is that the existence of God is just one of these revealed data which may count as a basic truth of revealed theology.

Kretzmann is a philosopher himself. He is particularly interested in those parts of Aquinas's thought which may contribute to the philosophical project of 'natural theology'. Natural theology is conceived of by him, very broadly, as the rational investigation of the first principles and most fundamental aspects of reality in general, and of human nature and behaviour in particular. It is not really different from metaphysics in its classical sense, but it includes anthropology and ethics. Natural theology aims at giving an ultimate explanation of reality, and therefore it deals with such traditional topics as God's existence, God's nature, and the relationships of all other things to God. It is a purely rational undertaking and as such not bound by a particular religious doctrine; nor does it accept any revelation. It speaks the (universal) language of reason without any commitment to a particular religious tradition.

Kretzmann acknowledges that the theological *Summa* is not meant to be a work of natural theology. In the *Summa* Aquinas intends to expound the science of sacred doctrine, which is clearly conceived as the doctrine of Christian faith. Inasmuch as Kretzmann regards the Five Ways as representing philosophical proofs for the existence of God, they are judged to be not necessary for the project of the *Summa*.

At the opposite pole of the spectrum of reason and faith we may meet an interpretation such as Velecky's, in his book on the proofs of God's existence in the *Summa Theologiae*.[2] According to Velecky, whose main target of attack is the straight philosophical approach of the Five Ways by Anthony Kenny,[3] Aquinas's arguments have usually been taken wrongly as purely philosophical proofs for the existence of God. It is more likely that they should be considered as ways of thinking about God from the perspective of the Christian belief in God. The arguments are not intended to prove, in a universally valid manner, the existence of a divine being independently of the Christian religion. They are arguments of an 'insider', which aim to give content to the notion of divinity

---

[2] Lubor Velecky, *Aquinas's Five Arguments in the Summa Theologiae Ia QQ. 2,3* (Kampen: Kok Pharos, 1994).

[3] Anthony Kenny, *The Five Ways: Saint Thomas Aquinas's Proofs of God's Existence* (London: Routledge & Kegan Paul, 1969).

by suggesting to the adherents of the Christian religion different ways of seeing the world of their experience as pointing to a transcendent being, which is worshipped by them as the God of Christian revelation.

For Kretzmann, as well as for Velecky, the *Summa* is definitely a work of Christian theology. Therefore, according to Kretzmann, the project of the *Summa* does not need philosophical proofs of God's existence, while in Velecky's view, the Five Ways are not intended to be philosophical proofs. They both seem to associate philosophical reason with an outsider's standpoint, aiming at a universal objectivity of rational justified truth, which requires a suspension of the 'subjective' claims of a particular historical revelation.

In what follows I would like to propose a different way of looking at the nature of what Aquinas is doing in his *Summa*. The question with which the interpretations of Kretzmann and Velecky confront us regards the precise meaning of Aquinas's claim that the doctrine of faith can be understood as a *scientia* and will be dealt with accordingly in the *Summa*. In what sense is theology a science of faith, and what exactly is the role of (philosophical) reason in this science? And finally, what makes it necessary to start this science with a demonstration of God's existence?

Why should there be a revelation?

Let us start by discussing the notion of revelation in Aquinas. How does he introduce the idea of a revealed doctrine in the *Summa*? And how does he account for its intelligible meaning? For Kretzmann, revelation seems to be primarily a positive and descriptive term. He speaks about 'revealed theology' and about 'data of revelation', which count as a given in the light of faith. The starting-points of revealed theology consist in what are supposed to be divinely revealed truths. This reference to a divine revelation, with which the attitude of religious faith is accompanied, escapes any verification by reason. From the viewpoint of reason one can recognise only what Christians take to be divinely revealed truths, a 'putative revelation'.[4] The articles of faith may be considered by the adherents of Christian religion as true, as expressing somehow the truth of God, but in Kretzmann's view this claim seems to be no more than a factual one, part of the positive religion of Christianity.

Aquinas, however, speaks from the outset of 'revelation' in the ideal and objective sense it has from the standpoint of faith. For him, revelation is not simply a factual claim attached to a class of propositions that are basic from the point of view of faith. Theology is the science of faith, not in the sense of the positive historical religion and its doctrinal state-

---

[4] See Kretzmann, *The Metaphysics of Theism*, p. 25.

ments, but in the sense of the intelligibility of faith. It is important to realise that from the moment the so-called data of revelation, the contents of Scripture, the ecclesiastical doctrines, the articles of faith, and so on, are conceived of as constituting a true revelation, as somehow expressing true knowledge about God, derived from God's own knowledge, the facts of revelation are seen in an intelligible light. Aquinas would probably identify this light as the light of faith, *lumen fidei,* by which consent is given to the object of faith, that is, the invisible reality of God, which is signified by the propositions of faith. For the believer, the data of revelation are not just positive facts, but they are invested with an intelligible meaning inasmuch as they are taken to signify something which is true of God in virtue of God himself. Now, if this is the case, the first issue to be dealt with when one wishes to treat the doctrine of faith, is how to account for the intelligibility of the notion of revelation. If Thomas does not want to restrict himself in the *Summa* to a 'putative' revelation, he should start by explaining that the idea of a revealed doctrine makes sense and can be understood to be what it is supposed to be. It is this question, concerning the existence (not *de facto* but *de iure*) of a revealed doctrine, which is the theme of the first article of the *Summa*.

In this article the question is asked whether we need any 'other teaching, besides philosophical studies'.[5] What is at issue here is the existence of a doctrine which has its origin in divine revelation and which as such stands apart from philosophical studies. Can an intelligible ground be given for the existence of such an, apparently additional, doctrine? In asking this question, Aquinas is referring to the historical Christian religion, which, according to its self-understanding, is founded on a divine revelation. For Aquinas, there exists as a matter of fact something like a holy doctrine of faith, distinct from the whole of human philosophy. As a theologian he wants to deal with the teachings of faith, which are claimed by the Christian tradition to be based on divine revelation in the Scriptures. What Aquinas is doing in the first article is arguing that this factual claim – of Christianity's being entrusted with a revealed truth about God – is an intelligible position, which makes perfectly good sense. The issue, one must stress, is not how one can demonstrate that the Christian religion is, in fact, right in claiming divine authority for its doctrine, but it is more a matter of showing that the Christian claim is not unreasonable, by arguing that the idea of God revealing knowledge about himself to man has indeed some moral necessity.[6]

---

[5] *ST* Ia, Q. 1, art. 1: 'Utrum sit necessarium, praeter philosophicas disciplinas, aliam doctrinam haberi.'

[6] Aquinas himself does not use the term 'moral necessity'; what he means, however, is not an absolute necessity, but a necessity in supposition of an end.

The argument of the first article can be regarded as a nice example of Aquinas's theological method. The truth of Christian doctrine is not simply taken for granted, but neither does he attempt to prove its divine origin and, consequently, its truth from the external standpoint of reason. I am inclined to say that, for Aquinas, there is no such external standpoint from which the way reality is pictured in the Christian tradition might be compared to reality itself. Aquinas places himself within the particular tradition of Christian faith, not simply by identifying himself with the particularity of its 'truth', but by arguing for the intelligibility of the Christian self-understanding. In this way he opens a universal perspective of truth, from within the particular tradition of Christianity, in so far as he aims to show that the notion of revelation has an intelligible sense.

Aquinas answers that revelation, on the part of God, is necessary for man's salvation. 'It was necessary for man's salvation that there should be a knowledge revealed by God (*revelatio*), besides the philosophical studies explored by human reason (*ratio*).'[7] Two reasons for this necessity are given. The first reason is that 'man is directed to God as to an end that surpasses the grasp of his reason'. What Aquinas is saying here is intended, in my view, as a rather simple assertion about human life, which does not yet imply much theory. Human life is characterised by a deep and fundamental desire for meaning and truth, ultimately for knowing the truth of the universe, in which consists the final perfection of human 'intellectual' life. That man finds his fulfilment in becoming united with God by way of knowledge is not Aquinas's personal opinion, which requires argument; it is a commonly accepted view in classical as well as in medieval thought. To this Aquinas adds a sharp sense of the mystery of God, who is inaccessible to the natural faculties of man. God exceeds the grasp of human reason. But human beings cannot live their lives in ignorance of what their life is ultimately about. They should have some knowledge of the ultimate goal of life in order to direct their intentions and actions toward it. 'It was therefore necessary for the salvation (*ad salutem*) of man that certain knowledge about God, which exceeds human reason, should be made known to him by divine revelation.'[8]

Thus, considering the necessity for human beings of having some foreknowledge of the end of their life in order to live and act in conformity with that end, and considering the transcendence of God, the idea of revelation, of God who makes himself known to men as their beatifying

---

[7] *ST* Ia, Q. 1, art. 1: 'Dicendum quod necessarium fuit ad humanam salutem, esse doctrinam quandam secundum revelationem divinam praeter philosophicas disciplinas, quae ratione humana investigantur.'

[8] *ST* Ia, Q. 1, art. 1: 'Unde necessarium fuit homini ad salutem, quod ei nota fierent quaedam per revelationem divinam, quae rationem humanam excedunt.'

end, does make sense. Revelation is shown to be an intelligible idea, and therefore the Christian talk about revelation cannot be dismissed as merely a product of mythical imagination or as a way of speaking. Of course, Aquinas's reasoning does not prove the truth of the claim of Christianity to have been granted with a doctrine of faith based on God's revelation in Scripture, but it does argue for its intelligibility.

Revelation, I must add, should not be seen here as an additional source of informative knowledge about God, beyond the limits of rational knowledge. For Aquinas, the issue is not so much that revelation provides us with an additional set of propositions about God, beyond those which are formed on the basis of human reason. The widespread view of the relationship between reason and revelation as constituting two different sources of knowledge about God – reason as leading to those universal truths about God which are part of philosophy, and revelation as source of the doctrinal statements of faith, only accessible in the light of faith – is really a distortion belonging to later times. Revelation, as distinguished from reason, pertains to the formality under which God is known as object of faith. God is known by faith in so far as he makes himself known. The propositions of faith relate to God as their object in the light of God's truth itself (*prima veritas*). The rationale behind the distinction between reason and revelation is not the (epistemological) question 'How do we know?', either by reason or by revelation, but the difference in the formal ground of truth by which a certain proposition about God is knowable.

Let us continue our reading of the first article in which Aquinas argues for the necessity of a sacred doctrine. The second reason why man should have some knowledge about God based on revelation is that man's salvation cannot be made wholly dependent on the work of human reason. 'For the truth about God, such as reason can know it, would only be known by a few, and that after a long time, and with the admixture of many errors.'[9] In view of human salvation, which consists in the full knowledge of God, the way of philosophy does not constitute an acceptable alternative to a religion which is based on divine revelation, even if philosophical reason is not confined to the finite being within the realm of human experience. One can know something about God by way of reason, but only in so far as finite being points beyond itself to an infinite cause of all being. Thomas does not question that the intelligible reality to which the name of God refers can be established by way of reason and through philosophy. The notion of 'God' is not tied up exclusively with faith and revelation.

---

[9] *ST* Ia, Q. 1, art. 1: 'Quia veritas de Deo, per rationem investigata, a paucis, et per longum tempus, et cum admixtione multorum errorum, homini proveniret.'

But perhaps one should say that the point of Aquinas's argument here is not so much reason's capacity to know something about God and to account for the intelligibility of the notion of 'God'. The emphasis is on the human condition of rational knowledge of the truth, as something which is intrinsically bound up with concrete human life and its practical limitations. The work of reason is a typically human, free and responsible activity, which requires practice, education, concentration, talent, leisure, and so on. Although no human life is without reason – to be human means to be rational – to dedicate one's life to reason and to the philosophical investigation of truth is, as a matter of fact, not granted to everybody. The argument presupposes that human salvation, or happiness, has something to do with knowing the truth of the universe. Happiness consists in the full realisation of the intellectual part of human nature. We must distinguish here between intellect and reason.[10] Reason pertains to the way man realises himself as an intellectual, that is, truth-apprehending being, in relation to his concrete bodily and sensory existence. The work of reason, broadly conceived, may be regarded as aiming at humanising and improving human life by means of culture, society, political institutions, science, morals, and the like. The work of reason essentially consists in making the world a human world. Now, as I wish to paraphrase Aquinas's view on this matter, the process of humanising, of becoming fully human within the temporal and contingent sphere of history, is not an infallible route to increasing perfection and happiness. Human reason at work in history does not offer any guarantee of final happiness. But without a sort of revelation by which the ultimate goal of human life is disclosed in the manner of a promise, thus as beyond what is humanly attainable, the infinite aspiration, which underlies the process of humanisation, would always be frustrated. Revelation is necessary in so far as it offers human life in this world a concrete orientation to the transcendent horizon of the good and the true.

The necessity of a revealed doctrine about God appears to be mainly of a moral and practical nature. In order to direct their intentions and actions towards God, human beings should have some foreknowledge of God. In this sense the notion of a revealed doctrine points forwards to the discussion of law and grace in the second part of the *Summa*. Law and grace, that is, God's rule of life and his assistance (*auxilium gratiae*) of human freedom, through which man can live up to that rule, refer to the practical aspect of divine revelation by which God instructs men how to live in view of the destination to which they are called.[11] In article 4 of

---

[10] For the distinction between *intellectus* and *ratio*, see *In BDT*, 6, 1.

[11] See the prologue of *ST* IaIIae, Q. 90: 'Principium autem exterius movens ad bonum est Deus, qui et nos instruit per legem, et iuvat per gratiam.' God as an externally moving principle is contrasted with God who as the Creator is active in the

the opening question of the *Summa*, Aquinas argues that although the knowledge of sacred doctrine has a practical aspect, it is primarily a speculative science, which is concerned with divine things (*de rebus divinis*). Compared to the Aristotelian division between practical and speculative sciences, the science of sacred doctrine has a mixed or hybrid character. It is a practical science in so far as sacred doctrine teaches men how to direct their intentions and actions to the ultimate end. Revelation is moral instruction. But because sacred doctrine is concerned with human acts, inasmuch as the moral life of man is ordained to the perfect knowledge of God, in which eternal beatitude consists, its knowledge is more speculative than practical.[12] It is primarily knowledge of God. In this sense revelation is self-revelation of God: God reveals knowledge of himself in order that men may have some foreknowledge of their end and direct their lives according to that end, which consists in enjoying the full knowledge of God (*visio beatifica*). In so far as God addresses himself through revelation to man in the midst of his historical life (*in statu viae*), revelation is moral instruction concerned with the means to the end; but in so far as God reveals himself as the very end of human life, revelation is concerned with the end itself, which is somehow present to man in faith. The knowledge of faith has, therefore, a speculative character in so far as God himself is present, in a mysterious and hidden manner, in his revelation. Although the knowledge of faith is not perfect knowledge of God, Aquinas conceives it as an inchoate beginning of the final and perfect knowledge, which is the vision of God. The hybrid character of the *scientia* of sacred doctrine, partly practical, partly speculative, is rooted in the dynamics of divine revelation by means of which God makes himself known to man, in his temporal and earthly existence (*in statu viae*), as the end of human life.

To sum up, sacred doctrine teaches the knowledge of God which is revealed by God for the sake of man's salvation; knowledge which is received by man in faith, and through which he has a certain anticipatory knowledge of the final and perfect knowledge of God, in which eternal happiness consists. Knowledge of sacred doctrine does not concern only the moral practice of human life on its way toward God as the end; it is also, and primarily, speculative knowledge of God himself, as God himself is present in his revelation as the source and object of man's beatitude.

---

operation of nature. In my view, the notion *principium exterius* should be interpreted as pertaining to God who enters through his revelation in the field of human history.

[12] *ST* Ia, Q. 4: 'Magis tamen est speculativa quam practica: quia principalius agit de rebus divinis quam de actibus humanis; de quibus agit secundum quod per eos ordinatur homo ad perfectam Dei cognitionem, in qua aeterna beatitudo consistit.'

Rudi A. te Velde

The doctrine of faith is a *scientia*

In the second article of the *Summa* it is argued that sacred doctrine, that is the doctrine of Christian faith, constitutes a *scientia*. After having been told that sacred doctrine is revealed knowledge of God, and as such distinct from all philosophical sciences, which are based on human reason, one might feel suspicious of this claim. How can a doctrine of faith be a science? The concept of science seems to be inextricably bound up with human reason, with rational method and with critical assessment of cognitive claims in the light of available evidence. But, as we have seen, the teachings of sacred doctrine surpass the scope of human reason (*supra rationem*) and should be accepted by faith on the authority of God who reveals himself in Scripture. Of course, one might apply rational procedures in expounding and clarifying the central tenets of Christian faith; one might even develop a rational theology within the institutional context of the university, in which the beliefs, the practices and the texts of Christian religion are investigated by means of available 'scientific' instruments and methods. To this purpose one can (or even must) make use of the resources of the philosophical disciplines. In this sense scholastic theology, in the days of Aquinas, had acquired a scientific appearance due to the development of the scholastic method and the abundant use of Aristotle's philosophical writings. But from a modern point of view theology cannot be a science in the proper sense of the word as long as its principles are not open to rational discussion and critical assessment.

Closer inspection reveals that it is not the rise of a 'scientific' theology in the medieval university, empowered by the use of Aristotle's philosophy, that Aquinas has in mind in asserting that sacred doctrine is a *scientia*. The point is not whether theology, considered as a human undertaking, may be practised according to a recognised scientific method and rational procedures, but whether sacred doctrine is, in itself, a *scientia*, regardless of the concern with the rationality of theological reflection in an academic context. The question that occupies Aquinas is whether the doctrine of faith, the revealed knowledge of God received by man in faith, can be understood to constitute a *scientia*. If it is a *scientia*, then, of course, the theological project of expounding the doctrine of faith may follow an order that is appropriate to its character as a science, an order that is derived from the intelligible structure inherent to all that belongs to this doctrine.

Before explaining in what sense the doctrine of faith is a *scientia*, a small but rather telling detail attracts our attention. In the *sed contra* argument of the second article, Thomas cites a passage from Augustine, in which the term *scientia* occurs in connection with the Christian doctrine of faith.[13] One must realise that Augustine, for Aquinas, is one of the most prominent *doctores ecclesiae*, whose writings have authority in matters of theology next to that of the canonical texts of the Christian religion. The use of the term *scientia*, with respect to the doctrine of faith, is thus sanctioned by the authority of Augustine himself. The way Aquinas is proceeding in this question is therefore as follows: given the fact that the Christian tradition, in the person of one of its most eminent teachers, speaks of the doctrine of faith in terms of *scientia*, how, then, can this doctrine be understood to constitute a *scientia*?

According to Aquinas, in order to fulfil the requirements of a *scientia*, knowledge must be true and certain in such a way that its truth is grounded in principles, which are known *per se*. A science is, essentially, *cognitio ex principiis*, cognition of propositions (conclusions) the truth of which depends logically on prior propositions, which are known through themselves (principles). It is essential for a *scientia* that its propositions – or that which is known by those propositions – must be completely determinate in their truth, so as to exclude the possibility of a propositional connection between two terms which is not sufficiently grounded.

As regards the principles on which the conclusions depend for their truth, there are two varieties of science. A science may proceed from principles immediately known as true in the natural light of the intellect. This constitutes a 'normal' human science based on self-evident principles, *principia per se nota*. But Aristotle also suggests the possibility of a subaltern science, which proceeds from principles known by the light of a higher science.[14] Optics, for example, is subaltern to geometry, because some propositions, which serve as principles in the *scientia* of optics, are not self-evidently known, but are conclusions demonstrated in the higher *scientia* of geometry. One might say that the *scientia* of optics borrows its principles from the higher science of geometry in which their truth is ascertained. Now, according to this model of a subaltern science, sacred doctrine can be understood, Aquinas says, to be a *scientia*, since its conclusions are based on principles known by the light of a superior *scientia*, namely the *scientia* of God and the saints.[15] These principles, from which the *scientia* of faith proceeds, are identified by Aquinas as the articles of faith, the concise summary of Christian faith, which contains the basic truths of sacred doctrine.

---

[13] Augustine, *De trinitate*, XIV, 1: 'Huic scientiae attribuitur illud tantummodo quo fides saluberrima gignitur, nutritur, defenditur, roboratur.'

[14] *ST* Ia, Q. 1, art. 2: 'duplex est scientiarum genus. Quaedam enim sunt, quae procedunt ex principiis notis lumine naturali intellectus ... Quaedam vero sunt, quae procedunt ex principiis notis lumine superioris scientiae'.

[15] *ST* Ia, Q. 1, art. 2: 'Et hoc modo sacra doctrina est scientia: quia procedit ex principiis notis lumine superioris scientiae, quae scilicet est scientia Dei et beatorum.'

One may certainly admire the ingenuity with which Aquinas argued for sacred doctrine's status as *scientia* by means of Aristotle's notion of subalternation. But is it also a convincing solution? To many, Aquinas's solution appears to be artificial and not really convincing. Sacred doctrine may be regarded as a science, but only so from the perspective of God and the saints in heaven, not from the perspective of ordinary humans in this life. It is not a science in any humanly recognisable sense, since no human being can grasp, or establish by argument, the truth of its principles. The principles must be accepted on the authority of faith. Should we conclude, following for instance the opinion of Chenu and of many others, that sacred doctrine is shown to be at most an imperfect science, or a science in a merely analogous sense?[16]

Let us first note that to regard sacred doctrine as but an imperfect science does not seem to be in accordance with Aquinas's intention. There is no suggestion that the science of faith somehow falls short of the standard of a pure rational science. On the contrary, compared to the other – human – sciences, sacred doctrine is even thought to be the most noble (*dignior*) science because of its greater certainty, since it is said to be a science that derives its certitude from the light of divine knowledge, not from the light of fallible human reason.[17] Because its intelligibility is founded in the light of the divine intellect, sacred doctrine is thought to be a superior science, even the highest wisdom, which includes in itself everything the lower human sciences contain of truth.

From a modern critical point of view this way of arguing may seem hopelessly question-begging: if sacred doctrine is what it is said to be, a partial expression of the divine truth itself, and if this divine truth is understood metaphysically as the 'first truth', on which every truth in the domain of human knowledge depends, then it is undoubtedly true and certain, and more so than any human science. But it is of course impossible to establish this claim from an independent standpoint.

For Aquinas, apparently, a science should not be judged by the extent to which its propositions can be epistemologically justified in the natural light of human reason itself. A presumed opposition between the autonomy of reason and the docility of faith is not at issue here. What he is mainly occupied with is to account for the intrinsic truth and certainty of

---

[16] According to Chenu, it is essential for a science in the Aristotelian sense that it proceeds from principles which are *per se nota*. The appeal to a higher authority, which should be obeyed in faith, is incompatible with the rational autonomy which is proper to a science. Chenu concludes that sacred doctrine can be a *scientia* 'only imperfectly'. M.-D. Chenu, *La Théologique comme science au XIIIe siècle*, 3rd edn (Paris: Vrin, 1969), p. 84.

[17] *ST* Ia, Q. 1, art. 5: 'Secundum certitudinem quidem, quia aliae scientiae certitudinem habent ex naturali lumine rationis humanae, quae potest errare: haec autem certitudinem habet ex lumine divinae scientiae, quae decipi non potest.'

the knowledge that pertains to sacred doctrine. In the Christian tradition, the propositions of faith are believed to be true in virtue of their being revealed by God himself. Now, what Aquinas does is no more than explain how their alleged character of being true in virtue of God's revelation can be made intelligible. Sacred doctrine, he argues, consists primarily in knowledge of God (in the sense of both the objective and the subjective genitive). This knowledge – the propositions of Christian doctrine – is true and certain because it is founded on a set of principles the truth of which is reducible to the knowledge God possesses of himself. So it is a *scientia*, not in spite of its being based on revelation, but, on the contrary, precisely because and in so far as its knowledge is reducible to the science of God himself. That the principles of this science are not known to be true in the light of the human intellect is not an objection to its alleged scientific status, so Aquinas argues, because there are more examples of sciences of which the principles are not self-evidently known but 'believed'. The epistemological access of human reason to the truth of the principles is not a criterion for a 'science'. And neither does an insurmountable gap exist between God who knows the truth about himself and the human intellect that merely believes it, since the distance between humans believing the truth and God's knowing that truth is bridged by the knowledge of the saints.[18] That is to say: it is part of the Christian understanding of 'faith' that its object can be known by the human intellect, and shall be known when human life has come to its final fulfilment. It belongs to the human perspective of faith to understand itself as relating somehow to, or sharing in, the divine perspective, which is the eschatological fulfilment of the dynamics of the human perspective.[19]

Now, sacred doctrine may be considered to be a *scientia* in the proper sense of the word.[20] It is a *scientia* based on revelation in the Scriptures and as such it is distinct from the philosophical sciences. However, this does not mean that it is a *scientia* about a distinct domain of reality. And neither is its consideration restricted to the contents of the positive revelation in Scripture. According to Aquinas, the *scientia* of sacred doctrine must have a unity that is grounded in its formal object, that is, the

---

[18] I take this to be the point of Aquinas's statement that the higher science concerns the 'science of God and the saints'.

[19] Compare Aquinas's view that through the theological virtue of faith (*fides*) the human intellect is brought to share in the knowledge God has of himself.

[20] There is no reason to consider the science of sacred doctrine to be a *scientia* in a mere analogous sense. The distinctive and proper character of a *scientia* consists in its being knowledge of conclusions, which are derived discursively from self-evident principles. This perfectly applies to sacred doctrine, since in sacred doctrine too, one has to distinguish between basic truths (the articles of faith) and derived truths (conclusions).

formality under which it considers reality. Now, being defined by the formality of Scripture, which considers some things as being revealed by God (*divinitus revelata*), sacred doctrine extends its consideration to all things that are 'revealable of God' (*divinitus revelabilia*).[21] The shift from sacred Scripture to sacred doctrine is accompanied by a widening of its gaze to the whole of reality. Being a *scientia*, sacred doctrine cannot be restricted to factual revelation in Scripture; rather, it considers the whole of reality under the aspect of the intelligibility which things have when seen in the light of God's revelation. On the one hand, one must acknowledge an essential distinction between philosophical knowledge and the knowledge of sacred doctrine. On the other hand, the diverse fields of knowledge of the philosophical sciences are subsumed by, and integrated in, the higher and more comprehensive intelligibility of the *scientia* of sacred doctrine.[22] Sacred doctrine is not a science about a different reality; it is about the same reality but seen under a different formality. The different intelligible aspects of reality that are disclosed and investigated by the different philosophical disciplines are included in this science in a more unified and comprehensive manner, notwithstanding the fact that its formal point of view is only accessible for humans through faith.

It appears now that sacred doctrine is not only a *scientia* which stands apart, separate from the disciplines of human knowledge; it is also related to the whole of human knowledge in so far as it considers the same reality and treats of the same subjects, but from a higher point of view. It is this complex relationship of inclusion that sanctions, in a certain way, the introduction and the use of philosophical rationality within the domain of sacred doctrine.

Let us clarify this with an example. It belongs to philosophy, particularly to metaphysics, to prove the incorruptibility of the human (intellectual) soul. According to Aquinas, the philosophy of Aristotle has correctly shown that the human soul, in so far as it is the principle of intellectual cognition, does not depend on matter but subsists in itself (*forma in se subsistens*). This same truth is also implied by the *scientia* of sacred doctrine, because the incorruptibility of the soul is presupposed by the Christian belief in the resurrection of souls. Although the mystery of the resurrection is *supra rationem,* beyond the grasp of philosophical

---

[21] *ST* Ia, Q. 1, art. 3: 'Quia igitur sacra Scriptura considerat aliqua secundum quod sunt divinitus revelata . . . , omnia quaecumque sunt divinitus revelabilia, communicant in una ratione formali obiecti huius scientiae'.

[22] See *ST* Ia, Q. 1, art. 3, ad 2: 'ea quae in diversis scientiis philosophicis tractantur, potest sacra doctrina, una existens, considerare sub una ratione, inquantum scilicet sunt divinitus revelabilia: ut sic sacra doctrina sit velut quaedam impressio divinae scientiae, quae est una et simplex omnium'.

reason, its truth presupposes the incorruptibility of the soul, which is open to philosophical demonstration. In so far as the incorruptibility of soul is presupposed by the teachings of faith, its truth must be held on faith, at least by those who are not acquainted with the demonstration.

The incorruptibility of the soul, considered as a presupposition of the truth of faith, is an example of what Aquinas used to call the 'preambles of faith', that is, those truths about God, presupposed by the articles of faith, which can be known by natural reason.[23] It is especially with respect to these 'preambles' that philosophy is put into use in the *scientia* of sacred doctrine. Although this *scientia* is conceived of as formally independent from the philosophical sciences, its exposition may use philosophical demonstrations in order to make the teachings of faith 'clearer' (*ad maiorem manifestationem*). In Thomas's view, sacred doctrine does not depend on the philosophical sciences, because it accepts its principles immediately from God through revelation.[24] It is not subordinate to any of the philosophical sciences. But although the *scientia* of sacred doctrine is founded in God himself, and as such superior to the whole of human philosophy, 'we' (the human intellect) may need the help of philosophy in order to obtain a clearer understanding of its truths. Aquinas thus distinguishes between the truth of sacred doctrine itself, absolutely certain and true by reason of its being grounded in God himself, and our apprehension and understanding of its truth, which is less certain 'because of the weakness of our intellect'.[25] It is at this point that philosophy enters the scene. Philosophy is put into service of sacred doctrine, not to prove its truth, but in order to make its contents more manifest (*ad maiorem manifestationem*). The need of philosophy is due to the imperfection of the human intellect, 'which is more easily led (*manuducitur*) by what is known through natural reason to that which is above reason'.[26]

---

[23] See *ST* Ia, Q. 2, art. 2, ad 1 ('praeambula ad articulos'); and IIaIIae, Q. 1, art. 5, ad 3.

[24] *ST* Ia, Q. 1, art. 5, ad 2: 'Haec scientia accipere potest aliquid a philosophicis disciplinis, non quod ex necessitate eis indigeat, sed ad maiorem manifestationem eorum quae in hac scientia traduntur. Non enim accipit sua principia ab aliis scientiis, sed immediate a Deo per revelationem.' For my interpretation of this statement concerning the relationship between faith and reason it is crucial to distinguish between the *scientia* of sacred doctrine in itself and our (imperfect) understanding and appropriation of its contents.

[25] *ST* Ia, Q. 1, art. 5, ad 1: 'propter debilitatem intellectus humani'.

[26] *ST* Ia, Q. 1, art. 5, ad 2: 'qui ex his quae per naturalem rationem (ex qua procedunt aliae scientiae) cognoscuntur, facilius manuducitur in ea quae sunt supra rationem, quae in hac scientia traduntur'.

The *manifestatio* through philosophy

Although these explanations with respect to the ancillary status of philosophy in theology are rather marginal and not much elaborated, they are still important to understanding something of what Aquinas is actually doing in the *Summa*. Let us return to the arguments for the existence of God at the beginning of the *Summa*. Following the *ordo disciplinae*, the order of learning by which one is introduced systematically into the body of knowledge constituting a *scientia*, one should begin with God, the subject-matter (*subiectum*) of the science of sacred doctrine. The reason is that in sacred doctrine all things are treated under the aspect of God (*sub ratione Dei*). Knowledge of God is presupposed by everything else that is treated in this science. Now, the first thing one must know of the subject of a science, is whether it exists (*an sit*).[27] We see Aquinas treating the first thing to know first: the second question of the *Summa* is devoted to the issue of God's existence: *an Deus sit*. Everything else that must be understood about God according to the doctrine of Christian faith, for example, that he is good, that he is triune, that he is the creator of everything that exists, and so forth, presupposes the knowledge that God is.[28] The knowledge that God is good, for instance, presupposes the truth that God is, since any predicate is a qualification of a thing's being. Being is the first predicate of a thing.

At first sight it seems quite reasonable to assume that the existence of God ('that God is') may count as a basic truth of the *scientia* of sacred doctrine, to be accepted on faith. This is in fact Kretzmann's view. Considering the nature of Aquinas's project in the *Summa*, it would be perfectly legitimate, according to Kretzmann, to accept the proposition 'God exists' as a principle, taken directly from revelation, from which the *scientia* of theology starts to argue. This suggestion is not wholly absurd. Beginning the exposition of sacred doctrine with what seems to be a philosophical proof of God's existence threatens, so it seems, the declared independence of sacred doctrine with respect to human philosophy. In Aquinas's view, the proposition 'God exists' is, considered in itself, a self-evident truth (since God is his being), but not self-evidently known by us.[29] The truth of God as known by himself (*prima veritas*), which includes the truth of his existence, is *supra rationem*, and as such

---

[27] *ST* Ia, Q. 2, art. 2, sed contra: 'primum enim quod oportet intelligi de aliquo, est an sit'.

[28] Because of this the translation of the Latin *esse* with 'existence' is not wholly adequate. Each predicate of God (being good, being one, etc.) presupposes the first predicate of being.

[29] *ST* Ia, Q. 2, art. 1: 'haec propositio, Deus est, quantum in se est, per se nota est . . . Sed quia nos non scimus de Deo quid est, non est nobis per se nota.'

has been communicated to us through revelation. Hence, we are allowed to give our consent to the truth that God exists in the light of revelation: God let himself be known. In this case the proposition of God's existence is not a *scibile* but a *credibile*, something the truth of which is affirmed in the light of faith. Now, we see Aquinas referring, immediately preceding the presentation of the Five Ways, to the self-revelation of God in Scripture, where God in person declares himself to exist (*Ego sum qui sum*).[30]

From a modern perspective, this authoritative appeal to God, who declares himself to exist, in the immediate context of the demonstration of God's existence might be thought to be very odd and even misplaced. In the modern project of natural theology, any reference to positive religion and a factual revelation is ruled out. One cannot assume the truth of any reference in the Scripture to the existence of God, since this is precisely what has to be demonstrated. But, seen from the perspective of Aquinas's theological method, it makes perfectly good sense. What he is saying is this: although there are several objections against the existence of God, which should be taken seriously, we Christians affirm, by the authority of Scripture itself, that God exists. Assuming that this is true, as we believe it is, let us try to show, through reason, how this truth that God exists can be made understandable to us. This seems to be a case of what Aquinas calls *manifestatio*, that is, a rational clarification of a truth of revelation by means of philosophical arguments.[31]

The philosophers offer several arguments by which they intend to demonstrate the existence of God, being the first cause of all things, through his effects. The theologian may employ these arguments in order to manifest the truth that God exists to the human intellect. The arguments show the way in which the truth that God exists can be affirmed in relation to the object of the human intellect. God, a word of faith, is posited in an intelligible form, in so far as he is conceived of as the 'first cause' or the 'first being', the existence of which is implied by the intelligibility of the object of human knowledge.

What should be stressed is that, according to Aquinas, God's being, as such, cannot be known, and that the conclusion of the Five Ways does not make the truth of his being knowable to us. God's being is not subject to a demonstration, nor to a definition, nor to any other rational form of knowledge. The arguments lead the human intellect to the insight into the truth of the proposition that God is, not into the truth of God's

---

[30] *ST* Ia, Q. 2, art. 3: 'Sed contra est quod dicitur Exodi 3,14, ex persona Dei: *I am Who am.*'

[31] In my view the *manifestatio*, mentioned in *ST* Ia, Q. 1, art. 5, ad 2, includes the rational form of demonstration, without, however, being limited to it. Even in the context of the Trinity one can speak of *manifestatio* by philosophical means.

being.[32] But still, one can say that the arguments show the intelligible sense of our affirmation that God exists, which is implied by the propositions of faith.

The 'Catholic truth'

There is unmistakably a strong philosophical dimension in the *Summa*, which cannot be reduced to a use of philosophy wholly internal to faith, aiming at an analytical and argumentative clarification of its doctrinal statements (*pace* Kretzmann). The distinctive feature of the philosophical in Aquinas is the particular focus on the truth of being. According to Aquinas, the truth of reality is disclosed to the intellect in virtue of its being. Any doctrine, if it is to constitute a *scientia*, that is, knowledge of the true, must somehow fall under the scope of the transcendental idea of being, since the true is convertible with being (*ens et verum convertuntur*).

At the same time one has to recognise that Aquinas does not proceed formally like a philosopher, and that the theological method of the *Summa* is conceived in contrast to reason's approach to the truth of reality. In the general prologue he presents himself as a *doctor catholicae veritatis*, a teacher of Catholic truth. The expression 'Catholic truth' demands some explanation. It refers, in the first place, to the truth of the Catholic faith. The truth about which Aquinas wishes to speak in the *Summa* is normatively determined by the founding texts and the doctrinal system of the Church. Still, the phrase 'Catholic truth' must be read, I think, in a speculative sense, and with the emphasis on 'truth'. If it is about 'truth', then it cannot be relative to a particular point of view or to a particular religious tradition by which 'insiders' (the faithful) are divided from the 'outsiders'. As truth, Catholic truth is not simply the truth as Catholics see it, that is, their particular perception of the truth. If it is the truth, then it can be seen, in principle, and acknowledged to be true by everyone, since the truth is universal. This is why, in my view, the *scientia beatorum* is indispensable for the concept of a *scientia* of faith. It is only in relation to a supposed *scientia beatorum* – a knowledge that consists in seeing the truth about God – that the factual claim of a doctrine of faith that entails the truth about God receives an intelligible sense.

The phrase 'Catholic truth' must be interpreted, I think, as referring to the intelligibility implicit in the positive tradition of Christian faith, its

---

[32] See *ST* Ia, Q. 3, art. 4, ad 2. The distinction between knowing God's being (*esse Dei*) and knowing that God is (*Deum esse*) is strongly emphasised by Velecky.

founding Scriptures, its beliefs and its religious and moral ideas. 'Truth' stands for something which transcends the realm of the positive given. It is like when one says: 'What I believe are not just propositions: I believe in the reality to which the propositions of faith refer, or are taken to refer, by signifying, albeit inadequately, the truth of that reality.' Now, the historical and positive doctrine of Christian faith is taken by its adherents to be a doctrine about God. To consider the doctrine of Christian faith as a 'doctrine' which discloses something about God (and not only empirically, that is, as how a particular historical tradition perceives 'God') is to consider that doctrine in the light of its truth. And to pursue its truth means to be involved in a proper theological undertaking which intends to make manifest the implicit intelligibility of the factual doctrine of Christian faith. So when Aquinas asserts that sacred doctrine is a *scientia*, this 'is' is not a matter of fact; it pertains to how this doctrine must be understood to be, if it is what it is claimed to be: a teaching received from God himself through revelation. If this is the 'Catholic truth', its intrinsic intelligibility, which it is supposed to possess, can only be accounted for if there is a way for us to affirm the very being of God, of whom the biblical revelation can be understood to be a revelation.

Throughout the whole of the *Summa* the rationality of philosophy remains formally external to what belongs to the doctrine of faith, since its teachings are beyond the reach of rational proof, not because faith is the domain of the irrational, but because its truth is, as it were, too bright to be grasped by an intellect which, in its rational-discursive manner of knowing, is adapted to the 'darkened' intelligibility of phenomenal reality. The doctrine of faith is an immediate, although veiled and partial, expression (*impressio*) of the 'first truth', of the 'in itself most manifest nature', to which our intellect relates but indirectly, through its darkened reflection in sensible reality.[33] From this one must conclude that the conception of a *scientia* of faith, which derives its truth directly from the 'first truth' itself, is only thinkable within the supposition of a metaphysical account of the truth of being. The theological science of the *Summa* is conceived against the background of a metaphysical picture of reality, in which the human intellect and its mode of apprehending the truth is positioned in distinction to the intrinsic truth of reality. The human intellect knows the essence of reality from the bottom up, so to speak, by reducing that which is more known to us (the sensible effects) to what is more known qua nature (the intelligible causes of those effects). This positioning of the human intellect as 'weak' and 'imperfect' in relation

---

[33] It is in this way that the so-called 'weakness' of the human intellect must be understood; see *ST* Ia, Q. 1, art. 5, ad 1: 'propter debilitatem intellectus nostri, qui *se habet ad manifestissima naturae, sicut oculus noctuae ad lumen solis*, sicut dicitur in II *Metaphys*'.

to the intelligible order of reality itself must be understood as a self-positioning in the light of the absolute idea of being, a self-positioning which entails the contrasting idea of a divine mode of knowing from the top down, that is, a way of knowing things through the 'first truth' itself. Now, the mode of knowing proper to the *scientia* of faith is derived from this divine mode of knowing the truth. In this way Aquinas can rightly claim the epistemological independence of the doctrine of revelation from philosophy, but only thanks to a metaphysical movement of thought by which the object domain of human knowledge is reduced to the first principle of being and truth. In this sense, the demonstration of the very being of God and the consequent determination of the divine being (*simplicitas*, *perfectio*, etc.) is indispensable for the idea of a science, which derives its truth and certainty from the truth of God himself.

The Summa's keyword with regard to the status of philosophical reason in the doctrine of faith is *manuductio*. By what is known through natural reason, the human intellect is led more easily to that which is above reason. Philosophy thus plays a mediating role: it mediates between the human intellect and the full intelligibility of revealed truth, which is beyond the grasp of reason. What Aquinas has in mind in speaking about the 'manuduction' of the human intellect is exemplified by the metaphysical reduction that is performed in the proofs of God's existence. Even when the truth of God (the 'first truth', upon which faith rests) is too bright to be grasped by way of an intellectual intuition, the human intellect is brought by reason to the insight that the darkened intelligibility of its proper object – the being of sensible things – points to a first principle of intelligibility which surpasses the object-domain of the human, sense-bound intellect. In this way philosophy does not prove the truth of faith, but it shows, by means of natural reason, that there must be a 'first being' and a 'first truth' in relation to which the claims of faith can be understood to be fulfillable. Without this philosophical *manuductio*, by which the (ontological) subject of the science of sacred doctrine is given an intelligible determination, the Christian *revelatio* cannot be understood to be what it is assumed to be: true knowledge that refers to the reality of God. Without the 'manuduction' of metaphysics, disclosing the field of the truth of being, the Christian revelation will lapse into the positivity of a historical religion.

Aquinas's Appropriation of *Liber de causis* to Articulate the Creator as Cause-of-Being

DAVID B. BURRELL CSC

Western medieval appreciation of the Hellenic philosophical tradition was first mediated through Islamic and Jewish thinkers who profited from the flurry of translating surrounding caliph al-Ma'amûn's founding of the Beit al-Hikma [House of Wisdom] in Baghdad in 830. Although the tensions were not immediately evident, the initial affinity which Muslim thinkers felt with this philosophy had to do with its inherent penchant for resolving all things to one source: be that Plato's *Good* or Aristotle's *prime mover*. For *tawhîd*, or faith-in-divine-unity, is the very watchword of Islam.[1] The result was something called *falsifa*, where the transliteration signals the importation. Both Jewish and Muslim revelation centred on a free creator, presupposing nothing, however, so the philosophical drive to unity would encounter significant constraints from the side of faith, which the philosophical legacy tended to sweep aside in favour of a neat and comprehensive intellectual explanatory scheme. Adapted from the formidable pagan alternative elaborated by Plotinus, notably by al-Farâbî, the axiomatic model left no room for freedom in the first cause, yet came to enjoy the authority of Aristotle, despite the fact that his *prime mover* fell far short of a primal source. So two thinkers of the Islamicate – al-Ghazali and Moses ben Maimon – confronted this powerful and attractive scheme with Qur'an and Torah, respectively. That was the problematic which Aquinas engaged, relying palpably on the key distinctions supplied by Maimonides, who was himself probably acquainted with Ghazali's arguments: that neither free creation nor necessary emanation were susceptible of demonstration. Aquinas would carry this strategy one step further, however, to probe the conceptual

---

[1] Cristina D'Ancona Costa, *La Casa della Sapienza: La trasmissione della metafisica greca e la formazione delle filosofia araba* (Naples: Guerini e Associati, 1996), pp. 17, 62–4.

possibility of a free creation without an initial moment of time – something both al-Ghazali and Maimonides tended to regard as oxymoronic.[2]

The lynchpin in his exposition of the possibility of a free everlasting origination was the proposition that creation, as the 'emanation of being entire from the universal cause',[3] could not itself take time, for no *process* can be involved in so primal an expression of *act*. It is this lapidary formula of Aquinas which I wish to explore here, showing how his encounter with the *Liber de causis* offered Aquinas a vehicle for introducing the creator as cause-of-being.[4] As his commentary on this seminal text (which he recognised to be an Islamic adaptation of Proclus) displays, however, the Neoplatonic scheme it followed and propagated could hardly on the face of it expound a free creator. So Aquinas's re-directing of the Arabic text *Kitâb al-khaîr* [Book of the Pure Good] will prove to be no less significant than the particular re-casting of Proclus by the anonymous Muslim writer. Yet the fact remains that Aquinas did fasten on this work as key to his endeavour to incorporate a free creator into the Hellenic heritage, just as he insisted on employing the term 'emanation' for creation, even after removing and gutting the scheme of necessary emanation enthusiastically adopted by the Islamic thinkers al-Farabi and Ibn Sina, ostensibly to articulate the revelation of a unitary creator of the universe. That same scheme, trenchantly attacked by al-Ghazali and Moses Maimonides in the name of revelation as impugning a free creator and so rendering revelation itself incredible, was rejected by Aquinas for mediating the act of creation. So another way to cast our net is to ask why Aquinas still felt that *emanation* offered the best metaphor for the *sui generis* activity of creation, even of a free creator?

Moreover, this inquiry is critical for me, since 20 years of comparative exploration into this question has been shaped by the initial opposition between 'necessary emanation' and 'free creation'.[5] Yet that bipolar frame can lead only so far. In fact, as we shall see that Aquinas realised,

---

[2] See David B. Burrell, *Freedom and Creation in Three Traditions* (Notre Dame, IN: University of Notre Dame Press, 1993).

[3] *ST* Ia, Q. 45, art. 1, resp. 'sed etiam emanationem totius entis a causa universali'.

[4] St Thomas Aquinas, *In LDC* [ET: *Commentary on the Book of Causes*, annotated English translation by Vincent A. Guagliardo OP, Charles R. Hess OP and Richard C. Taylor (Washington, DC: Catholic University of America Press, 1996)]. See *The Book of Causes*, trans. Dennis Brand (Milwaukee, WI: Marquette University Press, 1984), and Proclus, *Elements of Theology*, trans. Thomas Taylor (Somerset: The Prometheus Trust, 1994).

[5] David B. Burrell, *Knowing the Unknowable God* (Notre Dame, IN: University of Notre Dame Press, 1986). For a summary statement, see David B. Burrell, 'Aquinas and Islamic and Jewish Thinkers', in Norman Kretzmann and Eleonore Stump (eds.), *The Cambridge Companion to Aquinas* (Cambridge: Cambridge University Press, 1993), pp. 60–84.

formulating what it is that a free creator *does* in creating will require elements from the emanation scheme as well; hence his explicit retention of the term to define creation. For despite Aquinas's celebratory identification of Aristotle's *prime mover* with the liturgical formula: 'quod est Deus per omnia saecula saeculorum' (closing his commentary on the *Physics*), he realised full well that none of Aristotle's four causes could describe the act of creating. Indeed, his occasional use of 'efficient cause' to identify the creator of all is manifestly 'loose' or 'improper', and only intended to contrast this causality with others even less apt. For Aristotle's *efficient cause* always presupposes a subject upon which to work. So Aquinas needed a conception of *causality* not available from Aristotle, yet intimated (as we shall see) in *the Liber de causis*; indeed, a *cause-of-being*. Furthermore, one of the crucial arguments opposing free creation to necessary emanation had been that the axiomatic model used to propose emanation (and so make it *necessary*) failed to distinguish the originator from all that originated from it, since an axiom differs from other premises only by its prominent place in the deductive order. Yet 'the distinction' of creator from creation proves notoriously difficult to articulate, as Robert Sokolowski has shown so ably in his *God of Faith and Reason*.[6] Indeed, customary western attempts to separate creatures from the Creator falsify the relation as effectively as some 'eastern' attempts to collapse the two. Fear of pantheism has moved western thinkers to parse the *distinction* as a *separation*, yet I shall argue that this strategy has diluted the specific assertions of Jewish-Christian-Muslim faith in a creator, so demoting the creator to 'the biggest thing around' and promoting a secular ethos.[7]

Yet affirming that shared faith in a free creator will entail philosophical effort, and watching Aquinas adapt the *Liber de causis* to that end might encourage us to similar efforts. Allow me first to identify those who have helped me to the point of appreciating what *Liber de causis* must have meant for Aquinas, and how we might be enabled to make similar intellectual moves ourselves. I have already mentioned Sokolowski's careful and extended inquiry into 'the distinction' of creator from creation, to articulate its *sui generis* character. A trenchant remark by Bernard McGinn at our conference on 'God and Creation' (in which Sokolowski participated) alerted me to the partial and polemical way in which I was then (1989) opposing free creation to emanation, while Sara Grant's exploring Shankara's use of non-duality to probe 'the

---

[6] Robert Sokolowski, *God of Faith and Reason* (Notre Dame, IN: University of Notre Dame Press, 1982; Washington, DC: Catholic University of America Press, 1995).

[7] See David B. Burrell, 'Creation, Metaphysics, and Ethics', *Faith and Philosophy* 18 (2001), pp. 204–21.

distinction' which Aquinas proposed began to dispel my fears of pantheism.[8] Still more recently, and doubtless in conjunction with John
Milbank and Catherine Pickstock's 'radically orthodox' proposals for
reading the Christian tradition (including Aquinas), I have become fasci-
nated with two thinkers thus far relatively marginal to philosophical
theology: Scottus Eriugena and Meister Eckhart.[9] Their affinity with
Neoplatonic vehicles of thought to help articulate 'the distinction' *not* as
a *separation* has led me to find them to be better guides to what Aquinas
was trying to articulate in a 'cause-of-being' (and hence 'the distinction')
than what has often passed as canonical Thomist interpretation. And the
inquiry into Aquinas's use of the *Liber de causis* will, I hope, indicate
why this is the case.

Let us begin by posing a question which I have hitherto been content
simply to deconstruct: how is it that the One, whose proper effect is
things' very being, effects that? Given the precision of Aquinas – here can
be no *process* whereby things come to be – it is easy to deconstruct: there
is no *how*; coming to be takes no time, creation involves no *change* (in
Aristotle's sense) from one thing to another, requiring a substratum. But
is there then no way at all to articulate what happens in the infinite shift
from nothing to something? We could, as I have, simply reiterate
Aquinas's insistence that the 'proper effect of a creator is the to-be of
things', but that tells us very little indeed; and should we parse it as
'bestowing being on things', that way of speaking (we shall see) falsifies
the relation as well. Here is where the *Liber de causis*, as Aquinas adapts
it, may well lend a hand: think of creating as an ordering – a salient
feature of the emanation scheme, for things come to be according to their
kind, whether we are following Genesis or Aristotle! *Being*, of course, is
not a kind, but whatever is, is inanimate, animate, or intelligent, in the
sense that something may simply exist, or exist as a living being, or as an
understanding being. Now this fact of categorisation (or levels of *formal
cause* [Aristotle]) elicits two opposing pictures. One is additive: being +
self-motion + intention; and hence subtractive as well: taking away
intelligence will yield vegetative, removing that yields simple inanimate
being. The other retains the sense of modes of existing, regarding them as
ascending levels as well, but relates these levels not additively but virtu-

---

[8] See Sara Grant, *Towards an Alternative Theology*, which comprises the Teape
lectures given at Cambridge and Bristol in 1989, with the subtitle *Confessions of a
Non-dualist Christian* (Bangalore: Asia Trading Corporation, 1991; Notre Dame,
IN: University of Notre Dame Press, 2002).

[9] See John Milbank and Catherine Pickstock, *Truth in Aquinas* (London:
Routledge, 2000); the insightful introduction to his thought by Deirdre Carabine,
John Scottus Eriugena (Oxford: Oxford University Press, 2000); and Bernard
McGinn's masterful study, *The Mystical Thought of Meister Eckhart: The Man from
whom God Hid Nothing* (New York: Crossroad, 2003).

ally. That is, the being of inanimate things is regarded as restricted, those capable of growth and/or of self-motion more ample, and those also endowed with understanding and intention yet more fully realising the reaches of being.

Both pictures are present in the *Liber de causis* as well as in Aquinas, yet the effort to incorporate a free creator into the scheme of categorisation will inevitably privilege the *virtual* picture. The tension surfaces quite dramatically (for those who can unveil drama in ontology!) when Aquinas proposes to identify the creator God uniquely as the One whose very essence is to-be. This succinct formula offers *simpleness* as the 'formal feature' securing 'the distinction' by singling out God in the only way possible – without turning God into god, the 'biggest thing around', and so effectively eclipsing God's divinity as well as 'the distinction'.[10] Yet we must meet the *prima facie* objection that what is simple is ontologically 'lower' than what is composed or complex, much as animate things are more complex than inanimate. He does this by reversing the picture itself, proposing that the One whose essence is to-be (and so can cause all else to be) should not be conceived as 'mere being' but as the fullness of being, so that *simpleness* here denotes plenitude rather than a lack.[11]

But how can we execute such an about-face? What makes one see (as in Wittgenstein's duck/rabbit example) that the virtual picture of levels of being must take precedence over the additive? I suspect – along with and thanks to Josef Pieper – that the effort to incorporate and properly articulate a creator into one's metaphysics will decide it, but there are supporting arguments as well. The most telling, I believe, is one derived from Aristotle's argument to the unity of substantial forms, captured in the maxim: the being of living things is to live.[12] Indeed, contrary to the *prima facie* sense of the *Liber de causis*, levels of being are not separable or subtract-able. Take away *life* from a living thing and *it* remains inanimate for a very short while; indeed, what is left begins to decompose into elements and is soon no longer identifiable as one thing. This fact supports the virtual picture: being expresses itself in different ways. Moreover, if 'higher levels' were simply added, what would make the resultant being one sort of thing? This is what Aristotle meant by the

---

[10] See David B. Burrell, *Aquinas: God and Action* (London: Routledge; and Notre Dame, IN: University of Notre Dame Press, 1979).

[11] See *ST* Ia, Q. 3.

[12] St Thomas Aquinas, *In DA*, Leonine edition: lines 172–87, pp. 97–8; Marietti – Pirotta edition: paragraph 319. The reference is to τὸ δὲ ζῆν τοῖς ζῶσι τὸ εἶναί ἐστιν, Aristotle, *De anima*, Bk II, Ch. 4, 415b12–13 [ET: *Commentary on Aristotle's De anima*, trans. Kenelm Foster OP and Silvester Humphries OP, Book Two, Lecture VII (Notre Dame, IN: Dumb Ox Books, 1994), p. 102].

'unity of substantial form'. Moreover, a closer reading of the *Liber de causis* reveals just such a picture. The bestowal of being [*esse*] by the first cause is an orderly bestowal, yielding an inherent order structuring each existing thing so that higher levels are implicit in lower. Indeed, were this not the case, were *being* not an abundant source expressing itself in different ways, then *existing* would have to be pictured (as many do) as something added to a potential thing, as in 'actualising a possible state of affairs'. But that picture is doubly redundant, for it first presumes 'potential things', that is, an order or structure present before something exists; and then presumes existing to be a feature (or 'accident') which can be added to a non-existing 'thing'. These two incoherencies are in fact one, but it is instructive to see how *existing* must be construed as a feature once one adopts 'possible things'.

Ironically enough, so-called 'existential' readings of Aquinas, by their description of *esse* as 'act of existing', can unwittingly turn *esse* [to-be] into a feature. It is true, of course, that by identifying *esse* as *act* Aquinas expressly intended to eliminate that move, suggested by Avicenna's terminology of *existing* as an 'accident' [*'arad*]. Yet his own expression of 'receiving *esse*' could subvert his own intentions as well.[13] So how can we escape these traps? *The Liber de causis* offers a way: to see creation as the orderly bestowal of things' being, which adopts the metaphor of *emanation* and sees *existing* as a participation in being by virtue of the One whose very essence is to-be, and so alone can make things participate in being. And as a way of spelling out the metaphor of *participation*, we are invited to see it as an order inherent in each thing. So *existing* is no more something *added to* a thing than learning is something acquired, like a degree after one's name. The degree is acquired, of course, as a step in credentialing, but *learning* (as Socrates insisted) is really *recollection*, as we utilise others to hone the faculties already present in our being intentional persons. What comes with our mode of being is an ordered set of capacities, which stand to be perfected and need help to do so, but when perfected are so from within. Moreover, part of being intentional beings is that these capacities *desire* their perfection, that is (in *Liber de causis* terms), they are so shaped from within as to strive to return to their proper good, their source. Such is the power of a creation-centred picture of *being*: *virtual* (not additive), and *directional* towards its source. This picture is completed in fully intentional, or free agents, whose freedom can be expressed as a 'hunger for the good' and so best seen as a response rather than an initiative.[14] Such a picture underscores the antinomies

---

[13] See David B. Burrell, 'Essence and Existence: Avicenna and Greek Philosophy', *Mélanges de l'Institut Dominicain d'Etudes Orientales* (Cairo) 17 (1986), pp. 53–66.

[14] See David B. Burrell, 'Freedom and Creation in the Abrahamic Traditions', *International Philosophical Quarterly* 40 (2000), pp. 161–71; and the development

which Socrates had already exposed in the alternative view of freedom as 'doing what I want to do', which can so easily mean slavery to multiple desires; and also express Nietzsche's model of self-creation as exactly what one must undertake without a creator.

The fullness of the act of existing is displayed in its order, much as the efficacy of any of our actions is assured by the ordering it displays towards its goal. We focus authentically, not by eliminating all but one feature, but by aligning all the relevant features in a proper order, so that the effect is orchestrated. Notice that we cannot escape metaphors here, for there is no given ordering. Revelation assists by allowing us to name 'the Good'. And also by providing us with some strategies of ordering – the Torah, the example of Jesus, the Qur'an – yet here again, discernment is always needed, and traditions can subvert as well as elaborate a given revelation or way. The ur-pattern derives from creation, as conceived by the *Liber de causis*: orderly emanation from the One so that the intentional portion of creation desires to return to its source. Moreover, such an order is not imposed but inherent, as *existing* is not an added feature but an inherent gift. This is seen most fully, according to Aquinas, when we can appreciate this unitary source as freely bestowing what it truly is. For since its manner of being is triune, in creating it freely communicates the manner in which it naturally communicates.[15]

Before concluding, let us return to the original question: how is it that the One, whose proper effect is things' very being, effects that? The *Liber de causis* says: 'first cause infuses all things with a single infusion, for it infuses things under the aspect (*secundum rationem*) of the good'.[16] Aquinas concurs, reminding us that it had already been shown that 'the first cause acts through its being . . . [h]ence it does not act through any additional relation or disposition through which it would be adapted to and mixed with things'.[17] Moreover, 'because the first cause acts through its being, it must rule things in one manner, for it rules things according to the way that it acts'.[18] The following Proposition 21 links this 'sufficiency of God to rule'[19] with divine simpleness: 'since God is simple in the first and greatest degree as having his whole goodness in a oneness that is most perfect'.[20] Hence Proposition 23 can assert: 'what is essen-

by Eleonore Stump, 'Intellect, Will, and the Principle of Alternate Possibilities', in Michael Beatty (ed.), *Christian Theism and the Problems of Philosophy* (Notre Dame, IN: University of Notre Dame Press, 1990), pp. 254–85.

  [15] *ST* Ia, Q. 32, art. 1, ad 3 and resp. ad 3.
  [16] *In LDC* {110} [p. 123].
  [17] *In LDC* {111} [pp. 123–4].
  [18] *In LDC* {111} [p. 124].
  [19] *In LDC* {112} [p. 125].
  [20] *In LDC* {113} [p. 126].

tially act and goodness, namely, God, essentially and originally communicates his goodness to things'.[21] With such a One there can be no anxiety about 'control'; indeed, the simile which the proposition on divine rule elicits is that 'it is proper for a ruler to lead those that are ruled to their appropriate end, which is the good'.[22] For to 'infuse things under the aspect of the good' is precisely to bring all things to be in a certain order, inherent in their very existing, so there is nothing 'external' about divine providence, no imposition – neither 'inasmuch as it establishes things, which is called creation; [nor] inasmuch as it rules things already established'.[23] Indeed, the initial diversity comes from the first cause, who 'produces the diverse grades of things for the completeness of the universe. But in the action of ruling . . . the diversity of reception is according to the diversity of the recipients'.[24] Yet since the original order comes from the One, the One in ruling will 'effortlessly' adapt itself to the order established in creating. Another way of putting all this, and one which should dissolve most conundra regarding 'divine action', is to remind oneself that the creator, in acting, acts always as creator; and this proposition elucidates Aquinas's contention that *creating* and *conserving* are the same action, differing only in that conserving presupposes things present.

Yet since the manner of that action will ever escape us, for its very simplicity belies any *manner* at all – no 'relation or disposition', the best we can do is to remind ourselves that the creator ever acts by constituting the order which inheres in each existing thing, in the measure that it is. (And since essence measures *esse*, it is pointless to oppose essence to existing, in things that are.) Yet since 'order' is a consummately analogous term, we can never be sure we have detected the originating divine order in things, though our conviction that there is one, inscribed in their very being and our intentional attitudes towards them, will continue to fuel our inquiry. Crude classifications – inanimate, animate, intentional – can be supplemented by refined mathematical structures and symmetries (as in DNA), yet each stage of analytic tool will be serving our innate desire to unveil the activity present in these infused 'goodnesses'[25] which constitute our universe. And to grasp something of that constitutive ordering is to come closer to its source, 'because every knowing substance, insofar as it has being more perfectly, knows both the first cause and the infusion of its goodness more perfectly, and the more it both receives and knows this the more it takes delight in it, [so] it follows that

---

[21] *In LDC* {118} [p. 132].
[22] *In LDC* {118} [p. 132].
[23] *In LDC* {122} [p. 137].
[24] *In LDC* {123} [p. 137].
[25] *In LDC* {116} [p. 130].

the closer something is to the first cause the more it takes delight in it'.[26] All is not light or delight, of course, because in truth we cannot, ourselves, hope to *know* 'the first cause and the infusion of goodness'. Indeed, '[t]he most important thing we can know about the first cause is that it surpasses all our knowledge and power of expression',[27] for 'our intellect can grasp only that which has a quiddity participating "to-be" . . . [while] the quiddity of God is "to-be" itself'.[28] Indeed, that is why Aquinas can concur that 'the first cause is above being inasmuch as it is itself infinite "to-be"'.[29] Yet since '[w]hat belong to higher things are present in lower things according to some kind of participation',[30] we can be said to share, as beings, in this inaccessible One.

Reflecting on Aquinas's particular task, we can fairly say that he was concerned to show how *theologia* could be a *scientia* – with neither of those terms translatable into their current modern language cognates. To accomplish this task he received help from thinkers in the Jewish and Muslim traditions: from Maimonides the very strategy itself, and from the *Liber de causis* a philosophical focus on faith in divine unity [*tawhîd*]. Yet as we have noted, he managed as well to exploit the resources of his own tradition, notably in articulating creation according to processions within a triune God. We are placed to appreciate and to develop other features of his thought, as Eckhart did, underscoring the *sui generis* relation which creation is, and searching for metaphors to elucidate it. In this way, we can use his subtle appropriation of the *Liber de causis* to carry out similar adaptations of our own. For me, this has meant coming full circle to appreciate the mode of reflection enshrined in *emanation* to illuminate the uniqueness of the creation-relation, while realising that we shall never adequately articulate it. Yet we can reach for metaphors, as Aquinas did in appropriating the *Liber de causis*, or as Sara Grant has in expounding Shankara's *non-duality* in a vein reminiscent of Meister Eckhart. And should some be put off by the apparently disembodied 'intellectuality' of all this, they need only recall Pierre Hadot's reminders that such rarified modes of thought can only be executed in a milieu shaped by sustained and rigorous 'spiritual exercises'.[31] Such is the inherent *telos* of philosophical theology, as it strains, in the persons of its practitioners, to align itself with the goodnesses infused in things, the divinely ordained order of being.

---

[26] *In LDC* {123} [p. 138].
[27] *In LDC* {43} [p. 46].
[28] *In LDC* {47} [p. 52].
[29] *In LDC* {47} [p. 51].
[30] *In LDC* {17} [p. 20].
[31] For an illuminating introduction to the work of Pierre Hadot, see Arnold Davidson's translation and collection of some key articles in *Philosophy as a Way of Life* (Chicago, IL: University of Chicago Press, 1995).

In Matters of Truth:
Heidegger and Aquinas

LAURENCE PAUL HEMMING

Martin Heidegger suggested that inasmuch as Nietzsche based his understanding on the doctrine that truth is the correctness of the judging reason, then 'Nietzsche is unwittingly in perfect agreement with *Thomas Aquinas*, who said, on the basis of a particular interpretation of *Aristotle*: truth *principally* is in the intellect.'[1] In this short, pithily provocative statement, Heidegger manages to concentrate the entire scope of the question of his (Heidegger's) reading of, and relationship to, Aquinas. Even here the problem is not straightforward: how Heidegger read Aquinas (sometimes resolved as *which* Aquinas Heidegger is supposed to have been able to read) is not the same as how we bring ourselves into an understanding of the impact of Heidegger's own philosophical thought on how it is now possible to read St Thomas's work.

It has sometimes been presumed that Heidegger can only have been a product of the neo-Thomism that dominated theology in the early part of the twentieth century in the wake of the Encyclical *Aeterni Patris*, as if, therefore, this immediately settles the question of how Heidegger read Aquinas or what kind of understanding of Aquinas he might have had. There is, in truth, no evidence to support this claim, and indeed, it is a distraction from the very different and careful considerations Heidegger himself brought to this question. Above all, Martin Heidegger was a perspicacious and sensitive reader of *texts*, which means that he addressed himself to what Aquinas actually said, in the few places where he cites and discusses Aquinas's work.

Moreover, because, especially in English-speaking circles, Aquinas has been loosely understood to be the exemplar of the understanding that God and being are the same, and with a parallel crudity Heidegger has

---

[1] Martin Heidegger, *Grundfragen der Philosophie: Ausgewählte 'Probleme' der 'Logik'*, in *Gesamtausgabe*, vol. 45 (Frankfurt: Klostermann, 1992 (1984)), p. 102: '*Nietzsche*, ohne es zu wissen, [geht] vollkommen einig mit *Thomas von Aquin*, der aufgrund einer bestimmten Auslegung des *Aristoteles* sagt: veritas *principaliter* est in intellectu' (emphasis in original).

been understood to be the philosopher of being, then surely – or so runs the well-trodden thought-path – it is right to bring these two into a confrontation?

Thus from the outset, Aquinas and Heidegger are made to appear to differ on the ground of who, and this means *what* God is, as a difference about the meaning of the word 'being'. Much of the critique of Heidegger as a supposed 'immanentist' thinker, or a nihilist, has been in consequence of this artificial and manufactured confrontation, which penetrates and unfolds in any significant way neither the thought of Heidegger nor that of Aquinas. Heidegger's statement juxtaposing the doctrines of truth of Nietzsche and Aquinas appears, however, to locate Aquinas above all in the genealogy of the history of philosophy and in the history of being's forgettingness or *Seinsvergessenheit*. Moreover, in juxtaposing *Nietzsche* with Aquinas, not only is Aquinas apparently located with regard to the unfolding of metaphysics, but at the same time, it seems, we can place him with regard to the death of God and so to metaphysics' fulfilment. In this respect there appears to be no 'debate' between Heidegger and Aquinas that is possible – the relation between them is decided in advance of our entering the question. We have only to examine the relative 'positions' of these two thinkers with varying degrees of sophistication and then take sides.

This has been the approach, for instance, of the major English-speaking consideration of the work of Heidegger and Aquinas by John Caputo, above all in his book *Heidegger and Aquinas*. Caputo, having spent some time outlining the positions of both thinkers and directing us through various accounts of the two thinkers themselves and of various others into whom Heidegger especially enquired, finally leads us to what is to be *the* central concern. He proposes a section entitled '*Anwesen* and *Esse*: A Confrontation' which will deal with 'the confrontation of the conception of Being in Heidegger and St. Thomas'.[2] Certainly Heidegger occasionally uses the term *Anwesen* (presencing) to indicate *das Sein* (being).[3] Heidegger employs the term *Anwesenheit* (presence) to develop what he argues is the basic understanding of being that persists in all metaphysics. Heidegger understands presence as the ἀεί ὄν, *das Immer-seiende*, or 'being-always' that Heidegger takes as the way philosophy construes its understanding of God from Plato and Aristotle forward, right up to Hegel and Nietzsche. Although Heidegger does use the word

---

[2] John D. Caputo, *Heidegger and Aquinas* (New York: Fordham University Press, 1982), p. 198.
[3] Cf., for instance, Martin Heidegger, *Zur Seinsfrage*, in *Wegmarken*, *Gesamtausgabe*, vol. 9 (Frankfurt: Klostermann, 1996 (1967)), p. 395; *Wozu Dichter*, in *Holzwege*, *Gesamtausgabe*, vol. 5 (Frankfurt: Klostermann, 1994 (1950)), p. 301 and *passim*.

wesen as a verb (normally capitalised in German to mean the noun 'essence'), as in *das Dasein west* – '*Dasein* essences', in fact Heidegger argues that being is in itself to be understood through the pair presence/presencing (*Anwesenheit/Anwesende*).

In this section, Caputo continues: 'And let me now ask, in the light of this reading of Heidegger, whether it is possible to understand the metaphysics of St Thomas within the framework of Heideggerian alethiology'.[4] The neologism 'alethiology' Caputo understands to be 'the ἀλήθεια process',[5] although at best this is only a very loose understanding of what Heidegger understands by the Greek word we translate as truth (ἀλήθεια). For Heidegger, what ἀλήθεια indicates can never be reduced to a process (or even what is indicated in Greek by the term μέθοδος). Caputo says as he sets out in this confrontation: 'I find it difficult to imagine that in the texts of St. Thomas . . . there is to be found a philosophy of ἀλήθεια'.[6] He concludes then, that on the issue of the confrontation *as such* 'one takes a stand either with Thomas and against Heidegger or with Heidegger and against Thomas'.[7] It is only subsequent to this impasse that Caputo proposes to resolve the issue by 'deconstructing' St Thomas to find a theological mysticism within his texts that Heidegger himself had somehow overlooked, but that will allow 'an authentic alliance between St. Thomas and Heidegger'.[8] This mysticism is discovered as an underlying 'non-metaphysical experience of Being' that relies on what Caputo identifies in St Thomas as a commitment to an understanding of participation in being, albeit one which must be 'wrested from him'.[9]

Caputo's argument that there is in Aquinas an underlying theology of participation does not itself avoid metaphysics. This is neither because Heidegger's understanding that the ontological structures of *Dasein* can support a mystical soteriology of theosis – I have argued elsewhere that they can,[10] nor even that Aquinas's theology is shot through with precisely this soteriological understanding – I think it is. The word 'participation' (μέθεξις), heavily employed both by Plato and by Aristotle, relies metaphysically on what is common (κοινόν) across whatever participates

---

[4] Caputo, *Heidegger and Aquinas*, p. 198.

[5] Caputo, *Heidegger and Aquinas*, p. 208, but see the preceding discussion from the beginning of ch. 6.

[6] Caputo, *Heidegger and Aquinas*, p. 198.

[7] Caputo, *Heidegger and Aquinas*, p. 209.

[8] Caputo, *Heidegger and Aquinas*, p. 243. Caputo describes this mysticism (quite correctly) as: 'the end of the self is a non-metaphysical union with God' (p. 250).

[9] Caputo, *Heidegger and Aquinas*, p. 248: cf. pp. 242–3.

[10] See the final chapter of Laurence P. Hemming, *Heidegger's Atheism: The Refusal of a Theological Voice* (Notre Dame, IN: University of Notre Dame Press, 2002).

in what. Thus what is at stake is what is substantially common to both. Taken in relation to the question of being – which is exactly how Caputo wishes to take it – it is being itself which would have to be understood as what is common between the one being divinised and the divine.

Caputo cites Max Müller's study of Aquinas and Heidegger, and argues that it seeks in Aquinas an understanding of being not based on cause and effect, but which discovers rather (in Caputo's summary of it) that 'God is the presence which is concealedly present in everything present in the world.' Caputo argues that this discovery shows how the effects of Aquinas's doctrine of being thereby evades metaphysics, albeit through a 'deconstructive' reading.[11] In fact of course, it does nothing of the sort, since if the word 'being' is substituted for 'God' in this summary, it is possible immediately to see in this very sentence a recapitulation of Plato's (metaphysical) interpretation of Parmenides' doctrine of being, where being is distributed in equal parts throughout the whole.[12] What is at issue here? Two things: first, for Heidegger, either causally or non-causally, in this argument of Caputo's (and Müller's), divinity and being are understood to be the same thing – the one causes the other or participates in the other. Indeed, worse than this, it is precisely the understanding of what it is for beings to participate ($\mu\epsilon\tau\acute{\epsilon}\chi\epsilon\iota\nu$) in being that prepares the way later for being *as* God to be taken as an originating cause, especially in Descartes and the philosophy of subjectivity that he inaugurates. Second, what is really at stake for Heidegger is not whether or not a causal understanding of being is at issue in ontology, but what the *ground* is of the being for whom being is an issue (*Dasein*). Indeed this is precisely Heidegger's earlier definition of what *Dasein* is: 'To grasp the understanding of being means to understand *that* being to whose being-constituted the understanding of being belongs, the *Dasein*.'[13] In other words the question of being can only arise *as a question* for that being who can interrogate itself as the being that it itself is.

Every attempt to disclose the essence of God metaphysically, either through causation (meaning God as the prior cause of all things) or participation, makes the being of God the ground of the being of being human, which is metaphysics. This displaces the ground of the being of being human from the very self that I am, whose being I can then enquire into, onto a being whose being is not transparently interrogable for me,

---

[11] Caputo, *Heidegger and Aquinas*, p. 241, paraphrasing M. Müller, *Existenzphilosophie im geistigen Leben der Gegenwart* (Heidelberg: Kerle Verlag, 1964).

[12] Cf. Plato, *Sophist*, 244b–245a.

[13] Martin Heidegger, *Grundprobleme der Phänomenologie*, in *Gesamtausgabe*, vol. 24 (Frankfurt: Klostermann, 1997 (1975)), p. 322: 'Das Seinsverständnis begreifen heißt aber *das* Seiende zunächst verstehen, zu dessen Seinsverfassung das Seinsverständnis gehört, das Dasein' (emphasis in original).

namely God. It is Heidegger's challenge of this shift of the ground of being from human *Dasein* to the being of God that leads him to pronounce his shocking parody of Aquinas's most often-cited definition of the being of God in *Sein und Zeit*. Thus whereas Aquinas argues that only in God are essence and existence identical,[14] Heidegger argues that '*the "essence" of* Dasein *lies in its existence*'.[15] The reference to Aquinas, and its concomitant provocation, is ineluctable.

For Heidegger, it is the *Ab-grund* or without-ground (abyss) which *Dasein* is, which is the only possible (and therefore genuinely ontological) ground of the being of being human as far as philosophy is concerned, and therefore for whom the question of being can become a genuine question. Once this is understood, only then is human *Dasein* free to understand how *the human being itself* may be saved through divine revelation – even in a soteriology of theosis – but only because of the way in which human *Dasein* already comports itself to itself ontologically. The distinction may be made like this: the question of how Christian *Dasein* is to be saved belongs to faith and revelation, and to theology in so far as it reflects on these: the question of how as *Dasein* the human being itself understands this being-saved, and the basis on which this understanding unfolds for *Dasein* is a possible self-understanding itself only for human *Dasein*. This is because only as *Dasein* may human being enquire into its own ontological determinations and structures – it knows nothing of these determinations and structures as they belong to God as (if any such thing should be possible) God's self-enquiry – though it may know something of these things in so far as they are revealed by God's self-revelation of himself to humanity. This is not different to St Thomas's other most emphatic assertion: only God is transparent to God, God is known by the created intellect only in so far as it receives the light of glory.[16]

What Caputo inadvertently ends up attempting is to resolve the question of being in its relation to God. Thus Caputo concludes, 'we must hear in *esse* the intensely Christian experience of Being . . . We must find in God's relationship to the world not causality but presencing.'[17] What we actually witness here is a sleight of hand – for Christians, even thought non-causally, all that is said here is that God and being turn out to be the same after all: Caputo simply re-divinises being, not through thought, but faith. This is nothing other than an early form of the ever more popular word 'theo-ontology' that is nowadays being counter-

---

[14] Cf. *ST* Ia, Q. 3, art. 4, resp.

[15] Martin Heidegger, *Sein und Zeit*, in *Gesamtausgabe*, vol. 2, p. 56: '*Das "Wesen" des Daseins liegt in seiner Existenz*' (emphasis in original).

[16] *ST* Ia, Q. 12, art. 7, resp.

[17] Caputo, *Heidegger and Aquinas*, p. 283.

posed to the term 'ontotheology' by theologians sensitive to at least
something of Heidegger's critique of metaphysics. The ambiguity is to be
found in Caputo's use of the term 'presencing' (*Anwesen*): Caputo takes
Heidegger's claim that beings are dis-closed (ἀ-λήθεια) and un-covered *in*
presencing and transforms this into a concern about God. He thereby
suggests not that it is God (or something of God) that is disclosed
through the presencing that ἀλήθεια is and unfolds, but that God *is* the
very presencing that *is* this unfolding disclosure. Nothing could be further from what Heidegger understands as the 'truth of being', as ἀλήθεια.

Let us not even ask the question: need being be divine? A question
which I have asked elsewhere and concluded negatively, except to say
that for Heidegger being is always finite and so can *never* function as a
name for God: I would argue St Thomas never said otherwise. 'God is
God's own to-be' does not say, and never did say, God and being are the
same.[18] The question at issue here is also, which Aquinas is Caputo reading? For it is not a matter of concealment, and there is no need either to
deconstruct or destructure the texts, to find that there is in St Thomas a
fully worked out and operative theosis or theology of mystical union of
the human and divine as to what salvation is.[19] The question, 'Which
Aquinas is Caputo reading?' draws our attention to the fact that Caputo
can find in Thomas a metaphysician – indeed that there is something like
the 'philosophy' of St Thomas Aquinas. Mark Jordan has pointed out
that 'for Thomas, membership in a school of philosophy does not befit
Christians . . . Thomas speaks about philosophy, of course, as a habit of
knowing necessary for an educated believer . . . I cannot find that the
epithet *philosophus* is ever applied by Thomas to a Christian'.[20] Fergus
Kerr has not been alone recently in drawing attention to the extent to
which Aquinas, in his understanding of the being of God (a phrase that
even here does not say that being and God are the same), draws his
understanding *not* from the ὄν ἡ ὄν, the science of being in so far as it is
being of Aristotle's *Metaphysics*, but from a reading of the Vulgate's (and
behind that the Septuagint's) rendering of Exodus 3.14.[21] Étienne Gilson

---

[18] See Hemming, *Heidegger's Atheism*, pp. 190–9.

[19] See for a full discussion of this both in St Thomas and in the secondary literature, the chapter 'Deified Creaturehood', in Fergus Kerr OP, *After Aquinas: Versions
of Thomism* (Oxford: Blackwell, 2002), pp. 149–61. Kerr holds the view that
Aquinas 'had a rich conception of the transforming effect of divine grace on the individual believer which clearly amounts to the traditional patristic doctrine of
deification'. See especially A. N. Williams, 'Deification in the *Summa Theologica*: A
Structural Interpretation of the *Prima Pars*', *The Thomist* 61 (1997).

[20] Mark Jordan, *The Alleged Aristotelianism of St. Thomas Aquinas*, The Étienne
Gilson Series 15 (Toronto: Pontifical Institute of Mediaeval Studies, 1990), p. 6. See
also pp. 32–7.

[21] 'Dixit Deus ad Mosen ego sum qui sum'; καὶ εἶπεν ὁ θεὸς πρὸς Μωυσῆν ἐγώ εἰμι ὁ
ὤν.

argues that 'historians of philosophy find themselves confronted with this to them always unpalatable fact: a nonphilosophical statement which has since become an epoch-making statement in the history of philosophy'.[22] Heidegger believed no different – indeed, his stated concern was to strip out this biblical text together with the first verse of the book of Genesis and their combined subsequent effects so that philosophy *as* philosophy could live again. For Heidegger, to think beings in their being means to recognise that in Christianity above all, all beings are explained in their origin as *ens creatum*, 'and where the Creator is the most certain and all beings are the effect of this most beingful cause'.[23] This is what ontotheology is – the fusion of philosophical and theological concerns into one region of thought – so that questions concerning being are answered by means of an understanding derived from an article of faith. Elsewhere Heidegger speaks of how the very definition of modern metaphysics is the clamping together of '*two forces* . . . in the history of Western humanity: the Greek enquiry into beings and Christian faith in God'.[24]

In the first instance, therefore, Heidegger points us in his statement concerning the agreement of Nietzsche and Aquinas to what is *unwitting* about it – his point (contrary to Caputo's and every other attempt to wrestle Heidegger and Aquinas into cheerful agreement one with the other) is that it is an unexpected agreement. For what reason? Is it not surely that Nietzsche and Aquinas would *expect* to be doing different things, and that Heidegger is fully aware of this? Surely what Heidegger draws our attention to is that these two *fall in to agreement* for some reason of which neither would necessarily themselves be aware (if such a thing were possible to them), but which we are now able to see – and all, not because of something to do with whether or not *being* is derived either from Aristotle or from Exodus, but on the basis of an interpretation of the character of truth. Heidegger takes the understanding that truth is to be found more in the intellect than in things to be a standard position of metaphysics, in some sense tying these two figures together. Thus in a supplementary note to a lecture course of 1931–2 he says, 'the common, traditional and firm opinion: *veritas per prius in intellectu*

---

[22] Cf. Étienne Gilson, *God and Philosophy* (New Haven, CT: Yale University Press, 1992 (1941)), p. 40.

[23] Martin Heidegger, *Beiträge zur Philosophie (vom Ereignis)*, in *Gesamtausgabe*, vol. 65, p. 110: '. . . und wo der Schöpfer das Gewisseste ist, alles Seiende die Wirkung dieser seiendsten Ursache'.

[24] Martin Heidegger, *Sein und Wahrheit: 1. Die Grundfrage der Philosophie. 2. Vom Wesen der Wahrheit*, in *Gesamtausgabe*, vol. 36/37 (Frankfurt: Klostermann, 2001), p. 52: '*Zwei Mächte* . . . Mächte der Geschichte des abendländischen Menschen: die griechische Frage nach dem Seienden und der christlichen Glaube an Gott' (emphasis in original).

(Mediaeval), *proprie in solo intellectu* (Descartes), truth as holding-fortrue in thought and as "value" (Nietzsche), is prepared through Aristotle and Plato: ἀλήθεια and ψεῦδος are ἐν διανοίᾳ'.[25] This is an amplification of his statement concerning the unwitting agreement that exists between Nietzsche and Aquinas.

In fact Heidegger is uninterested in any quarrel or congruence between himself and Aquinas – the one recorded time he is asked about it (where Heidegger mentions that he is asked to explain something like this almost every fortnight) he gives a delphic, mocking answer which is no answer at all – when asked if God and being are identical he replies: 'I have asked an old Jesuit friend of mine to show me the place in Thomas Aquinas where he says what "esse" specifically means and what the proposition means that says "Deus est suum esse". I have to this day received no answer.'[26] The Jesuit in question is clearly Suárez – Heidegger's point is that the 'answer' is to be found, not in Aquinas, but in metaphysics, and yet, this answer cannot be found because it is answered in advance, answered with regard to the *ens creatum*. Before even we proceed a step further, we are required – required even by Heidegger – to ask whether simply because Aquinas speaks of being and Heidegger speaks of being, they are speaking in the same way or with the same concern. On this, Heidegger's remarks are now famous – he counterposes the situation of one who asks the question of being (*Seinsfrage*) to that of anyone who believes that in the beginning God created heaven and earth, and comments this 'can supply no answer to our question because they are in no way related to it'.[27] Indeed he concludes they can in no way be brought into relation to it. Those who understand being on the basis of the *ens creatum* are not speaking of the same being in the same way as those who raise the question of being as an ontological question.

Already we are far from the region in which Caputo (and Lotz, Siewerth, Müller and many others) attempt to relate Heidegger to Aquinas, by setting their faces in opposition or by reconciling them. For we set out accepting that what Heidegger is concerned with and what

[25] Martin Heidegger, *Vom Wesen der Wahrheit: Zu Platons Höhlengleichnis und Theätet*, in *Gesamtausgabe*, vol. 34 (Frankfurt: Klostermann, 1997 (1988)), p. 332: 'Die gewöhnliche, überlieferte und feste Meinung: veritas per prius in intellectu (Mittelalter), proprie in solo intellectu (Descartes), Wahrheit als Fürwahrhalten im Denken und als "Wert" (Nietzsche), ist vorbereitet durch Aristoteles und Platon: ἀλήθεια und ψεῦδος sind ἐν διανοίᾳ.'
[26] Martin Heidegger, *Seminare*, in *Gesamtausgabe*, vol. 15 (Frankfurt: Klostermann, 1986), p. 436: 'Ich habe einen mir wohlgesinnten Jesuiten gebeten, mir die Stellen bei Thomas von Aquin zu zeigen, wo gesagt sei, was "esse" eigentlich bedeute und der Satz besage: Deus est suum esse. Ich habe bis heute noch keine Antwort.'
[27] Martin Heidegger, *Einführung in die Metaphysik*, in *Gesamtausgabe*, vol. 40 (Frankfurt: Klostermann, 1983 (1953)), p. 9: 'er kann überhaupt keine Antwort auf unsere Frage darstellen, weil er auf diese Frage keinen Bezug hat'.

Aquinas is concerned with are not commensurate, neither on their own terms, nor on any we might set for them. And we have been able to do this precisely by appeal to the word 'being' which, superficially at least, appeared to link them together. We discovered that Aquinas understands being to be unfolded from out of the *ens creatum*, whereas Heidegger unfolds the question of being through *Dasein*'s existence as that being for whom being is a self-enquiry, a concern for itself.

We can go further than this, however, which is to say that Heidegger is uninterested in intruding on the specifically theological questions which Aquinas raises: he did not, and explicitly rules out, ever wishing to unfold the question of man's salvation from a theological point of view.[28] For Heidegger, however, what remains to philosophy in its conversation with the ontic science of faith that theology (for him) is, is that 'ontology functions therefore only as a corrective of the ontic, and to be precise, the pre-Christian content of theological basic-concepts: here one must note this correction is not grounding'.[29] Pre-Christian does not indicate here what precedes Christianity as a whole, but rather what ontologically lies prior and makes possible the content and structure of faith itself. This lying prior and correcting is not *positively* determining for the content of faith – it does not say what the content of revelation can be, but it is *negatively* determinative, in that it can open up the self-concerning self-understanding of what the content of revelation can be *for me*. This is not in the sense, for instance, of disbarring belief in miracles or a resurrection as 'impossible on rational grounds' or the suchlike, but rather asks what the ontological basis of such a belief could be. Thus in response to the seemingly reasonable question, informed by all the demands for objectivity set up by Enlightenment scepticism, 'Why is there no independent witness to the resurrection?', ontology can uncover that any witness who would have been present to such an event either would ineluctably be drawn into belief or into disbelief – it is simply not possible 'dispassionately' or 'objectively' to be witness to a dead body rising from its tomb. To see a dead body come to life, and witness this independently of the existential meaning and force that such an event would engender (in this sense 'this body was not really dead' or 'I am being deceived' are as ontologically legitimate in their content as 'now this dead man lives') in the one witnessing it, would be impossible. Indeed something like this, if

---

[28] See again his remarks in Heidegger, *Seminare*, pp. 436–7.

[29] Heidegger, *Phänomenologie und Theologie*, in *Wegmarken*, p. 64: 'Die Ontologie fungiert demnach nur als ein Korrektiv des ontischen, und zwar vorchristlichen Gehaltes der theologischen Grundbegriffe. Hier bleibt aber zu beachten: diese Korrektion ist nicht begründend.' Heidegger was so concerned to emphasise the point that it was italicised in the text. The lecture *Phänomenologie und Theologie* was given in 1927, but there is every reason to believe that Heidegger held fast to this view up until the end.

believed, would demand that the witness find and supply a meaning for
it.

If Heidegger is not interested in confronting Aquinas with regard to the
question of being, why does he engage with Aquinas on the question of
truth? More significantly, why does he raise this in relation specifically to
an interpretation of Aristotle, which therefore has nothing obvious to do
with the interpretation of *esse* as *ens creatum*, and still further, why does
he suggest that Aquinas is in unwitting agreement with Nietzsche?

In his *Beiträge zur Philosophie* Heidegger distinguishes the leading
question of metaphysics – τί τὸ ὄν – 'What is the being?' from the grounding question, the question of being as such as the ground of the truth of
being: 'the *grounding* of truth as the truth of being (the *Da-sein*)'.[30] I have
already indicated the character of this grounding question as it is asked
both in *Sein und Zeit* and elsewhere. In this we can see immediately
the extent to which a question concerning truth will help us into a more
genuine confrontation between Aquinas and Heidegger. If for Heidegger,
the grounding of truth as the truth of being is the same as the being of
being human (*Dasein*), then the question of the relation of Aquinas's
understanding of truth to how Heidegger himself understands truth will
indicate how they relate one to the other.

What therefore is at issue in the question of truth, both as Heidegger
and as Aquinas understand it? For clearly, as they have with being, they
have a different understanding of truth. The answer must surely lie in
this: while on the one hand Heidegger seeks to ground the being of beings
in *Da-sein*, in the being of being-human, Aquinas grounds being in the
actus essendi not of human being but of God. Although it is possible to
show how this grounding, taken metaphysically, arises out of the
forgetfulness-of-being, the *Seinsvergessenheit* that metaphysics is, such a
demonstration is further complicated by the fact that the God of faith is
for Aquinas a living and saving force who becomes intruded into philosophy for quite other reasons than for resolving the question of human
salvation. It is legitimate, in the region of faith, to believe that 'in the
beginning God created the heavens and the earth'. On the other hand, the
understanding of truth which Aquinas has and which continues up to
Nietzsche has an ontological grounding, and therefore in some sense
both at the same time springs from the originary grounding Heidegger
seeks to demonstrate for it, and (at the same time) covers over that originary grounding in virtue of being's forgettingness, *Seinsvergessenheit*. It is

---

[30] Heidegger, *Beiträge zur Philosophie*, p. 9: 'Die Gründung der Wahrheit als der
Wahrheit des Seyns (das Da-sein).' It should be noted here that Heidegger uses the old
form *das Seyn*, which after about 1934 he uses to indicate being when it ceases to be
forgotten, i.e., as it is and can be thought after the fulfilment of metaphysics.

easier to see, therefore, what is at issue with relation to truth in Aquinas and for Heidegger than it is on the issue of being.

In *Sein und Zeit* Heidegger notes, again with regard to Aristotle, that the priority of *Dasein* was seen from early on, although not grasped in its genuine ontological structure. He immediately quotes as evidence for this view, Aristotle: 'ἡ ψυχή τὰ ὄντα πώς ἐστιν. "The soul (of man) is in a certain way, beings" '.[31] He points in this very passage to how this understanding of Aristotle's is taken up by Aquinas, in his definition of the soul as the 'ens quod natum est convenire cum omni ente' and notes 'here the emergent, although not ontologically clarified, priority of "*Dasein*" before all other beings has obviously nothing in common with a terrible subjectivisation of the totality of beings'.[32] From this passage, therefore, it is possible to see that Heidegger understands Aquinas as also asserting the priority of *Dasein* in his thinking. Heidegger quotes Aquinas's definition of the soul from the *Quaestiones disputatae: de veritate*, from the first question, on the character of truth itself. Thus from the outset, Heidegger is able to argue that although Aquinas takes for granted the priority of *Dasein*, and in the very heart of the question with which we are concerned, in the establishment of the question of truth, he is unable to give it an ontological determination, because he takes for granted that the demonstration of this determination has already been undertaken in Aristotle.

The tendency to interpret Aquinas in relationship to Heidegger as being one of 'fitting Aquinas in' to the history of being, the *Seinsgeschichte*, as if simply piecing together the parts of a jigsaw puzzle, therefore turns out to be erroneous – rather what Heidegger offers us is a way into Aquinas from the perspective of ontology, that is to say, from within philosophy's concerns.

Aquinas asks the question 'what truth might be' at the opening of the *Quaestiones disputatae: de veritate*.[33] Here Aquinas actually gives three definitions of truth. The first 'is defined according to that which precedes the reckoning of truth and in which the true is founded';[34] the second 'is

[31] Heidegger, *Sein und Zeit*, pp. 18–19: 'ἡ ψυχή τὰ ὄντα πώς ἐστιν. "Die Seele (des Menschen) ist in gewisser Weise das Seiende" '; citing Aristotle, *De anima* III, 431 b 21.

[32] Heidegger, *Sein und Zeit*, p. 19: 'Der hier hervortretende, obzwar ontologisch nicht geklärte Vorrang des "Daseins" vor allem anderen Seienden hat offensichtlich nichts gemein mit einer schlechten Subjektivierung des Alls des Seienden.' In the passage cited from Aquinas (*QDV*, Q. 1, art. 1, resp.) Aquinas proceeds immediately to quote the Latin translation of the same passage of Aristotle: 'hoc autem est anima, quae quodammodo est omnia'.

[33] *QDV*, Q. 1, art. 1: 'Quid sit veritas'.

[34] *QDV*, Q. 1, art. 1, resp.: 'secundum id quod praecedit rationem veritatis, et in quo verum fundatur'.

defined according to that which formally satisfies the reckoning of the true';[35] the third 'defines the true according to [its] consequent effect'.[36] Of these it is the second which interests Heidegger, and which he correctly identifies as the most fundamental for St Thomas, that 'truth is the adequation of thing and intellect'.[37] Indeed, in the *Summa Theologiae* Aquinas says that this definition in some sense satisfies and explains all the others.[38]

Heidegger takes the *adequation* or what is more commonly called the 'correspondence' definition as the standard one, having a particular medieval origin.[39] However, he notes a particular ambiguity in the definition:

> This can mean: truth is the enlikening of the matter to knowledge. It can however also say: truth is the enlikening of knowledge to the matter . . . Both concepts of the essence of *veritas* have continually in view a conforming to . . ., and hence think truth as correctness. Nonetheless, the one is not the mere inversion of the other.[40]

'Enlikening' here translates the German term *Angleichung*, but clearly what Heidegger actually has in mind is Aristotle's word ὁμοίωσις – making like to – in relation to Aristotle's discussion of truth.[41] Elsewhere, Heidegger notes that the two halves of the ambiguity, which he names as on the one hand represented by Kant (i.e., by the philosophy of subjectivity), and on the other by Aquinas (and specifically with reference to

---

[35] *QDV*, Q. 1, art. 1, resp.: 'definitur secundum id quod formaliter rationem veri perficit'.

[36] *QDV*, Q. 1, art. 1, resp.: 'definitur verum secundum effectum consequentem'.

[37] *QDV*, Q. 1, art. 1, resp.: 'veritas est adaequatio rei et intellectus'. This is also how St Thomas defines it in the *Commentary on the Sentences*, where he speaks of the 'relatio adaequationis, in qua consistit ratio veritatis' (*In I Sent*, Ds. 19, art. 5, resp.; cf. Ds. 40, art. 3, resp. and *In IV Sent*, Ds. 46, Q. 1, resp.) and in the *SCG*, Bk 1, Ch. 59, no. 2, as well as the *ST* Ia, Q. 16, art. 1, resp.

[38] *ST* Ia, Q. 16, art. 1, resp. Here, after giving an almost identical list of the various definitions of truth to that found in the *de veritate*, Aquinas concludes that the 'adequation' definition (which he places on this occasion last in the list) 'can pertain to any of them' ('potest ad utrumque pertinere').

[39] Attributed by Aquinas to Isaac, although it is more likely that its origin is in fact Avicenna.

[40] Martin Heidegger, *Vom Wesen der Wahrheit*, in *Wegmarken*, p. 180: 'Das kann bedeuten: Wahrheit ist die Angleichung der Sache an die Erkenntnis. Es kann aber auch sagen: Wahrheit ist die Angleichung der Erkenntnis an die Sache . . . Beide Wesensbegriffe der veritas meinen stets ein Sichrichten nach . . . und denken somit die Wahrheit als Richtigkeit. Gleichwohl ist der eine nicht die bloße Umkehrung des anderen'.

[41] Cf. Aristotle, *De interpretatione*, 16a5–8. Heidegger has a discussion of this passage in *Vom Wesen der Wahrheit: Zu Platons Höhlengleichnis und Theätet*, p. 8. Again here he specifically mentions Aquinas's definition of truth in the *QDV*.

the first question of the *Quaestiones disputatae*) together with Aristotle, represent not simply 'three steps, but three worlds' in the unfolding of the meaning of correctness, but that they spring from a 'singular force from which human *Dasein* can withdraw itself only with difficulty'.[42] Thus the interpretation of truth that unfolds through this interpretation is constitutive and definitive for what follows from it – it has a certain force about it which is both unavoidable and unleashes a history from which whole worlds, whole spheres of interpretation follow. These worlds are decisive for humanity in its understanding of truth.

Heidegger notes that on each side of the ambiguity the terms *intellectus* (mind, intellect) and *res* (thing) are thought differently. In the first case he points out, the correspondence definition does not mean in its medieval form what it comes to mean in Kant, that objects conform to our knowledge, but rather 'it implies the Christian theological belief that, with respect to what it is and whether it is, a matter, as created (*ens creatum*), is only in so far as it corresponds to the idea preconceived in the *intellectus divinus*, i.e. in the mind of God, and thus measures up to the idea (is correct) and in this sense is "true"'.[43]

Heidegger argues that the full explication of the 'correspondence' definition found in the *Quaestiones disputatae* is that the truth of created things, having been already intended and made (literally created) to correspond to the ideas in the divine intellect, thereby supplies a guarantee for the correctness of the correspondence of things to the human intellect. In this sense, truth in the human intellect becomes a kind of passive faculty, which can always rely on the correctness of what it knows because what it knows has been intended to be so known by one no less than God himself. Moreover, all of this may rely on the consonance of all things to each other because they spring from the divine plan for the whole of creation. This is how Aquinas takes the second half of the ambiguity (truth is the enlikening of knowledge to the matter) to refer to truth in the human mind.

Heidegger's point, therefore, is that Aquinas's understanding of truth has an explicitly theological resolution, and moreover, works within the understanding of being that I have already indicated Heidegger sees as differing radically from his own, that is the createdness of all things (beings) in God, the *ens creatum*. Are we not back where we started?

---

[42] Heidegger, *Sein und Wahrheit*, p. 121: 'Nicht einfach drei Stufen, sondern drei Welten . . . Demnach doch eine eigentümliche Macht, der sich das menschliche Dasein schwer entziehen kann.'

[43] Heidegger, *Vom Wesen der Wahrheit*, in *Wegmarken*, p. 180: 'Sondern [meint] den christlich theologischen Glauben, daß die Sachen in dem, was sie sind und ob sie sind, nur sind, sofern sie als je erschaffene (ens creatum) der im intellectus divinus, d.h. in dem Geiste Gottes, vorgedachten idea entsprechen und somit idee-gerecht (richtig) und in diesem Sinne "wahr" sind.'

Have we not indicated that, not only is Heidegger's understanding of being incommensurate with Aquinas's, but also that because Heidegger already sees the medieval interpretation of 'correspondence' springing out of the *ens creatum*, their understandings of truth must also be incommensurate in the same way and for the same reason, and that Aquinas's definition of truth is in fact a definition springing, not from a philosophical ground at all, but from one of faith? Indeed, recent attempts to develop an 'overcoming of metaphysics' out of Aquinas's appeal to correspondence, which have made special reference to the participation of the human mind in the divine mind through the human mind's adequation to things and with regard to this half of the ambiguity, have entirely overlooked what must be for them a devastating criticism. This is that the way in which *Aquinas* defines truth as far as it is understood in the human mind is so far uninvolved with a genuinely philosophical or ontological determination of truth that it can be seen *only* as a statement of theological belief. It can hardly overcome what it itself does not even touch – except in so far as this overcoming is a matter purely of faith and assertion and not demonstration or argument. In other words, in so far as this overcoming has already decided *in advance* that human beings are created in such a way that they could never, through faith, be trusted to discover this for themselves (which would be an ontologically grounded, and so thoughtful, discovery of their faith in a matter of divine revelation, rather than their unthinking conformity to a simple assertion of faith).[44] It is only what comes after Aquinas, that is, subsequent attempts to bend this theological understanding of truth back into the matter of philosophy, that result in the very construction of the metaphysics that the *adaequatio* as it is understood by Aquinas is supposedly said to be able to overcome.

Still worse than this, Heidegger himself understands the supposedly non-theological development of the 'correspondence' understanding that succeeds Aquinas's explicitly theological account not to be able to exceed its theological determination, albeit under a different guise. Thus he

---

[44] It could be doubted that Aquinas privileges faith over the thinking enquiry into causes (*rationes*), and so allows a place for thinking and philosophy apart from divine revelation. In fact St Thomas proceeds in the opposite direction, arguing that although there is a kind of intelligibility of the Divine which the enquiry of reason can reach, and another which can only be given by divine revelation, 'it is fitting that both of these truths be proposed to man for believing' ('utraque convenienter divinitus homini credenda proponitur' [*SCG*, Bk 1, Ch. 4, no. 1]). This is because otherwise few would possess the knowledge of God. The consequence of this is that 'If the only way open to us for the knowledge of God were solely that of the reason, the human race would remain in the greatest shadows of ignorance' ('Remaneret igitur humanum genus, si sola rationis via ad Deum cognoscendum pateret, in maximis ignorantiae tenebris' [*SCG*, Bk 1, Ch. 4, no. 4.]).

notes that 'the theologically conceived order of creation is replaced by the capacity of all objects to be planned by means of a world-reason that supplies the law for itself and thus also claims that its procedure is immediately intelligible (that which is considered logical)'.[45] Hence in the *Beiträge* Heidegger argues that liberalism is simply the manifestation of a de-divinised form of Christianity, as much as philosophy after the Enlightenment and up to and even beyond Hegel has fused theological and philosophical concerns in such a way that the enquiry into being that philosophy is disappears altogether and loses its ground (which means, loses its *explicit* connection to the God of reason, whilst this connection *implicitly* remains). The extreme result of this is that

> so-called natural knowledge not based upon any revelation, therefore, did not have its own form of intelligibility or grounds for itself, let alone from out of itself. Thus what is decisive for the history of know-ledge is not that all truth of natural knowledge was measured by the supernatural. Rather it is that this natural knowledge, disregarding this criterion, arrived at no independent foundation and character out of itself.[46]

Heidegger's point is that by basing the being of all things on the *ens creatum* and by determining their truth as our own measuring-up to what God intends for things – discovering the 'correctness' of what we know about them – then knowledge of the natural world loses its genuinely ontological foundation. From now on the sciences will search in vain for an ontological foundation worked out through the self-enquiry that is possible only for human *Dasein*, even when things are no longer understood to be grounded in God. In the *Quaestiones disputatae* Aquinas had made this question of the 'measuring' of the correctness of our knowledge explicit in relation to the divine intellect. Thus he argues that 'The divine intellect measures and is not measured; a natural thing both measures and is measured, but our intellect is measured, and meas-ures only artifacts, not natural things.'[47] Heidegger notes in relation to

[45] Heidegger, *Vom Wesen der Wahrheit*, in *Wegmarken*, p. 181: 'An die Stelle der theologisch gedachten Schöpfungsordnung rückt die Planbarkeit aller Gegenstände durch die Weltvernunft, die sich selbst das Gesetz gibt und daher auch die unmittel-bare Verständlichkeit ihres Vorgehens (das, was man für 'logisch' hält) beansprucht.'

[46] Martin Heidegger, *Die Frage nach dem Ding*, in *Gesamtausgabe*, vol. 41 (Frankfurt: Klostermann, 1984), p. 97: 'Das sogenannte natürliche, nicht offen-barungsmäßige Wissen hatte daher für sich und gar aus sich keine eigengestaltete Form der Wißbarkeit und Begründung. Nicht dies also ist wissenschaftsgeschichtlich das Entscheidende, daß alle Wahrheit des natürliche Wissen, unbeschadet jener Messung, aus sich zu keiner eigenständigen Begründung und Prägung gelangte.'

[47] *QDV*, Q. 1, art. 2, resp.: 'Sic ergo intellectus divinus est mensurans non mensu-ratus; res autem naturalis mensurans et mensurata; sed intellectus noster est mensu-ratus, non mensurans quidem res naturalis, sed artificiales tantum.'

this passage that as a result the speculative human intellect is only reproductive, and so only mimetically representative of the divine intellect.[48]

In pursuing this line of enquiry, however, we get ahead of ourselves.
For although it becomes possible to gain clarity, at least in outline, with
regard to Heidegger's claim that Nietzsche and Aquinas are in unwitting
agreement, this is the effect of the way in which the ambiguity of the
'correspondence' or adequation understanding of truth gets folded back
into philosophy through an intrusion of the *ens creatum* into the understanding of being. And indeed we have space and time for no more than
the outline, except to say that it becomes clear exactly why Heidegger
understands that for Nietzsche the proclamation of the death of God and
his commitment to truth as a form of error are related. Heidegger interprets the position that God is the *ground* of all things as the way in
which, after Descartes (and incidentally Newton) the *ens creatum* construes all thought of being in philosophy. Therefore Leibniz's principle
'nichts ohne Grund' (nothing is without reason/ground) becomes the
expression of this construal, so that with Nietzsche's declaration of
the death of God, the unifying effect of ground and reason is thereby
disbanded. This dissolution leaves intact the correspondence, the
adaequatio or ὁμοίωσις, of thing to intellect, so that the individual, sub-
jectival, intellect become the source of the truth of the thing, but now
(because there is no exterior unifying ground) the being of the thing is
grounded purely through the will. Willing becomes the basic determination of the being of things, following Nietzsche. Moreover, every attempt
to reassert the unity of the ground of all things, because this unity is
no longer able to be taken for granted (else why would it need to be re-
asserted), can resolve itself only as and through the will to power.
Heidegger remarks with regard to this that Nietzsche interpreted the
metaphysics of subjectivity 'on the basis of the will to truth, and this as a
kind of will to power'.[49] Thus the will to power is the final step in the
unfolding of the history of the interpretation of the *adaequatio*, but as
understood as the culmination of the metaphysics of subjectivity, and
after the death of God.

This, exactly, leads us back to the other half of the ambiguity (truth is
the enlikening of the matter to knowledge) which Heidegger traces and
which he suggests in his consideration of the *adaequatio* formula. For as
Heidegger points out, 'the *intellectus humanus* is also an *ens creatum*'.[50]

---

[48] Cf. Heidegger, *Sein und Wahrheit*, p. 285.
[49] Martin Heidegger, *Der europäische Nihilismus*, in *Gesamtausgabe*, vol. 48
(Frankfurt: Klostermann, 1986), p. 312 (cf. his *Nietzsche*, in *Gesamtausgabe*, vol.
6.1 (Frankfurt: Klostermann, 1997 (1961)), p. 211). 'aus dem Willen zur Wahrheit
und diesen als eine Art des Willens zur Macht'.
[50] Heidegger, *Vom Wesen der Wahrheit*, in *Wegmarken*, p. 180. 'Ein ens creatum
ist auch der intellectus humanus.'

Now the original question with which Heidegger had associated Nietzsche and Aquinas did not concern the *adaequatio*, but in fact appeared only as the answer to the topic of the second article of the question on truth in the *Quaestiones disputatae*: 'whether truth might principally be found more in the intellect than in things'.[51] If we are to understand Heidegger's comment linking Nietzsche and Aquinas, we have to realise that in relation to the *adaequatio*, we are to a certain extent looking in the wrong place if we ask ourselves whether what is at stake in the *ontological* grounding of the question of truth is the question of what occurs in the *human* mind. This is because, precisely because being is determined out of the *ens creatum*, it is not the human mind (*intellectus humanus*) which is at issue in unfolding the *ontological ground* of truth – at least not until Nietzsche's proclamation of the death of God. For Aquinas, the genuinely *ontological* adequation of thing to intellect is between the thing and the intellect or mind of *God* – exactly as it becomes in the *human* mind in Nietzsche when God (because God is now dead) is no longer the guarantor of the correctness of the truth, passively received, in the human mind. For Aquinas, things are true because God actively intends them to be in the way that they are. Indeed he says as much: 'Therefore, a natural thing . . . is said to be true inasmuch as it corresponds to the divine intellect in so far as it fulfils that which has been ordained for it by the divine intellect'.[52] Thus the mind of God as Aquinas understands it functions in the same way as the human mind functions in Nietzsche, at least as far as truth is concerned. The question whether truth is found more in the intellect rather than in things is so, not because of any kind of relation, although a relation is required to discover it, but because of a willed intention, a decision of the intellect as such.

The place where we should look, therefore, for a full description of the ontological grounding of truth in Aquinas in the *Quaestiones disputatae* and the corresponding questions on the two *Summas* and the *Commentary on the Sentences* is not Question 1, *concerning truth*, not even Question 2, *on the knowledge of God*, but Question 3, *concerning ideas*. Here we find the way in which Aquinas is constantly synthesising and drawing together the ancient ontologies (admittedly in the very modified forms in which he has received them) of Plato, Aristotle, and Neoplatonism, but locating them not as applied to the human intellect, but to the divine intellect alone. It is for this reason that the first article of this

---

[51] *QDV*, Q. 1, art. 2: 'Utrum veritas principalius inveniatur in intellectu quam in rebus.'

[52] *QDV*, Q. 1, art. 2, resp.: 'Res ergo naturalis . . . secundum adaequationem ad intellectum divinum dicitur vera, in quantum implet hoc ad quod est ordinata per intellectum divinum.'

question asks 'whether there are ideas in God'.[53] Aquinas begins by explaining how the Greek term ἰδέαι will be understood: he answers, as species or forms. Here then, we discover an astonishing parallel between Aquinas and Nietzsche, at least with regard to the primacy of the will in the production and valuation of truth (where valuation is heard in its full meaning of 'counting up' and so 'estimating', and *ratio* is translated as 'reckon' as in the 'reckoning up of accounts' rather than as 'reason'): 'Similarly those who say that all things proceed from God by a necessity of nature and not by a decision of will cannot admit ideas, since those who act impelled by the necessity of nature do not determine the end for themselves.'[54] For this reason there are ideas in God, and they are the forms or species of things which God has chosen and activates (in so far as he chooses) by means of his will. Aquinas concludes his discussion by saying 'and therefore Plato . . . affirmed ideas to be'.[55] Aquinas derives his understanding of the being of ideas, and therefore the ontological basis of the truth of things, by means of an explicit reference to Plato. It is in this that Aquinas and Nietzsche are unwittingly linked, since, as Heidegger so determinedly shows throughout his engagement with Nietzsche, it is Plato whom Nietzsche seeks to be the inversion (*Umkehr*) of. Heidegger concludes with regard to this that Nietzsche 'thinks being in a thoroughly Platonic and metaphysical way – even as the over-turner of Platonism, even as the anti-metaphysician'.[56]

We know already from the answers given to the questions on truth that whatever God determines as true is true as such. Here, concerning the ideas, we discover the genuine connection between truth and the *ens creatum* on the other side of the ambiguity (truth is the enlikening of the matter to knowledge) earlier named by Heidegger, for Aquinas proceeds to say with regard to this question of the primacy of the decisive will in God, that we understand God to be 'the first cause of all beings'.[57] Heidegger had noted in connection with this that exactly as the speculative intellect in humanity was reproductive (*nachbildend*), the divine intellect was productive (*vorbildend*).[58] The prefix 'pro' here must be

[53] *QDV*, Q. 3, art. 1: 'An sint ideae in Deo.'

[54] *QDV*, Q. 3, art. 1, resp.: 'Similiter etiam secundum eos qui posuerunt quod a Deo procedunt omnia per necessitatem naturae, non per arbitrium vountatis, non-possunt poni ideae: quia ea quae ex necessitate naturae agunt, non praedeterminant sibi finem.'

[55] *QDV*, Q. 3, art. 1, resp.: 'Et ideo Plato . . . posuit ideas esse'.

[56] Heidegger, *Der europäische Nihilismus*, p. 302 (Cf. his *Nietzsche*, pp. 201–2): '[Nietzsche] denkt das Sein durchaus platonisch und metaphysisch – auch als Umkehrer des Platonismus, auch als Anti-Metaphysiker.'

[57] *QDV*, Q. 3, art. 1, resp.: 'Quia omnes loquentes de Deo intelligunt eum esse causam primam entium.'

[58] Cf. Heidegger, *Sein und Wahrheit*, p. 285.

taken in its causal priority, as what comes prior to the matter, that is, knowledge determines in advance what the matter will be.

Precisely because we can now see how it is that Nietzsche and Aquinas are in unwitting agreement, we can understand both what rescues Aquinas and how what Nietzsche brought to light enables Heidegger to announce the need in theology to establish 'wholly new distinctions and delimitations'.[59] Provided that we accept that Aquinas is using the language of philosophy to elaborate and unfold the concerns of faith (true, because they are revealed to be so by God), we need have no more difficulty in accepting or rejecting what Aquinas says outside the normal concerns of the engagement with his thought that is our own taking up and reflecting on the experience and understanding of faith. In so far, however, as we convert Aquinas's *theological* reflection into *philosophy*, only disaster can ensue, for precisely the reasons which Heidegger makes plain – such an event results in the deprivation or the removal of the onto-logical ground of knowledge, and at the same time results in a situation from which human *Dasein* can withdraw itself only with great difficulty. However, this disaster also brings the disastrous character of the disaster to light, since it culminates ineluctably with the need to proclaim *in philosophy* the death of God – which throws the determination of the essence of truth back into open question, because if God is dead the pri-macy of the human being – *Dasein* – is brought to the fore as what needs to become interrogable in thinking.[60] At the same time it exposes the extent to which the question of truth has unfolded through the will to power – thus (for Heidegger) it actually opens up all over again the ques-tion of the meaning and ground of the term ἀλήθεια, and what he calls the 'truth of being'. In this, however, we can see how Heidegger took up the interpretation of Nietzsche that he did, both in his lectures, seminars and writing on Nietzsche between 1937 and 1946 and elsewhere. It also explains Heidegger's comparative silence with regard to Aquinas, and why the only question he receives concerning Aquinas results in a mock-ing and delphic answer: he believed himself not to be implicated in the same question of being as that one in which Aquinas was involved, although at the same time he believed that the *consequences* of not only Aquinas's but the whole medieval engagement with Aristotle and Plato were decisive for what followed them from Descartes to Nietzsche and

---

[59] Heidegger, *Seminare*, p. 437: 'ganz neue Unterscheidungen und Abgrenzungen'.

[60] We should note here that for Heidegger this does not resolve the question of being, or even demonstrate that the question appears, but it does demonstrate the uttermost *need* for the question to be asked. It is for this reason that Nietzsche's thought is in its very essence ambiguous, pointing at the same time back into meta-physics and forward to what will overcome metaphysics. It is only *after* Nietzsche that the question of being emerges *as a question*.

Hegel and even today – even though what followed the medieval understanding declared itself to be a wholesale overthrow of it. Nevertheless it worked out of the same ground.

Do we need to compel Heidegger and Aquinas to sit down together in agreement? The answer to this question can only be 'No'. Can Heidegger shed light on how we are to understand what it is that Aquinas undertakes in his thinking, and thereby place ourselves both within and in relation to what it is that Aquinas has to say? The answer to this can only be a resounding 'Yes'. And therein lies the task.

Thomas at Utrecht

HERWI M. RIKHOF

Introduction: a short history

It started with a question. How could a theologian who had dominated Catholic theology in manuals and articles, in seminaries and faculties disappear so suddenly and so completely from curricula and theological discussions? A question asked out of astonishment, not just because it happened so suddenly and completely in the period after Vatican II, but mostly because it happened without further discussion or arguments, without attempts to explain this remarkable development. Did it take place for good reasons, and if so, which were those reasons? Alternatively, did it happen because of certain misunderstandings and misconceptions? If so, should one leave it at that?

The second alternative formed the basis for the hypothesis with which a research program was started at the Katholieke Theologische Universiteit Utrecht. Looking back several elements can be discerned.

1. The theology after Vatican II showed not just a difference in style and content with the theology before the council, but it exhibited an explicit break with the theology of the neo-scholastic manual and even a rejection of that type of theology.[1]
2. In the neo-scholastic period Thomas figured prominently, but the manuals *ad mentem Sancti Thomae* provided an interpretation of Thomas that was strongly philosophical and apologetic in tone and interest.
3. The disappearance of Thomas was more due to this neo-scholastic interpretation than to his genuine theological views.
4. Consequently, the disappearance of Thomas from the theological agenda was a regrettable mistake.

---

[1] A good example is M. Schmaus, who before Vatican II wrote a manual (*Katholische Dogmatik*) that belonged more or less to the neo-scholastic type and who wrote after the Council another comprehensive dogmatic theology in which he explicitly takes leave of his earlier work: *Der Glaube der Kirche*, 2 vols. (Munich: Max Hüber Verlag, 1969).

As is clear from these elements a certain negative or defensive tone can be noticed in the formulation of the hypothesis. Underneath, though, a more positive conviction was present, namely that Thomas's theology contains important insights that could and should play a significant role in the current theological discussions. But at first this conviction did not surface. In the first research project, a pilot study about the reception of Thomas's theology, the negative hypothesis was dominant even to the extent that not just the neo-scholastic period was charted, but also some other periods were included: early Thomism, the Reformation, the Catholic theology of the sixteenth and seventeenth centuries.[2]

The negative hypothesis was not completely new. Long before the Council, theologians had discovered the difference between Thomas and (neo)-Thomism, but a thorough historical investigation exploring this distinction and evaluating was lacking.[3] Therefore, research projects should contribute to such an investigation. However, when the first projects were executed, the internal dynamism of research made it necessary to concentrate on Thomas's theology itself and to abandon more or less the reception. This dynamism did not only occur in dissertation projects of doctoral students, but also in other research projects. This happened partly because research into the reception, certainly if reception is understood as a comparative and evaluative investigation, appeared to require more than a superficial knowledge of the authors involved, partly because the evaluation required not just some basic knowledge of Aquinas, but also a reasoned interpretation of his theology. This second reason proved to be decisive. The dissertation projects were so formulated (or reformulated) that the main emphasis came to lie on Thomas's theology: on his Christology,[4] on his views on evangelical poverty,[5] on his account of divine foreknowledge and will,[6] on his exposé of the life on earth and after death.[7] In other projects, a similar shift can

[2] J. van den Eijnden, *Thomas van Aquino in de theologie: Een draaiboek voor receptieonderzoek* (Utrecht: Werkgroep Thomas van Aquino, 1985).

[3] Cf. O.-H. Pesch in his contribution on Thomism in *Lexicon für Theologie und Kirche* (2nd edn, 1965). In his book, *Thomas von Aquin: Grenze und Größe mittelalterlicher Theologie* (Mainz: Matthias-Grünewald Verlag, 1988), he dedicates part of the first chapter to the relation between Thomas and the various forms of Thomism, pp. 27–38.

[4] H. Schoot, *Christ the 'Name' of God: Thomas Aquinas on Naming Christ*, New Series, vol. 1 (Louvain: Publications of the Thomas Instituut te Utrecht, 1993).

[5] J. van den Eijnden, *Poverty on the Way to God: Thomas Aquinas on Evangelical Poverty*, New Series, vol. 2 (Louvain: Publications of the Thomas Instituut te Utrecht, 1994).

[6] H. Goris, *Free Creatures of an Eternal God: Thomas Aquinas on God's Infallible Foreknowledge and Irresistible Will*, New Series, vol. 4 (Louvain: Publications of the Thomas Instituut te Utrecht, 1996).

[7] C. Leget, *Living with God: Thomas Aquinas on the Relation between Life on*

be noticed.[8] This does not mean that the reception aspect completely disappeared, but that research in Thomas's theology became the primary focus.[9]

Another dissertation project that was reformulated during the process was the research project into Thomas's use of Scripture. Originally, it was designed as a comparative study on the place and function of Scripture in Thomas, in Reformational Scholasticism and neo-Scholasticism. On the one hand, the choice for the authority of Scripture was determined by exploring Thomas's theological attitude; on the other hand, the choice for the comparison with Reformational Scholasticism was inspired by the institutional setting: the co-operation between the Katholieke Theologische Universiteit and the (Protestant) Theological Faculty of Utrecht University.[10]

When the research programme started it was in a certain sense a continuation of an already existing tradition in the Netherlands to read Thomas theologically. G. Kreling, who was professor of dogmatic theology at the Theological Faculty of the Katholieke Universiteit Nijmegen from 1928 till 1957, read and interpreted Thomas without the customary recourse to the 'great' commentators and outside the various Thomistic schools.[11] E. Schillebeeckx, his successor as professor of dogmatic theology, brought with him the influence of a historical approach

---

Earth and 'Life' after Death, New Series, vol. 5 (Louvain: Publications of the Thomas Instituut te Utrecht, 1997).

[8] H. Rikhof, *Over God spreken: Een tekst van Thomas van Aquino uit de 'ST' (ST I, q. 13): Vertaald, ingeleid en van aantekeningen voorzien* (Delft, 1988).

[9] F. de Grijs, 'Notitie: Filosoof over theoloog. Het Thomasboek van Delfgaauw', *Bijdragen* 43 (1982), pp. 199–204; F. de Grijs, 'Christologie en Thomasinterpretatie', *Bijdragen* 45 (1984), pp. 350–73; F. de Grijs, 'Spreken over God en Thomasinterpretatie', in *Jaarboek Werkgroep Thomas van Aquino 1984*, pp. 7–38; J. van den Eijnden, *Poverty*, ch 5.1 for a comparison between Thomas and Johannes Olivi; H. Rikhof, 'Das Geheimnis Gottes: Jüngels Thomas Rezeption näher betrachtet', *Dialektische Theologie* 6.1 (1990/91), pp. 61–78; H. Rikhof, 'De paradox van de neo-scholastiek. Eclips van taal en traditie: De dogmatische theologie van J. B. Heinrich', in E. Borgman and A. v. Harskamp (eds.), *Tussen openheid en isolement: Het voorbeeld van de katholieke theologie in de negentiende eeuw* (Kampen: Nijmegen, 1992), pp. 115–33.

[10] P. Valkenberg, *Did Not Our Hearts Burn? Place and Function of Holy Scripture in the Theology of St. Thomas Aquinas* (Louvain: Publications of the Thomas Instituut te Utrecht, 1990). See pp. 2–3 for this background. Valkenberg published a revised and updated version of his dissertation under the title *Words of the Living God: Place and Function of Holy Scripture in the Theology of St. Thomas Aquinas*, New Series, vol. 6 (Louvain: Publications of the Thomas Instituut te Utrecht, 2000).

[11] E. Schillebeeckx, 'Kreling en de theologische situatie van zijn tijd', in F. de Grijs et al. (eds.), *Het goddelijk geheim: Theologisch werk van G.P. Kreling OP* (Kampen: Kok Pharos, 1979), pp. 47–68, esp. pp. 59–61; for a theological portrait of Kreling see also the contribution of de Grijs, 'De beschouwende theologie van G.P. Kreling', in *Het goddelijk geheim*, pp. 69–121.

to Thomas. During his years at Le Saulchoir, he met Chenu and was deeply impressed by him and his theology.[12] F. de Grijs, professor of dogmatic theology at Utrecht, made his studies under Kreling and Schilleebeeckx, who was the director of his dissertation on the *imago Dei* in the *Scriptum*.[13] De Grijs initiated the research programme, founded in 1979 a 'working group' that in 1990 became the Thomas Instituut te Utrecht, and started the *Jaarboek* (1981).[14] His publications mirror, not surprisingly, the interests and developments sketched above.[15]

But apart from this influence, two other authors have to be mentioned explicitly: D. Burrell and M. Corbin. Their publications have shaped the research. Burrell emphasises both the continuous importance of the negative theology in Aquinas and Aquinas's use of linguistic theories in his theological analyses.[16] In particular, Burrell's analysis of the opening of the *Summa Theologiae* has influenced profoundly the way Thomas is read at Utrecht. According to him Thomas is, in Questions 3–11 of the Prima Pars, 'engaged in the metalinguistic project of mapping out the grammar appropriate *in divinis*. He is proposing the logic proper to dis-

---

[12] For Schillebeeckx see, e.g., his *De sacramentele heilseconomie: Theologische bezinning op S. Thomas' sacramentenleer in het licht van de traditie en van de hedendaagse sacramentenproblematiek* (Antwerp: H. Nelissen, 1952) and part III of *Openbaring en Theologie*, Theologische Peilingen deel I (Bilthoven: H. Nelissen, 1964), pp. 185–261. The following example may show that among Dominicans this theological approach to Aquinas was not exceptional. Professors of the 'Filosoficum' of the Dutch Dominicans published in 1963 a collection of 'philosophical considerations': R. Thuijs (ed.), *Mens en God: Wijsgerige beschouwingen over het religieuze* (Utrecht: Erven Bijleveld, 1963). Among the articles is one by J. Willemse about the hidden God in Thomas Aquinas: 'De verborgen God bij Thomas van Aquino', pp. 120–35. In it he argues that Thomas wrote the *ST* 'explicitly as a theologian' and that the theological perspective should be kept in mind even if Thomas uses 'apparently' philosophical terms and arguments (p. 121).

[13] F. de Grijs, *Het goddelijk mensontwerp: Een thematische studie over het beeld Gods in de mens volgens het Scriptum van Thomas van Aquine*, 2 vols. (Hilversum: Brand, 1967).

[14] L. Winkeler, 'Van tekstlezing tot Thomas Instituut: De geschiedenis van de Werkgroep Thomas van Aquino', in *Jaarboek 1995*, pp. 65–78.

[15] F. de Grijs, 'Thomas' Schriftgebruik bij de systematische overdenking van het willen van Christus', in *Jaarboek Werkgroep Thomas van Aquino 1981*, pp. 38–84; 'Het Schriftgebruik in *de Regno* van Thomas van Aquino', in *Jaarboek Werkgroep Thomas van Aquino 1985*, pp. 34–72; 'The Theological Character of Aquinas' *de aeternitate mundi*', in J. B. Wissink (ed.), *The Eternity of the World in the Thought of Thomas Aquinas and His Contemporaries* (Leiden: Brill, 1990), pp. 1–8. The complete bibliography of de Grijs is provided by H. Schoot (*Jaarboek 1995*, pp. 79–83). H. Rikhof gives an overview of de Grijs's work under the title 'A Theology of Provocative Receptivity', in *Jaarboek 1995*, pp. 11–42; part 3 of that article is about de Grijs's publications on Aquinas.

[16] D. Burrell, *Aquinas: God and Action* (Notre Dame, IN: University of Notre Dame Press, 1979). See also his *Knowing the Unknowable God: Ibn-Sina, Maimonides, Aquinas* (Notre Dame, IN: University of Notre Dame Press, 1986).

course about God'.[17] Consequently *quaestio* 13, the *quaestio* in which Thomas deals with the possibilities and limitations of our language about God and analyses the analogical use of certain words, becomes an important *quaestio*.[18] That 'linguistic' way, though, has provoked some controversy. J. Aertsen, for example, has made some critical remarks about 'the Thomas of Utrecht'.[19]

Corbin influenced the way Thomas is read at Utrecht in at least three ways.[20] First, in his analyses of Thomas's four major methodological texts (*Scriptum, In Boethius de Trinitate, Summa contra Gentiles, Summa Theologiae*), he has followed Aquinas's struggle in coming to terms with Aristotle's third entrance and has shown how in the end Thomas is able to formulate a new theology as *fides quaerens intellectum*. The analysis of the first *quaestio* of the *Summa Theologiae* shows that Thomas gives Scripture a crucial place and function within his systematic theology. Second, because of his very detailed analyses, Corbin has shown how important it is, certainly for the *Summa Theologiae*, to read the texts closely and carefully and to read the texts (*articuli* and *quaestiones*) as a whole. Third, his 'speculative reading', that is, to read texts that cover the same ground as stages in a not always linear development, has made us sensitive to the possibilities of development, not just in the cases where Thomas explicitly has changed his mind, but also in other texts, where this development is more subtle. It has made us cautious to put texts from various periods together too quickly.

After the completion of some dissertation projects on Thomas's theology, research into the reception of Thomas's theology again became a topic. Some postdoctoral and other projects were developed.[21] Another fruit of this return to reception was the second conference of the Thomas Instituut (December 2000) on Aquinas as Authority. Some of the papers presented at that conference showed the work in progress at the Instituut.[22] In these papers, one can see on the one hand a historical

---

[17] Burrell, *Aquinas*, p. 17.

[18] See also R. Sokolowski, *The God of Faith and Reason: Foundations of Christian Theology* (Washington, DC: Catholic University of America Press, 1992 (1982)), esp. chs. 1–4.

[19] J. Aertsen, 'Thomas van Aquino en Thomas van Utrecht: Kritische kanttekeningen bij de Utrechtse lezing van de *ST*', *Bijdragen* 55 (1994), pp. 56–71. For a reaction: H. Rikhof, 'Een kwestie van lezen? Een antwoord aan Jan Aertsen', *Bijdragen* 56 (1995), pp. 429–50.

[20] M. Corbin, *Le chemin de la théologie chez Thomas d'Aquin* (Paris: Beauchesne, 1974).

[21] P. van Geest, Gabriel Biel, a devout theologian; H. Goris, The reception of Aquinas's doctrine of God in the fifteenth and the beginnings of the sixteenth century; C. Leget, Life is always a good (about Ricoeur); H. Schoot, Christologia Recepta: On the reception of Aquinas's theology 1300–1600.

[22] Paul van Geest, Harm Goris and Carlo Leget (eds.), *Aquinas as Authority*, New

approach and on the other hand a systematic theological interest. In the planning for future projects this systematic interest will play a predominant role. The dissertation projects currently being executed are concerned with Thomas's theology of the sacraments (penance, Eucharist) and his doctrine of God (God's almightiness and the suffering of Christ) and plans have been developed to study Thomas's treatment of the theological virtues.

After this historical survey, I now want to show how we read Thomas at Utrecht. I want to do that by concentrating on four characteristics we have discovered. These four determine what kind of theologian Thomas is. This frame allows me also to present briefly the main publications of the Thomas Instituut.

Thomas the theologian

On rare occasions, Thomas shows something of himself, of how he understands himself, of what his intentions and motives are. In the *Summa contra Gentiles*, a work that probably can be considered as his most personal work, he makes a saying of Hilary his own. 'I am aware that I owe this to God as the chief task of my life: that all my words and thoughts speak of him.'[23] In the prologue to the *Summa Theologiae*, Thomas presents himself as *catholicae veritatis doctor*. These sayings, but also his various jobs at the university or within the Dominican order,

---

Series, vol. 7 (Louvain: Publications of the Thomas Instituut te Utrecht, 2002): H. Goris, 'Thomism in Fifteenth Century Germany', pp. 1–24; H. Schoot, 'Early Thomist Reception of Aquinas' Christology: Henry of Gorkum', pp. 25–39; P. van. Geest, 'Influence of Thomas Aquinas in the *via moderna* and the *devotio moderna*? Gabriel Biel's Debt to Thomas Aquinas', pp. 39–64; H. Rikhof, 'Aquinas' Authority in the Contemporary Theology of the Trinity', pp. 213–34; F. Vosman, 'Thomas Aquinas, Founder of Modern Political and Social Thought? Aquinas' Political-Ethical Philosophy According to John Finnis', pp. 253–76; C. Leget, 'Authority and Plausibility: Aquinas on Suicide', pp. 277–94. See also H. Schoot, 'Christologia Recepta: Fray Luis de León (Deel I)', in *Jaarboek 1996*, pp. 91–119; H. Schoot, 'Christologia Recepta: Fray Luis de León (Deel II)', in *Jaarboek 1998*, pp. 95–129; H. Schoot, 'Friars in Negative Christology: Thomas Aquinas and Luis de León', in T. Merrigan and J. Haers (eds.), *The Myriad Christ* (Leuven: Uitgeverij Peeters, 2000), pp. 329–48; H. Schoot, 'Language and Christology: The Case of Henry of Gorkum (+ 1431)', *Recherches de Théologie et Philosophie Médiévales* 68 (2001), pp. 142–62.

[23] SCG, Bk 1, Ch. 2, no. 2. Thomas refers to Hilary, but in *De Trinitate* I, 37 Hilary addresses God: 'Ego quidem hoc vel praecipuum vitae meae officium debere tibi Pater omnipotens Deus, conscius sum ut te omnis sermo meus et sensus loquatur.' For a survey of the discussion about the *Summa contra Gentiles* see J.-P. Torrell, *Initiation à saint Thomas d'Aquin: Sa personne et son oeuvre* (Fribourg: Éditions universitaires Fribourg, 1993), pp. 153–6, and Corbin, *Le chemin de la théologie chez Thomas d'Aquin*, pp. 475–89, for the suggestion that this summa is a personal work.

point towards a characterisation as theologian. To consider Thomas as a theologian, though, is not enough. One has to specify what kind of theologian he is. The quote from Hilary suggests a 'theo-centric' theologian. When Thomas in *quaestio* 1 of the first part of the *Summa Theologiae* discusses his discipline, more specifically the scientific character of it, he clearly gives God the central place: 'not about God and creatures equally, but about God principally and about the creatures in so far as they refer to God, either as their beginning or as their end'.[24] In the bare outline of the *Summa Theologiae* this theo-centricity can be noticed as well: 'First, we will discuss God; second the movement to God of reasoning creatures; third Christ who as man is our way to God.'[25]

But even this specification, theo-centric, is not sufficient. For how does he understand God, how does he proceed, what is his point of departure, what are his tools and how does he use them? A first answer to these questions is that Thomas is a biblical theologian, that he is a negative theologian, that he is very well aware of the limitations and constrictions of human knowledge and language vis-à-vis God and that he is a systematic theologian. This is still a rather formal answer. Formal because it is short and because it points to method. But by unpacking these formal characteristics one can see how decisive these features are and also how filled with content. The best way to unpack these characteristics is to have a closer look at some texts. In this manner, it will become clear as well that these characteristics are not the product of some strange imagination, but come out of the texts themselves. In this manner, finally, it will become clear that these features cannot be separated neatly. Their interaction makes Thomas such a fascinating theologian.

Thomas the 'biblical theologian'

While studying at Naples, Thomas decided to join the Dominican order, against the will of his parents who had sent him as an oblate to the Benedictine monastery of Monte Cassino when he was a young boy.

---

[24] *ST* Ia, Q. 1, art. 3, ad 1: 'sacra doctrina non determinat de Deo et creaturis ex aequo, sed de Deo principaliter et de creaturis secundum quod referuntur ad Deum ut ad principium vel finem'. Cf. also *ST* Ia, Q. 1, art. 4, resp.: 'quia principalius agit de rebus divinis quam de actibus humanis, de quibus agit secundum quod per eos ordinatur homo ad perfectam Dei cognitionem in qua beatitudo aeterna consistit'; *ST* Ia, Q. 1, art. 7, sed contra: 'sed in hac scientia fit sermo de Deo, dicitur enim theologia quasi sermo de Deo'; *ST* Ia, Q. 1, art. 7, resp.: 'omnia autem pertractantur, in sacra doctrina sub ratione Dei vel quia sunt ipse Deus; vel quia habent ordinem ad Deum ut ad principium et finem'.

[25] *ST* Ia, Q. 2, intro.: 'Primo tractabimus de Deo, secundo de motu rationalis creaturae in Deum, tertio de Christo, qui secundum quod homo via est nobis tendendi in Deum.'

Thomas's decision did not only mean a choice for an 'evangelic' life, but also for a life dedicated, to contemplate and to transmit what has been contemplated to others. A prominent source for that contemplation was Scripture.[26] Later in life as Magister in *Sacra Pagina* his task in the university was to read, to discuss and to preach Scripture.[27] It would be rather strange to suppose that each of these different tasks was executed in isolation and even stranger that they would be isolated from the religious life. Thomas the biblical theologian is not just the commentator of Scripture, but also the theologian who in his systematic works uses Scripture as a primary source. Thomas gives Scripture that role in his methodological reflections with which he starts his major systematic theological works. M. Corbin has studied Thomas's four major methodological texts in great detail and has presented a 'speculative reading' of those texts, a reconstruction of Thomas's searching for an adequate explanation of his practice. As already indicated, his analyses have influenced our understanding of Thomas (see below). But methodological reflections are necessarily secondary and might not adequately reflect the actual practice. Therefore, an additional inquiry is called for, concentrating on that practice. P. Valkenberg has done that.[28] He has developed a heuristic device for tracing the place and the function of Scripture in Thomas's systematic theological works (see further below).

Theology: 'scientia' between 'sacra doctrina' and 'sacra scriptura', Summa Theologiae *Ia, Q. 1*

Three terms dominate the very first *quaestio* of the *Summa Theologiae*: *sacra doctrina*, *scientia* and *sacra scriptura*. The way Thomas organises and formulates the various questions of the ten articles reveals how these three terms are related and how they together determine his concept of theology.

Thomas starts with a question about *sacra doctrina*, to be more precise, about its necessity. This necessity can be qualified as an existential one, since the question is discussed with regard to human salvation and the direction of human life. God, the centre of the *sacra doctrina*, is 'our end' and our salvation.[29]

The term *doctrina* suggests knowledge. This suggestion is confirmed by other words that belong to the field of 'knowledge' like *disciplina*,

---

[26] Cf. Thomas's view on religious life in *ST* IIaIIae, Q. 188, esp. arts. 5 and 6.

[27] M.-D. Chenu, *Introduction à l'étude de saint Thomas d'Aquin*, 4th edn (Montreal/Paris: Institut d'études médiévales, 1984), pp. 199–255; Torrell, *Initiation à saint Thomas d'Aquin*, pp. 79–108.

[28] Valkenberg, *Words of the Living God.*

[29] *ST* Ia, Q. 1, art. 1, resp.: 'homo ordinatur ad Deum sicut ad quemdam finem . . . tota hominis salus, quae in Deo est'.

nota, *praecognitum* and *cognitione*. The qualification *sacra* suggests another field: that of religion, faith, God. This suggestion, too, is confirmed in the rest of the article, since Thomas adds several times that this *sacra doctrina* is revealed by God. One could therefore translate *sacra doctrina* as 'revelation', be it that the term should not be understood in the rather formal way it has been used in theology since the seventeenth century, but rather in the way it is used in *Dei Verbum*, the Dogmatic Constitution on Revelation of Vatican II. Revelation is then primarily God communicating himself as Father, Son and Spirit. For the *responsio* points to God as the core of that *sacra doctrina*.

In the *sed contra* of that first article the term *sacra scriptura* occurs. The quotation from 2 Timothy 3.16 contains the two elements one can discern in *sacra doctrina* (*sacra*, revelation and *doctrina*, *docere*, *arguere*, etc.) but now connected with *scriptura*: 'all Scripture inspired by God is profitable to teach, to reprove, to correct, to instruct in righteousness'. This reference to Scripture is not accidental. There is a strong connection between this first article and the two final articles of the *quaestio*. Thomas announces at the beginning of the *quaestio* that in articles 9 and 10 he will discuss topics related to Scripture. It is not surprising that Thomas in these articles uses *sacra scriptura* repeatedly. But the term *sacra doctrina* occurs also both in the *objectiones* and in the *sed contra* of article 9. *Sacra doctrina* therefore determines the problem to be discussed in that article on Scripture. This suggests, like the *sed contra* of article 1, a link between the two. That link is confirmed by Thomas's saying that God is the author of Sacred Scripture (article 10). A further specification of this link is to be found in the focus of the questions. In both articles about Scripture, Thomas is interested in the intelligibility of Scripture. The reason for this focus becomes clear when one takes a closer look at the precise problems Thomas mentions and the way he formulates these. In article 9, the question is about metaphorical or symbolic language. The suggestion is that this type of language is not appropriate. The answer is that it is fitting (*conveniens*) that God has used this type of language and one of the arguments is that Sacred Scripture therefore becomes accessible to everyone, including the non-educated. So, the theme of the existential necessity of revelation, which is central to article 1, returns in article 9. There is another aspect to this link, which explains not only why Thomas finishes his discussion about theology with a discussion about Scripture but also why he does so with a focus on intelligibility. This is found in the discussion of *scientia*, which is the central part of this *quaestio* (articles 2 and 8).

The historical background for the discussion whether *sacra doctrina* is a *scientia* can be noticed in the way Thomas phrases the question in article 1: whether another *doctrina* is necessary apart from the philosophical doctrines. The 'philosophical doctrines' refer to the well-organised body of knowledge that is available since Aristotle's so-called third entrance. The concept of *scientia* Thomas uses is also Aristotelian. In article 2 Thomas makes uses of a distinction which is based on the place of the principles or the premises of a *scientia*. There are sciences that work with premises formulated within that science (e.g., arithmetic) and there are sciences that work with premises formulated in another, higher science (e.g., music that uses the arithmetical principles). Thomas argues that theology is a science of the second kind, for it receives its principles: they belong to a higher science, namely, God's knowledge, and are revealed by God. Theology proceeds from them. In the final article of this series on *scientia* (article 8), Thomas specifies this proceeding by discussing the argumentative nature of theology. Theology does not argue to establish these principles, but proceeds from them to show something.[30] These principles are to be found in Scripture. *Sacra doctrina* and *sacra scriptura* allow and call for a *scientia*, a theological explication. Precisely because the principles form the starting-point of the whole process of 'scientific' explanation and understanding which is theology, the intelligibility of Scripture is the focus of Thomas's two final articles on *sacra scriptura*.[31]

The practice

Does Thomas practise what he says in his methodological considerations? Does he give Scripture that crucial place and function in his theology? Valkenberg's research shows that Thomas does precisely that and increasingly so.

In order to appreciate Thomas's practice one has to pay attention to quantitative data. How often does Thomas quote Scripture explicitly and implicitly? How do these quotations compare to quotations from other works? Which books from Scripture does he quote? These quantitative analyses show the place of Scripture. But one has to investigate also the qualitative data and to discover how the (explicit or implicit) quotations from Scripture function theologically. An important distinction Valkenberg makes is the one between the theological primary function (singular) and the theologically secondary functions (plural). The theological primary function of Scripture refers to a special function that other sources (like Church Fathers, other theologians, philosophers) do not

---

[30] *ST* Ia, Q. 1, art. 8, resp.: 'haec doctrina non argumentatur ad sua principia probanda, quae sunt articuli fidei, sed ex eis procedit ad aliquid ostendendum'.

[31] Cf. Thomas's remarks in *ST* IaIIae, Q. 1, art. 9 (whether it is fitting that the articles of faith are put in a symbolum): 'veritas fidei in sacra Scriptura diffuse continetur et variis modis et in quibusdam obscure; ita quod ad eliciendum fidei veritatem ex sacra Scriptura requiritur longum studium et exercitium'.

have. In this unique function, Scripture is 'the framework and source of the theological text itself'. That is to say, the reference to Scripture in the text shows an 'encompassing function of Scripture before the text. In this function, Scripture is received as the Word of God.'[32] The theological secondary functions refer to functions Scripture has like other sources or *auctoritates*.

Valkenberg has mapped out the place Scripture occupies and has traced the primary function and secondary functions of Scripture by analysing a number of discussions in the *Summa Theologiae*: resurrection, the christological discussions about hypostatic union, assuming *persona*, assumed nature, and the use of 'person' in *divinis*. He has also compared the *Summa Theologiae* with other texts about the resurrection. These analyses show that

> the theologically primary function of Scripture [can be found] everywhere in Aquinas' theology, because it is essential to a theology proceeding from the principles of faith known through revelation; the place and the theologically secondary functions of Scripture, however, may vary depending on the influence of subject matter, literary genre and sources.[33]

The analyses of all of Aquinas's texts on the resurrection allow also for a historical perspective. Over the years, Thomas uses Scripture more and more prominently in his systematic works. An explanation is not just that by understanding Aristotle better he relies less on Aristotle and more on Scripture, but also that his work as Magister in *Sacra Pagina*, his lecturing on Scripture, has influenced profoundly his systematic theological work. This conclusion is corroborated by comparing Thomas's use of other sources when he discusses the resurrection in the *Scriptum* and the *Summa Theologiae*. In the *Scriptum*, Thomas is rather dependent on some of his predecessors, in the *Summa Theologiae* his sources are the *glossae* and his own commentaries on Scripture.[34]

Thomas the 'negative' theologian

To qualify Thomas as a negative theologian might cause some confusion, certainly since in recent postmodern philosophical debates negative theology has become a popular theme. As will become clear, though, the core of Thomas's negative theology is not a lack of knowledge or the

---

[32] Valkenberg, *Words of the Living God*, p. 134; cf. pp. 48–53.
[33] Valkenberg, *Words of the Living God*, p. 141.
[34] Valkenberg, *Words of the Living God*, pp. 188–9, 201–10.

impossibility of knowledge, but the constant awareness of *Deus semper major*. His negative theology therefore does not mean that one cannot truthfully speak about God, but that that speaking always is inadequate.[35]

In the very first *quaestio* of the *Summa Theologiae*, Thomas makes comments about God exceeding the comprehension of human reason and about the impossibility to know what God is.[36] He repeats these remarks when introducing the first part of the *Summa*: 'But because we cannot know about God what he is but what he is not, we cannot consider about God how he is but rather how he is not. Therefore, first we have to consider how he is not.'[37] How do we have to understand and to appreciate these sayings? Are they just pious remarks to be expected from a theologian at the beginning of his work, as an example of true or token humility, uttered without much consequence for what follows? Or should one take these sayings seriously, as a heading for the following discussion and as a key to understanding the opening *quaestiones*?

It seems fair and quite normal to start with taking an author's indication seriously, certainly if the author, as in Thomas's case, starts with saying that he will present the material in a precise and orderly way.[38] Of course, the author might in fact not do what he says he intends to do. But it seems correct that one has to prove that and not to assume it. Nevertheless, due to historical developments in reading Thomas and especially in reading the beginning of the Summa, it was (and still is) necessary to argue that those sayings are not just pious remarks and to show that he really keeps to the programme indicated by that short *quomodo non sit*.

'quomodo non sit': Summa Theologiae *Ia, QQ. 3–11*

In the introduction to the *quaestiones* 3–11, Thomas announces the two principles that will govern his analyses of the *quomodo non sit*: to remove what is inappropriate to God and to pay attention to God's perfection. The phrase 'to remove from him what is inappropriate' can

---

[35] See J. Wissink, 'Enkele theologische reflecties over negatieve theologie toegelicht aan de hand van Thomas van Aquino', in I. Bulhof and L. ten Kate (eds.), *Ons ontbreken heilige namen. Negatieve theologie in de hedendaagse cultuurfilosofie* (Kampen: Kok Pharos, 1992), pp. 46–65.

[36] *ST* Ia, Q. 1, art. 1: 'a Deo . . . qui comprehensionem rationis excedit'; *ST* Ia, Q.1, art. 7, ad 1: 'de Deo non possumus scire quid est'.

[37] *ST* Ia, Q. 3, intro.: 'Sed quia de Deo scire non possumus quid sit sed quid non sit, non possumus considerare de Deo quomodo sit sed potius quomodo non sit. Primo ergo considerandum est quomodo non sit.' Cf Q. 2, intro.: 'quomodo sit vel potius quomodo non sit'.

[38] *ST* Ia, *Prologus*.

easily be misunderstood. For the temptation is great – almost a natural one – to think or conclude that the appropriate remains when the inappropriate is removed. In other words, to think that Thomas indicates here a negative way in order to reach a positive description and to conclude that the terms he introduces, 'simplicity', 'perfection', 'infinity', 'immutability' 'unity', are to be considered as attributes, which form the basis of an informative doctrine of God. But this line of thought is not correct: the method of removing shows only the how-not. Nothing more.

Thomas starts with inquiring into God's simplicity, 'by which composition is removed from him'.[39] Here again it is crucial to look carefully at what Thomas in fact does. He indicates that the inquiry will be about God's simplicity and *quaestio* 3 is an inquiry into God's simplicity. But the way he approaches the simplicity is revealing. In the eight questions he announces he is going to discuss, *simplex* is mentioned only once and even then not as the only or central term: in all cases *compositio* is the central term.[40] Moreover, in answering those questions in all cases *compositio* is removed or denied. 'Simplicity' appears only at the end of the inquiry, and only as the result of a series of denials. Thomas does not give one positive argument for simplicity, he only gives arguments against composition. 'Simplicity' is therefore to be understood as a summary of a series of denials, as shorthand for those denials. 'Because God is in no way composite, he must be altogether simple.'[41] The inquiry Thomas undertakes in the *quaestio* about the simplicity sets the pattern for the inquiries in the following *quaestiones*. In those inquiries finiteness, change, temporality and multitude are denied and these denials lead to the conclusion of God's infiniteness, immutability, eternity and unity.

Therefore, no positive information is given when God is said to be altogether simple, or infinite, or immutable or one. But that also makes clear that the type of negative theology Thomas is practising does not, in the end, yield something positive. The way Thomas proceeds does not resemble sentences like 'He did not help us', or 'He did not refrain from action'. The denials in the *quaestiones* showing how God is not are not a means to a purpose, but the purpose itself. Thomas's negative theology is a radical one.

---

[39] *ST* Ia, Q. 3, intro.: 'Primo ergo inquiretur de simplicitate ipsius, per quam removetur ab eo compositio.'
[40] *ST* Ia, Q. 3, intro.: 1. 'utrum Deus sit corpus' ['quasi compositionem habens ex partibus quantitativis', the ed. Piana adds]; 2. 'utrum sit in eo compositio formae et materiae'; 'utrum sit in eo compositio quidditatis sive essentiae vel naturae et subjecti'; 4. 'utrum sit in eo compositio quae est ex essentia et esse'; 5. 'utrum sit in eo compositio generis et differentiae'; 6. 'utrum sit in eo compositio subjecti et accidentis'; 7. 'utrum sit quocumque modo compositus vel totaliter simplex'; 8. 'utrum veniat in compositionem cum aliis'.
[41] *ST* Ia, Q. 3, art. 7, resp.: 'manifestum est quod Deus nullo modo compositus est sed omnino simplex'.

The second principle Thomas announces (to pay attention to God's perfection) is related to this negative theology. For, as Thomas indicates, the denial or removal of compositeness in our material world means imperfection and incompleteness.[42] So, the procedure to show *quomodo non sit* would result in a God who would be imperfect and incomplete. To counter this suggestion, attention has to be given to perfection. Thomas repeats this procedure several times. After removing limitation he discusses God's existence in things, after removing motion he discusses God's eternity, after removing multiplicity he discusses God's unity.

Even if one sees how Thomas in these opening *quaestiones* combines a strong and radical negative theology with considerations about God's perfection and therefore with some biblical notions (good, eternal) his decision to start with concepts like *compositio, finitas, motus* remains puzzling and strange, especially if one takes seriously what he says in *quaestio* 1 about Revelation/Scripture as the source of the theological *scientia*.

Before one can conclude that these *quaestiones* belong rather to philosophy than to theology or rather to natural theology than to revealed theology, one has to ask why Thomas has chosen to start with *composition* and the like, and not with love or mercy or with God as Creator, Redeemer and Sanctifier, terms used in the Creed. Thomas does not give the reasons for his choice explicitly, but they can be discovered by looking carefully at the concepts analysed and the questions answered.[43] The topics he discusses with regard to *compositio* show that the *compositio* he has in mind is not the composition that belongs to our daily or normal experience. The composition we experience is the composition, for example, of a sauce, of concrete, of a sweater. The compositions Thomas has in mind are different: it is the composition of quantitative parts, of form and matter, of nature and subject, of nature and existence, of genus and difference, of substance and accidents. They are the compositions we have to think in order to explain and understand our daily experience. These compositions belong to the deep-structure of our experience. So, by choosing *compositio* he indicates that he moves on a meta-level: on the level of thinking and talking about the structure of our experience, on the level of ways of thinking and talking that mirror the deep-structure of our experience, on the level of language-rules and thought-patterns.

There is another feature that indicates that Thomas in these *quaestiones* is engaged in an analysis on the meta-level. That is the connection between the topics he discusses: composition, finiteness, motion, time,

---

[42] *ST* Ia, Q. 3, intro.: 'Et quia simplicia in rebus corporalibus sunt imperfecta et partes, secundo inquiretur de perfectione eius.'

[43] The following analysis of *quaestiones* 3–11 is inspired by Burrell, *Aquinas: God and Action*, pp. 12–41.

multitude. In his analyses, Thomas indicates repeatedly the conceptual linkage between these concepts: motion presupposes composition, time presupposes motion, and so on.[44] So, he indicates that in these analyses he does not add something new every time he discusses another topic, but that he shows the implications, basically the implications of Question 3.[45] So, the strangeness of the way Thomas starts the *Summa* disappears when one realises that he moves on a meta-level, that he analyses fundamental structures of our experience of reality, of our thinking and talking about reality.

Formulated in this way, Thomas's negative theology seems to be something primarily of the theologian. The *Summa Theologiae* would then start with an exercise in modesty, an exercise especially relevant for beginning theologians. That is only one side. Thomas is not primarily interested in the theologian: he is primarily interested in God, the mystery of our God. That is ultimately the basis of his negative theology. This implies that negative theology is not restricted to these opening *quaestiones*, but permeates also the rest.[46] An example can show this.

God's knowledge of the future: Summa Theologiae Ia, Q. 14, art. 13.[47]

A topic which shows nicely how Thomas maintains and employs the insights of the *quomodo non sit* is one discussed throughout the ages including ours: how is God's foreknowledge, providence, predestination related to our free will and to the contingencies of our reality?[48]

According to Thomas's analysis of the issue, two problems should be distinguished.[49] The first one concerns the diachronic relation between (our statements about) God's eternal knowledge and the future. If we say

---

[44] Cf., e.g., *ST* Ia, Q. 9, art. 1, resp.: 'et sic in omni eo quod movetur, attenditur aliqua compositio'; *ST* Ia, Q. 10, art. 1, resp.: 'Sicut igitur ratio temporis consistit in numeratione prioris et posterioris in motu'; *ST* Ia, Q. 10, art. 2, resp.: 'ratio aeternitatis consequitur immutabilitatem, sicut ratio temporis consequitur motum'.

[45] Cf. the beginning of *ST* Ia, Q. 9, art. 1: 'Dicendum quod ex praemissis ostenditur Deum esse omnino immutabilem'; and the beginning of *ST* Ia, Q. 11, art. 3: 'Dicendum quod Deus esse unum ex tribus demonstratur. Primo quidem ex eius simplicitate . . . Secundo vero ex infinitate eius perfectionis.'

[46] See, e.g., J. Wissink, 'Aquinas: The Theologian of Negative Theology: A Reading of *Summa Theologiae* I qq 14–26', in *Jaarboek 1993*, pp. 15–84; P. Bakker, M. Brinkhuis, A. Kamp and H. Rikhof, 'Een hypothese getoetst: Een lezing van enkele *quaestiones* uit Thomas' *ST* ', in *Jaarboek 1989*, pp. 65–118 (the *quaestiones* read are *ST* Ia, Q. 21 and Q. 34; *ST* IIIa, Q. 1 and Q. 24). See also Schoot, *Christ*, for a 'negative' Christology.

[47] See, for the following, Goris, *Free Creatures of an Eternal God*.

[48] See Goris, *Free Creatures of an Eternal God*, pp. 66–89 for an outline of the present discussion.

[49] Goris, *Free Creatures of an Eternal God*, pp. 54–66.

that God foreknows or foreknew the whole future, does it not follow that the future is as determinate as the past and that chance and freedom do not really exist? The other problem has to do with the synchronic relation between (our statements about) God's will as necessarily efficacious cause and its effects in creation. Only the first problem will be discussed here. Because Thomas deals with it in the context of God's eternity, a first step is to see how he understands eternity.

When Thomas in *quaestio* 10 discusses God's eternity, he starts, as so often, with a conceptual clarification. Is Boethius' definition – 'eternity is the all-at-once and perfect possession of interminable life' – suitable?[50] Thomas argues it is. Remarkable, though, is his negative interpretation of that definition. He stresses two elements in particular as crucial: eternity has neither beginning nor end (article 1), and eternity lacks successiveness (*tota simul*). Thomas's next step is to ask whether this concept applies to God (article 2) and to God alone (article 3). For a positive answer to the first question Thomas appeals to the implication mentioned already: eternity is implied in unchangeableness. But in the course of the article, he makes also two additional comments that clarify his understanding of God's eternity further. First, commenting upon another saying by Boethius about eternity, that it is *nunc stans*, an abiding instant, Thomas points to our way of understanding. Time we understand as a flowing instant, eternity we grasp by understanding it as an abiding instant. The starting-point is our understanding (or experience) of time as duration or flow concentrated in 'now'. That 'now' becomes the focal point, the point of similarity between time and eternity, for 'instant' suggests a timelessness. But there is a greater dissimilarity while our now is always part of duration, of before and after, that is not the case with God's eternal now.[51] Second, responding to the objection that in Scripture verbs with past, present, and future tenses are used for God, Thomas states that God's eternity includes all time. So, eternity is not to be understood as everlasting within time (omnitemporal). Eternity is more than that, although that more is difficult to specify or even impossible to express.[52]

Thomas's answer to the question whether God knows future contingencies is that God knows. When he formulates this positive answer at

---

[50] 'Aeternitas igitur est interminabilis vitae tota simul et perfecta possessio', Boethius, *Philosophiae Consolationis* V pr. 6:9-10.

[51] Or 'atemporal duration' as Kretzmann and Stump have suggested: see Goris, *Free Creatures of an Eternal God*, pp. 45–8 for a presentation of their views and for references to the discussion their suggestion has provoked.

[52] See Goris, *Free Creatures of an Eternal God*, pp. 49–52 for a discussion of the grammatical consequences. Goris stresses, too, that Thomas does not understand God's eternity in terms of the atemporality of universals or mathematical concepts (p. 44).

the beginning of the *responsio* of article 13, he refers to an earlier article (article 9) in the same *quaestio* where he has argued that God knows everything whatsoever (*omnia quaecumque sunt quocumque modo*). Thomas is there at pains to elaborate *omnia*. The key to understanding why he is so concerned that nothing should be excluded is to be found in the term he uses several times: *creatura*. Thomas, in other words, makes a remark that belongs to the theology of creation and hints at the fundamental difference between God the Creator and the creatures that is the central insight of that theology. Everything is created. God, as beginning and end of everything that is created, is not part of everything, but is different. This difference is not the same as the differences within the whole of creation, but 'differently different' and therefore hardly imaginable.[53] If something would be excluded from everything created, it would amount to denying that creation is *ex nihilo* and to accepting something on a par with God the Creator. That argument Thomas uses again in his discussion of future contingencies.

In the same article 9, Thomas makes another remark that he repeats almost verbatim in article 13. That remark is about eternity. God's knowing is measured by eternity 'which is without succession and embraces all time'. That means that God's knowing extends over all time, and to all that is, in whatever time. In article 13, Thomas applies this to future contingencies. While we know things as they become actual successively, God does not. He knows simultaneously (*simul*) 'for his knowledge is measured by eternity as is his being'.[54] All that is in time is present to God eternally (*ab aeterno*).

To understand this argument and to appreciate it, one has to pay attention to the terms Thomas uses and the way he argues. Thomas uses terms like *intuitus, conspectus, visio*; terms that connote some immediacy, a kind of knowledge or understanding that happens in a flash and that is different from the kind of knowledge that is the result of long and laborious searching and arguing. Thomas makes the same point in an example: someone on the road cannot see those who come after him, for he cannot oversee the whole road, but someone standing on some height has a better view and can.[55] But it would be inadequate to leave it at that and not to notice that Thomas corrects these insights radically. He does that in the way he presents his argument, by distinguishing on the one hand between how things are and how they are known and on the other

---

[53] Schoot, *Christ*, p. 232; see Thomas's illuminating discussion of the concept of creation in *ST* Ia, Q. 45.

[54] In article 9 the connection between eternity and God's being is more indirect: via knowledge (God's knowing which is his being).

[55] *ST* Ia, Q. 14, art. 13, ad 3. See Goris, *Free Creatures of an Eternal God*, p. 245 for a discussion of this example and for another example.

hand how God is and knows. He does not say that the future things are already there somehow, but says that God is present to them. The reason why all temporal beings are said to be present to God is not that they have some kind of timeless existence, but God's own, incomprehensible mode of being, namely, eternity.

Thomas the 'theo-logian'

If one compares Heinrich's *Dogmatische Theologie*, a popular and representative nineteenth-century manual, with the *Summa Theologiae*, one can notice some remarkable differences.[56] These differences are remarkable since Thomas is not only frequently quoted and presented as the theologian *par excellence*, but Heinrich also wants to return qua content and structure to the traditional theology, the theology of the *Vorzeit*. Two differences are especially interesting. First, one finds a greater attention to our knowledge of God. Moreover, that discussion about knowledge combines the three separate discussions that can be found in the Prima Pars of *Summa Theologiae* (Q. 2, art. 2; Q. 12; Q. 32).[57] Second, one discovers that hardly any attention is paid to language. *Quaestio* 13 with its famous discussion about analogy is treated as a discussion about concepts, about attributes.[58] These differences one can notice, too, in a manual that belongs to the neo-scholastic tradition, but that at the same time is more personal, Scheeben's *Handbuch der Dogmatik*.[59]

These differences result also in a different structure. If one combines the three discussions about knowledge Thomas inserts at three rather different moments of his inquiry, one has to change the overall structure. In the manuals the discussion about knowledge becomes the first part of the doctrine of God and so forms an introduction to the discussion of the divine attributes. This in fact means that they start with a treatise *de Deo Uno*, which is understood to be 'natural theology', or 'philosophical

---

[56] J. B. Heinrich (1816–91), *Dogmatische Theologie* (Mainz: F. Kirchheim, 1881–1904: vol. 1, 1873 (1881); vol. 2, 1876 (1882); vol. 3, 1879 (1885); vol. 4, 1881 (1885); vol. 5, 1884 (1888); vol. 6, 1887 (1900). Vols. 7–10 were published by C. Gutberlet (1896, 1897, 1901, 1904); Vol. 7 was still mainly written by Heinrich.

[57] Heinrich even combines these discussions with that belonging to the anthropology of *ST* Ia, QQ. 84, 88 and 89.

[58] Heinrich, *Dogmatische Theologie*, vol. 3, pp. 310, 312.

[59] M. Scheeben, *Handbuch der katholischen Dogmatik*, vols. 1–3 (Freiburg im Breisgau : Herder, 1873–1903). See vol. 1, par. 63 about our conception of the divine essence and attributes; par. 66 about the supernatural knowledge of God; and par. 69 about the divine attributes.

theology': a doctrine of God based upon 'natural reason'. Question 13 is also moved forwards and serves to introduce the distinction between negative and affirmative attributes of God. Among the negative attributes ones finds simplicity, unchangeability, infinity with references to Thomas's discussions of those terms. As the term 'negative attribute' already indicates, there is a substantial difference between the way these theologians read the opening *quaestiones* of the *Summa Theologiae* and the interpretation presented above. Both types of attributes are part of a descriptive *de Deo Uno*.

These differences and structural changes are important since they betray on the one hand the concern of these nineteenth-century theologians and the frame of mind with which they read Thomas. They clearly share the modern concentration on knowledge and the equally modern neglect of language.[60] Developments in contemporary philosophy, the so-called linguistic turn, has put language back on the philosophical agenda and had made us aware of the influential role language plays in human existence. But research into the medieval period has shown too that this contemporary discovery of the importance of language is also a rediscovery. On the other hand, these nineteenth-century theologians do not seem to notice a real difference with Thomas. Heinrich is aware that his structure is different from Thomas's, but he presents his structure as being according to Thomas and his changes as improvements (more effective, more understandable). This judgement about in fact radical changes makes sense only if one presupposes that Heinrich takes his way of treating the doctrine of God as part of natural theology and of structuring it accordingly as shared by Thomas. But the formulations *de Deo Uno* or *de Deo Trino* are not used by Thomas. Neither does he use terms like *tractatus*.[61] It is also highly questionable whether the distinction natural–supernatural captures adequately the discussions about knowledge in Questions 12 and 32. However, even more importantly, they do not seem to appreciate Thomas's reasons for inserting at three different moments a discussion about knowledge and for connecting to one of these a discussion about 'theological language' (Question 13). The reason for discussing knowledge and language after the *quaestiones* in which Thomas shows how God is not is to be found in that inquiry: they are part of showing how God is not, be it on an even more reflective level. The negative thrust of *quaestiones* 3–11 asks for a fundamental discussion about knowing and naming God. If God is so different, can we know him and speak about him at all? In *quaestiones* 12 and 13 Thomas

[60] F. Kerr, *Theology after Wittgenstein* (Oxford: Blackwell, 1986), esp. pp. 3–52.
[61] Rikhof, 'Aquinas' Authority in the Contemporary Theology of the Trinity', pp. 217–19.

addresses these questions. In *quaestio* 13 Thomas does not only exhibit his familiarity with 'language analysis' but also shows his skills by using this analysis 'theo-logically'. A closer look at *quaestio* 13 reveals this (see below) and an important issue in Thomas's Christology confirms this (see further below).

Limitations and possibilities: Summa Theologiae *Ia, Q. 13*

Thomas starts his inquiry into our talking about God with the fundamental question whether our language is adequate for such a purpose. Thomas formulates this problem on two levels: on the level of religious language and on the technical level of language analysis. Both Scripture (Proverbs 30.4) and the theological tradition (Pseudo-Dionysius) suggest a negative answer (obj. 1). On the other hand, Scripture itself talks about God 'Almighty is his name' (Exodus 15.3) (*sed contra*). By formulating the problem this way, Thomas shows not only the principal and fundamental character of the question, but also indicates that it is a problem belonging to faith and provoked by faith. The problem of talking about God mirrors the tension between revelation and hiddenness. The seriousness of this inner faith problem is underlined by more technical *objectiones* (obj. 2 and 3). In these the basic structure of our language – all our nouns are either concrete or abstract, and our nouns, verbs, participles, pronouns refer always to something 'in connection with' (time, place, etc.) – is contrasted with the denials of composition and the like, which form the main outcome of the earlier *quaestiones*. So, right at the beginning, the connection is made with the analyses of *quaestiones* 3–11 and the conclusion is drawn that our language is so tied up with creation that it cannot be used for the Creator.

In his *responsio*, Thomas does not alter the limits set by his earlier analyses. On the contrary, the basis of it (we do not know the essence of God, but know him only from creatures as their principle) and the consequences (by way of excellence and denial) are repeated. This determines the nuanced and qualified conclusion: we cannot talk about God as we can about a creature, whose essence we can capture. Nevertheless, we can talk about him, only this talking is and remains 'from creatures' and requires therefore some operation. The limits leave some space, enough space not to be forced into silence. Something can be said, however inadequate, or perhaps more precisely, something can be suggested and shown in our use of language. As a telling example of how in faith language is used to suggest and to show what cannot be said, Aquinas refers to the fact that for God we use both abstract and concrete terms. So, we say, for example, 'God is good' and 'God is goodness' (not just 'God has goodness'). Each expression on its own is inadequate, but in combination, the inadequacies are used to suggest more.[62] This type of argument Aquinas uses again and again when he explores in the following articles little by little the space between silence and talking about God straightforwardly.

But in the second article this little space is immediately questioned and threatened: we may be able to speak about God because we know of him from creatures, but does that mean that we therefore can talk about God self? Should we not be content with only negative and relative terms, that is with words 'that deny something of him or words that refer to his relation to something else, or rather of something else to him'?[63] Thomas thinks such a reduction of positive sayings to negative or relative ones to be incoherent with regard to actual religious language and the intention of the speakers. Therefore, something else must be the case: those positive sayings refer to God self, predicate of him something *substantialiter*, but they fail in representing him.

Thomas's appeal to the actual practice is significant and revealing. Thomas's reflections presuppose that practice and are directed to clarify it. He is engaged neither in construing some ideal language – that would be impossible, for it would remain a creature-language – nor in reforming the existing religious language – that would be superfluous since such a 'clean' language would fall short too.[64]

Thomas clarifies this position by appealing to creation or creation theology, but this is not an easy appeal. A creature is a representation of God, is similar to him as far as perfections are concerned. Only this representation or similarity does not put them in the same category; it represents God as the transcending principle.[65] The appeal results in a heavily qualified 'yes', or in an almost emptied 'yes', in the same way 'creation' is thought about as a form of production of which all the characteristic features are denied.[66] The answer amounts to accepting

---

[62] *ST* Ia, Q. 13, art. 1, ad 2: 'Quia et Deus simplex est et subsistens est, attribuimus ei nomina abstracta ad significandam simplicitatem eius et nomina concreta ad significandum subsistentiam et perfectionem ipsius, quamvis utraque nomina deficiant a modo ipsius, sicut intellectus noster non cognoscit eum ut est secundum hanc vitam.'

[63] *ST* Ia, Q. 13, art. 2, resp.: 'remotionem alicuius ab ipso, vel relationem eius ad alium, vel potius alicuius ad ipsum', cf. obj. 3 for the first part of the question. The formulation 'vel potius alicujus ad ipsum' reveals nicely how Thomas keeps to the limits and reminds his readers of them.

[64] He argues that the reduction does not explain why we are saying that God is good or living and not that he is a body, that it would follow that all religious language is second hand, and that it does not value the intention of the speakers.

[65] *ST* Ia, Q. 13, art. 2, resp.: 'Unde quaelibet creatura intantum eum repraesentat et est ei similis, inquantum perfectionem aliquam habet, non tamen ita quod repraesentat eum sicut aliquid eiusdem speciei vel generis, sed sicut excellens principium.'

[66] See, e.g., *ST* Ia, Q. 45, art. 1 and art. 2.

that we do talk about God self and say something 'really' about him, but this applies only to some words, namely indicating a perfection, like 'good', 'living', 'being' and even these should not be understood as straightforward descriptions.

Article 3 again questions and probes this result. If we speak about God on the basis of creatures, and if this basis remains present in the way we talk, what is its worth? Does that not imply that all language about God is metaphorical, or are some words used *proprie*?[67] In answering that question, Thomas uses distinctions developed in a long tradition of thinking about language and shows the sensitivity for the variety and flexibility of language which is the basis for that kind of reflection.

We can refer to the same object in different ways. To use an example that is famous in the modern philosophy of language, 'Hesperus is Phospheros', or 'the evening star is the morning star'. 'Hesperus' and 'Phosphorus' have the same 'reference' but have a different 'sense'. The point of this example is not just that we refer to the same object in different ways, but also that all referring is 'mannered'. The distinction *modus significandi – res significata* expresses this and Thomas appeals to this point when he addresses the problem whether the perfection terms we use to refer to God *substantialiter* are *proprie* or not. He argues that with regard to the *res*, the perfections, these are properly attributed to God, but that with regard to the *modus* our language remains creatural and therefore 'not proper' for God. Again a nuanced and qualified answer and again a heavily qualified one, for it applies only to the category of the perfection words and the distinction is an analytical and theoretical one.

In his argument, Thomas also makes use of a peculiar feature of perfection words like 'good', 'living', and 'being'. While some words have a fixed meaning, regardless of their linguistic context, others depend on their linguistic context for their precise meaning. Words with a fixed meaning like 'surgeon', 'author' or 'under age' determine the she or he who is the subject of these predicates. In the case of words with a vague and open meaning, the subject determines the meaning of the predicate: 'car', 'wine' or 'lecture' all give a specific meaning to 'good' or 'bad'. Moreover, within this category of open, vague and flexible words, a special category allows for gradation and more importantly for growth. Words like 'pregnant' or 'dead' do not allow for gradation: one either is pregnant or not: to be 'a little pregnant' is nonsense. Words like 'taciturn' allow for gradation ('rather', 'very'), but there are limits: it does not make sense to call somebody 'taciturn' who never says anything. But in the case of 'good', 'wise' and the like, one can always think about

---

[67] *ST* Ia, Q. 13, intro.: 'Utrum aliqua nomina dicta de Deo proprie dicantur de ipso an omnia attribuantur ei metaphorice.'

something more: there are no limits and it does make sense to use qualifications like 'totally', 'completely', 'perfectly' in connection with 'good' or 'wise'. Given these characteristics of words we use in ordinary language, we can understand why they are used religiously. They are appropriate, or least inappropriate, for God, because they are so open that God determines their meaning (and not vice versa) and they allow for infinite growth, and can therefore suggest what cannot be said.

It is not surprising that in the discussion about *proprie*, Thomas uses a few times the qualification *metaphorice*. Traditionally – that is to say since Aristotle's observation about metaphors – the distinction proper–non-proper belongs to the theory of metaphor. Aristotle determines metaphor as a word that, for various reasons, is being used instead of another word that is the proper word. In principle, the metaphor-word can be replaced by the proper term. So, the metaphor is an ornament, used to say nicely or beautifully what can be said simply and properly. In this traditional theory, the metaphor is judged rather negatively. It can be effective in poetics, but should be avoided in reasoning and argumentative discourse.[68]

Thomas returns to metaphors when, in the final stage of his inquiry into the words we use of God *substantialiter*, he further determines these perfection words and asks whether some words we use for both God and creature are used univocally or equivocally.[69] Whether a word is univocal or not depends on its having one *ratio* (meaning) or more and different *rationes*. The word 'bank' is equivocal because it has the *ratio* 'slope', the *ratio* 'money institution', and the *ratio* 'row' or 'line'. Whether a word is univocal or equivocal can be discovered in a dictionary, a sign it is a question of meaning. Or to use another important distinction developed in the reflection on language: univocity and equivocity are concerned with *significatio* not with *suppositio*.[70] *Significatio* is used to refer to the meaning of a word; *suppositio* is used to refer to its use, to what it stands for. *Significatio* can be translated with connotation or sense, *suppositio* with denotation or reference. The two are connected: given its meaning (*significatio*; connotation) a word designates something (*suppositio*; denotation).[71] So, when Thomas asks the question whether words are used

---

[68] Thomas accepts this negative evaluation, but argues that in the case of religious language this is not a disadvantage: see, e.g., *ST* Ia, Q. 1, art. 9.

[69] *ST* Ia, Q. 13, intro.: 'Utrum nomina aliqua dicantur de Deo et creaturis univoce vel aequivoce.'

[70] See, for an extended discussion with references to other literature: Schoot, *Christ*, pp. 41–73.

[71] Several types of *suppositio* are distinquished. The distinction *materialis–formalis* is fundamental. 'The word *curro* is a verb' is an example of *suppositio materialis*, the term is standing for itself; in all the other cases a *suppositio formalis* (a term having a *suppositio* on the basis of its *significatio*) takes place. The *suppositio*

univocally or equivocally of God and creatures he is concerned with
significatio.

Article 5 has a striking structure that mirrors the content. The arguments in the three *objectiones* reach the conclusion 'univocal', the two
arguments in the *sed contra* the opposite: 'equivocal'. In the corpus of the
article Thomas discusses first these two extremes, rejects both and then
points to yet another type of meaning: analogy. In this article, Thomas
does not only respond to the *objectiones* but also to the arguments in
contrarium. The problem is put as a dilemma; the reaction is to reject the
dilemma. By putting the problem as a dilemma, Thomas suggests that
either extreme solves the problem by denying it. The univocity view
denies there is a difference between Creator and creatures; the equivocity
view denies that we can speak meaningfully about God. So, there must be
another solution.

But a closer look at the corpus shows an even more interesting picture.
Thomas rejects both extremes, but spends much more time and effort in
rejecting the univocity view than its opposite.[72] Apparently, the first is
more appealing, more 'natural' if one thinks about language; it certainly
is more dangerous. For although Thomas locates this third type 'in
between pure equivocation and simple univocity',[73] that phrase is
somewhat misleading. The phrase suggests a scale, but the distinction
univocal–equivocal is not a matter of more or less. It is a matter of either–
or. Either a word has one *ratio* or it has several different *rationes*. In the
case of analogy, a word has several different *rationes*, but that difference
does not imply, as in the case of 'pure' equivocity, disparity and incom-
mensurability, but relationship and order. The various *rationes* have
something in common (*ratio communis*). In one case, one can find that
ratio communis as the *ratio propria* (so to say most condensed), but in all
the other cases the *ratio communis* is present as well, be it not as 'condensed' as in the central case. Therefore all cases of analogical use are
'proper' use of language. Thomas's favourite example is 'healthy': we can
say 'a medicine is healthy', 'the urine is healthy', 'that person is healthy'.
In this example 'that person is healthy' is central; it contains the *ratio
communis* as the *ratio propria*. In the other cases 'healthy' is used properly, but not as 'condensed'. There is, one might say, a hierarchy and a

---

formalis is then further distinguished. See Schoot, *Christ*, p. 61 for the further division.

[72] Thomas's discussion of the univocity view is considerably longer than his discussion of the other viewpoint; he also uses stronger terms: '*impossibile univoce* . . .
nullum nomen univoce' form the frame of his argument.

[73] *ST* Ia, Q. 13, art. 5, resp.: 'Et iste modus communitatis medius est inter puram
aequivocationem et simplicem univocationem.'

family resemblance between the various uses of words that can be used analogically.

At this point, the difference between analogical and metaphorical use as Thomas sees it can become clear. A metaphor-word is neither equivocal (a sheer difference of *rationes*) nor analogous (a plurality of related *rationes*) but univocal. There is one *ratio*, one meaning. In, for example, 'God is my rock and my shield', 'rock' and 'shield' have both one meaning, are both univocal. The specific and decisive feature of a metaphor-word is that that word refers (designates, denotes) not properly. In terms of the distinction mentioned earlier: metaphors belong to the level of *suppositio*, analogical words to the level of *significatio*.

When Thomas applies this general analysis of analogous use of words theologically, he again makes use of the other distinction: *modus–res*. In article 5 Thomas points to this 'third way' and argues very quickly that this applies to 'some' words used for God and creatures, but in article 6 he is more specific: given that words are used analogously, are they used primarily of God or of creatures?[74] His answer is again nuanced. In the case of metaphors, words are primarily said of creatures and secondarily of God.[75] But in some other cases (the perfection words) the *res significata* is primarily (*per prius*) said of God. Still the way remains primarily that of creatures.[76] The possibilities of our human language are limited when we speak about God.

The unity of Christ: Summa Theologiae *IIIa, Q. 17, art. 1*

A central theme in that part of theology that is concerned with the person of Christ is the union of the divine and the human nature in him. The discussion of the so-called hypostatic union contains a number of important issues, but a key question is how to understand that union. How to understand that Christ is truly God and truly man? Thomas addresses that question in a way that shows his theo logical acumen and skill.[77]

Acumen and skill are shown, first, when Thomas reflects upon the union as such, the 'and' in 'truly God and truly man'. Thomas discusses

---

[74] *ST* Ia, Q. 13, intro.: 'Supposito quod dicantur analogice utrum dicantur de Deo per prius vel de creaturis.'

[75] *ST* Ia, Q. 13, art. 6, resp.: 'omnia nomina quae metaphorice de Deo dicuntur, per prius de creaturis dicuntur quam de Deo, quia dicta de Deo, nihil aliud significant quam similitudines ad tales creaturas'.

[76] *ST* Ia, Q. 13, art. 6, resp.: 'quod quantum ad rem significatam per nomen per prius dicuntur de Deo quam de creaturis, quia a Deo hujusmodi perfectiones in creaturas manant; sed quantum ad impositionem nominis per prius a nobis imponuntur creaturis, quas prius cognoscimus. Unde et modum significandi habent qui competit creaturis'.

[77] See, for the following, H. Schoot, *Christ,* ch. 4, 'The Naming of the Unity of Christ Incarnate', pp. 110–55.

the examples presented to him in the history of theology, but with a clear feeling for the limitations of those examples.[78] This can be noticed even more when Thomas analyses the ways two or more constitute one. First, a union of two complete things which remain in their perfection (e.g., a house built of stone and timber); second, a union that is made up of several things that are perfect but are changed in the process (e.g., a mixture of elements); third, a union of imperfect things that do not change (e.g., various members). Each time he concludes that this type of union does not fit the hypostatic union.[79]

When Thomas reflects upon another relevant theme – the way God and creature can be united – he presents a hierarchy of unions: God's union with creation by essence, presence and power, God's union with the faithful by operation (knowing and loving God) and God's personal union in Christ.[80] The qualification 'hierarchy' is apt because of the order of lower and higher, but it suggests also an order of less and more and first and later, an order that belongs to analogy. We can understand what the personal union, the hypostatic union means by starting from the general union with God that can be found in creatures and from the graceful union with God that can be found in the faithful. But we only understand it adequately if we see the difference and if we realise that the way (*modus*) we try to capture something that is unique necessarily falls short. To use another element from the reflections about the analogous use of words: the meaning of 'union with God' is primarily (*per prius*) determined by the personal union in Christ.[81]

Thomas's theo-logical acumen and skill is shown especially when he turns his attention to the 'is' in 'Christ is truly God and truly man'. While the analyses of *unum* and *unio* take place on the level of signification or connotation, the reflection about the 'is' belongs to the level of supposition or denotation. The fascinating feature of Thomas's dealing with the hypostatic union is that he uses that level to clarify the hypostatic union itself. A text in which this can be seen is the first article of *quaestio* 17.

Thomas asks the fundamental question whether Christ is either one or two. The argument in the *sed contra* concludes Christ is one since something that is, is one. The arguments in the *objectiones* go into the opposite direction: God and man, therefore two. In these arguments, the kenosis hymn from Philippians 2 shines through in the quotations from Augustine, and the dogma of Chalcedon is constantly in the background.

---

[78] Examples are garment, body–soul, marriage; see for references and analyses: Schoot, *Christ*, pp. 129–30.

[79] *ST* IIIa, Q. 2, art. 1, resp.; cf. also In III Sent, 1.1.1, for a somewhat different analysis but with the same tenor.

[80] *ST* IIIa, Q. 2, art. 10, resp. and ad 2; cf. art. 9, resp.

[81] Schoot, *Christ*, pp. 133–5.

Using the distinction *significatio–suppositio* one can say that the *objectiones* are concerned with *significatio*, the *sed contra* with *suppositio*.

In his response, Thomas starts with two preliminary remarks. The first one is concerned with the difference between abstract and concrete words, a distinction on the level of *significatio*. Thomas appeals to that distinction as part of a reminder about grammar *in divinis*. In the case of God we can say (or even have to say) what we cannot not say in the case of human beings. Of a human person (including Jesus Christ) we cannot say that he or she is human nature. Human nature *in abstracto* cannot be said of a person, cannot be predicated of a *suppositum*. If that were done, it would entail that there is only one human being. We can, though, predicate human nature *in concreto* of a human person in the sense that he or she has a human nature. The divine nature, however, can be said both *in concreto* and *in abstracto*: 'for, we say that the Son of God, who is the *suppositum* of the name Christ, is the divine nature and is God'.[82]

The second remark is a remark on the level of supposition and concerns the distinction between having either humanity or deity *distincte* or *indistincte*. The (proper) name Jesus (or Peter) has 'the ability to denote' a distinct human person; the term *homo* does not: *homo* denotes *indistincte*.[83] The name Son of God has the ability to denote a distinct divine person, the term *deus* does not.

The first remark leads to the conclusion that with regard to nature one could only say that Christ is two if one understands the two natures *in abstracto*.[84] But that cannot be done, for the human nature cannot be predicated *in abstracto* of one person. Both natures are therefore predicated *in concreto*. But that means that they are predicated of a *suppositum*. The consequence of this is that in order to decide the question of one or two, one has to take the *suppositum* into consideration.[85] The unity of Christ has to be approached not (or not only) on the level of signification, as the arguments in the *objectiones* suggest, but on the level of supposition as the *sed contra* argument indicates. Moreover, the second remark leads to the conclusion that because *homo* and *deus* are used *indistincte*, 'Jesus Christ is God and man' does not entail or presuppose two distinct *supposita*.[86]

---

[82] *ST* IIIa, Q. 17, art.1, resp.: 'Dicimus enim quod *Filius Dei*, qui supponitur in hoc nomine *Christus, est divina natura et est Deus*.'

[83] For the formulation 'the ability to denote', see Schoot, *Christ*, p. 140.

[84] *ST* IIIa, Q. 17, art. 1, resp.: 'Si ambae naturae in abstracto praedicarentur de Christo, sequeretur quod Christus est duo.'

[85] *ST* IIIa, Q. 17, art.1, resp.: 'Sed quia duae naturae non predicantur de Christo nisi prout significantur in supposito, oportet secundum rationem suppositi praedicari de Christi *unum* vel *duo*.'

[86] Cf. *ST* IIIa, Q. 17, art. 1, ad 6: 'duo dicitur quasi habens dualitatem non quidem in aliquo alio sed in ipso de quo duo praedicantur. Fit autem praedicatio de

So, in this discussion, Thomas points to a feature in our ordinary language which 'concerns the very structure of our language'.[87] The distinction between signification and supposition is at the heart of our speaking. Moreover, the subject–predicate structure enables us to express difference and identity. Thomas uses this 'logical relation of supposition', this relation between subject term (*suppositum*) and the predicate terms (*significatio*), as a model to understand the hypostatic union. In this model, one can do justice, on the one hand, to the 'two-ness' and, on the other hand, maintain firmly the one-ness: 'a good theory of supposition enables one to safeguard the unity of Christ'.[88]

Thomas the 'systematic theologian'

To call Thomas a systematic theologian is at first an obvious qualification. But upon reflection it is a classification that becomes more complicated and more interesting. If one considers Thomas the father of Thomism or neo-Thomism, one can easily portray him as a builder of a system and see his theology in terms of a Gothic cathedral.[89] But if this picture of Thomas the system builder is not correct – because the relationship between Thomas and the various forms of Thomism is far from simple and easy, because the *Summa contra Gentiles* and the *Summa Theologiae* are so different, because the *Summa Theologiae* is not finished – the question becomes whether 'systematic' is an adequate label and if so, in what sense it can be used for Thomas.

The 'nexus mysteriorum'

If one considers the *Summa Theologiae*, one can say that Thomas is systematic in the sense that he discusses issues in a clear order. He indicates that order (be it often too scantily) and he thinks that the order matters.[90] One might sometimes be puzzled by that order: is *exitus-reditus* the scheme that Thomas uses? One might disagree with it or question its biblical or theological validity: is the place of Christ in the Tertia Pars

---

supposito, quod importatur per hoc nomen Christus. Quamvis igitur Christus habet dualitatem naturarum, quia tamen non habet dualitatem suppositorum, non potest dici esse duo.'

[87] Schoot, *Christ*, p. 143.
[88] Schoot, *Christ*, p. 142. This does not mean, though, that it ceases to be a *model* and that it fits completely: see Schoot's remarks on p. 139.
[89] See, e.g., M. de Wulf, *Histoire de la philosophie médiévale* (Louvain: Institut supérieur de philosophie, 1939), vol. 2, p. 179.
[90] See the introduction to the *ST*.

really correct? But one cannot deny that there is a determining order. Moreover, there is not such an order only in the overall structure of the *Summa Theologiae* but also on the level of *quaestiones* and *articuli*. Thomas presents his analyses and arguments in a systematic order: for example, conceptual clarifications precede other questions. Anyone reading an article from the *Summa Theologiae* discovers quickly that Thomas's arguments are difficult to summarise – they rather ask for analysis and commentary – and that one often has to read previous articles as well, since he presupposes or appeals to those earlier considerations.

But there is still another sense in which Thomas can be called a systematic theologian, which is theologically more interesting and important. For underneath the surface of *quaestiones* and *articuli* lies a kind of interconnection that is not so easily detected: a system of interrelated mysteries. Thomas is a theologian who is sensitive, to use a phrase from the First Vatican Council, to the *nexus mysteriorum*. That is to say, Thomas does not present in works like the *Summa Theologiae* a 'system' that is constructed apart from the data of faith and in which those data are forced, but he exhibits a 'system' that arises out of the data of faith and that is called for by those data. That he wants to be a systematic theologian in this sense is clear from his methodological reflections.

When Thomas in article 8 of the first *quaestio* of the *Summa Theologiae* finishes his discussion of the *sacra doctrina* as *scientia*, he does so by raising the question whether this doctrine is *argumentativa*.[91] His answer is a qualified 'Yes', for one has to take into account who the opponent is. If one argues with someone who does not accept anything from revelation, one can only solve the arguments put forward against faith. If the opponent accepts some points of revelation but denies others, one can argue properly. That is to say, one can appeal to sacred texts, one can use what is accepted and argue from it to what is denied. This procedure presupposes a connection and a consistency within revelation, within the articles of faith. It is this feature which Thomas points to at the beginning of his *responsio*, and this reveals another aspect of *argumentativa*. While one could call the two procedures just mentioned 'apologetical' or 'defensive', Thomas starts his *responsio* with a procedure that one could call 'systematic' or 'contemplative'. Theology does not argue in order to establish its principles or premises (the articles of faith): theology argues by showing something from them.[92] Thomas illustrates this with

---

[91] See Corbin, *Le chemin*, pp. 807–54, for an extended analysis of this article.

[92] *ST* Ia, Q. 1, art. 8, resp.: 'haec doctrina non argumentatur ad sua principia probanda, quae sunt articuli fidei, sed ex eis procedit ad aliquid ostendendum sicut Apostolus 1 *ad Cor.* xx resurrectione Christi argumentatur ad resurrectionem communum probandam'.

a short but extremely revealing example. Paul points in 1 Corinthians
15.12 to the resurrection of Christ to prove our resurrection. To understand this example it is absolutely necessary to realise that our resurrection is an article of faith. So, Paul does not conclude to our resurrection
on the basis of the resurrection of Christ, but Paul clarifies our resurrection with the help of Christ's. In other words, Thomas sees the primary
task of a theologian to contemplate the mysteries of faith and to illuminate and clarify them mutually. Thomas's example suggests also a theme
with which this contemplative, systematic theology can be shown: life.

Life and eternal life[93]

Life, death, life after death raise perennial questions. To ask the question
how eternal life is related to life on earth is to ask a theological question.
Not only because Paul in the passage Thomas refers to argues that belief
in the life eternal belongs to the centre of the Christian faith, but also and
ultimately because God is life and to know God is to live (cf. John 17.3).
Given the biblical background it is not surprising to find in the *Summa
Theologiae* a *quaestio* about life (or living) as a name for God.[94] Given
Thomas's awareness of the limitations of our language with regard to
God it is not surprising to discover that 'life' is used analogously and
most properly of God. Given Thomas's negative theology it is not
surprising to discover that 'life' refers to God's 'incomprehensible self-
determination', and 'incomprehensible movement', 'a direction being
pointed, based on the created effects of God we know'.[95]

To ask the question how eternal life is related to life on earth is also to
ask a systematic question, for it is a question about the relationship
between two articles of faith. 'Eternal life' (or 'life of the world to come')
is mentioned explicitly at the end of the Creed. 'Life on earth' is implied
in the confession that God is the Creator of heaven and earth. Even
stronger, the belief in God the Creator, since it is the belief in God as the
origin of all (*causa prima*) and as the purpose of all (*finis ultimus*), provides Thomas with the basis for a systematic treatment of life. The biblical vision of the goodness of creation helps him to appreciate the value
and the importance of the various levels of life in creation (plants,
animals, human beings, angels). The biblical vision of the human person
as the centre of the cosmos helps him to reflect on the human person as
'a small world'.[96] Consequently, the human soul consists of the *vita*

---

[93] See, for the following, C. Leget, *Living with God*.
[94] *ST* Ia, Q. 18; cf. also *In DDN* 6; *In Joh* 14, 2; *In XII Met.* 8 and *SCG*, Bk I, Chs.
97–9. See, for an analysis of Q. 18, Leget, *Living with God*, pp. 25–46.
[95] Leget, *Living with God*, p. 45.
[96] Cf. *ST* Ia, Q. 91, art. 1, resp.

vegetativa, sensitiva and *intellectiva*. These three form a dynamic unity.[97] This unity does not only show materiality and time as the co-ordinates of the human condition, it reveals also the perfection in the *vita aeterna* to be dependent on this earthly life. In the human person life as way of being is the foundation of life as specific to the human person (the operations of knowing and willing) and this determines life in the sense of direction and perfection.

The richness contained in 'God the *causa prima* and *finis ultimus*' is unfolded by Thomas in a *quaestio* about the *missiones* of the divine persons. That *quaestio* is at the same time the culmination of his discussion of the *distinctio personarum* and the transition to his discussion of God's creative activity.[98] In a discussion about the basis (or the impact) of the missions of Son and Spirit Thomas distinguishes between two ways God is in creatures. These two ways can be connected with *causa* and *finis*.[99] The one way God is in creatures is common to all creatures 'as the cause in the effects that share his goodness'.[100] The other way is particular to rational creatures, and according to 'this special way God is not only said to be in a rational creature, but to dwell in it as in his temple'.[101]

Thomas calls this second way also 'a new way'. This qualification is revealing. 'New' might suggest that the other way is old and passé. This suggestion is incorrect, for God remains present in all creatures. 'New' refers more to 'renewed', or perhaps better to 'surprising' or 'un-expected', for the new way is a higher quality of relationship, a more intense, more personal kind of relationship. For this new way is due to the missions of Son and Spirit. It is the Triune God who comes to dwell in the human person. It is a presence which is built upon and presupposes the other, common presence. Each creature is called to perfection, but the rational creatures are called in a special way that fits their knowing and willing. 'New' contains yet another revealing element. It might suggest a change on the side of God. But Thomas corrects this too: the newness, the

---

[97] See Leget, *Living with God*, pp. 73–6 for Thomas's insistence on the unity of the soul and its consequences.

[98] *ST* Ia, Q. 43; see for a commentary on (parts of) this *quaestio*: H. Rikhof, 'Trinity in Thomas: Reading the *Summa Theologiae* against the background of modern problems', in *Jaarboek 1999*, pp. 83–100.

[99] This is somewhat too schematic, since God is the *finis ultimus* of everything.

[100] *ST* Ia, Q. 43, art. 3, resp.: 'Est enim unus communis modo quo Deus est in omnibus rebus per essentiam, potentiam and presentiam, sicut cause in effectibus participantibus bonitatem ipsius.'

[101] *ST* Ia, Q. 43, art. 3, resp.: 'secundum istum specialem modum Deus non solum dicitur esse in creatura rationali, sed etiam habitare in ea sicut in templo suo'.

change is on our side.[102] Our intellect, our knowing is illuminated by the Son (*Verbum*), our affect, our willing is enkindled by the Spirit (*Amor*), we are assimilated to the divine persons sent to us, we become conformed to God.[103]

Thomas's discussion of the missions of Son and Spirit and of the indwelling of the Trinity is a discussion of grace, of the life of grace. This life of grace is presented in the other articles of faith ('for us and our salvation'; 'Lord and giver of life'). And Thomas reflects upon the foundations of this life, its dynamism and its perfection.[104] In these reflections on the mysteries of faith he shows that this life of grace is 'the perfection of natural life and the beginning of eternal life', that life after death is 'the copious consummation' of the friendly relationship of the human person with Father, Son and Spirit which can exist and flourish in the conditions of materiality and time.[105]

Conclusion

Via a short history and via a longer discussion of Thomas the theologian I have presented the way we at Utrecht read him. A focus on the way of reading implies a concentration on method. I have consequently used work that has been done in our research-group on that aspect of Thomas's theology. However, I have also concentrated on the somewhat formal questions of method because that type of attention is part and parcel of the way we read Thomas. Not because we are not interested in content, but precisely because the way Thomas does theology helps us to do theology now.

---

[102] *ST* Ia, Q. 43, art. 2, ad 2: 'divinam personam esse novo modo in aliquo vel ab aliquo haberi temporaliter non est propter mutationem divinae personae sed propter mutationem creaturae, sicut et Deus temporaliter dicitur Dominus propter mutationem creaturae.' Thomas refers in the final part in fact to his discussion in *ST* Ia, Q. 13, art. 7.

[103] Cf. *ST* Ia, Q. 43, art. 5, ad 2 and ad 3.

[104] Leget, *Living with God*, ch. 2: foundations of life with God; ch. 3: dynamism of life with God; ch. 4: perfection of life with God.

[105] Leget, *Living with God*, pp. 63, 263.

Recent Work on St Thomas in North America: Language, Anthropology, Christology

ROBERT C. MINER

Language

Do words signify things? In his first book, *Thomist Realism and the Linguistic Turn*, John O'Callaghan draws upon the thought of Aquinas to argue that they do. One may be surprised to learn that an affirmative answer to the question requires much defence. But, as the middle section of *Thomist Realism* reminds us, the dominant tradition in modern philosophy conspires to deny that words signify things. Instead, words are taken to signify concepts in the mind, which in turn problematically correspond to or represent things. Concepts, usually construed as mental representations, are 'third things' that stand between the mind and the world. From this way of setting up the relation between words, concepts and things, the questions of modern epistemology arise. How can the mind know the world, if it has access only to its concepts, strictly speaking? If the mind's access is limited to private mental representations, how is it possible to grasp a world beyond those representations? Does it even make sense to posit a world apart from representations, or the conceptual scheme in which representations are embedded?

Concepts are private, but language that signifies concepts is public. The linguistic turn is, or aspires to be, a response to the apparently solipsistic tendencies of modern epistemology. It is plausible, then, to suppose the possibility of significant affinities between the linguistic turn and the Thomist tradition. To the latter O'Callaghan ascribes a 'willingness and sense of obligation to engage contemporary modes of thought'.[1] O'Callaghan's book is an attempt to discharge this obligation by taking exemplars of the linguistic turn as primary interlocutors. Before turning to the work of Putnam, Fodor, McDowell and others, O'Callaghan

---

[1] John P. O'Callaghan, *Thomist Realism and the Linguistic Turn* (Notre Dame, IN: University of Notre Dame Press, 2002), p. 12.

frames his treatment by focusing on the Aristotelian 'semantic triangle'. The semantic triangle is O'Callaghan's preferred metaphor for indicating the multiple relations between word, concept and thing. It may seem that any consideration of the relation between words, concepts and things will be triadic, since the three relations of word–concept, concept–thing, and word–thing naturally arise from such consideration. But this appearance is deceptive. Acknowledging a debt to Walker Percy, O'Callaghan suggests that many accounts of the relations between word, concept and thing are only superficially triadic. They tend to reduce to a linear dyad: words signify concepts; concepts represent things. What would be the third side of the triangle, the word–thing relation, is not in fact basic, since it can be constructed out of the relations word–concept and concept–thing. Thus the triad is reduced to a conjunction of dyads.

Against the reduction of the semantic triangle to a line, O'Callaghan wants to show that words signify both concepts in the soul (*passiones animae*) and things outside the soul (*res extra animam*), and that neither relation can be reduced to the other. Both modes of signification are related (language does not err in using the verb 'to signify' in each case), but distinct, which suggests that 'signification' is an analogical term. For the sake of clarity, O'Callaghan uses 'signification$_1$,' to denote the word–concept relation and 'signification$_2$,' to denote the word–thing relation. The third leg of the triangle is the concept–thing relation. This latter relation is not an instance of signification. It is a *similitudo*, a likeness between concepts in the soul and things outside the soul.

Any successful escape from some form of representationalism requires the presence of a defensible word–thing relation that is not derivable from the word–concept and concept–thing relations. In positive terms, the task is to vindicate the possibility of a genuinely irreducible semantic triangle. O'Callaghan's overarching argument is that such a thing exists in the work of Aristotle and is coherently developed in the work of Aquinas. As a kind of preliminary exercise, O'Callaghan defends the proposition that the semantic triangle is authentically Aristotelian. He does so through a detailed examination of an attempt found in the work of Norman Kretzmann to deny the existence of the semantic triangle in Aristotle. Kretzmann's central contention is that interpretation of Aristotle on word, concept and thing has been radically distorted by Boethius's Latin translation of a central passage from Aristotle's Περὶ ἑρμενείας. The suggestion that Aristotle intended a direct relationship between words and things rests upon the tradition's acceptance of Boethius' decision to translate both the Greek συμβόλα and σημεῖα with the Latin term *notae*. This distinction, according to Kretzmann, obscures a crucial distinction between 'symbol' and 'sign'. Sufficient appreciation of the distinction will, according to Kretzmann, furnish grounds upon which to deny that Aristotle intended to affirm any irreducible relationship between word and thing. Words are primarily natural signs of mental impressions, and secondarily symbols that are conventionally related to mental impressions to the extent that they represent or encode mental impressions in a different medium. O'Callaghan's critique of Kretzmann is both philosophical and philological. His philosophical argument is that Aristotle correctly saw no need to posit a natural relation between sign and mental impression as the ground for a conventional relation between word and concept. Even if a mental impression is a necessary condition for a conventional symbol, the need for an additional class of 'natural symptoms' corresponding to these impressions does not arise.[2] For the philological side of his critique of Kretzmann, O'Callaghan deploys the work of John Magee on Boethius. We may pass over O'Callaghan's careful handling of the philological issues, and simply note his success in exhibiting the connection between Kretzmann's denial of the semantic triangle in Aristotle and his lingering commitment to the assumptions of mental representationalism.

In his commentary on the passage from the Περὶ ἑρμενείας, Aquinas isolates the vertices of the semantic triangle: there are articulated sounds, passions of the soul (identified as conceptions of the intellect), and things outside the soul. Articulated sounds signify conceptions of the intellect without mediation, and things by mediation. Is not the affirmation that articulated sounds signify things outside the soul *mediante* tantamount to saying that words signify things only indirectly? If it is, does not Aquinas also reduce the semantic triangle to a dyad? O'Callaghan's response to this charge is to distinguish between the thesis that the concept mediates the relation of word to *res extra animam*, which Aquinas certainly accepts, and the proposal that the relation between word and *res extra animam* is only secondary and indirect, as the mental representationalist would hold. O'Callaghan illustrates the distinction with an analogy from artistry. A carpenter uses instruments to make a table, his relation to the table is 'mediated' by the tools he uses. But qua artisan, he is defined primarily by the work he produces, and related but secondarily to the tools that he uses, however immediate his relation to them. The carpenter does not use tools, which then make the table; he directly makes the table by means of tools. By denying the synonymy of 'immediate' with 'direct' or 'primary', and that of 'mediate' with 'indirect' or 'secondary', O'Callaghan prepares the ground for a more detailed interpretation of how Aquinas thinks words signify things mediately (by means of concepts) and yet directly. 'Mediate' in this context means 'by means of'; it does not mean 'indirectly' or 'secondarily'.

---

[2] See O'Callaghan, *Thomist Realism*, pp. 50–1.

O'Callaghan does not pretend that this distinction settles all the issues. On the contrary, he takes seriously the claim (made by Putnam and Dummett) that mental representationalism does not begin with early modern epistemology, but has deep roots in Aristotle and Aquinas. For the mental representationalist, knowledge is mediated by entities in the mind – concepts, representations, ideas – which, as Bertrand Russell puts it, threaten to 'become a veil between us and outside things'.[3] The worry, as Russell comments, is that 'we never really, in knowledge, attain to the things we are supposed to be knowing about, but only to the ideas of those things'.[4] Is Aquinas committed to mental representationalism, or something like it? O'Callaghan explains why some have been tempted to ascribe the view. Aquinas holds both that signs are associated with concepts (by convention), and that concepts correspond to things (by nature). Is he not thereby committed to a view of concepts as screens between the mind and reality? Putnam levels this charge at Aristotle, but O'Callaghan suggests that *prima facie* it applies to Aquinas as well, in so far as Aquinas holds a broadly Aristotelian account of naming and knowing.

O'Callaghan begins his dialogue with Putnam by recalling the main lines of the latter's critique of mental representationalism. One may, following Frege, distinguish between sense (*Sinn*) and meaning (*Bedeutung*), from which follows a parallel distinction between two kinds of meaning: 'intention' and 'extension'. O'Callaghan provides an informal illustration of the distinction: intention is meaning, as we use the term in the question 'What did you mean when you said the captain was sober this morning?' Extension is meaning, as captured in the question 'Whom did you mean when you said the captain was sober this morning?'[5] Two phrases may possess different intentions but share the same extension: for example, 'rational animal' and 'featherless biped'. Thus sameness of extension does not determine intention. But intention does determine extension, from which it follows that a difference in extension determines a difference in intention. How do we know what the intention of a term or phrase is? The mental representationalist holds that we answer this question by inspecting the content of the mental entity signified by the term or phrase. Putnam's critique of the mental representationalist is to show the utter absence of any connection between intention and mental or psychological states. As the famous 'Twin Earth' experiment shows, Earthlings and Twin Earthlings are both

---

[3] Bertrand Russell, 'Knowledge by Acquaintance and by Description', in *Proceedings of the Aristotelian Society* (London: Aristotelian Society, 1910–11), p. 119, quoted in O'Callaghan, *Thomist Realism*, p. 81.

[4] Russell, 'Knowledge by Acquaintance', in O'Callaghan, *Thomist Realism*, p. 81.

[5] O'Callaghan, *Thomist Realism*, p. 142.

in the same psychological state when they use the term 'water', yet 'water' has different extension, since the thing picked out by 'water' on Twin Earth is not the same thing as the thing picked out by 'water' on Earth (*ex hypothesi* only water on Earth is H_2O). The point is that mental representation determines neither extension nor intention: 'words do not have the same intention when they are associated with the same mental representation'.[6]

In making this point, Putnam supposes himself to have undermined the Aristotelian account of meaning, since he assumes that the Aristotelian takes mental representation to constitute or determine intention. O'Callaghan agrees with Putnam on one key point. If mental states are understood as 'third things' in addition to the mind and objects, it is clear that mental states cannot determine meaning, and that we are better off without them. But why must one construe mental states as 'third things'? Is there not another and better way to relate meaning to mental states? O'Callaghan argues that Putnam feels compelled to abandon the task of relating meaning to mental states, because (like his representationalist opponents) he is able to conceive of mental states only as third things. Against the contemporary tendency to conceive semantics and the philosophy of mind as entirely distinct disciplines, O'Callaghan opposes Aquinas's dictum 'we name as we know' and cites a contemporary parallel to Searle and Fodor, both of whom argue (in ways that differ both from one another and St Thomas) that any satisfactory account of signification requires an account of the knowing mind that produces language.[7]

What prevents Putnam from being able to conceive of mental states in a non-representationalist manner is his commitment to 'methodological solipsism' (a kind of residual Cartesianism). This residual Cartesianism enables him to assume that we can talk about the mind prior to talking about the world, as if we were capable of knowing the mind and its contents while bracketing anything we know about the world in which the mind is found (perhaps one may even say 'thrown'). Against this, O'Callaghan seeks to construct an alternative account according to which the human being uses concepts in signifying and knowing, without these concepts assuming the status of third things (pictures, images, appearances, effects) that interpose themselves between the mind and its objects. In positioning himself to construct this account, O'Callaghan attends not only to the 'Third Thing Thesis', but also to two other related (but logically separable) positions. These he calls 'the Intro-spectibilty Thesis' and the 'Internalist Thesis'. The Introspectibility

---

6 O'Callaghan, *Thomist Realism*, p. 148.
7 O'Callaghan, *Thomist Realism*, p. 26.

Thesis holds that mental objects (including but not limited to representations) are introspectible, knowable independently of reflection on the world outside the mind. According to the Internalist Thesis, there is no intrinsic relationship between concepts and their objects; the associations between the two are contingent and may even vary with change between or within cultures.

These theses, taken together, state central assumptions of post-Cartesian philosophy of mind. In keeping with his aim of emphasising the contrast between Aquinas and post-Cartesian thought, O'Callaghan expounds his reading of St Thomas in chapters that correspond to each thesis.[8] Common to each chapter is the prosecution of two objectives: to show how Aquinas thinks about concepts in a way that decisively sets him apart from the thesis in question, and to confute other readings that would assimilate Aquinas (whether implicitly or explicitly) to these theses. First, O'Callaghan shows that Aquinas does not conceive of concepts as 'third things' that stand between the mind and the objects it knows. This requires demonstration because Aquinas does hold that the mind thinks with concepts, and it seems natural to assume that concepts are objects that we 'have' – and that we have them 'in' our minds. O'Callaghan begins with the latter point: we may say that we have concepts 'in' our minds, but the relevant sense of 'in', for both Aristotle and Thomas, does not at all involve the spatial metaphors endemic to modern philosophy (at least in its 'canonical' form) and its picture of the mind. In some of its uses, 'in' denotes a mode of existence, not a mode of location. When Aquinas says that concepts exist in the mind, he means that they depend upon the mind for their existence. To say this is not to say, even metaphorically, that they exist within some internal space in the chamber of the mind.

Even if concepts do not spatially exist within the mind, are they still not 'third things'? O'Callaghan acknowledges some ground for reading St Thomas in this manner. In the *Summa Theologiae*, Thomas writes: 'articulated sounds do not signify the intelligible species, but rather that which the intellect forms for itself to judge of exterior things'.[9] As O'Callaghan notes, the passage seems to suggest that 'the possible intellect forms some being, some thing when it forms definitions, combinations, and divisions'.[10] O'Callaghan responds to this appearance in several ways. First, he observes that for Aquinas, a reflective analytic study may distinguish multiple features that demand examination, without affirming that these features are in reality separate. Against 'the error of the Platonists', Thomas does not suppose an absolute correspondence

---

[8] O'Callaghan, *Thomist Realism*, chs. 6, 7, 8.
[9] *ST* Ia, Q. 85, art. 2, ad 3; quoted in O'Callaghan, *Thomist Realism*, p. 166.
[10] O'Callaghan, *Thomist Realism*, p. 167 (emphasis in original).

between what the mind distinguishes in the order of knowing and what exists in the order of being.[11] Concepts are not the objects of under-standing, according to O'Callaghan's reading; they are that which express our understanding. He supports this point by adverting to Thomas's use of the distinction between immanent and transitive acts. Thinking and understanding are immanent acts.[12] We may figuratively describe immanent acts with transitive language, but the termination of the act remains within the agent ('he took a stroll' – there is no stroll apart from the act of walking). Thus O'Callaghan concludes that 'con-cept' for Aquinas 'is a nominalized form of talking about our act of conceiving, not a way of referring to an additional class or category of objects or things in addition to our acts'.[13] To say this differently: in con-ceiving, we do not grasp concepts; we grasp things by means of concepts.

Some of this will sound familiar to those aware of Aquinas's use of *quo* and *quod* in texts that treat of knowledge by concepts. The concept is that by which (*quo*) the mind grasps, not what (*quod*) it grasps. But does it not remain the case that, as O'Callaghan summarises an objection, 'concepts are had, not done'?[14] If so, is it not true that concepts are 'third things' the mind has, even if we agree that they have no life apart from thinking? O'Callaghan answers this objection by acknowledging that in

---

[11] Cf. *ST* Ia, Q. 50, art. 2 resp., where Aquinas criticises Avicebron for supposing that 'whatever things are distinguished by the intellect are really distinct' ('quae-cumque distinguuntur secundum intellectum, sint etiam in rebus distincta'). One may compare this to Descartes: 'the fact that I can clearly and distinctly understand one thing apart from another is enough to make me certain that the two things are distinct'. Descartes, *Meditations on First Philosophy*, *Meditation VI*, in *The Philo-sophical Writings of Descartes*, vol. 2, trans. John Cottingham, Robert Stoothof and Dugald Murdoch (Cambridge: Cambridge University Press, 1988), p. 54. 'satis est quod possim unam rem absque altera clare & distincte intelligere, ut certus sim unam ab altera esse diversam'. Descartes, *Meditationes de prima philosophia*, bilingual edi-tion, ed. George Heffernan (Notre Dame, IN: University of Notre Dame Press, 1990), p. 194.

[12] The character of thinking as an immanent act may receive further illustration in the comparisons of human thinking to the divine generation of the Word. See, for example, *ST* Ia, Q. 34, art. 2 and Ia, Q. 27, art. 2. O'Callaghan excludes the *verbum mentis* from consideration on the ground that the *verbum mentis* doctrine belongs to his theology rather than his philosophy, and serves no philosophical purpose (*Thomist Realism*, p. 300, n. 16). Whether or not one is persuaded by this claim, the exclusion is understandable, because a misreading of the *verbum mentis* in Aquinas can easily lead to a conflation of the Thomist view with the mental representational-ism of those (e.g., Fodor) who posit a *lingua mentis*. As Mark Jordan observes, it is tempting (but erroneous) to conclude that 'Thomas's account of language rests mere-ly on the positing of an interior speech, as if he had wanted to explain language by creating a small speaker within the mind.' See Mark Jordan, *Ordering Wisdom* (Notre Dame, IN: University of Notre Dame Press, 1986), p. 38.

[13] O'Callaghan, *Thomist Realism*, p. 169.

[14] O'Callaghan, *Thomist Realism*, p. 174.

one sense, it is legitimate to say that we 'have' knowledge, thoughts and concepts. This is the sense in which we possess a reliable capacity to engage in thinking, a habitus that is formed by multiple acts. One can understand habitually, without exercising one's understanding at the moment. For example, one may be said to know the calculus – to know it actually, not merely potentially as an ordinary pre-schooler potentially knows it – without engaging in the act of taking a derivative. This does not show that concepts are third things which the mind has, but only that we are capable of having dispositions to know, which correspond to what Aristotle calls the 'first act of intellect'. Thus O'Callaghan plausibly claims to attribute 'the ordinary language of "having concepts" to the structured habits of the power of intellect'.[15]

The sixth chapter of *Thomist Realism and the Linguistic Turn* closes by considering a recent attempt to saddle Aquinas with a variant of the Third Thing Thesis. In *Theories of Cognition in the Later Middle Ages*, Robert Pasnau reads Aquinas as holding that in addition to a cognitive power and an external object, any particular occurrence of cognition requires an intellectual species.[16] This species or form is what causes cognition to occur; it is the efficient cause of cognition. O'Callaghan calls Pasnau's reading into question by exhibiting his failure to consider the distinction between efficient and formal causes. When Aquinas says that an intellectual species makes cognition occur, he does not suppose that the species exists as a prior efficient cause. His actual view, as O'Callaghan shows in detail, is that the species is a formal cause of cognition. Aquinas does occasionally say that the species 'makes' (*facere*) cognition occur, but as O'Callaghan observes, *facere* is 'a common locution for St. Thomas in the context of formal causality'.[17] What blinds Pasnau to the relevance of the agent causation/formal causation distinction, O'Callaghan suggests, is that he 'chooses to read Aquinas through Ockham's eyes'.[18]

To dispose of the Third Thing Thesis is to invite the suspicion that little hope remains for the Introspectibility and Internalist Theses. It is logically possible, however, to deny the Third Thing Thesis while affirming the Introspectibility Thesis, on the ground that 'an act of understanding need not take as its object a being other than itself'.[19] Even if concepts are not distinct from acts of conceiving, it remains possible that we perceive these acts through a feat of introspection that occurs without regard to the

[15] O'Callaghan, *Thomist Realism*, p. 175 (emphasis in original).
[16] Robert Pasnau, *Theories of Cognition in the Later Middle Ages* (Cambridge: Cambridge University Press, 1997).
[17] O'Callaghan, *Thomist Realism*, p. 181.
[18] O'Callaghan, *Thomist Realism*, p. 178.
[19] O'Callaghan, *Thomist Realism*, p. 200.

world outside the mind. Here O'Callaghan is concerned to vindicate Thomas from Putnam's charge that any Aristotelian account of the mind presupposes an introspective access to its concepts, and thus lacks credibility for contemporary philosophers. O'Callaghan traces Aquinas's denial of this possibility first by a valuable clarification of what Aquinas means by *obiectum*. An 'object' for Aquinas is not simply a thing. It is a thing 'taken as either moving a power to act or terminating the act of a power'.[20] Through careful exegesis, O'Callaghan concludes that for Aquinas, there is no knowledge of the mind's powers independently of the knowledge of its acts, and there is no knowledge of its acts independently of the knowledge of the objects of those acts. Thus when the intellect knows, it knows both the *passiones animae* and the *res extra animam* of which the *passiones* are likenesses, but it primarily knows things beyond the soul. The effect is not to refute scepticism, but to bypass it altogether. As O'Callaghan puts it, Thomas does not try to cross a chasm between what appears to him 'in his skull' and what he hopes exists outside it.[21] The problem does not arise, because on O'Callaghan's reading of Aquinas, we cannot even talk about the mind except in so far as we are 'always already' talking about the world. O'Callaghan makes this point forcefully. For Thomas, the way into the soul 'is by considering how the human being, a material being, acts in the world'.[22] We do not know ourselves introspectively; 'we come to knowledge of ourselves through knowledge of others'.[23] In one of the most quotable sentences of the book, O'Callaghan concludes: 'If for Socrates an unexamined life is not worth living, for St. Thomas an unlived life is not a life worth examining.'[24]

Concepts are neither 'third things' nor acts knowable by introspection apart from living in the world. But what is their relation to the world? Putnam's 'methodological solipsism' suggests one answer to this question: mental states simply are what they are, determined by factors internal to the subject apart from his world or environment. On this view, the concept has an 'in itself' character.[25] The concept can be related to the world, but any such relation will have to be imposed or wilfully instituted. Against this view – the Internalist Thesis – O'Callaghan opposes St Thomas's view that the being of concepts is essentially related to things outside the soul, because concepts are likenesses (*similitudines*) of these things outside the world. Once again, O'Callaghan sets his exegesis in

---

[20] O'Callaghan, *Thomist Realism*, p. 206.
[21] See O'Callaghan, *Thomist Realism*, p. 213.
[22] O'Callaghan, *Thomist Realism*, p. 227.
[23] O'Callaghan, *Thomist Realism*, p. 227.
[24] O'Callaghan, *Thomist Realism*, p. 227.
[25] See O'Callaghan, *Thomist Realism*, p. 237.

opposition to Putnam, while acknowledging a certain reasonableness to the latter's impatience with the Aristotelian tradition. Putnam is 'perfectly legitimate', O'Callaghan thinks, to be exasperated by the tendency of some Aristotelians merely to assert the 'formal identity' of the concept and the thing outside the soul.[26] This habit of mere assertion, unaccompanied by any real effort at elucidation, may be what prompts Charles Taylor to write that once the Aristotelian theory of species is dropped, the participational conception of knowledge is 'untenable and rapidly becomes almost unintelligible'.[27] The task of the eighth chapter of *Thomist Realism* is to acknowledge this state of affairs and to explain the notion of formal identity in a way that restores the intelligibility of the Aristotelian account.

O'Callaghan performs this task by demystifying the notion of 'formal identity'. The 'form' of a dog simply consists in those features that pertain to dogs as such, rather than this dog or that dog.[28] This is the nature of the dog 'absolutely considered'. What is the identity of the concept? O'Callaghan argues that if we ask what it means to conceive a dog, absolutely considered, we will ascribe precisely the same features to the concept of the dog as we do to the nature of the dog absolutely considered. Thus the nature of the dog absolutely considered is both the form of the object known and the form of the knowing (though it is not one single being that is both). The concept of the dog exists only as a (non-pictorial) likeness of the dog. This account of the ontology of concepts has epistemological implications. O'Callaghan argues that '*res extra animam* are not identified by attending to the concept. On the contrary, the concept is identified by attending to the *res extra animam*'.[29] What makes this identification possible is the presumption of formal identity between thing and concept. O'Callaghan stresses that formal identity, though it may require elucidation, is not an explanation of how concepts 'hook on to the world'.[30] The demand for any such explanation assumes that we have an account of concepts prior to our engagement with the world. O'Callaghan argues that we have no reason to embrace, and every reason to reject, this assumption. It remains, however, that we require some account of the relation between concepts and the things of which concepts are *similitudines*. The Aristotelian notion of formal identity, according to O'Callaghan, provides resources for constructing an account of this relation that is both intelligible to contemporary readers

---

[26] O'Callaghan, *Thomist Realism*, p. 239.

[27] Charles Taylor, *Philosophical Arguments* (Cambridge, MA and London: Harvard University Press, 1995), p. 3.

[28] Here O'Callaghan is evidently in dialogue with Kant, *Critique of Pure Reason*, B180.

[29] *Thomist Realism*, p. 241.

[30] See O'Callaghan, *Thomist Realism*, p. 244.

and faithful to St Thomas. As elsewhere, *Thomist Realism* makes its case here through both exegesis of historical texts and argument with recent proposals in *soi-disant* philosophy of mind.

Perhaps the most striking conclusion O'Callaghan reaches is that Putnam, despite his energetic avoidance of representationalism in the context of semantics, ends up affirming a version of the Third Thesis, precisely because his methodological solipsism survives his embrace of the linguistic turn. In making the linguistic turn, Putnam relocates concepts from the mind into the space of public language. But, according to O'Callaghan, his assumption of methodological solipsism still causes him to occupy a standpoint from which

> we introspect the linguistic concepts of our scientific language, and by such introspection we come to know the world as mediated by that scientific language as it determines for us the natures or essences of things. Even though concepts are 'in the mouth', they are just as intro-spectible and mediating as they ever were; giving them the aura of scientific descriptions doesn't make them less so.[31]

The implication is that Putnam never fully makes the linguistic turn. If O'Callaghan is correct, his attachment to the Cartesian legacy prevents him from understanding what is crucial in either Aristotle or Wittgen-stein.

O'Callaghan is not the first to fuse a Wittgensteinian sensibility with profound sympathy for the texts of St Thomas. The debt of *Thomist Realism and the Linguistic Turn* to Anscombe, Geach and Burrell is clear enough. But the thoroughness and depth of this work make it anything but a predictable repetition of familiar themes. What other author has used Putnam to correct Fodor, McDowell to correct Putnam, McGinn to correct McDowell, and Walker Percy to correct them all? Far from posing as a neutral expositor, O'Callaghan writes as a passionate, pene-trating and faithful reader of St Thomas. Thomists will have no difficulty recognising the basic theses, but they will profit by following the careful development of these theses in dialogue with a number of contemporary philosophers.

Anthropology

Two North American scholars have recently published books devoted to an examination of Aquinas on human nature. These are Robert Pasnau's *Thomas Aquinas on Human Nature* and Thomas Hibbs's *Virtue's*

---

[31] O'Callaghan, *Thomist Realism*, p. 266.

Splendor.[32] The subtitle of Pasnau's book is '*A Philosophical Study of Summa Theologiae Ia QQ. 75–89*'. Pasnau begins the first part of his book with an exposition of the Questions on the soul's essence. He suggests that Aquinas vindicates his own account indirectly, by showing the untenability of the accounts he wants to reject. These accounts, which Aquinas attributes to Averroes and Plato, Pasnau labels as 'nonreductive'. They aspire to 'unify soul and body without reducing them to one single thing'.[33] Pasnau holds that Aquinas's aim is to show the 'failure of nonreductive theories'.[34] Aquinas's own account of the soul–body union, Pasnau supposes, is well described as a 'reductive' theory. This supposition is credible only if one uses 'reductive' in a peculiar sense – that is, not to suggest that the corporeal is analysable into the incorporeal, or vice versa, but to restate Aquinas's view that the human being is one simply (*unum simpliciter*), rather than one in a qualified sense (*secundum quid*).

But what does Aquinas mean by *unum simpliciter*? The anachronistic description of Aquinas's account as 'reductive' does not shed much light on the question, as Pasnau tacitly admits when he acknowledges that he is using the word 'in a very broad sense'.[35] Pasnau allows that Aquinas is not reductive to the extent that he 'finds it explanatorily useful to distinguish between matter and form'.[36] Pasnau argues that for Aquinas, the distinction between form and matter is conceptual rather than real: in reality, everything is act.[37] As a reading of Aquinas, this claim is problematic. If actuality is all there is, it would follow that the distinction between act and potency is merely conceptual. But Aquinas does not hold 'reductive actualism'.[38] If he did, he would be unable to affirm the ontological distinction between angels and God (angels are a composite of potency and act, God is pure act).[39] Pasnau's treatment, which appears at this point to be coloured by Scotist and Ockhamist assumptions, would undermine distinctions between types of being that are absolutely central to Aquinas. For Aquinas, if not for Scotus and Ockham, a 'real distinc-

---

[32] Robert Pasnau, *Thomas Aquinas* (Cambridge: Cambridge University Press, 2002); Thomas Hibbs, *Virtue's Splendor* (New York: Fordham University Press, 2001).

[33] Pasnau, *Thomas Aquinas*, p. 75.

[34] Pasnau, *Thomas Aquinas*, p. 73.

[35] Pasnau, *Thomas Aquinas*, p. 80.

[36] Pasnau, *Thomas Aquinas*, p. 131.

[37] Pasnau, *Thomas Aquinas*, p. 133.

[38] The phrase 'reductive actualism' is not used by Pasnau, but it aptly describes his attempt to read Thomas as one who reduces all that is to actuality (see especially Pasnau, *Thomas Aquinas*, p. 135). As a reading of Aquinas, reductive actualism is incoherent. Any creature is limited act. To have limited act is to have act limited by something other than act. In the human case, the limiting principle is material potentiality. In the angelic case, it is non-material potentiality.

[39] See *ST* Ia, Q. 50, art. 2, ad 3.

tion' between x and y does not entail that x and y exist apart from one another. A real difference of things is not the same as really distinct things.

Both Pasnau and Hibbs understand that much of the difficulty of Aquinas's thought on the soul–body union lies in his attempt to understand how the intellectual soul can be embodied without being immersed in matter. Aquinas rejects the position that he attributes to Plato because he thinks it entails the merely accidental unity of soul and body. In his formulation of the problem, Hibbs displays a remarkable sensitivity to both the Aristotelian dimension of Aquinas's resolution and the sense in which Aquinas goes beyond Aristotle. For Aristotle, the problem of the soul–body union arises only for those who fail to understand that the soul is the form of the body. If we grasp that the soul is the form of the body, related to the body in the same way as form is related to matter and act to potency, we will see, as Hibbs puts it in his paraphrase of Aristotle, that 'it is as redundant to ask whether soul and body are one as it is to ask whether an act and that of which it is the act are one'.[40] But the question cannot so easily be dismissed for the Christian believer, who knows that the soul has its own *per se* operation and is a subsistent thing. Hibbs provides a clear statement of the problem: 'On the one hand, what subsists is capable of independent existence; on the other hand, soul is the form of body, to which it is naturally united. How can we affirm both?'[41]

Pasnau and Hibbs give strikingly different answers to the question. Pasnau's solution is to read Aquinas as if he were approaching the altar of modern naturalism. We are told that Aquinas understands form as the structure and function of material things, that his emphasis upon actuality is 'consistent with materialism in its modern form'.[42] His commitment to the absolute unity of substance ensures that 'he does not ascribe [sic] to a metaphysical dualism of matter and form, potentiality and actuality. His is a reductive hylomorphism.'[43] It is difficult to reconcile this astonishing conclusion with the end of Question 75, where Aquinas concludes that 'the soul in a certain way requires the body for its operation',[44] but does not reduce the distinction between the soul and body to a conceptual difference. Unlike Pasnau, Hibbs understands that Aquinas's aim is not to blur the distinction between the corporeal and incorporeal, but to account for their union in a way that does not make their relation accidental or inscrutable. If Aquinas were interested in performing the

---

[40] Hibbs, *Virtue's Splendor*, p. 45.
[41] Hibbs, *Virtue's Splendor*, p. 47.
[42] Pasnau, *Thomas Aquinas*, p. 39.
[43] Pasnau, *Thomas Aquinas*, p. 44.
[44] *ST* Ia, Q. 75, art. 7, ad 3: 'quod anima quodammodo indiget corpore ad suam operationem'.

sort of reduction described by Pasnau, it would be hard to see what
the former means when he claims that 'the body depends on the soul, not
the soul on the body'.[45] Aquinas does not want to reduce soul to body, or
body to soul, but to insist upon the teleological relation of one to the
other. What prevents the soul–body union from being merely accidental
is that the body acts for the sake of the intellectual soul, so that the latter
may perform its own *per se* operation in the manner appropriate to
embodied existence. 'To understand through a phantasm is the proper
operation of the soul by virtue of its union with the body. After separation from the body it will have another mode of understanding, similar to
other substances separated from bodies.'[46] In this life, Aquinas holds, the
body acts for the good of the soul.[47] Both Aristotle and Plato properly
distinguish between the sense and the intellect, but Plato's way of making
the distinction assumes that the body is essentially an obstacle to overcome. For Aquinas, if this were true, it would mean that human cognition would be nothing more than frustrated angelic cognition.

Aquinas's speech about the embodied creature does not proceed from
any particular interest in reductive actualism. His primary aim is to
affirm the goodness of incarnate creatures as such. Far from regarding
embodiment as a tragedy, he understands it as the condition appropriate
to human beings who occupy a certain place within the created order.
The perfection of the universe requires creatures both incorporeal and
corporeal.[48] Aquinas's detachment of the soul's act from anything
material – 'understanding is an act which cannot be performed by a
corporeal organ'[49] – is meant to negate the view that the soul is immersed
in matter. Properly understood, the Aristotelian maxim does not imply
the immersion of soul in matter, since the principle of a body is not a
body. Aquinas is confident that the root of the inability to distinguish
between the incorporeal and corporeal has little to do with reason. It is
simply a failure of imagination, as exemplified by the ancient naturalistic
philosophers. There is no textual evidence for Pasnau's claim that in
engaging with the *antiqui*, 'Aquinas clearly takes himself to be refuting a

---

[45] *ST* Ia, Q. 91, art. 4, ad 3: 'de corpore, quod dependet ex anima, et non e con-
verso'.
[46] *ST* Ia, Q. 75, art. 6, ad 3: 'Ad tertium dicendum quod intelligere cum phantas-
mate est propria operatio animae secundum quod corpori est unita. Separata autem
a corpore habebit alium modum intelligendi, similem aliis substantiis a corpore
separatis'.
[47] See *ST* Ia, Q. 89, art. 1, resp.
[48] See the important study of Oliva Blanchette, *The Perfection of the Universe
According to Aquinas: A Teleological Cosmology* (University Park, PA: Pennsylvania
State University Press, 1992).
[49] *ST* Ia, Q. 76, art. 1, ad 1: 'intelligere enim est actus qui non potest exerceri per
organum corporale'.

serious philosophical error.'[50] Aquinas's aim is not to refute material-ism.[51] It is to provide an account of the soul–body relation that illumi-nates the essence and operations of the embodied creature within the hierarchy of being.

The oddity of some of Pasnau's conclusions may be a product of his narrow focus. If the goal is to understand Aquinas on human nature, it is difficult to justify the decision to select only a small section from the Prima Pars. Why not also treat the Questions occurring in the Secunda Pars, which considers the rational creature's advance toward God? One may grant that any worthwhile study must limit its scope, while suspect-ing that Pasnau has failed to appreciate Alasdair MacIntyre's salutary reminder that parts of the *Summa* receive their meaning from their place in the whole, and that it is therefore 'a good deal more difficult to encounter, let alone to evaluate, Aquinas's thought than either Thomists or their opponents have sometimes supposed'.[52] MacIntyre's own example of the tendency to illegitimately isolate parts from the whole is the habit of publishing Questions 90–97 of the Prima Secundae as the *Treatise on Law* – a 'fictitious treatise', as he observes, since Aquinas neither wrote isolated, autonomous treatises nor prefaced clusters of questions with the word 'treatise'. That Pasnau speaks of the *Tractatus de homine* and wonders how to render the phrase in English suggests that he is simply unaware of this lexical fact.

Pasnau will occasionally advert to structural matters, as when he claims that the Questions on the human soul in the Prima Pars are 'part of a larger project to understand God via creation'.[53] Unfortunately for Pasnau, this gets it backwards, at least with respect to the *Summa*. The project of the Prima Pars is to understand creation via God, as attention to the actual shape of the text would suggest. The Questions on creation and created things follow, and are understood in light of, the preceding Questions on God and the Trinity. Confusion is compounded when Pasnau registers an objection that he takes to be derived from Thomas's texts. Why try to understand creation by focusing on human beings, he asks, when '[a]ll of creation provides a kind of image of God, and some parts of creation – specifically, the angels – provide a better image of God'?[54] Aquinas does not straightforwardly hold that the angels provide a better image of God. Their status as an *imago Dei* is superior with

---

[50] Pasnau, *Thomas Aquinas*, p. 39.

[51] As Chesterton noted, materialism may not be amenable to internal refutation. See G. K. Chesterton, *Orthodoxy* (New York: Image Books, 1908), pp. 23–6.

[52] Alasdair MacIntyre, *Three Rival Versions of Moral Enquiry* (Notre Dame, IN: University of Notre Dame Press, 1990), p. 135.

[53] Pasnau, *Thomas Aquinas*, p. 19.

[54] Pasnau, *Thomas Aquinas*, p. 19.

respect to intellectual nature, but not with respect to the imitation of God. In this respect, humans are superior images of God, or so Aquinas argues by appeal to analogies of generation and of the omnipresence of the soul in the body. Moreover, Aquinas does not hold, as Pasnau suggests, that 'all of creation provides a kind of image of God'.[55] He explicitly rejects this view in Question 93, where he argues that irrational creatures possess the *similitudo* but not the *imago*.[56] The shape of the *quaestio* as a whole confirms the point. Aquinas ends Question 93 with an article that underscores the proper distinction between *similitudo* and *imago*. The unsatisfactory character of Pasnau's discussion on this point illustrates the difficulty of encountering Aquinas's thought as a whole.

Like Pasnau, Hibbs privileges the *Summa Theologiae*, but is alert to the problems involved in the decision to consider only part of that text.[57] (An example: his observation that when the Questions on natural law are cut off from the whole of Thomas's moral teaching, 'the discussion of law becomes problematic, if not unintelligible'.[58]) His attempt to attend to the anthropological foundations of Aquinas's thought comprehends not only Questions 75–89 of the Prima Pars, but also a judicious selection of Questions from the Secunda Pars on action, virtue, law and grace. Hibbs's decision to consider these Questions is not informed by a desire to cover material for its own sake. It stems from his awareness that any treatment of Aquinas on human nature that does not consider the question of human freedom, which in turn requires an account of law, is radically incomplete.

Hibbs develops this point by drawing an extended comparison to both Suárez and Kant. Like Aquinas, Suárez assigns our knowledge of the content and reasonableness of the natural law to the intellect. Suárez departs from Aquinas, however, in holding that natural law precepts are obligatory only by dint of their derivation from divine command, that is, the will. As Hibbs notes, Suárez explicitly denies Aquinas's view that the *imperium rationis* is sufficient to obligate. Hibbs argues that Aquinas

---

[55] Pasnau, *Thomas Aquinas*, p. 19.

[56] See *ST* Ia, Q. 93, art. 2, resp.

[57] Both Pasnau and Hibbs often consult parallel passages from the *Summa contra Gentiles*. Pasnau also makes frequent reference to loci from the Aristotelian commentaries, assuming that what Aquinas writes by way of expounding Aristotle may be unproblematically identified with his own teaching. Pasnau seems entirely unaware of the contested character of this assumption. For a critique of the assumption, see Mark Jordan, 'Thomas Aquinas's Disclaimers in the Aristotelian Commentaries', in R. James Long (ed.), *Philosophy and the God of Abraham: Essays in Memory of James A. Weisheipl, OP* (Toronto: Pontifical Institute of Mediaeval Studies, 1991), pp. 99–112 and Mark Jordan, *On the Alleged Aristotelianism of Thomas Aquinas* (Toronto: Pontifical Institute of Mediaeval Studies, 1992), especially pp. 8–21.

[58] Hibbs, *Virtue's Splendor*, p. 86.

does not have a 'theory of obligation' of the sort that modern moral philosophers have come to expect.[59] His account implies that contemporary 'divine command' theorists who would enlist Aquinas for their cause have not read the *Summa Theologiae* well, perhaps because they have confused sections of that text with Suárez's *De legibus*. Aquinas's authentic teaching is that moral action is best conceived not as obligatory response to a divine command, but as a fulfilment of natural tendencies and desires. The source of these tendencies and desires, seated in the rational appetite, is not arbitrary will, but the act of creation itself. The priority of reason to will, which Hibbs interestingly links with a grammatical observation of Thomas about the dependence of the imperative on the indicative,[60] ensures the intelligibility of our natural inclinations. To understand how Thomas thinks about these inclinations, which he takes to be constitutive of human nature, we must attend both to the Questions of the Prima Pars on the rational appetite and to the Questions on the precepts of the natural law in the Prima Secundae. These precepts merit examination not because they provide a list of moral rules (Hibbs emphasises the contrast with Kantian models of ethical reasoning), but because they illuminate our natural inclinations and the objects toward which those inclinations are directed. For Aquinas, unlike Kant, free ethical action is that which fulfils our natural inclinations (when rightly ordered), not that which defies them. Hibbs concludes that Thomas has a compelling doctrine of moral action, but that it is intelligible only in light of 'a moral anthropology that had fallen into desuetude by Suárez's time'.[61]

Central to this anthropology is the view that rational perception of the good that we seek has the power to draw us nearer to that good, and that no special theory of obligation is required to explain, as Hibbs puts it, the transition from perception to action. The link between the two is virtue.[62] Pasnau notices that Aquinas has much to say about virtue, but reduces this to a sort of pragmatism. Aquinas talks about virtue, he claims, because discussions about virtue are 'useful to us'.[63] In contrast to Pasnau, Hibbs's consideration of a wider range of texts enables him to provide the deep anthropological reasons that motivate Thomas to devote the bulk of the Secunda Pars of the *Summa Theologiae* to an account of virtue in general, followed by discussions of particular virtues. The banality of Pasnau's explanation for Thomas's discussion of virtue may be rooted in a tendency toward anachronism characteristic of

---

[59] See Hibbs, *Virtue's Splendor*, p. 65.
[60] Hibbs, *Virtue's Splendor*, p. 71.
[61] Hibbs, *Virtue's Splendor*, p. 83.
[62] Hibbs, *Virtue's Splendor*, p. 85.
[63] Pasnau, *Thomas Aquinas*, p. 20.

philosophers with an exclusively 'analytic' training. This tendency is illustrated by his discussion of how to justify a 'philosophical study' (as he describes his own work) of what is evidently a theological text. Pasnau thinks that 'the most superficial examination' of Questions 75–89 of the Prima Pars will show that 'the topics are philosophical: mind and body, free will, knowledge, intellect, perception . . .'.[64] But why should we rest content with superficial examination? Pasnau's sole ground for maintaining a doctrine of strong continuity between medieval theology and contemporary philosophy – 'theology for him is continuous with philosophy for us'[65] – seems to be that both medieval theologians and modern philosophers employ 'reason' to talk about 'soul' and its relation to body, with a proclivity to abstract from physiological data. But do either *ratio* or *anima* bear the same sense for the thirteenth-century magister and the twenty-first-century professor of philosophy? Pasnau's casual supposition that they do recalls Collingwood's analogy between the man who could never shake the notion that τριήρης was the Greek for 'steamer' and the modern philosophers who imagine that πόλις means the same as 'state', or δεῖ means 'ought'.[66]

Pasnau claims that 'the real heart of Aquinas's theological project corresponds quite closely with what we consider the project of philosophy'.[67] Unfortunately, Pasnau does little to reassure the reader that 'we' is more than shorthand for a small group of professors who regularly attend the annual conventions of the American Philosophical Association. As for the 'real heart of Aquinas's theological project', Pasnau's book conspicuously lacks a scholarly discussion of the topic. It does not acknowledge the multiple attempts made over the last one hundred years to grapple with this question, from Chenu through Corbin and de Lubac to the recent work of A. N. Williams.[68] To observe, as countless others have done, that Aquinas supports many claims in the *Summa Theologiae* without direct appeal to revelation, does nothing to support the claim that Aquinas's 'theology . . . is thoroughly philosophical in its methods'.[69] On Pasnau's own reckoning, Aquinas may

---

[64] Pasnau, *Thomas Aquinas*, p. 10.
[65] Pasnau, *Thomas Aquinas*, p. 22.
[66] See R. G. Collingwood, *An Autobiography* (Oxford: Clarendon Press, 1939 (1982)), pp. 63–4.
[67] Pasnau, *Thomas Aquinas*, p. 16.
[68] See A. N. Williams, *The Ground of Union: Deification in Aquinas and Palamas* (Oxford: Oxford University Press, 1999), and her earlier pair of articles: 'Deification in the *Summa Theologiae*: A Structural Interpretation of the *Prima Pars*', *Thomist* 61 (1997), pp. 219–55; 'Mystical Theology Redux: The Pattern of Aquinas's *Summa Theologiae*', *Modern Theology* 13 (1997), pp. 53–74. Any serious attempt to capture the real heart of Aquinas's theological project will have to engage with Williams's imaginative and careful readings.
[69] Pasnau, *Thomas Aquinas*, p. 16.

derive 'guidelines' for his work from revelation. If this is the case, why should his work count as philosophy? Are not his conclusions ultimately restricted by the content of revelation? One may observe that any hasty resolution of the question in this direction assumes, without justification, a particular conception of philosophy.[70] But if Pasnau is to answer Russell's charge that 'there is little of the true philosophic spirit in Aquinas'[71] (and we agree with Pasnau that the charge should be answered) he would have to reflect more deeply on the question, 'What is philosophy?'

What enables Pasnau to suppose that Aquinas's theology is continuous with recent philosophy is the assumption of shared topical organisation. It is not that Pasnau is altogether unfamiliar with those who would contest the assumption. He construes John Inglis as a 'prudent scholar' who reaches the somewhat boring conclusion that neither medieval theology nor medieval philosophy is much like contemporary philosophy.[72] In fact, Inglis's conclusion is far more subtle and interesting. His work, which is too complex for brief summary (although it deserves consideration as a specimen of recent excellent work on Aquinas in North America), provides a helpful formulation of a view that many have taken for granted. This is the view that medieval thinkers are well understood by the dissection of their works into easily digestible parts, which happen to correspond to the standard branches of philosophy. Inglis's work provides both specimens of the view and a detailed genealogy showing how this view came to be.[73] It also contains some daring (not merely 'prudent') suggestions as to what a more authentic approach to medieval thought would look like. These involve, *inter alia*, a willingness to read Aquinas and other medievals on their own terms, rather than pressing them into alien moulds.

That Pasnau is less interested in understanding Aquinas's anthropology for its own sake than in promoting a version of Aquinas designed for the tastes of modern secularists is strongly suggested by the bizarre inclusion at the end of Part One of his book of a section on 'infusion and abortion'. Here we discover that the 'Church has identified itself with a noxious social agenda – especially on homosexuality, contraception and abortion – that has sadly come to seem part of the defining character of

---

[70] For a development of this argument, see Mark Jordan, 'The Terms of the Debate over "Christian Philosophy"', *Communio* 12 (1985), pp. 293–311.

[71] Bertrand Russell, *A History of Western Philosophy* (New York: Simon & Schuster, 1945), p. 463, quoted in Pasnau, *Thomas Aquinas*, p. 15.

[72] See Pasnau, *Thomas Aquinas*, pp. 13 and 405 n. 4.

[73] See John Inglis, *Spheres of Philosophical Inquiry and the Historiography of Mediaeval Philosophy* (Leiden: Brill, 1998). For an attempt to summarise this important work, see my review in *Review of Metaphysics* 53.3 (March 2000), pp. 706–8.

Catholicism'.[74] There are at least three (unintended) ironies here: (1) the appearance of a section on these topics within a work that is supposed to be a careful reading of Questions 75–89 of the Prima Pars, in which the topic of abortion is never discussed; (2) the use of the above language by an author who would contrast the character of his own discourse with the utterance of those who resort to 'rhetoric'; (3) the claim that Aquinas's discussion of ensoulment is not widely known, and 'those who do know are generally not eager to advertise it, and indeed have often attacked it in scholarly circles'.[75] If the *cognoscenti* are so eager to conceal his true position, why do they make a habit of attacking it? One might think that the practice of frequent attack would draw more attention to it, defeating the purpose of keeping it hidden.

In sharp contrast to Pasnau's book, Hibbs's discussion of Thomas's anthropology does not approach Aquinas under the aspect of anti-Catholicism. It leaves open the possibility that an account of Aquinas's anthropology based on the first two Parts of the *Summa* requires completion through a consideration of its third Part, which treats of Christ as man's way to God.

Christology

Even those broadly sympathetic to Aquinas have paid little attention to his Christology, contained in the Tertia Pars of the *Summa Theologiae*. In his first book, *Christ's Fulfillment of Torah and Temple*, Matthew Levering aims to change this state of affairs. Levering attempts to expound Thomas's christological doctrines by locating them within his theology of salvation. In the wake of Pinckaers, Torrell and Valkenberg, Levering interprets Thomas in a way designed to dispel the impression that a sound reading of Aquinas can afford to neglect his handling of Scripture. What Chenu says about the growing importance for the Old Testament among twelfth-century theologians applies equally to Aquinas, according to Levering, particularly to his later work. In contrast to the *Sentences* Commentary, which 'contains almost no discussion of the Mosaic Law and lacks a carefully organised exposition of the mysteries of Christ's life', the *Summa Theologiae* includes both in a 'mature theology of salvation'.[76] Levering seeks to expound this theology of salvation by careful attention to the way in which Aquinas understands Christ to fulfil the covenants with Israel. A primary aim of

---

[74] Pasnau, *Thomas Aquinas*, p. 105.
[75] Pasnau, *Thomas Aquinas*, p. 115.
[76] Matthew Levering, *Christ's Fulfillment of Torah and Temple* (Notre Dame, IN: University of Notre Dame Press, 2002), p. 6.

Levering is to articulate, guided throughout by Thomas, a contemporary theology of salvation that does justice to the essential relationship between theology and revelation, metaphysics and history. As such, his approach stands in sharp contrast to tendencies exhibited among both the heirs of Schleiermacher and transcendental Thomists 'to ground theology in universal anthropological categories abstracted from the history of God's revelation'.[77]

Levering divides his exposition into two parts, corresponding to the distinction between the Mosaic Law (Torah) and the renewal of the covenant with David (Temple). He begins his exploration of Christ's fulfilment of Israel's Torah with a summary of recent debates about the relationship between the Old Law and the New Law. These debates centre around the question: Do the Passion, death and resurrection revoke the Old Law? Those who take the answer to this question to be an unequivocal 'yes' are (in contemporary parlance) 'supersessionists'. Although Aquinas holds that some precepts of the Old Law have been superseded, he nonetheless places the law 'within the heart of his theology of salvation'.[78] He thereby avoids the charge of supersessionism. Aquinas insists on both the insufficiency and indispensability of the Old Law. The Old Law is insufficient because it does not fully direct human beings to their supernatural end. It leads them in that direction by the ordering of their exterior acts, but it does not effect the necessary transformation of the interior principle that is required 'to direct human acts, at their root, toward the supernatural end of knowing and loving the triune God'.[79] Despite this deficiency, the Old Law is good because it bears witness to Christ by prefiguring him, and it prepares for Christ by its pedagogical potency, that is, by its ability to direct people away from idolatry and toward the one God. 'Far from being a husk that is to be thrown out', Levering concludes, the Old Law 'possesses a permanent goodness'.[80]

The care of Levering's exposition is shown by his attention to both the permanent goodness of the Old Law and its historical character. God's love operates continuously throughout history, but if 'history' is to function as a meaningful category, difference as well as sameness must be acknowledged. Levering argues that Aquinas does justice to both. 'Aquinas does not "flatten" history, as if all times were really the same and the historical enactment of the passion hardly mattered'.[81] Although God's love is eternal, rooted in the life of the Trinitarian Persons, the

---

[77] Levering, *Christ's Fulfillment of Torah and Temple*, p. 9.
[78] Levering, *Christ's Fulfillment of Torah and Temple*, p. 18.
[79] Levering, *Christ's Fulfillment of Torah and Temple*, p. 22.
[80] Levering, *Christ's Fulfillment of Torah and Temple*, p. 22.
[81] Levering, *Christ's Fulfillment of Torah and Temple*, p. 24.

mode of pedagogy that is appropriate to the direction of fallen humanity is tailored to fit particular historical circumstances.[82] It is not that Aquinas conceives of a period before Christ where grace was absent. As the grace of the Holy Spirit, the New Law is found in all places and times. But the 'state of the new law', which begins after the New Law, is a distinct historical period in which, according to Aquinas, grace is given most abundantly. Such grace is nothing abstract, but is available concretely in the sacraments of the Church.

The use of 'history' as a category requires the presence of both continuity and discontinuity. Levering's argument is that Aquinas honours both by construing Christ as a fulfilment of the Old Law. He recognises, however, a worthy challenge to this conception in the work of the Jewish theologian Michael Wyschogrod, with whom he enters into respectful and fruitful dialogue.[83] Wyschogrod contends that Aquinas fails to allow for true continuity. Because Aquinas thinks that the requirement to obey the ceremonial and judicial precepts comes to an end with Christ, he regards the Old Law as essentially discontinuous with the New Law. Wyschogrod observes that with respect to some of the ceremonial precepts which Aquinas claims are no longer to be observed, God expressly commands (in Exodus) that they are to be observed forever. Moreover, he adds that Jewish Christians continued to observe these precepts, as documented by Acts. From these observations, Wyschogrod concludes that when Aquinas holds that precepts of the Old Law no longer bind Christians who live under the state of the New Law, he does not sufficiently allow for continuity.

Levering's response to this challenge is simple and stunning: 'the Mosaic Law, in a real sense (though not one that would be recognized by Wyschogrod), is still observed by Christians'.[84] This is true not only with regard to the moral precepts of the Old Law, but even with respect to the ceremonial precepts, which, in Aquinas's words, 'lasts forever in respect of the reality which those ceremonies foreshadowed'.[85] Christ does not destroy the Old Law, but fulfils it completely. It is 'end' in the sense of 'fulfilment', not 'destruction', that Levering wants to emphasise: 'the ceremonial and judicial precepts are taken up and fulfilled, not revoked, by Christ. They come to an end in the positive (teleological) sense of attain-

---

[82] This is an important theme for St Augustine as well. See, e.g., *Confessions* 3.7.

[83] As Alasdair MacIntyre observes in connection with his conception of tradition-constituted enquiry, 'Christians need badly to listen to Jews'. See MacIntyre, *Whose Justice? Which Rationality?* (Notre Dame, IN: University of Notre Dame Press, 1988), p. 11. Levering's book, particularly in its first and fourth chapters, is an exemplary attempt to meet this need.

[84] Levering, *Christ's Fulfillment of Torah and Temple*, p. 28.

[85] Levering, *Christ's Fulfillment of Torah and Temple*, p. 28.

ing their ultimate end, in which they rest or last forever.'[86] As for the observance of the Mosaic Law by early Jewish Christians, Aquinas provides what Levering judges to be a convincing response to Wyschogrod's challenge. The early Christians were allowed to observe the Mosaic Law during a 'middle period' in which Gentiles were in the process of being brought under the new covenant, for the sake of emphasising the unity of divine law. After that period, Jewish Christians who continued legal observance of the ceremonies of the Mosaic law would be in a state of mortal sin.

Grounded in the theology of Thomas, Levering undertakes to present a 'theology of history' that undercuts, by its participatory dimension, all naively supersessionist language. The New Covenant itself is a mere participation in the state of glory. History is thus understood as participating in eternity, thereby abolishing the strictly linear model upon which supersessionism thrives, without denying the radical newness and influence of particular historical events, pre-eminently Christ's Paschal mystery at the centre of history. By construing history as participation, Levering is able to articulate the sense in which the Old Law is more than a tool to be discarded, or a husk to be left behind. Christ's saving work cannot be entirely understood in abstraction from the Old Law, since it takes the form of a fulfilment of that very law.

This conviction leads Levering to expound the main lines of Aquinas's Christology under the heading 'Incarnate Wisdom in Israel'. Here Levering turns more directly to the Tertia Pars of the *Summa Theologiae*, probing the relation of Christ's divine knowledge to his human knowledge. Levering candidly acknowledges that some of the best interpreters of Thomas have not been satisfied with Aquinas's treatment of the question. Aquinas's resolution, as understood by Jean-Pierre Torrell and summarised by Levering, is that Christ 'had the ability to concentrate perfectly (without distraction) on each object proper to his rational powers and thus was able to contemplate God fully even while engaging fully with the world around him'.[87] Torrell's objection to this strategy is that it makes a '"flagrant exception" to Christ as regards his human psychology'.[88] It renders Aquinas able to secure the beatific knowledge of Christ, but at the price of conflating his (human) intellect with the angelic intellect. Levering develops a constructive response to Torrell's objection by considering the role of the Holy Spirit in the meeting of divine wisdom and human wisdom in Christ. When Aquinas teaches that

[86] Levering, *Christ's Fulfillment of Torah and Temple*, pp. 28–9.
[87] Levering, *Christ's Fulfillment of Torah and Temple*, p. 32.
[88] Jean-Pierre Torrell, *Le Christ en ses mystères: La vie et l'oeuvre de Jésus selon saint Thomas d'Aquin* (Paris: Desclée, 1999), pp. 338–9, quoted in Levering, *Christ's Fulfillment of Torah and Temple*, p. 32.

the Son alone assumed a human nature, he does not mean to deny the involvement of the other Persons in the Incarnation. Against the appearance that the Holy Spirit is excluded from a significant role in the Incarnation, Levering shows that for Aquinas, 'the work of the Incarnation proceeded in a trinitarian way'.[89] According to Levering, it is too weak to say that the work of the Holy Spirit in perfecting Christ's human nature is merely compatible with a strong appreciation of his humanity. The involvement of the Holy Spirit in his earthly ministry, by elevating Christ's human knowing to intimate (non-conceptual) contemplation of God, allows Christ to embody, in his words and deeds, divine Wisdom for human beings. As Levering puts it, the unique involvement of the Holy Spirit in gifting Christ's humanity 'actually enables him, precisely in his historical life, to perform the historical work of salvation in the personal way that it must be performed'.[90]

Levering's treatment of the Incarnation suggests the deficiency of any treatment that would speak of Christ as the embodiment of wisdom, but fails to add that the embodiment of wisdom necessarily occurs in a particular time and place. He approvingly quotes N. T. Wright's suggestion that apprehending the Incarnation requires attention to the fact that 'Jesus is enacting the great healing, the great restoration, of Israel'.[91] In accord with this suggestion of Wright, Levering proceeds to give a detailed examination of the Questions in the Tertia Pars that treat of the life of Christ as prophet, priest and king, in connection with both the Incarnation and the Passion. Following Aquinas, but interpreting him in an innovative fashion, Levering shows that Christ in his Passion fulfils the Old Law in a threefold way that manifests – as one would expect from the one who fulfils Israel's law – Christ as true prophet, priest and king. Levering employs this reading of the Passion to illumine the entire pattern of Christ's life, as presented by Aquinas. After a detailed exegesis of Questions 36–44, Levering concludes:

> as prophet, he gives humankind the interior law of love that is the grace of the Holy Spirit. As priest, he reconciles humankind to God by offering himself as a holy sacrifice. As king, he reconciles human beings to each other by suffering for all. In this way, he perfectly fulfils and transforms Israel's Torah.[92]

Dialectical excitement increases in the second part of the book, in which Levering focuses on Christ as fulfilment of Israel's Temple. As a

[89] Levering, *Christ's Fulfillment of Torah and Temple*, p. 37.
[90] Levering, *Christ's Fulfillment of Torah and Temple*, p. 40.
[91] N. T. Wright, *Jesus and the Victory of God* (Minneapolis, MN: Fortress Press, 1996), p. 130, quoted in Levering, *Christ's Fulfillment of Torah and Temple*, p. 41.
[92] Levering, *Christ's Fulfillment of Torah and Temple*, p. 79.

prolegomenon to a detailed exposition of Question 45 on the transfigura-
tion, Levering confronts the objection that any strongly christological
reading of the Old Testament is 'fundamentally antihistorical'. Following the model of Thomas himself, Levering chooses a formulation of the
objection that is succinct and to the point. The charge, in the words of
Baruch Halpern, is that worshippers

> seek behind the events a single unifying cause that lends them meaning,
> and makes the historical differences among them irrelevant. In history,
> the faithful seek the permanent, the ahistorical; in time, they quest for
> timelessness; in reality, in the concrete, they seek Spirit, the insubstan-
> tial.[93]

Levering refrains from observing the philosophical crudity contained in
the final appositive of the preceding sentence. His *respondeo dicendum* is
that the view of history according to which history necessarily lacks any
unified meaning is itself radically anti-historical. He adds that for
Aquinas, the 'spiritual' sense of the biblical text can only be attained
through the historical sense. 'Lacking knowledge of the historical sense
of the text, one has no basis to speculate about possible spiritual
senses.'[94] Any exploration of the sense in which an Old Testament passage prefigures aspects of Christ or the Church requires, according to
Aquinas, careful exploration of 'what the particular law or precept might
have meant for the ancient Israelites'.[95] Thus 'attention to the "historical" sense and attention to the "spiritual" or "confessional" sense is a
false opposition'.[96]

Having overcome this opposition, Levering proceeds to establish that
for Aquinas, Christ's Paschal mystery fulfils Israel's Temple. As the
embodiment of divine Wisdom and as the perfect sacrifice, Christ
engages the central motifs of Israel's Temple and fulfils them by enacting
God's perfect presence with his people. Just as Christ's members participate in his fulfilment of Torah, so also his members – pre-eminently Mary
– participate in his fulfilment of Temple, as the Mystical Body of Christ.
Israel, divinely constituted by Torah and Temple, thus receives her
Messiah and is reconstituted around the divine Messiah, in a way that
completes, rather than negates or discards, the role of Israel's covenantal

---

[93] Baruch Halpern, *The First Historians: The Hebrew Bible and History* (University Park, PA: Pennsylvania State University Press, 1996), pp. 3–4, quoted in
Levering, *Christ's Fulfillment of Torah and Temple*, p. 89.
[94] Levering, *Christ's Fulfillment of Torah and Temple*, p. 90.
[95] Levering, *Christ's Fulfillment of Torah and Temple*, p. 90.
[96] Levering, *Christ's Fulfillment of Torah and Temple*, p. 90.

life. For Aquinas, the new creation in the crucified and risen Christ is nothing other than a transformation and fulfilment of the Temple of Israel. Where the Temple of Israel was, there the mystical body of Christ is and will be. Once again, however, Israel's Temple is not thereby made obsolete or superfluous. The participatory theology of history that Levering, following Aquinas, has set forth militates against any derogation of Israel. Israel's Temple, like the Church, participates in the Heavenly Jerusalem. Reflection on both Torah and Temple – which, as Levering emphasises throughout, are ultimately one – shows that, for Aquinas, 'in fulfilling Israel's Torah and Temple, the Messiah himself becomes the perfect embodiment of Torah and Temple, which are thus radically transformed'.[97]

---

[97] Levering, *Christ's Fulfillment of Torah and Temple*, p. 142.

Concerning Natural Law: The Turn in American Aquinas Scholarship

SUSAN F. PARSONS

Of the many ways in which the works of St Thomas have been scrutinised, interpreted and used since the call for renewed study of him was issued in 1879, few have proved quite so delicate to negotiate or so urgently driven as that on which moral philosophers and theologians find themselves. For throughout modernity, which is to say since Thomas's own day, the expectations that have been laid upon moral thinking and the restless confluence of ideas within which these are supposed to be worked out have together shaped a discourse that would bear the load of redemption, that would operate as a fulcrum to carry us over from where we are to where we ought to be, and would do so effectively in whatever circumstance and with whatever given material. Here was to be 'the science of those principles which should direct man towards the supreme end of his existence', which above all forms of knowledge should lead us into our destiny that is the absolute good, yet which is ever tangled up in the contingent messiness of scientific and popular opinion, threatened constantly with the discrediting of its fundamental principles, and under considerable strain from the weight of its burden.

Not long after the publication of *Aeterna Patris*, Thomas Bouquillon was to decry the sorry state of moral theology at the end of the nineteenth century which seemed merely to have made things easy for itself. For it was being widely taken as 'simply a *method of applying certain principles* to human conditions', and was thereby 'dwarfed beyond recognition', reduced to being 'an adjunct, a mere technical necessity for the priest' in operating the mechanics of salvation.[1] This diminishment of its lofty responsibilities was to him the result of its loss of proper place

---

[1] Thomas Bouquillon, 'Moral Theology at the End of the Nineteenth Century', in Charles E. Curran and Richard A. McCormick SJ (eds.), *The Historical Development of Fundamental Moral Theology in the United States* (New York: Paulist Press, 1999), pp. 93–4 [first published in *Catholic University Bulletin* 5 (1899)]. Bouquillon is partly quoting here from a description of moral theology given with some approval (as indicated by the original emphases) by Rev. J. Talbot Smith in a book then recently published, *Our Seminaries*.

and character, both among the diverse physical and human sciences that had by then sprung up, but also within the whole framework of theological truths. Moral theology had not only become cautious about relating to the other sciences, many of which also understood themselves to be normative, so that the distinctive contribution it might make to a common consideration was no longer clear, but also, he claimed, had 'practically lost contact with the Gospel', so that whatever it might have had to convey of that Truth within whose life it most intimately belonged had become endangered.[2] Among the things that contributed to this weakening, he emphasised particularly 'the surrender of the Summa of St Thomas where all is unity'.[3] For he believed the synthesis so carefully formulated there had been destroyed, separating moral theology from dogma and disturbing the systematic order of his thought. It was no surprise then that Bouquillon's hope lay in the 'impetus [that] has already been given in the admirable encyclicals of Pope Leo XIII'.[4]

There is evident strain in this reflection, a spirit of anxiety, even regret, about the disordered confusions generated throughout modernity, and a keen determination to recover a ground that has been lost in order to start again. St Thomas has come to figure prominently in this, as though he were a kind of high point from which the modern has fallen and strayed, so the guidance he might give for thinking is more desperately sought. His understanding of the natural law in particular has come to represent a hidden treasure of wisdom whose time for full appreciation may now be upon us. For may not his teaching, taking us deeply as it does into the matter of who we are and of what is to become of us as creatures, setting out the reasons and principles of things in a comprehensive whole held in the loving will of the Creator – and this in the midst of a situation whose complexity resonates with our own – may it not provide a framework of moral decision and action that will commend itself to a bewildered and anguished humanity, thereby securing the ground for renewed confidence in the moral in the particular concerns and unprecedented dilemmas that present themselves in our day? May not his teachings yield to us again the way of our salvation?

In this hope, Leo XIII urges that we attend again to the golden wisdom of St Thomas whose systematic philosophical reflection carried out in the light of 'the splendour of divine truths',[5] might disclose the foundation

---

[2] Bouquillon, 'Moral Theology', p. 103.
[3] Bouquillon, 'Moral Theology', pp. 107–8.
[4] Bouquillon, 'Moral Theology', p. 110.
[5] 'Those, therefore, who to the study of philosophy unite obedience to the Christian faith, are philosophising in the best possible way; for the splendour of the divine truths, received into the mind, helps the understanding, and not only detracts in nowise from its dignity, but adds greatly to its nobility, keenness, and stability.'

for a moral philosophy that could provide guidance for the ordering of 'domestic and civil society'.[6] This intention is to be echoed a century later by John Paul II in *Veritatis splendor*. Amidst the wreckage brought about within the late-twentieth-century culture of death, he too assures us that only a renewal of moral theology in this way can answer the human search for meaning and so show us the way to have eternal life. For the *ordinem ethicum* is not separable from the *salutis ordinem*.[7] For both of them as pastors, the matter of the foundation is crucial, for only what is set upon solid ground can provide a 'firm, and stable, and robust' philosophy,[8] and so for both as teachers, the declaration of this foundation to be the universal, constant and absolute truth of God and the demonstration of its shining forth in all creation is to provide the basis for an understanding of the good, of that which is for us freedom and fullness of life. Participation in the *missio ad gentes* may then proceed with confidence.

Those whose *munus* it is to be theologians and philosophers are given here a direction for the recovery of St Thomas, and are encouraged in this task by the expectation that the demonstration of this foundation in his setting out of the natural law will make present to us the grounds on which redemption may be worked out in our living. Yet fundamental questions appear here that prevent this from being a simply straightforward, or indeed a detached, undertaking. For this matter of the foundation is disclosive to us of who we are and of what we have come to be in our present condition, as the latest generation of a philosophical tradition, whose laying down of this ground for truth was established early on among the Greeks, and whose securing of this ground by means

---

'Quapropter qui philosophiae studium cum obsequio fidei christianae coniungunt, ii optime philosophantur: quandoquidem divinarum veritatum splendor, animo exceptus, ipsam iuvat intelligentiam; cui non modo nihil de dignitate detrahit, sed nobilitatis, acuminis, firmitatis plurimum addit.' *Aeterna Patris* §9.

[6] 'Domestic and civil society even, which, as all see, is exposed to great danger from this plague of perverse opinions, would certainly enjoy a far more peaceful and secure existence if a more wholesome doctrine were taught in the universities and high schools – one more in conformity with the teaching of the Church, such as is contained in the works of Thomas Aquinas.' 'Domestica vero, atque civilis ipsa societas, quae ob perversarum opinionum pestem quanto in discrimine versetur, universi perspicimus, profecto pacatior multo et securior consisteret, si in Academiis et scholis sanior traderetur, et magisterio Ecclesiae conformior doctrina, qualem Thomae Aquinatis volumina complectuntur.' *Aeterna Patris* §28.

[7] *Veritatis splendor*, §37, and see §§28–64 *passim*.

[8] 'For, a multiform system of this kind, which depends on the authority and choice of any professor, has a foundation open to change, and consequently gives us a philosophy not firm, and stable, and robust like that of old, but tottering and feeble.' 'Etenim multiplex haec ratio doctrinae, cum in magistrorum singulorum auctoritate arbitrioque nitatur, mutabile habet fundamentum, eaque de causa non firmam atque stabilem neque robustam, sicut veterem illam, sed nutantem et levem facit philosophiam.' *Veritatis splendor* §24.

of the idea of the good has been formative of subsequent thought. And because today this way of thinking is so deeply called into question and at the same time brought to a kind of end in what is known as nihilism, truth itself and the relation of the good to it are seen to be at risk, deemed to require our renewed articulation of them, else all is lost.

These things sit heavily in the midst of moral thinking today, generating their own demands upon us as we strain to hear the call of truth and as we know our own self-understanding also to be at stake in speaking of it. This essay is an exploration of the unfolding of this foundational tradition in the throes of its overturning, particularly as this has taken shape in American Aquinas scholarship. For it is in that context that some of its most contentious implications are being worked out, and therefore that the distressing character of our situation and our receptiveness to this direction is made so painfully obvious. It is not accidental that the focal point of these concerns has come to rest on the question of the natural and its law, as will be evident in the ensuing discussion; and, while no full alternative is to be drawn up or, least of all, envisioned, in this piece, it is hoped nonetheless that something of an understanding of what is happening here may clear a way for us yet to learn from St Thomas in these matters.

It is in Plato's teaching about truth, particularly in the *Republic*, that a founding event of western thinking takes place. For he understands the natural, what for the Greeks is φύσις or that which comes forth, in terms of its standing presence before us, and accordingly for him, truth becomes a matter of determining the correctness of one's judgement of what is present there. For this, a sure ground is needed. Among the Greeks, what is natural was understood to come independently of us and so of its own accord, but for Plato the dimension that matters is its being able to be seen, its accessibility by means of its visible form, its εἶδος, by which it is made possible for us to apprehend the things of nature in their disclosure to us. His innovative proposal is that such apprehend-ability is granted to each being by the ἰδέα, for it is this essence or *quidditas* of a being, by which each is brought into view and is given a permanence of presence, that allows us surely to know it. If the ἰδέα is the basis for a natural thing's remaining present to us and so available for knowing, there must then be a further ground upon which these many forms of things are themselves to be secured.

So Plato considers what is the ground of grounds, what it is that both causes this apprehension by which we are able to know, and ensures its truthfulness. This would hold together our seeing and knowing of what is there with the things that are there to be seen and known, giving ground for our certain and true knowledge of the various φύσει. In the allegory of the cave, the discovery of this ground takes place in the rising above beings, the ἐπικείνα τῆς οὐσίας, a transcending by means of thought, from which one comes to know the idea of ideas, namely the idea of the good, ἰδέα τοῦ ἀγαθοῦ, by and in whose light all beings can be viewed and so measured. It is the idea of the good which is the yoke, the ζυγόν, that holds together the knower and the known by keeping the εἴδη together in its field of light. The ἰδέα τοῦ ἀγαθοῦ is thus understood by Plato to be both the cause, the αἰτία, and the enabling power of truth itself.[9] Truth now is taken to be correctness of apprehension and so of thinking, ὀρθὸς λόγος or *recta ratio*, in the light of the idea of the good. With the joining together of truth as visibility and being as presence, under the rule of the good, a lead is given for the moral to occupy a place of privilege in subsequent western thinking.

That Aristotle will describe the investigation of this foundation as πρωτὴ φιλοσόφια, and so as enquiry into τὸ θεῖον, the highest being, opens the way for later Christian thinkers to articulate faith in the God who reveals himself as Creator and Redeemer, and it gives way to a most troubled consideration of the relationship between the will and power of this God of faith to the good conceived philosophically. The ramifications of this founding event thus move also among theologians who come to speak of God as ultimately the One from whom all things come forth, by whose benevolent provision of order they are sustained in appearing independently of us, and in whose presence all will be brought to complete fulfilment. With such thoughts, Plato's teaching about truth may be gathered up into that Truth which is highest of all, and the investigation of φύσις so carefully undertaken by Aristotle's physics can be placed into the care of a strong and loving Creator God. These things are at work in St Thomas who performs such patient reconciliation of these philosophical ideas with what is revealed through faith in Christ.

But what renders our approach to his accomplishment so problematic is that other things have happened to shape our ways of thinking. For we have heard the announcement that the central thrust of the tradition that formed his thought and from out of which he speaks, the way of this thinking as a whole, has come to an end, culminating in its most logical outcome as the death of the God it has posited to be above us all and so as the collapse of its transcendent source into the sheer ordinary banality of human resolve. Nietzsche's word, 'Gott ist tot', resounds in our time, even when we turn away from its discomfort, for it necessitates our look-

---

[9] 'Thus that which provides truth to the thing known and also gives power to the knower, this I say is the idea of the good; you must understand it to be the cause of knowledge and of the knowledge of truth.' Τοῦτο τοίνυν τὸ τὴν ἀλήθειαν παρέχον τοῖς γιγνωσκομένοις καὶ τῷ γιγνώσκοντι τὴν δύναμιν ἀποδιδὸν τὴν τοῦ ἀγαθοῦ ἰδέαν φάθι εἶναι, αἰτίαν δ' ἐπιστήμης οὖσαν καὶ ἀληθείας ὡς γιγνωσκομένης μὲν διανοοῦ. Plato, *Republic* VI, 508E.

ing at what has been made of God since Plato first saw that all is yoked together by the good, thereby determining already what the god was to be. For it is '[t]he God seen in terms of "morality" and only this is meant, when Nietzsche says, "God is dead" '.[10] This seeing of what has been happening in the metaphysics of morals as itself an exercise of will to power is of the essence of the nihilism in which we live.

For in this event a turn takes place, an overturning of a way of thinking by which it is thrown into reverse, revealing what has been at work all along within it and defining the necessities of our being-in-the-world in a new way. Thus it is can be seen that human beings have come to assume the place of the god, as subjects who now must be the pivot around which the world is to be stretched out, a world delineated into objects of attention and value and becoming itself as a whole an object of conceptualisation and assessment, and so as ones upon whom the continuation of the moral has come entirely to depend. And this, not because of some inherent wilfulness that requires firmer resolve or discipline. This is not a problem of the subject who might be cured or set free of such influence, if only it grasped some still higher responsibility. Rather is it a further unfolding of a way of thinking made explicit by Descartes's ordering of perception to the *cogito* and by Kant's setting forth of the conditions and categories of representation and judgement, until it has become for us a law of the subject.[11] The necessity for the revaluation of values that Nietzsche foresaw has thus become in postmodernity the full living out of subjectivity by which the world itself is now to be framed.

So it is precisely the matter of this foundation and of its declaration, indeed of our having to declare it, to look for its signs and bring it to stand under us – these things bring to light the postmodern condition which, in its very striving to produce an encounter with truth, thereby enacts a distance from it that is declared to be overcome, but cannot be bridged, by sheer determination. Few concerns are more evident of the end of a path of thinking than that of foundations, for it speaks the emptiness it seeks to fill, throwing back into the past or out into some transcendent realm the exact shape and requirements of the lack we experience from here, which the moral is to bridge for us. This situation can only be one of self-defeating measures, of strategies to make something of the nothing that this speaking of foundations bears, and so it fulfils the nihilism it seeks to overcome.

The reading of St Thomas is marked by this difference, which cries out

---

[10] 'Der "moralisch" gesehene Gott und nur dieser ist gemeint, wenn Nietzsche sagt: "Gott ist tot." ' Martin Heidegger, *Die ewige Wiederkehr des Gleichen*, in *Nietzsche*, vol. 1 (Pfullingen: Verlag Günther Neske, 1961), p. 321.

[11] See the dense investigation of this issue in Judith Butler, *The Psychic Life of Power: Theories in Subjection* (Stanford, CA: Stanford University Press, 1997).

through the various earnest and noble attempts at recovering the natural law for our use in moral thinking today. In looking to restate this foundation or to recover it as already prepared by the tradition, our very search becomes a further instance of the problematic it resists. Thus it happens that considering natural law has become itself a project, its features rendered into a methodology, so that we seekers of truth can only hear the debate under the form of power. What have become highly contentious issues in American political and ethical debates are themselves the anguished indications of the horns of this dilemma in which moral discourse generally is trapped.

Such things have particular poignancy in the American situation as the outworking of this tradition in a new land. In the rhetorics of liberalism and of liberation with which America was founded, the mature emergence of the human person as sovereign subject of a will made in the image of the divine has been proclaimed. The subject's power to exercise the capacity for reason and to determine its own agency in the world became key emphases of Enlightenment politics and ethics, from out of which the events of history were now to be shaped by human direction. Accordingly nature came to represent an opposing force of unchanging a-historical determinations with which reason must struggle in order to shape the future. Kant's understanding of *Aufklärung* as a way out, *einer Ausgang*, claims the work of transcending reason for the individual, whose nature must be understood to be rational free agency for any upholding of the moral to be possible.[12] Laws then must not only be formed intentionally by such rational agents for the guidance of their public decision-making and the constraint of their private passions and relationships, these being the defining characteristics of a democratic politics. But something like law itself becomes a requirement of the system, serving as that to which subjects must make themselves subject to ensure the functioning of the moral realm at all. Here one notices the overturning, for law has become the means by which the moral retains its power over subjects, who are left with the happy idea of freedom and the barest bones of its reason.

While the American debate about the nature, purpose and content of moral discourse has been lively, energetic and passionate, nonetheless one feels this nihilism to be at work within it. These discussions not only engage thinkers of many backgrounds and commitments in a common concern for the shape of the πόλις, which today is understood to be nothing less than the world, but they also manifest in diverse strands a central and pragmatic conviction that the proper relationship of belief and action is the hinge upon which the good life depends, so that much is

---

[12] See Immanuel Kant, 'Beantwortung der Frage: Was ist Aufklärung?', in *Berlinische Monatsschrift*, No. 2, 1784, pp. 481–94.

expected of its outcome for the completion of subjectivity. The pressure under which guidelines are to be forged for what must now function as a global ethic, serving to bind together disparate peoples and cultures, and the growth of the ethics industry in every area of human affairs, providing the equipment required for effective performance of the business of life – these are indications of an underlying, and in places quite forceful, cultural determination that the moral is yet to save us, if not as redemptive politics, then at least as efficient management of life in the world.

The work of Charles Curran gives poignant illustration of what is going on here. Asserting that '[t]he question of stance or perspective is the most fundamental and logically first consideration in moral theology',[13] the human person as 'agent and subject' is assumed here to be the one who adopts this stance, and who from that position reflects on life and actions in the world and judges the adequacy of the various methods available for making decisions. The subject described is not one who is subject *to* something, but one who is the subject *of* growth and development, change and fulfilment, and so is capable of reaching for perfection in and through its own agency, and must be free in determining its relationship to those things it wills to submit to.[14] To take up this subject position is to embark on the journey of authentic life, which means nothing other than the subject's own completion, even though one expects and hopes there may be many such subjects included in this realisation. For its success in this enterprise, the broadest horizon must be brought into view. Citing Bernard Lonergan's description of horizon 'as a maximum field of vision from a determinate viewpoint', he urges the importance of providing ourselves with a horizon 'comprehensive enough to include all the elements which enter into the way in which the Christian understands reality and the world',[15] a field that, from Curran's particular Christian perspective, is to include also what is 'outside time and beyond history'.[16]

Whatever else may be said about the entanglements in which Curran's work found itself, it is noteworthy here that the stance of the subject has become foundational. It becomes the basis on which an assessment of the natural law approach to moral concerns is to be made. Curran argues from the standpoint labelled 'human', that such approach 'is deficient because it does not integrate the natural or creation into the total Christian perspective',[17] and so is not large or inclusive enough for the

---

[13] Charles E. Curran, *Directions in Fundamental Moral Theology* (Notre Dame, IN: University of Notre Dame Press, 1985), p. 5.
[14] Curran, *Directions*, ch. 3.
[15] Curran, *Directions*, p. 35.
[16] Curran, *Directions*, p. 33.
[17] Curran, *Directions*, p. 7.

flourishing of what belongs to human subjects. Furthermore it puts the subject who makes decisions constantly at risk of 'the danger of physicalism', in consequence of which a person is rendered incapable of the agency by which it is distinguished.[18]

To engage in this kind of critique of the natural law shows the extent to which it has itself become an identifiable cluster of beliefs and concepts, complex and subtle to be sure, but nonetheless an object in the field of the subject's attention, before whom it is being brought for assessment as a useful tool in the methodological kit of moral decision-making. So it is to be evaluated as a possible method or approach to the living of the moral life and is found wanting. The basis on which this assessment rests is the subject, who is now responsible for the good in which this evaluation can be made. The need of the subject to provide itself with the grounds for its moral life could not be more plainly expressed.

If this is but one position among many others that may be taken up with regard to the natural law, it is yet the merest hint of the strife which cuts so deeply into the fabric of this moral debate. Indeed the editors of a new collection of essays suggest that a climate of adversity may precisely be what has stimulated the current 'revival of natural law theory', urging that something of a tenacious spirit may yet uncover its value and show the 'substantial gains (that) remain to be made from engaging with it'.[19] This revival of the value of St Thomas has gained pace in America, offering presentations of nature that might be more congenial in that context, and that indeed might lay to rest some of the more disputed questions that lie between moral theologians and philosophers. Could it become our common ground? This way of speaking about nature as something that might serve us has its roots in the new mood of scholarship influenced by horrifying experiences in the Second World War and by encouragement of the Second Vatican Council for a greater humanisation of the Church's witness.

The voice of Bernard Häring was not alone in calling for 'a new strategy of liberation'[20] which moral theology may serve, for 'its basic task and purpose is to gain the right vision, to assess the main perspectives, and to present those truths and values which should bear upon decisions to be made before God'.[21] In his writings, the natural is worked out in an exercise of vision, by means of an envisioning of that which will 'broaden the horizons of freedom', and so have the power to hold open

---

[18] Curran, *Directions*, pp. 127–8.

[19] Nigel Biggar and Rufus Black (eds.), *The Revival of Natural Law: Philosophical, Theological and Ethical Responses to the Finnis-Grisez School* (Aldershot: Ashgate, 2000), p. xiii.

[20] Bernard Häring, *Free and Faithful in Christ: Moral Theology for Priests and Laity*, vol. 1 (Slough: St Paul Publications, 1978), p. 3.

[21] Häring, *Free and Faithful*, p. 6.

the wide space in which creative fidelity may be exercised. The natural, as this broadest horizon, is to represent and to shape 'man's total environment and life',[22] and thus provide the context for the formation of 'a Christian mind set and that profound vision which is essential for Christian maturity'.[23] Like St Thomas, who apparently was himself 'a creative theologian' in this sense,[24] the moral theologian must embark on a work of 'wholistic understanding', trying to comprehend 'man's total vocation',[25] so that within a vision of wholeness gleaned from biblical and traditional perspectives, 'the value and meaning of Christian life' could be seen, learned from, and adapted into contemporary situations.[26]

Evident in Häring's approach to the natural law tradition is the fact that the distinction of what is eternal and unchanging, which for Plato was the distinguishing character of the transcendent realm of the εἴδη and so of the divine as ὁ ἀεὶ ὄν, is now understood to reside within human nature, so that what is abiding – those 'abiding truths', 'abiding human rights and moral values', 'one abiding design for humankind', and so on[27] – these must be worked out by reflection on our humanness and so from the human perspective, and must reach out towards the broadest possible world-view, projecting out from the individual subject towards that which is most inclusive. It is inevitable then that revelation will provide only a further specification of this vision, which itself merely opens up 'new dimensions and orientations',[28] giving a unique tinge to 'a distinctively Christian vision of the natural law'. This is evidently what Häring considers most urgent 'in view of the Church's dialogue with the modern world, where the first necessity is our own Christian identity'.[29] How much this bears the anxieties of a new world.

The constructed character of the natural here, presented to us as the outcome of the productive imagination, thinking as widely and deeply as possible of that which may encompass the whole, such an oddly fabricated world appears too in Alasdair MacIntyre's study in moral theory. After acknowledging that 'the language and the appearances of morality persist even though the integral substance of morality has to a large degree been fragmented and then in part destroyed',[30] he too offers us an exercise in imagination in order to show us what is happening 'in the

---

[22] Häring, *Free and Faithful*, p. 3.
[23] Häring, *Free and Faithful*, p. 6.
[24] Häring, *Free and Faithful*, p. 43.
[25] Häring, *Free and Faithful*, p. 317.
[26] Häring, *Free and Faithful*, pp. 7–8.
[27] Häring, *Free and Faithful*, p. 323.
[28] Häring, *Free and Faithful*, p. 335.
[29] Häring, *Free and Faithful*, p. 333.
[30] Alasdair MacIntyre, *After Virtue: A Study in Moral Theory* (London: Duckworth, 1981), p. 5.

actual world which we inhabit'.[31] This curious inversion of the Platonic allegory of the cave is performed to bring us before a choice – Nietzsche or Aristotle? – for these are the 'genuine theoretical alternatives confronting anyone trying to analyse the moral condition of our culture'. To be placed before these alternatives reveals the need for 'a vision' that will enable us to see what is happening to us and provide a place from which to make such a fundamental choice about our future.[32] MacIntyre himself, without comment on the already nihilistic character of his own question and of these conditions for its resolution, seeks to make a new start by attending to the virtues, another treasure that the tradition might yield to us.

Even his 'partial and tentative definition' of virtues cannot hold however without some whole to which these are ordered.[33] So this must be found, and we must undertake *to* find it, in the envisioning of a *'telos* which transcends the limited goods of practices by constituting the good of a whole human life, the good of a human life conceived as a unity'. Only this will protect us from arbitrariness in our choices and provide specification of the contexts in which virtues are to inform practice.[34] In St Thomas, he believes, one finds a strong claim (assuming of course that Thomas's teaching is constructed of claims), for 'the unity of the virtues', based on Thomas's assumption 'that there exists a cosmic order which dictates the place of each virtue in a total harmonious scheme of human life. Truth in the moral sphere consists in the conformity of moral judgment to the order of this scheme.'[35] Contemporary moral philosophers are without this world, as MacIntyre is well aware, and so are left adrift with only the bare question, 'Is it rationally justifiable to conceive of each human life as a unity?' and, once this is established, with the project of setting about 'the construction of local forms of community within which civility and the intellectual and moral life can be sustained', work to which much of MacIntyre's later writing is directed.[36] Yet the awkward place of the one who is doing this conceiving remains – the builder of worlds known from the outset to be virtual, blinded – and by now surely also exhausted and bored – by the endless recycling of bright ideas, and anxious about his? her? identity.

The vulnerability of this position is evident also in Jean Porter's work, who writes with some sensitivity to the dilemmas that have arisen recently in the logic of moral reasoning. In her argument for 'reclaiming

---

[31] MacIntyre, *After Virtue*, p. 2.
[32] MacIntyre, *After Virtue*, pp. 104–5.
[33] MacIntyre, *After Virtue*, p. 178.
[34] MacIntyre, *After Virtue*, p. 189.
[35] MacIntyre, *After Virtue*, p. 133.
[36] MacIntyre, *After Virtue*, p. 244.

the tradition for Christian ethics', she sets out to demonstrate that the medieval version of natural law reflection is 'both cogent and supple enough to allow for development and appropriation in our own context' and so to 'serve as a basis for fruitful moral reflection'.[37] She argues that in our interpretation of the tradition, we can fuse together our field of vision with that of an earlier era, and in the new insight gained as these pictures become one, provide the ground for bridging the rifts that perplex and threaten the fruitfulness of moral theologians today.[38] It would be ungenerous to say that the various steps taken in this project are contrived, but there is a sense in which the insistent concern to describe social and intellectual contexts, the twentieth century set alongside the Scholastic, forces us still to map out horizons and place ourselves within them. This yields a definition of nature as 'an ordered totality', a purportedly neutral and inclusive description that is made to seem exactly what both we and the Scholastics are thinking about. Not only does this notion disclose a modern idea of the whole as the biggest imaginable gathering together of everything, and of nature as that space within which human beings make their special appearance and in which diversities of all kinds can be seen and located and so valued.[39] It also skirts entirely the question of what is involved in the thinking of it, of what it means to think in this way.

For the modern way of speaking about nature as a largest conceiveable whole within which everything can be classified and located has turned into the definitively postmodern project of producing the most adequate concept of nature to serve as the context for the re-presenting and re-valuing of all that is, a turn that in itself reveals the supremacy of the moral and its relentless demand on thinking. Indeed her assumption that there is such a thing as a 'concept' of nature at all already reveals this difference, carrying forward as it does the distance between knower and known which was opened up by Kant. For the gap contained by this word allows her to state that 'the natural [is] seen as the ground of human action',[40] a claim that at once hides the different things the

---

[37] Jean Porter, *Natural and Divine Law: Reclaiming the Tradition for Christian Ethics* (Grand Rapids, MI: Eerdmans, 1999), p. 18.

[38] Porter, *Natural and Divine Law*, p. 29. Porter is here aligning her aim with Hans-Georg Gadamer's recommendations in *Truth and Method* (London: Sheed & Ward, 1975).

[39] There is no reference in her book to the work of Fr James Weisheipl OP whose studies of these matters throughout this period would seem to be directly of relevance here, but attention to contexts seems not to permit this. See especially his *Nature and Motion in the Middle Ages*, ed. William E. Carroll (Washington, DC: Catholic University of America Press, 1985). See also Helen S. Lang, *Aristotle's Physics and its Medieval Varieties* (Albany, NY: State University of New York Press, 1992).

[40] Porter, *Natural and Divine Law*, p. 98.

Scholastics have to show us, and performs a reification in seeming to produce a stable foundation to meet our crises. The strangeness of these texts cannot then speak, drawing us into questions that might disturb our understanding, and the very things we think we need to believe are made to seem more sure as a result of their purported endurance over time.

This base provided by nature so conceived gives rise to further 'moral concepts' that are to be tested in their application.[41] Again it is a modern invention of a method for decision-making that requires the positing of concepts as 'prior to theological reflection', and indeed as prior to social expressions that vary across time, a last pale shadow of divine providence.[42] What is going on here but the construction of a realm of concepts as the *a priori*, the always-already-there set up to mediate our salvation by bringing the world and human life into conformity with them according to the requirement of the moral?

The presentation of nature as this large and generally benign space within which things of all kinds come to be seen, is posited as the container of all the values and goods generated within it, a spaciousness whose capacity for diversity appears to be infinite. In its being-posited and being known as such, it is present to us as the simulacrum, the feigning of what is not present which is to serve as the real for us, and so becomes that weightless simulation of the traces of God's existence as sustaining presence.[43] So impelling and yet so hidden is the movement of thought here that one barely may notice the overturning that is taking place through it, and its costs. Lisa Cahill, whose work explicitly reflects upon the problematic of postmodernity, yet enacts it in her continuous use of scare quotes around the word 'nature', and in her claim that 'In a Thomist perspective, the concept "nature" is a means to establish moral goods or ends on the basis of human experience itself.'[44] Nature here is heuristic device. Filling up this receptacle with generalisations derived from experiences, it is noteworthy that women have come into particular prominence in the field of American Aquinas scholarship and in philosophical explorations of natural law.[45] Yet without any consideration of what is being carried out by this machinery of the hyperreal, they assume the place of ματήρ, no longer as any kind of merely natural place but as a

---

[41] Porter, *Natural and Divine Law*, p. 187.

[42] Porter, *Natural and Divine Law*, p. 216. The fact that these concepts are required in a special way in a discussion of 'Marriage and Sexual Ethics' deserves comment at greater length elsewhere.

[43] Jean Baudrillard, 'Simulacra and Simulations', trans. Paul Foss, Paul Patton and Philip Beitchman, in *Selected Writings*, ed. Mark Poster (Oxford: Polity Press, 1988), pp. 166–84 [original publication (New York: Sémiotext(e), 1981), pp. 1–13, 23–49].

[44] Lisa Sowle Cahill, *Sex, Gender and Christian Ethics* (Cambridge: Cambridge University Press, 1996), p. 46.

[45] Martha C. Nussbaum is surely the most prolific and influential of the latter.

declared position of power, claiming themselves to be ones who bear forth the fullness of earth's rich possibilities and protect its entire flourishing from harm.[46]

Such language of moral goods is not unique to women in this revival however, for there are few more ardent spokesmen of their role in 'a sounder theory of morality' than John Finnis, Joseph Boyle and Germain Grisez.[47] Once again a mediation is being sought amid contemporary diremptions of moral discourse, this time between deontology and teleology, with nature serving as the provider of the goods by which this can be accomplished. It is human goods, 'the goods of real people living in the world of experience', in which is the grounding of ethics, and which 'explains both human life's constant and universal features, and its diversity and open-endedness'.[48] Such goods are not only the 'already given ("natural") aspects' that are essential to our being human at all and in that sense are 'obvious' to us, but also extend 'beyond what is naturally given' by providing occasions for us to synthesise and harmonise various elements in the choices we make. What the moral foundation determines then is merely 'the rightness and wrongness of choices by differentiating attitudes toward basic goods', since it is according to one's disposition towards these given but extendable goods that an individual's will is aligned, is disposed toward the entire moral foundation with an attitude of appreciation.[49] In this way Grisez declares and demonstrates the needful foundation of the moral.

At least one outspoken critic of this approach notes the way in which the principles of practical reason have here become mere mechanisms to 'generate the field of possibilities in which choices are necessary', that must be further determined by the will itself.[50] In such a scheme, good too has been emptied of any meaning other than to function as a place-marker for any of the basic and multiple goods that might come to occupy it.[51] Thus, as nature is filled to overflowing with goods, so is our final end evacuated. It is perhaps unsurprising then that, after its many journeys through modernity, the path of natural law theory should come

---

[46] These are themes to be found not only in Cahill's work, but in those of numerous feminist writers who disclaim naturalism while adopting it in another guise. For another feminist recovery of St Thomas, see Christina Traina, *Feminist Ethics and Natural Law: The End of the Anathemas* (Washington, DC: Georgetown University Press, 1999).

[47] John Finnis and Joseph M. Boyle, Jr, 'A Sounder Theory of Morality', in Curran and McCormick (eds.), *Historical Development*, pp. 200–18.

[48] Finnis and Boyle, 'Sounder', p. 202.

[49] Finnis and Boyle, 'Sounder', p. 207.

[50] Ralph McInerny, 'Grisez and Thomism', in Biggar and Black (eds.), *Revival of Natural Law*, p. 67.

[51] McInerny, 'Grisez', p. 69.

to an end in a 'natural law without nature'.[52] Here we find the complete reversal accomplished in Finnis's claim that St Thomas was reasoning from morality to nature, so that 'the teleological conception of nature was made plausible, indeed conceivable, by analogy with the *introspec-tively* luminous, self-evident structure of human well-being, practical reasoning, and human purposive action'.[53] The conclusion of Pauline Westerman is inevitable here, that what we witness in this way of pre-senting the natural is nothing other than 'the disintegration of natural law theory', nature no longer its foundation but an afterthought, and its τέλος, a projection devised from out of human experience.[54]

If thinking of nature has come to an end in this way, what then remains of its law? In an important sense, this is just what we are left with, for what has been outlined in this essay so far is indicative of the overriding tendency of modern thinking towards legalisation precisely in the assertion of its freedom. The prevalence of language of autonomy and of legitimacy in political and ethical thought is entirely at one with the *Drang nach Autonomie* of physics, after which, as Jeffrey Stout has noted, the cosmos can no longer be conceived 'in a moralized, teleologi-cal fashion',[55] but rather is understood to have an independent life, governed by its own law under the axiomatic ideal and connected to con-cepts of 'global constraint, necessity and universality'.[56] The *lex naturæ,* now detached from eternal and human law and turned into another kind of rational consideration altogether, as a description of the laws of nature, cannot merely be brought to us again, without reinforcing the overriding concern with law in which thinking is now ensnared. For this 'juridification' of thinking is disclosive of our situation, illuminating a preoccupation with 'the extrinsic, formal, juridical, certitude of faith' and of moral teaching, that now characterises the contemporary way of understanding.[57]

One indication of this has been the perceived threat of committing the

---

[52] This phrase forms the title of ch. 4 in Lloyd L. Weinreb, *Natural Law and Justice* (Cambridge, MA: Harvard University Press, 1987).

[53] John Finnis, *Natural Law and Natural Rights* (Oxford: Clarendon Press, 1987), p. 52.

[54] Pauline C. Westerman, *The Disintegration of Natural Law Theory: Aquinas to Finnis* (Leiden: Brill, 1998), p. 249.

[55] Jeffrey Stout, 'Truth, Natural Law, and Ethical Theory', in Robert P. George (ed.), *Natural Law Theory: Contemporary Essays* (Oxford: Clarendon Press, 1992), p. 95.

[56] Stout, 'Truth', p. 74.

[57] Ignatius Theodore Eschmann OP, *The Ethics of Saint Thomas Aquinas: Two Courses*, ed. Edward A. Synan (Toronto: Pontifical Institute of Mediaeval Studies, 1997), p. 4. See also a discussion of 'the obsession with law' following the Council of Trent in John Mahoney SJ, *The Making of Moral Theology: A Study of the Roman Catholic Tradition* (Oxford: Clarendon Press, 1987), pp. 35–6.

naturalistic fallacy that has constantly troubled modern moral philosophy, and is encountered throughout considerations of natural law
thinking. As a question about the legitimacy of deriving ethical impera-
tives from statements of fact about nature, it has driven an enquiry into
what might serve as law, that would both indicate and maintain the connection between our knowledge of the world as it is and our practical
reasoning from which decisions arise. Stout claims that '[n]atural law
theory in its traditional form was intertwined with the realist metaphysics of traditional natural philosophy. It sought to provide a kind
of correspondence to the real that would explain what makes moral
sentences true.'[58] The legitimacy of the claims of practical reason are considered to depend upon what Stout and others call 'moral realism', which
like scientific realism, can be the ground that secures our thinking about
truth. So to avoid accusation of this fallacy in considerations of natural
law, we must look for a contemporary way of grasping the *adaequatio ad
rem* of St Thomas and the ὀρθὸς λόγος of Plato. Stout sets himself the task
of providing such assurance. Claiming that he wants to construct 'a conception of higher law suited to a secular moral philosophy . . . keeping
metaphysical assumptions to a minimum' and then 'determine what
additional assumptions would be needed to make it serve the purposes of
a natural law theory of ethics', his essay exemplifies the unstable yet
necessary partnership of realism and constructivism that now characterises the postmodern situation, a realism that is not one except as it is
made so by the constructive enterprise of a subject.[59]

   A second concern with the promulgation of the law is manifest here,
for what would determine the legitimacy of this higher law and by what
authority would it be compelling? As Stout expresses it, how 'can one
make sense of a higher law, if not by defining it in reference to a divine
promulgator?'[60] This question speaks of the empty place that the rise of
humanism has filled, first in its Kantian form as the self-legislation of
rational agents, but more recently as a categorical conception of what is
most universally human, of what most essentially belongs to human
nature in general. The emphasis on the *humanum* by those like Joseph
Fuchs reveals the way in which the end of human life, that *telos* towards
which human life is to be directed with the help of law, is rather brought
to stand behind and before us, as that which is already there and from
out of which each one's life is a necessary unfolding. The being of being
human, no longer futural, is thus made into a prior authority and
measure of value that compels attention to what is called natural by its

---

[58] Stout, 'Truth', p. 95.
[59] Stout, 'Truth', pp. 74–5.
[60] Stout, 'Truth', p. 73.

preceding and so determining every decision, even those that would oppose its influence.

On the whole, moral theologians have depended upon the human sciences, rather than the natural or physical ones, to yield insights, broadly understood as anthropological, by which to formulate the category of this 'morality of genuine being-human'.[61] On this basis, Fuchs can claim that norms of conduct 'to the extent to which they proclaim truth . . . are universally human',[62] with the result that the distinctively Christian, only related to truth in so far as it too speaks from this *humanum*, becomes simply a matter of 'intentionality', of a 'full, personal decision' and of the 'actual presence' of this intention in one's 'particular attitude and conduct'.[63] Does this not rather fulfil the very counter-resonance that is the essential movement of Nietzsche's philosophy by carrying out its will to invert in favour of the subject, and so does not this way of thinking complete the humanisation of being to which his doctrine of the return tends, rather than provide any kind of a foundation for its overcoming?[64]

The aim of this essay has been to explore the turn of events that renders the contemporary way to St Thomas problematic, that discloses the striving to appropriate his teaching into the service of contexts as these are represented by intentional Cartesian subjects, within which horizon what he has to say can be assessed and used. The projects of envisioning, construction and valuation by which contemporary thinking is consumed are not of course phenomena exclusive to American Aquinas scholarship, but manifest, as this essay has argued, the overturning of a way of thinking that has prevailed throughout the western tradition into the nihilism that lay waiting within. The extent of its possibility has unfolded through modernity, and bequeaths to those who come after it, a nostalgia for remaking what has been lost and a stubborn

[61] Joseph Fuchs SJ, 'Is There a Christian Morality?', in Charles E. Curran and Richard A. McCormick SJ (eds.), *Readings in Moral Theology, No. 2: The Distinctiveness of Christian Ethics* (New York: Paulist Press, 1980). This piece was originally given at a conference in Zurich in 1968 and published in 1970 in *Stimmen der Zeit*. See also his more full and systematic treatment of this theme in Josef Fuchs SJ, *Lex naturæ: zur Theologie des Naturrechts* (Düsseldorf: Patmos, 1955) [ET: *Natural Law: A Theological Investigation*, trans. Helmut Reckter SJ and John A. Dowling (Dublin: Gill & Son, 1965)].

[62] Fuchs, 'Christian Morality', p. 3.

[63] Fuchs, 'Christian Morality', p. 6.

[64] 'Dieses Auszeichnende betrifft, wenn anders dieser Gedanke der Grundgedanke von Nietzsches Philosophie ist, diese in ihrem Wesen. Sie ist in ihrer inneren Denkbewegung eine Gegenbewegung . . . Das, *wogegen* es denkt, will es nicht ablehnen, um anderes an seine Stelle zu setzen. Nietzsches Denken will *umkehren*.' Martin Heidegger, 'Der Bereich des Wiederkunftsgedankens: Die Wiederkunftslehre als Überwindung des Nihilismus', in *Nietzsche*, vol. 1, p. 433.

adherence to the skeleton of its way of thinking as mere methodology. If this is at the same time a disclosure of what has become of the moral as the way of thinking by which the working out of the subject's salvation was to be accomplished, then we who have come into the end of this way are standing at a most distressing threshold, rendered vulnerable at a place that cannot be traversed.

It is striking then that St Thomas may have things to teach us that run against the grain of the recovery traced here, precisely by turning our attention to the grasp of reason and the manner of its producing, and by showing us at that point a way for the reception and articulation of what is known to faith. For his consideration of the whole that we call nature is only as this comes to appear to the eye of faith, and so as it is seen, not from what we can make out of it, however dimly or expansively, but from what God has made of it, for it is here that its nature is disclosed as creation. This is the place at which St Thomas speaks of *totius entis*, and it is here no intellectual or philosophical concept that would bind all together. Rather is this speaking the unveiling of a relation with that in which is the beginning, the *principium*, ἀρχή and αἰτία, of all that is.[65] So this is for him the place of an encounter, where the hold upon what can be thought is known to be a limit precisely as it is opened from without, made known as the difference that lies between God and all that is dependent for being upon God. The breaking-through into thought that occurs in faith's receiving of what is revealed here does not happen by means of some necessary securing of an outside for the inward certainty of a thinking subject, for this would only bind the subject endlessly to its own presupposition and so produce an outside in name only. Rather are we shown that this break-through takes place as one rises up to the threshold that is the furthest reach of reason's possibilities, and as one is oneself disclosed there in the futility of all attempts to know as God knows and in the sheer graciousness of which one's own thinking participates.

Each of the points made in this question concerning the mode of emanation of all things from the First Principle is indicative of this difference, in pointing us both to the distinction of creation that is 'the proper act of God alone',[66] and to that *principium* to which everything that is is ordered as effects to a cause, and furthermore in bringing us into

---

[65] *ST* Ia, Q. 45, art. 3, resp.: 'Unde relinquitur quod creatio in creatura non sit nisi relatio quaedam ad Creatorem, ut ad principium sui esse . . .' [ET: 'Hence creation in the creature is only a certain relation to the Creator as to the principle of its being . . .' Fathers of the English Dominican Province (Allen, TX: Christian Classics, 1981)].

[66] *ST* Ia, Q. 45, art. 5, resp.: 'Unde manifestum est quod creatio est propria actio ipsius Dei'. ['Hence it is manifest that creation is the proper act of God alone'.]

this difference by the way of our thinking, so that it takes place in us. For St Thomas, we are thus to find ourselves as ones so ordered among the things of creation to the First Principle. Unlike reason's work of envisioning that always bears its own assumptions, 'creation is not from anything presupposed' but is rather 'what is presupposed to all other effects'.[67] To come upon this point is for reason to be unburdened of its instrumentalising and to stand before what cannot be produced. Yet it is also the case that 'in all creatures there is found the trace of the Trinity', which is what it is for each creature to be at all,[68] and here is reason given its task of understanding, which means of coming to realise itself as that in which is found the divine image. To hold to the twofold character of this difference, that both preserves and distinguishes what is of God, and that simultaneously makes of me as creature the place for this illumination of the world and of God together, this is of utmost significance for the consideration of natural law.

For St Thomas, the primary concern is with the *manner* of our coming together with God, of our being brought together with the Creator, as ones who already find ourselves cast about among the things of the world that concern us, that take us up in their affairs. So the natural law must be considered as a further working out of the doctrine of creation. These questions about the extrinsic principles by which human acts are instructed by God, these are to guide us in considering how this beginning that is the principle of my being created, how this beginning that comes from without myself, can take place in me, and in its preparation of me, in its shaping and guiding of my life, so move me to the good which is my end in God.[69] Reason is brought out into its fullest stretch as 'the rule and measure of human acts', distinctly as it directs us to this end, and this means as it accomplishes, as it carries out, that to which it is ordered, and so binds us to the Creator.[70] Such work is done, not by a willed appeal to nature as that which is brought to stand under us to

---

[67] *ST* Ia, Q. 45, art. 5, resp.: 'Unde non potest aliquid operari dispositive et instrumentaliter ad hunc effectum, cum creatio non sit ex aliquo praesupposito, quod possit disponi per actionem instrumentalis agentis.' ['Hence nothing else can act dispositively and instrumentally to this effect, since creation is not from anything presupposed, which can be disposed by the action of the instrumental agent.']

[68] *ST* Ia, Q. 45, art. 7, resp.: 'Sed in creaturis omnibus invenitur repraesentatio Trinitatis per modum vestigii, inquantum in qualibet creatura inveniuntur aliqua quae necesse est reducere in divinas Personas sicut in causam.' ['But in all creatures there is found the trace of the Trinity, inasmuch as in every creature are found some things which are necessarily reduced to the divine Persons as to their cause.']

[69] *ST* IaIIae, Q. 90, prologue.

[70] *ST* IaIIae, Q. 90, art. 1, resp.: 'Regula autem et mensura humanorum actuum est ratio, quae est primum principium actuum humanorum, ut ex praedictis patet: rationis enim est ordinare ad finem, qui est primum principium in agendis, secundum Philosophum.'

carry us across a threatening chaos, but rather by a coming to understand, and this means by a letting be known to one, that from which one is ruled and measured. The 'from which', *a Deo ordinatur*,[71] that reason stretches to grasp, but that can only be received at this threshold, is the marker of this difference in which the natural law is a participation.[72]

To think through the nature of the natural law in St Thomas is thus and necessarily to be taken into a hierarchy of thinking, by which is meant, that thinking is directed to the place of the crossing over of the divine and the human, to where what is unattainable through itself is granted in order to be taken up, assumed in one's life. How entirely this is lost in the flattening of contemporary discourse concerning natural law, which renders it into a set of requirements for the full flourishing of life, that are easily grasped and set into a formula readily adaptable to one's particular circumstances, as if there were nothing further to consider than the practical details of a scheme ordered only to its own efficiency. Have we too fallen into empty formulaic applications, more sophisticated though they may sound to us, which cannot bring us into the life that is promised?

The burden that lies upon the natural law in St Thomas is to provide a way for creatures to realise their being created *ad imaginem Dei*, to the image of God, and so of their being moved towards that final good which is *beatitudo*.[73] This is a way that we can try to delineate to the best of our knowledge, but that for St Thomas cannot be fully specified or insured. Any description of nature and of what is natural is something that must be worked out from among the accidents in which our belonging to God is hidden in this world,[74] a task that we may not assume has already been completed for us. It is not just that details change with context and circumstance, which St Thomas himself acknowledges, but that there is always more to what is meant by 'nature' than can be said, so that every specification will fall short of a total grasp. This way is always therefore a following after that elusive richness of meaning, that disclosure of what is yet unsaid that is always ahead of us, that lies not in our past but in our

---

[71] *ST* IaIIae, Q. 91, art. 1, ad 1: 'secundum quod a Deo ordinatur ad gubernationem rerum ab ipso praecognitarum'. Cf. art. 2, resp. 'a lege aeterna regulentur et mensurentur'. [The English translation has this: 'in so far as it is ordained *by* God to the government of things foreknown by Him' (my emphasis). However, the prepositions 'from' and 'to' give a better sense of the movement of St Thomas's thought here.]

[72] *ST* IaIIae, Q. 91, art. 2, resp.: 'Unde et in ipsa participatur ratio aeterna, per quam habet naturalem inclinationem ad debitum actum et finem. Et talis participatio legis aeternae in rationali creatura lex naturalis dicitur.' ['Wherefore it has a share of the Eternal Reason, whereby it has a natural inclination to its proper act and end: and this participation of the eternal law in the rational creature is called the natural law.']

[73] *ST* IaIIae, prologue.

[74] As St Thomas particularly undertakes in *ST* Q. 94, art. 2, resp.

future as who we are to be in God. Accordingly, the leading question of any enquiry into natural law is never in our possession, but always is heard from beyond, beckoning us into our own coming-to-be.

St Thomas is a consummate teacher in this way. He speaks at every point from faith towards faith, in order that the love of God may touch the intellect and will, and so move that which awaits his coming.[75] To learn from him is to understand that the work of moral theology is entirely a formative enquiry, not a construction in the modern sense of a project, but an undergoing of the soul by which it is made over into that for which it has been made. One's own life is entirely at stake in this pedagogy, for the soul is being informed by that which is sought, and so itself becomes the founding place, the ground that is prepared for the coming of God. This must then, in the end, be a way of redemption, that lifts us on to the point we cannot cross as now having been broken open, and so takes us to the place of the Crucified One by whose death and resurrection we are taken over into God. St Thomas is fixed on this point, drawn steadfastly to it, as one who knows life utterly to depend upon the mercy that overflows here, that lays itself across the aporia of reason, and that opens to us the door of heaven. In considering natural law, is the time for this teaching now once again upon us?

---

[75] *ST* IaIIae, Q. 9, art. 6; Q. 10, arts. 1–2.

Thomas Aquinas and Contemporary Theology

OTTO-HERMANN PESCH

The silence surrounding Thomas Aquinas

'So that everyone knows where they stand, it should be said right at the outset what the issue is here. It is a warning against the forgetting of Thomas Aquinas in contemporary Catholic theology.' Thus Karl Rahner in a talk on Bavarian Radio on 29 December 1970.[1] He went on to say:

> On the whole an uncanny silence surrounds Aquinas in theology today. One has only to consult the lists of major new theological publications to see how far he has lost his position just in terms of the counts of the number of theologians quoted here and there by authors trying to appear scholarly.[2]

Only eight years earlier the same Karl Rahner had published an introductory essay to the dissertation of his pupil Johann Baptist Metz on Christian anthropocentrism in Aquinas's thinking.[3] His theme was that one should understand the familiar teachings of the Church and even the prescriptions of canon law with regard to the study of Thomas Aquinas and his decisive importance in the training of Catholic theologians in order *not* to accord an intolerably absolutist status to Thomist doctrine.[4]

---

[1] Karl Rahner, 'Bekenntnis zu Thomas von Aquin', in *Schriften zur Theologie*, vol. 10 (Zurich: Benziger, 1972), pp. 11–20, p. 11: 'Gleich am Anfang soll gesagt werden, worum es hier geht, damit jeder weib, woran er ist. Es handelt sich uns eine Mahnung, Thomas von Aquin in der heutigen katholischen Theologie nicht zu vergessen.'

[2] Rahner, 'Bekenntnis zu Thomas von Aquin', p. 11: 'Im ganzen wird es . . . um Thomas unheimlich still in der heutigen Theologie. Man muß nur einmal die Register großer theologischer Neuerscheinungen aufschlagen, um zu sehen, wie weit Thomas zurückgezuckt ist in die Zahl der vielen Theologen, die man, wenn man gelehrt tun will, da und dort einmal zitiert.'

[3] Karl Rahner, 'Einführender Essay', in J. B. Metz, *Christliche Anthropozentrik: Über die Denkform des Thomas von Aquin* (Munich: Herder, 1962), pp. 9–20.

[4] *Codex Iuris Canonici* (Vatican, 1917), Canon 1366, §2.

Here, then, are two essays on the significance of St Thomas for (then) contemporary theology that have exactly opposing thrusts: playing it down on the one hand, commending it on the other, rejecting absolutist claims here, warning against neglect there! Admittedly these eight years cover the major historical event for the Church of the Second Vatican Council and the exciting years of its first effects. The Council still refers expressly in two texts to St Thomas's importance in the sphere of ecclesiastical education.[5] But it already all sounds much 'quieter' than previously.[6] The 'quieter' note of the Council is however only the restrained echo of new tones long-since struck. Following the Council, these admittedly swelled, as they did elsewhere, into a mighty new sound: one which silenced the old music, or, where it was still played, drowned it out. Hence the warning to continue to keep an ear open for Aquinas.

Is the loss of interest in St Thomas, then, more, or other, than a swing of the pendulum to the opposite extreme, a swing whose impulse derives from the fact that the pendulum was held over to one side for so long? In any event, to reflect on the theme of 'Thomas Aquinas and Contemporary Theology', is to attempt nothing less than to address our thoughts to the situation of Catholic theology and theology in general against the background of the challenges and developments of the twentieth century. In 1974, the year of the 700th anniversary of Aquinas's death, the Catholic Academy in Bavaria could hold an Aquinas conference with the provocative title 'Authority without Weight'.[7] Did this properly repre-

---

[5] See *Gravissimum educationis* (Declaration on Christian Education), Art. 10; *Optatam totius* (Decree on the Education of Priests), Art. 10, in *Sacrosanctum Oecumenicum Concilium Vaticanun II: Constitutiones, Decreta, Declarationes: Cura et studio Secretariae Generalis Concilii Oecumenici Vaticano II* (Vatican, 1966) [ET: in A. Flannery OP, *Vatican Council II: The Conciliar and Postconciliar Documents* (Northport, NY: Costello Publishing Company, 1992 (revised))]. The first text refers to the speech of Pope Paul VI to the Sixth International Thomist Congress on 10 September 1965, the second to the addresses of Pope Pius XII of 24 June 1939 and Pope Paul VI of 12 March 1964.

[6] Rahner, 'Bekenntnis zu Thomas von Aquin', p. 11.

[7] The conference took place on 16–17 February 1974 in Munich. Documentation of the conference papers is unfortunately not available. The following papers have been published singly: J. Baur, 'Fragen eines evangelischen Theologen an Thomas von Aquin', in L. Oeing-Hanhoff (ed.), *Thomas von Aquin 1274/1974* (Munich: Kösel Verlag, 1974), pp. 161–74; W. Kluxen, 'Metaphysik und praktische Vernunft: Über ihre Zuordnung bei Thomas von Aquin', in *Thomas von Aquin 1274/1974*, pp. 73–96. Much expanded statements based on papers presented at the conference are: L. Oeing-Hanhoff, 'Thomas von Aquin und die gegenwärtige katholische Theologie', in W.-P. Eckert (ed.), *Thomas von Aquino: Interpretation und Rezeption: Studien and Texte* (Mainz: Matthias-Grünewald, 1974), pp. 245–306; U. Horst, 'Thomas von Aquin – Ein Heiliger ohne Autorität?', *Die neue Ordnung in Kirche, Staat, Gesellschaft, Kultur* 28 (1974), pp. 171–8; R. Heinzmann, 'Anima unica forma corporis: Thomas von Aquin als Überwinder des platonisch-neuplatonistischen Dualismus', *Philosophisches Jahrbuch* 93 (1986), pp. 236–59.

sent the situation? If not, what basis is there for objecting to the thesis of the 'silence surrounding Aquinas'? If the answer is yes, does it still hold true today, in the opening years of a new millennium?

The course of Aquinas scholarship in the twentieth century

Which present, and which St Thomas?

We must first clear about dating the 'present' within which we examine St Thomas's importance. However many-layered and unclear, this begins where a prior phase in theology has irrevocably ended, and any return is precluded by the insight gained for all time after historical thinking entered theology in the first half of the twentieth century. This insight runs as follows: the history of the Church and of theology is not just made up of a handing-on intact of unchangeably formulated truths in the form of doctrinal phrases through the vicissitudes of time and allowing change only as a greater formulaic precision. It is made up in real historical change in articulating a truth of faith itself, thus no longer disputing epoch-making breaks or new beginnings. Historical circumstances themselves have a role in writing these formulations of faith. The continuity of the one truth, to which the Church and its tradition of faith always adheres through the working of the Holy Spirit, is not to be sought in the surface aspects of linguistic formulation. It is to be sought in its 'intention', in whatever the thrust of its meaning, to articulate ever anew God's one mystery, historically disclosed for us in Jesus Christ, in the light of the presuppositions of each age and the conceptual means available to it. Even if unable to specify a particular date, one can point to dates of symbolic significance when the impact of an insight can be publicly noted and the way back is increasingly closed off. For Germany, such symbolic dates would perhaps be the appearance of Karl Adam's two repeatedly republished books, *Das Wesen des Katholizismus* and *Jesus Christus*, or the appearance of the first edition of Michael Schmaus's *Dogma*. In France one thinks of the numerous essays by Marie-Dominique Chenu, begun already in the 1920s, the epoch-making and repeatedly republished book, *Catholicism*, by Henri de Lubac as well as his historico-theological essays appearing in collected form in his 1946 book *Surnaturel*. This book became the classic text of the *Nouvelle théologie*.[8]

---

[8] K. Adam, *Das Wesen des Katholizismus* (Düsseldorf: Patmos Verlag, 1957 (1924)); *Jesus Christus* (Düsseldorf: Matthias-Grünewald Verlag, 1933); for translation, see M. Schmaus, *Dogma*, 6 vols. (New York: Sheed & Ward, 1968–77); Chenu's articles are collected in: M.-D. Chenu, *La Parole de Dieu*, vol. 1: *La foi dans l'intelligence*; vol. 2: *L'Evangelie dans le temps* (Paris: Éditions du Cerf, 1964) [ET: in one volume as *Faith and Theology* (Dublin: Gill & Son, 1968)]; de

The processes represented by these works and their times of appearance all have to do indirectly, but also in many ways directly, with Aquinas.[9] Michael Schmaus as a writer on patristics is thus also known as an eminent scholar of the Middle Ages.[10] The contributions of both French theologians referred to are in part direct investigations of the theology of St Thomas. For Aquinas also had first to be freed from the unhistorical perspective into which he had slipped and where he had remained until the time he could achieve new and fruitful importance in the developments of Catholic theology indicated. Were he really as one had hitherto understood him and claimed him to be, one could have expected nothing from him.

The historically-informed re-orientation in theology and the historically-informed inquiry into Aquinas thus go hand in hand, the latter deriving from an attempt at an answer to the former. And like the new departures in theology generally, the new view of St Thomas also has a symbolic date: 1950, the year of the first appearance of the introduction to Aquinas by Marie-Dominique Chenu.[11] His preliminary works stemmed from the 1930s.[12] They triggered the debate lasting several decades over the plan of the *Summa Theologiae*. The question, 'Which present, and which Aquinas?' can thus be answered as follows: we are dealing with the theology following the rejection of the neo-scholastic understanding of faith and theology, and with the historical St Thomas, who, as was recognised under the impulse of the new theology, had been

---

Lubac, Cardinal H.: *Catholicisme: Les aspects sociaux du dogme* (Paris: Éditions du Cerf, 1938) [ET: *Catholicism: A Study of Dogma in Relation to the Corporate Destiny of Mankind* (London: Burns & Oates, 1950)]; *Surnaturel: Études historiques* (Paris: Aubier, 1946) [ET: *The Mystery of the Supernatural* (New York: Herder and Herder, 1967)].

[9] For reviews and insights: H. J. Schultz (ed.), *Tendenzen der Theologie im 20. Jahrhundert* (Stuttgart: Kreuz-Verlag, 1966); H. Vorgrimler and R. van der Gucht (eds.), *Bilanz der Theologie im 20. Jahrhundert: Perspektiven, Strömungen, Motive in der christlichen und nichtchristlichen Welt*, 3 vols. [supplementary volume *Bahnbrechende Theologen*] (Freiburg im Breisgau: Herder, 1969-70); O.-H. Pesch, 'Sachliteratur zur katholischen Theologie', in R. Radler (ed.), *Kindlers Literaturgeschichte der Gegenwart: Die deutschsprachige Sachliteratur nach 1945* (Munich: Kindler Verlag, 1978), pp. 204–42.

[10] See R. Heinzmann, 'Die Identität des Christentums im Umbruch des 20. Jahrhunderts', *Münchener Theologische Zeitschrift* 38 (1987), pp. 115–33; R. Heinzmann, 'Michael Schmaus zum Gedenken', *Münchener Theologische Zeitschrift* 45 (1994), pp. 115–35.

[11] M.-D. Chenu, *Introduction à l'étude de saint Thomas d'Aquin* (Paris: Éditions du Cerf, 1950) [ET: as *Toward Understanding Saint Thomas* (Chicago: Henry Regnery, 1964)].

[12] M.-D. Chenu, 'Le plan de la somme théologique de saint Thomas', *Revue thomiste* 47 (1939), pp. 93–107.

elevated incorrectly and mistakenly to being the key spokesman for neo-Scholasticism.

At this point it is worth taking a look back to get as clear a view as possible of the changed perspective we now have on Aquinas before turning to the matter in hand. Of course, we can only do this with a few key words and headlines which do not amount even to so much as an outline sketch, concentrating on the German-language literature. Nevertheless, in the meantime all the relevant aspects are now relatively easy to follow in the literature.[13]

From 'true teacher' to 'Father of the Church'

It is ironic that St Thomas owes his normative position as 'true, authentic teacher' of the Church – or better put in view of the often distressing consequences, tragic – to the historical event of the Reformation.[14] It was in the late Middle Ages, and only in the Thomist school that took its name from him, that Aquinas has been the definitive figure, his teaching dictating the definitive orientation.

As Martin Luther, for reasons that we cannot go into here, cut himself free of his theological roots in the *via moderna* of the late medieval Ockhamist thinking, turned to St Augustine, after whom his order was named, and on this basis criticised the practice of indulgences and the doctrine of grace and the sacraments and the ecclesiology that this implied, his first theological and clerical opponents were Thomists.[15] These refused to view the conflict that had broken out as a mere argument among schools of thought but, in opposing Luther, asserted that Thomist teaching was the uniquely binding doctrine of the Church. This made Aquinas *the* enemy for Luther. He did not realise that in his struggle to overcome Ockhamism, he would have had St Thomas on his side as far the decisive points of the doctrine of grace and the sacraments

---

[13] It would be desirable here to consult a history of Thomism – if one existed! See in lieu of one, O.-H. Pesch, *Lexikon für Theologie und Kirche*, vol. 10, 1965, pp. 157–67 and the literature cited there; O.-H. Pesch, *Thomas von Aquin, Grenze und Größe mittelalterlicher Theologie: Eine Einführung* (Mainz: Matthias-Grünewald Verlag, 1995 (1988)), pp. 27–38; D. Berger, 'S. Thoma praesertim magistro . . . Überlegungen zur Aktualität des Thomismus', *Forum Katholischer Theologie* 15 (1999) pp. 80–202.

[14] O.-H. Pesch, *Martin Luther, Thomas von Aquin und die reformatorische Kritik an der Scholastik: Zur Geschichte und Wirkungsgeschichte eines Mißverständnisses mit weltgeschichtlichen Folgen*, No. 12 (Hamburg: Verlag Vandenhoeck & Ruprecht, 1994).

[15] For summary see O.-H. Pesch, *Hinführung zu Luther* (Mainz: Matthias-Grünewald Verlag, 1983), pp. 48–115; and then B. Lohse, *Luthers Theologie in ihre, historischen Entwicklung und in ihrem systematischen Zusammenhang* (Göttingen: Vandenhoeck & Ruprecht, 1997), pp. 29–40, 47–61.

were concerned. And so the Council of Trent went back with greater emphasis to St Thomas and the Thomist school and, with due caution, to a Thomist interpretation of Augustine. The consequence was that a Thomist interpretation of the decisions of the Council of Trent prevailed, at least in the doctrine of justification.[16]

At any event, in the period following the Council of Trent the Ockhamist tradition fell into abeyance and the teachings of Duns Scotus lived on only in the colleges and faculties of the Franciscans. In their place new schools formed, based on Thomist thought, which had now become the norm. This held especially for the faculties of the young Jesuit order.

All the competing 'Thomist' positions were overtaken by the challenges of the Enlightenment in the eighteenth century. A rediscovery of Thomas Aquinas started at the end of the eighteenth century, with the beginnings of neo-Thomism. Thus for early nineteenth-century Catholic theology Aquinas became a bulwark against the new philosophical and political movements of the time – Rationalism, German Idealism, Liberalism, Socialism, critical religious studies. In the second half of the century St Thomas the theologian became the key figure invoked in support of a re-invigorated papacy and the First Vatican Council, whose climax is the Thomist Encyclical *Aeterni Patris* of 4 August 1887. In this Encyclical Pope Leo XIII presents Aquinas as *the* true teacher of the Church and exhorts all theologians to adopt his methods.[17] The Church's law book, the *Codex Iuris Canonici* of 1917, elevates this exhortation to a canonical prescription.[18]

Thus the philosophy and theology of Aquinas held an unchallenged position in the Catholic Church until well into the years following the Second World War. Arguments like the following were held to be substantiated even after the war: it is unthinkable that the true teacher of the

---

[16] See on this and the following O.-H. Pesch and A. Peters, *Einführung in die Lehre von Gnade und Rechtfertigung* (Darmstadt: Wissenschaftliche Buchgesellschaft, 1981), pp. 169–221, and pp. 260ff.; O.-H. Pesch and A. Peters, 'Kernpunkte der Kontroverse. Die antireformatorischen Lehrentscheidungen des Konzils von Trient (1545–1563) und die Folgen', in B. J. Hilberath and W. Pannenberg (eds.), *Zur Zukunft der Ökumene: Die 'Gemeinsame Erklärung zur Rechtfertigungslehre'* (Regensburg: Friedrich Pustet, 1999), pp. 24–57, where specialist literature is cited.

[17] Cf. *Acta Sanctae Sedis*, vol. 11 (Vatican, 1878–9), pp. 98ff. [ET: by J. Wynne SJ in *The Great Encyclical Letters of Pope Leo XIII* (New York: Benziger Brothers, 1903)].

[18] See note 4 above. The prescription is sharpened by the 24 'anerkannten Thesen der thomistischen Philosophie' of 27 July 1914, with documentation Denzinger-Schönmetzer (eds), *Enchiridion symbolorum definitionum et declarationum de rebus fidei et morum* [hereafter abbreviated (DS)], §§ 3601–3624. For the background and on the argument about the binding nature of the 'theses', which began immediately, and on further ecclesiastical pronouncements, see the editorial introduction in DS, and also Rahner, 'Einführender Essay'.

Church teaches otherwise than the Church itself – even the latter day Church. In case of doubt as to the correct interpretation of St Thomas, therefore, the Church's teaching, even though a later one, is the appropriate criterion to apply.[19]

This universal validity claimed for Thomas Aquinas is overlaid in philosophy and theology by the assumed correspondence between Aquinas himself and the tradition of the Thomist school – in so far as this itself has a unanimous view. The historical research into Thomas Aquinas beginning in the second half of the nineteenth century also expected to find, and therefore had first to look for, confirmation of the neo-scholastic picture of Aquinas. A distinction between Thomas Aquinas and Thomism long remained unremarked.[20] Below the surface of this armour-plated certainty of Catholic theology under the banner of Aquinas, however, change had long been under way, occasionally in such a way as to arouse mistrust in certain 'high quarters' and to provoke 'measures' against, for example, Chenu and Congar. This change has four aspects, which again we can only point out headline form.[21]

The first stage consists of the discovery of the *Christian* philosopher Thomas Aquinas, whose philosophy is more than, and different from, a more or less laboured reconciling of a new version of the Aristotelian philosophy with Christian belief. This new view is exemplified in France by Étienne Gilson, and in Germany by Joseph Pieper.[22] The second stage is generally an increased attention to Aquinas's *theology*. The new intellectual mood within the Catholic theology after the First World War – despite the blockade imposed by the anti-modernist decisions of Rome – gave added weight to the question of what the *theology* of Aquinas might have to contribute to the renewal of ecclesiastical thought. In the German-speaking countries researchers like Martin Grabmann, Arthur

---

[19] See, for example, A. Michel, 'La grâce sanctifiante et la justice originelle', *Revue thomiste* 26 (1921), pp. 424–30, see esp. pp. 424–5.

[20] Details are to be found in Pesch, *Thomas von Aquin*, pp. 31ff.

[21] The best overview is that by the Protestant theologian U. Kühn, *Via caritatis: Theologie des Gesetzes bei Thomas von Aquin* (Berlin: Vandenhoeck & Ruprecht, 1964), pp. 21–48. Protestant study of Aquinas and ecumenical discussion of him does not *begin* with Kühn, but he is one of its pioneers and remains its most representative voice, at any rate in the German-speaking countries, until the present time.

[22] See J. Pieper: *Philosophia negativa: Zwei Versuche Über Thomas von Aquin* (Munich: Hochland-Kösel, 1953); *Thomas von Aquin: Leben und Werk* (Munich: Kösel Verlag, 1986); *Scholastik, Gestalten und Probleme mittelalterlicher Philosophie* (Munich: Kösel Verlag, 1986). See also Étienne Gilson: *L'esprit de la philosophie médiévale* (Paris: J. Vrin, 1944 (1932)); *Le thomisme: Introduction à la philosophie de saint Thomas d'Aquin* (Paris: J. Vrin, 1972) [ET: *The Philosophy of St. Thomas Aquinas* (Cambridge: Heffers, 1929)]. Reducing Aquinas to his philosophy began as early as the fourteenth century and has exercised an influence down to the present day.

Michael Landgraf and their students represent this second step in Aquinas scholarship.[23] In France there are, besides de Lubac and Chenu, the theologians of the Dominican college in Le Saulchoir near Paris, and among these especially Yves Congar.

The third stage, triggered by the discovery of history in the theology of both confessions, leads to what is surely the most surprising discovery of modern Aquinas scholarship. This is that the picture of an Aquinas free of historical context and merely indulging in conceptual speculations is a myth. It is especially here that the discussion on the theological meaning of the construction of the *Summa Theologiae*, begun by Chenu in 1939, assumes its importance.[24]

Having reached this point – and this is the fourth stage – research on Aquinas becomes a theme for both confessions. Released from the protective custody of Thomism, and revealed as a Christian philosopher and an authentic theologian interpreting history in terms of salvation, Aquinas can now be a real conversation-partner for Protestant theology.[25] The latter is now producing its own Aquinas research, which, through publications and academic lecture series, in all seriousness poses questions about St Thomas as a part of the 'patrimony' (*Vätererbe*, Ulrich Kühn) of Reformation theology too. Are we thus to see St Thomas as a 'Father of the Church' also for Protestant theology? This last stage of course also clearly interacts with processes and events at the Second Vatican Council which we must now briefly relate.

Aquinas and the Second Vatican Council

Roman theologians of neo-Thomist persuasion had produced for the Council a draft submission *De doctrina S. Thomas servanda*. In this text, a sort of canonisation of Thomist *philosophy* was proposed to the Council in all seriousness. Also, it was proposed, the philosophical methods and principles of Aquinas should be adhered to without discussion and should be approved as a 'dogmatic fact' by all believers because

---

[23] A true reflection of this situation in research is to be found not only in the collected essays of M. Grabmann, *Mittelalterliches Geistesleben*, 3 vols. (Munich: Kösel Verlag, 1926–56), but also especially in the *Festschrift* for Martin Grabmann: A. Lang, J. Lechner and M. Schmaus (eds.), *Aus der Geisteswelt des Mittelalters*, 2 vols. (Münster: Aschendorff Verlag, 1935).

[24] See M.-D. Chenu, 'Le plan de la somme théologique de saint Thomas', *Revue thomiste* 47 (1939), pp. 93–107. This became chapter eleven of *Toward Understanding Saint Thomas*, with slight alterations.

[25] Symptomatic here are the numerous references in the edition of *Bekenntnisschriften der Evangelisch-Lutherischen Kirche* (BSLK) (Göttingen: Vandenhoeck & Ruprecht, 1959), where Aquinas is presented as the key figure in medieval theology, also where he is not named at all in the text.

of their close connection with the dogmas of the Church![26] The Council did not in the event accede to this absolutist claim of neo-Thomism, but came down instead on the side of the new view of Aquinas. Aquinas is mentioned twice. How 'Faith and Reason come together in the one Truth' is shown by the example of the 'Teachers of the Church, especially St. Thomas Aquinas'.[27] Students of theology must 'learn with St. Thomas as their master to penetrate by their speculations deeper into the secrets of salvation in their totality and to understand their interconnections, in order as far as possible to illuminate them'.[28] No less, but also no more! The new canon law of 1983 draws the consequences. Missing now are the old obligations and strictures, missing too is the ban on deviant opinions.[29]

It was through this break with the body of neo-Thomist thought that there first came about that silence surrounding Aquinas in the first decade following the Council that prompted Karl Rahner's warning. It was precisely at this point that a new 'Aquinas wave' broke out, especially in Germany, the USA and the Netherlands, that has lasted until today, and has embraced Protestant theology. It discloses the real Aquinas with his limitations and in his greatness, in a word, in *his* time – so that he becomes a model for a theology for *our* time which is at one and the same time appropriate, accords with the Bible, has regard to tradition, and fearlessly poses questions. And so, before addressing ourselves directly to contemporary theology, we must cast a brief glance over this new Aquinas wave, again only in headlines.

---

[26] Relevant here is chapter 3 of the draft by the Preparatory Commission for Studies and Seminars for a decree *de obsequio erga Ecclesiae magisterium in tradendis disciplinis sacris*. See on this Giovanni Caprile, 'Entstehungsgeschichte und Inhalt der vorbereitenden Schemata. Die Vorbereitungsorgane des Konzils und ihre Arbeit', in *Lexikon für Theologie und Kirch: Das Zweite Vatikanische Konzil: Konstitutionen, Dekrete und Erklärungen*, 3 vols. (Freiburg: Herder, 1966–8), vol. 3, pp. 665–726, pp. 706–7. If this attempt had been successful, the remark by L. Oeing-Hanhoff, *Thomas von Aquin 1274/1974*, p. 245, would have been a sad statement of the facts. He states that it was Aquinas himself who gave a place to independent philosophy within the Church and recognised the right of free philosophising even against the objections of the Church and the theology of his time. Therefore, it is difficult to think of a worse perversion of his inheritance.

[27] *Gravissimum educationis*, §10.

[28] *Optatam totius*, §16.

[29] *Codex iuris canonici* (Vatican, 1983), canon 252, §3 – with an almost literal quotation from the text of the Council. Berger's contribution, D. Berger, 'S. Thoma praesertim magistro', is an attempt to reinforce these sentences in a new normative Thomist direction. I cannot wish this attempt any success in the sense that is intended. However, the contribution is valuable not only because of its copious references to literary sources, but also because of the insight it affords into a current conflict.

Aquinas research continues

Precisely if we wish St Thomas to have further influence in contemporary theology, and indeed in the theology of all the confessions, we cannot know enough of the significance of his teaching. The most important contribution of Aquinas's lasting influence in contemporary theology is Aquinas scholarship, which continues on its unwavering way, equipped with ever better means. For what is no longer of interest to historical research can no longer exert any influence in the present.

General comments

Mention must first be made of the progress with constantly improved working editions and translations into major languages. These are mostly bilingual, and render the main works of Aquinas more and more readily accessible to those interested. Adherents of other great theologians of the Middle Ages cannot even imagine such a situation.[30]

To assist the study of Aquinas's works there are both the complete working editions, and separately, aids and indexes which are partly computer-supported, and so approach the ideal.[31] Moreover there exist numerous organs and journals of Aquinas studies, and Thomas Aquinas research institutes on a national and international basis. International Aquinas conferences and symposia take place regularly in various places, with published proceedings.[32]

---

[30] In German, see Appendix I in Pesch, *Thomas von Aquin*, pp. 404–9.

[31] They are listed in Pesch, *Thomas von Aquin*, pp. 408ff.

[32] Here are at least the most important organs of Aquinas research. For bibliography and reviews see: *Bibliotheca Theologica* (Göttingen) [up to 1965]; *Rassegna di letteratura tomistica* (1966–); Richard Ingardia, *Thomas Aquinas, International Bibliography 1977–1990*. Journals, in German: *Zeitschrift für Theologie und Philosophie, Theologie und Philosophie, Miscellanea Mediaevalia, Philosophisches Jahrbuch*; in Italian: *Angelicum, Doctor Communis, Divus Thomas* (Piacenza), *Gregorianum*; in Spanish especially: *Ciencia Tomista*; in French: *Ephemerides theologicue Lovanienses, Nouvelle Revue Théologique, Revue Philosophique de Louvain, Revue des sciences philosophiques et théologiques, Recherches de théologie ancienne et médiévale, Revue thomiste*; in English: *Dominican Studies, Irish Theological Quarterly, New Scholasticism, The Thomist*; in Dutch: *Jaarboek Thomas Instituut te Utrecht* (English articles), *Tijdschrift voor Filosofie, Tijdschrift voor Theologie*. Most of these journals are no longer specialist organs of Aquinas scholarship in a narrow sense, but general theological technical journals in Thomistic tradition, and so reflect for their part the change in Aquinas research already described.

The most important institutes of Aquinas studies are: the Papal Thomas University of the Dominican Order in Rome (the *Angelicum*), which is also the official seat of the *Editio Leonina* (work office in Grottaferrata); the Grabmann Institute for Research into Mediaeval Philosophy and Theology at the University of Munich; the Thomas Institute of the University of Cologne; the Pontifical Institute of Mediaeval Studies at the University of Toronto, Canada; the Thomas Institute of Utrecht (Interuniversity

If the appearance of Chenu's *Introduction* in 1950 was the symbolic turning point which showed that there could from now on be no possible going back to the neo-scholastic view of Aquinas, then the jubilee year of 1974, the year of the 700th anniversary of Thomas Aquinas's death, marks something like a first harvest thanksgiving, amounting to an interim balance of Aquinas research as regards his importance for contemporary theology.[33]

Perhaps the most important fruit of the jubilee year is that since then we have once again a scholarly biography of Aquinas based on the state of knowledge at the time, namely that by James Weisheipl. The book appeared in 1983 in a revised American version.[34] For two decades this work was the standard biography, distinguished on the one hand by its sober exposition and interpretation especially of those aspects of the life of Thomas Aquinas which had become encrusted with legend – such as the abduction of the young Aquinas by his brothers on the way to Paris or the events of 6 December 1273 – and on the other hand by taking up a carefully argued position on traditional problems of scholarship. It remained the standard biography until the arrival in 1994 of a counterpart in the biography from the pen of the old master of historical Aquinas research, and former member of the Leonina Commission, Jean-Pierre Torrell. This stressed different points in detail, and has happily appeared in the meantime in German and English.[35]

Themes and thematic areas in recent Aquinas studies

We shall divide these into four aspects.

Thomas Aquinas without Thomism

Today's definitive standard works of reference, like the specialist journals too which owe a debt to the Aquinas tradition, have come with

---

institute of the Catholic Theological University of Utrecht and the Tilburg Faculty of Theology). In a broader sense all faculties and colleges of the Dominican Order are naturally places of Aquinas studies, and generally also publishers of Aquinas editions in the languages of the respective countries. We may mention Walberberg near Bonn, St Jacques in Paris (previously Le Saulchoir near Paris), the Dominican study centres in Oxford and Washington, DC and the theological faculties in Salamanca and Fribourg.

[33] See the collected volumes cited in note 7. *The Thomist* devoted its whole annual volume, and the *Freiburger Zeitschrift für Theologie und Philosophie* a whole issue to the state of Aquinas scholarship.

[34] J. A. Weisheipl, *Friar Thomas d'Aquino: His Life, Thought and Works* (New York: Doubleday, 1983 (1974)).

[35] J.-P. Torrell, *L'Initiation à saint Thomas d'Aquin: Sa personne et son œuvre* (Paris: Éditions du Cerf, 1993) [ET: *Saint Thomas Aquinas*, vol. 1: *The Person and His Work* (Washington DC: Catholic University of America Press, 1996)].

gratifying rapidity to take seriously the fundamental insight of recent Aquinas studies, namely the distinction between the historical Thomas Aquinas and the Thomist school. Following on this, the question of the theological methods of Aquinas constitutes an interesting and engaging topic in recent Aquinas studies.

Once this is addressed, the simple and schematic way in which questions of method, and especially the relationship of reason and faith, philosophy and theology are viewed in school Thomism and in the ecclesiastical directives based upon it, can no longer be held to represent the last word in scholarship.

It is more than incidental to the issue here, and rather a fruit of the insights brought together above all by Chenu into the basic impulses of scholastic theology, at least that of the twelfth and thirteenth centuries, that the researcher's attention is drawn with striking frequency in the period in question to Aquinas exegesis and particularly to his exegetic methods. The lectures of Master Thomas represent after all an interpretation of Holy Scripture.[36] It was to be expected that at some stage a complete account of the theology of Aquinas would be published based on recent Aquinas studies, just as there has been a complete account of Aquinas's philosophy which is still readable today, although it is not our business to discuss these here. Strangely, however, the former is still awaited.[37] One will probably have to be content for some time yet with the existing more limited 'introductions', which make no claim to being a complete account.[38]

---

[36] It begins with the chapter on Thomas Aquinas in Henri Cardinal de Lubac's monumental work, *Exégèse médiévale: Les Quatres sens de l'Écriture*, 2 vols. in 4 books (Paris: Éditions Montaigne, 1958–69); cf. also O.-H. Pesch, 'Paul as Professor of Theology: The Image of the Apostle in St. Thomas' Theology', *The Thomist* 38 (1974), pp. 584–605; W. G. B. M. Valkenberg, *Words of the Living God: Place and Function of Holy Scripture in the Theology of St. Thomas Aquinas* (Louvain: Peeters, 1999). See also B. Smalley, *The Study of the Bible in the Middle Ages* (Oxford: Clarendon Press, 1941). The time is past when classical and/or modern commentators more or less ignore the three great sections of the *Summa Theologiae*, i.e. *ST* Ia, QQ. 65–74 (creation, the biblical account of creation); *ST* IaIIae, QQ. 98–108 (The old and the new law); *ST* IIIa, QQ. 30–45 (The life of Jesus) or leave them to biblical studies. Typical instances in this regard are Cajetan, who makes only very brief remarks about *ST* IaIIae, QQ. 102–5 and *ST* IIIa, QQ. 35–45 in his printed commentary in the Editio Leonina (*Omnia clara sunt*), and R. Garrigou-Lagrange, who in his commentary on *ST* IIIa, QQ. 35–45 leaves things to the *biblicis*.

[37] The only notable attempt to present an account of the situation existing at that time is *Initiation théologique*, 4 vols. (Paris 1950–4).

[38] See my essay in *Thomas von Aquin* and also B. Davies, *The Thought of Thomas Aquinas* (Oxford: Clarendon Press, 1992); J.-P. Torrell, 'Saint Thomas d'Aquin: Maître spirituel', in *Vie Spirituelle* (Paris: Cerf, 1993).

Major themes

If I judge aright, the question of Aquinas's understanding of *faith* emerged as the first major topic in point of time. This is readily explained by the new reworking of the concept of faith in contemporary (Catholic) theology. A second major theme, which has remained so until today, is clearly anthropology. Here the main interest concerns the unity of body and soul in Man on the one hand, and the problem of free will on the other; in both cases with express regard to the implications for eschatology.

In the time period in question, the issue of major interest seems to be topics related to Aquinas's theological ethics. The roots of this interest are obvious: the crisis in the thinking on natural law of the kind usual hitherto, thinking which found its strongest support in the Thomist school.[39] Scholarly interest therefore lies particularly in substantive individual questions, in the problems of the basis of Aquinas's ethics. The interest lies also in the theological impulse of his philosophical-ethical reflections, the question of the moral autonomy of Man, the doctrine of virtue, and, not least from impulses arising from ecumenical discussion, to his theology of law.[40]

Relegated to the shadows

In comparison with the 1930s and 1940s, there is strikingly less topical work on the details of Thomist Christology. The same is even more true of the doctrine of the Trinity, and also for the doctrine of angels and the doctrine of sin.[41] But among the new directions in the theology of our

---

[39] Typical of the perception and treatment of this crisis are the two collected volumes by F. Böckle (ed.), *Das Naturrecht im Disput: 3 Vorträge beim Kongress der Deutschsprachigen Moraltheologen 1965 in Rensberg* (Düsseldorf: Patmos Verlag, 1966); F. Böckle and W. Böckenförde, *Naturrecht in der Kritik* (Mainz: Matthias-Grünewald Verlag, 1973); and J.-M. Aubert, 'Le droit naturel, ses avatars historiques et son avenir', *Vie Spirituelle, Supplément* 80–83 (1967), pp. 282–322. Summing up and further references in *Deutsche Thomas Ausgabe, Das Gesetz* (Graz: Verlag Styria, 1977), pp. 568–85, 619–29.

[40] See the collected volume by Elders and Hedwig cited in note 63, but especially U. Kühn, *Via caritatis: Theologie d. Gesetzes bei Thomas von Aquin* (Göttingen: Vandenhoeck & Ruprecht, 1965 (1964)), and W. H. J. Schachten, *Ordo Salutis: Das Gesetz als Weise der Heilsvermittlun: Zur Kritik des hl. Thomas von Aquin an Joachim von Fiore* (Münster: Aschendorff Verlag, 1980).

[41] See the works on Christology listed in O.-H. Pesch, *Theologie der Rechtfertigung bei Martin Luther und Thomas von Aquin: Versuch eines systematisch-theologischen Dialogs* (Mainz: Matthias-Grünewald Verlag, 1967), pp. 567–77 and pp. 468–84 on the doctrine of sin. On Christology see H. J. M. Schoot, *Christ the 'Name' of God: Thomas Aquinas on Naming Christ* (Louvain: Peeters, 1993). On the doctrine of sin, see H. J. M. Schoot (ed.), *'Tibi soli peccavi': Thomas Aquinas on*

century the problems and solutions of medieval theology have in fact run their course.[42] The many specific arguments, in clear contrast to the specific arguments on the other topics mentioned, strike today's reader as more frustrating than stimulating, not so much perhaps from slothful thinking on the reader's part as because, but precisely for *theological* reasons, they are not felt to permit going into as much detail as Aquinas does because there are no compelling grounds for doing so in the documented traditions of faith.

The 'said but unspoken'

Finally, with regard to contemporary theology, we must point to a completely heterogeneous subject area of recent Aquinas research: to Aquinas's inquiries into theological topics which he did not subject to formal treatment, but on which he expressed views, sometimes directly, if only in passing or for some immediate reason; sometimes only indirectly as 'something said but unspoken', in implicit theological premisses that he must have adopted in order to treat the express subject matter of his theology.

The first thing to mention here is the doctrine of the Church. There are good reasons for the view that the omission of a thematic ecclesiology in Aquinas is neither an accident nor due to an inadequate awareness of the problem, but the consequence of at least an implicit decision deriving from the interior logic of his theological approach.

Closely linked to the doctrine of the Church is the question, in this case really an implicit one of Aquinas's historical theology. This has to do indirectly with views of the nature of the Church in that it turns out that St Thomas in this regard, far removed from juridical and institutional constraints, views the Church as an instance of historical salvation,

---

Guilt and Forgiveness (Louvain: Peeters, 1996), and O.-H. Pesch, 'Die Sünde: Kommentar zu Thomas von Aquin, Summa Theologiae I-II 71-89', in *Deutsche Thomas-Ausgabe*, vol. 12 (Graz: Verlag Styria, 2002). On the doctrine of angels see J.-M. Vernier, *Les anges chez saint Thomas d'Aquin* (Paris: Nouvelles Éditions Latines, 1986). An example of both the historical and neo-Scholastic interest in a detail of Thomist Christology – in the context of Thomist thinking, even a very important one – is the controversy between A. Patfoort, *L'unité d'être dans le Christ, d'après saint Thomas d'Aquin: À la croisée de l'ontologie et de la christologie* (Paris: Desclée de Brouwer, 1964), and J.-H. Nicolas, 'L'unité d'être dans le Christ d'après saint Thomas', *Revue thomiste* 65 (1965), pp. 229–60.

[42] Which does not mean that there are no systematic-theological and ecumenical questions and impulses residing in these didactic pieces! In the area of christology new ground was broken in the great work by E. Schillebeeckx, *De sacramentele heilseconomie: Theologische bezinning op S. Thomas' sacramentenleer in het licht van de hedendaagse sacramentenproblematiek* (Antwerp: 't Groeit, 1952).

standing at the end of history.[43] Finally, late in the day, but directly related to current problems, there has been a growth in recent years of the number of studies on the themes of 'St Thomas and the Jews', 'St Thomas and Islam', and not least, 'St Thomas and Women'. Did St Thomas conduct a genuine Christian-Jewish dialogue, like his predecessors in twelfth-century Paris? Did he debate with Islam, not just in terms of apologetics, but in something at least approaching the manner of an 'inter-religious dialogue'? Did he, who, after all struck off so decisively in new directions and without fearing conflict in the sphere of philosophical and theological anthropology, transcend the usual social view, and the related medieval theological view of women that had an interactive relationship with it?[44]

Thomas Aquinas and contemporary theology

Viewing the themes of this more recent Aquinas scholarship leads us directly to the heart of the actual matter of our current considerations. There is of course a difference between Aquinas research in the technical sense and recourse to St Thomas in the 'normal' work of current theology, most obviously in systematic theology. Nevertheless, as has been shown, research on Aquinas poses questions and draws its main themes from impulses deriving from the 'normal' work of theology. And conversely, the latter can the more effectively use St Thomas as a support the better Aquinas scholarship addresses it. Thus it is apparent that the ways in which Thomas Aquinas can have contemporary significance or has benefit to contemporary systematic theology relate precisely to those areas to which specialised Aquinas research has been devoted. We now seek to illustrate this again in the following overview, pointing out the

---

[43] See O.-H. Pesch, '"Behold, I am doing a new thing" [Is. 43:19]: History of Salvation and Historic Moments of Transition in Thomas Aquinas and Martin Luther', *Science et Esprit* 2001 [forthcoming]. There are still other indirect themes in St Thomas's theology which research pursues at appropriate points, such as the theology of church service or liturgy, recently treated by D. Berger, *Thomas von Aquin und die Liturgie* (Cologne: Editiones Thomisticae, 2000). There is also the problem of beauty, philosophy and theology of language, of the word, of music, of ecology, also St Thomas's utterances on animals, the Earth, and many other topics.

[44] On the subject of 'Jews', see D. Berg, 'Servitus Judaeorum: Zum Verhältnis des Thomas von Aquin und seines Ordens zu den Juden in Europa im 13. Jahrhundert', in Z. Zimmermann (ed.), *Thomas von Aquin: Werk und Wirkung im Licht neuerer Forschungen* (Berlin: de Gruyter, 1988), pp. 439–58. On the subject of 'Islam' see L. Hagemann, *Missionsteoretische Ansätze bei Thomas von Aquin in seiner Schrift 'De rationibus fidei'*, in *Thomas von Aquin: Werk und Wirkung*, pp. 459–83. On 'women', see the reference list and sketch of the problem area in Pesch, *Thomas von Aquin*, pp. 208–27.

problems and giving an indication rather than presenting a research report.

St Thomas and Catholic dogmatics

The general line here can again be formulated in terms of the headline: from 'true teacher' to 'Father of the Church'. A 'true teacher' *must* be quoted, and with the underlying thought: 'That finally settles the issue!' A 'Father of the Church' *may* be quoted, with the underlying thought, 'What a joy to read that a theologian who lived, thought and worked hundreds of years before our time had something to say on the issue that can still help us today.' Thus, in the preconciliar handbooks of Catholic dogmatics, especially in those consciously intended as 'Thomist' handbooks, the so-called 'speculative investigation', following the exposition of the 'sources of revelation', was always related to Aquinas's work, with precise references, in some cases with further ones to authorities of the Thomist school. In the didactic literature on dogmatics in the post-council period however, St Thomas is *one* key spokesman for tradition. In some situations, he is the one most heavily relied on for guidance, but in no way is his solution to problems fundamentally the last word on the matter. Even St Thomas, then, is just *one* of the voices of the tradition: certainly a loud voice but, just as St Augustine before him had to retreat when St Thomas 'knew better', so must St Thomas today, when we know 'better' or have questions which St Thomas could not yet pose. And beside Thomas Aquinas there stand, though with less weight certainly, the other great figures of the Middle Ages, Bonaventure, Duns Scotus, Nicholas of Cusa and others.

Even if prompted by the tension between the two Rahner essays with which our consideration began, one can nevertheless detect fine differences in the dogmatics following the Council. St Thomas is cited most persistently by those scholars of dogmatics who began their scholarly careers studying the Middle Ages, by Johann Auer, Joseph Ratzinger for example and, most especially, Michael Schmaus. At any event, the background of medieval study of these authors ensures that from the outset St Thomas remains bound up with the whole body of medieval thought which in any case retains something of the status of being the measure of all things in post-medieval and modern theology. By contrast, the great contribution of Gottlieb Söhngen on the conception of theology as wisdom and scholarship in the first volume of the handbook *Mysterium Salutis* again strikes one as a symbolic milestone. Söhngen, as an original interpreter of medieval theology, equally known until his death as a strong advocate of the transformation toward historical thinking and a participant in ecumenical debate, has a masterly ability to place St

Thomas's theological conceptions in the historical stream of reflection on faith, and then, standing with both feet in this stream, point the way to hitherto unknown banks.[45] In short, his contribution is quite typical – also as to its date of publication – of the transformation of St Thomas that occurred through the Second Vatican Council, from the dogmatically binding head of the Thomist school to the most significant medieval impulse to modern theology as before.

He has maintained this position over the ten-year period that *Mysterium Salutis* has been appearing. One finds St Thomas repeatedly, although in contrast to earlier times, mainly in the dogmatic and historical theological expositions and reviews under each of the subdivided themes, in which medieval tradition often enough takes up only three to five pages.

From another perspective – more precisely, from a different kind of view on the theme of history – the same can be seen in the leading textbooks and didactic expositions in the same period. One thinks for example of *Church* by Hans Küng, and even more of his book *Infallible? An Enquiry.*[46] Here St Thomas is admittedly cited throughout but, as is often the case with the voices of tradition with Küng, less by way of exposition than as a more or less disastrous misinterpretation of the original Bible message. Not quite so critically – or to be more precise, perhaps with even more profoundly radical criticism – St Thomas is referred to in the older works of Walter Kasper, for example, especially in his *An Introduction to Christian Faith* and in *Jesus, the Christ.*[47] Influenced by his immersion in the historical thinking of the nineteenth century in connection with the philosophy of freedom in German Idealism, Kasper goes so far as to hold that the basic categories of Greek philosophy are little suited in principle to handle the core of the biblical witness of a God intervening in human history. St Thomas then hardly plays a significant role in these works either, at least not as a leading initiator of thought.

A much altered situation by contrast is apparent, one which once more relativises Karl Rahner's pessimism considerably, when Walter Kasper in his discussion of the doctrine of the nature of God in 1982 expressly confesses that for this book he had gone back to school for intensive study with the Fathers of the Church in a way that he himself would not have

[45] See G. Söhngen, 'Die Weisheit der Theologie durch den Weg der Wissenschaft', in *Mysterium Salutis* (Cologne: Benziger, 1965), vol. 1, pp. 905–80.

[46] Hans Küng, *Die Kirche* (Freiburg: Herder, 1967) [ET: *Church* (London: Burns & Oates, 1967)]; *Unfehlbar? Eine Anfrage* (Zürich: Benziger, 1970) [ET: *Infallible? An Enquiry* (London: Collins, 1971)].

[47] Walter Kasper, *Einführung in den Glauben* (Mainz: Matthias-Grünewald Verlag, 1971) [ET: *An Introduction to Christian Faith* (London: Burns & Oates, 1980)]; *Jesus der Christus* (Mainz: Matthias-Grünewald Verlag, 1974) [ET: *Jesus the Christ* (London: Burns & Oates, 1976)].

imagined beforehand.[48] Could it be that a somewhat naïve upsurge of the theme 'history of salvation' has passed its peak? Where it is appropriate in any event to *think* about precisely the *historical* presence of one who is *eternal*, St Thomas automatically becomes the major figure in theological formulation once more – as can again be confirmed by consulting the index of persons!

St Thomas and foundational theology

Thomas Aquinas obviously did not know a 'foundational theology' as a separate discipline in today's sense. But St Thomas has not only left us a set of very unambiguous statements on the question of how one should conduct arguments with those who question Christian belief.[49] In the Thomist view, a decidedly optimistic established relationship between faith and reason and a thoroughgoing 'natural theology' as the basis, the entry hall (*praeambulum*), for belief in revelation, are the hallmark of St Thomas. Aquinas has been the key witness for that version of Catholic fundamental theology which saw itself unreservedly as 'Apologetics'. This has become problematic today, at least in the way it is conceptually presented, as has St Thomas as the advocate of such apologetics. The theological reorientation of the second half of the twentieth century, which naturally concerned itself intensely especially with foundational theology, consequently took place in the first instance without St Thomas, more so than was the case in dogmatics. It is shown in a particularly exemplary way by the voluminous literature of the concept of faith and the so-called 'reason for faith' of recent decades.[50]

Now something similar is happening in dogmatics. Anxiety at handling the topic has dissipated, and it is no longer necessary to dissociate oneself because there is no longer a fear of misunderstanding. For a good decade or so, several textbooks of fundamental theology have been available, according St Thomas the status of an important voice of tradition in the same way as the most recent dogmatic literature gives him a special

---

[48] See Walter Kasper, *Der Gott Jesu Christi* (Mainz: Matthias-Grünewald Verlag, 1982) [ET: *The God of Jesus Christ* (New York: Crossroad, 1984)], Preface. He had already rehabilitated metaphysical thought in his contribution 'Zur gegenwärtigen Situation und zu den gegenwärtigen Aufgaben der systematischen Theologie' [ET: 'The Present Situation and the Present Tasks of Systematic Theology'], in *Theologie und Kirche* (Mainz: Matthias-Grünewald Verlag, 1987), pp. 16–18 [ET: *Theology and Church* (London: SCM Press, 1989)].

[49] See especially *SCG* I, Q. 2; *ST* Ia, Q. 1, art. 8; and the opusculum *De rationibus fidei* (see also note 44); *QQ*, IV, 18, Q. 9, art. 3.

[50] On the most recent developments see P. Neuner (ed.), *Theologie und Rationalität* (Freiburg: Herder, 2001).

solo role in orchestral sound in efforts at theological synthesis.[51] This relates first and foremost to St Thomas's basic understanding of theology as the scholarly study of faith, which has enjoyed a renaissance above all in Max Seckler's *Handbuch der Fundamentaltheologie*.[52]

It relates to single topics on a case-by-case basis, among these, surprisingly, to St Thomas's ecclesiology. Although, as already noted, this is only indirect, this is not from a lack of awareness of the problem, but is based on a very conscious theological view of the Church on St Thomas's part, a view whose possibilities in terms of foundational theology and ecumenism, if they were realised, could have a healthy critical effect in many arguments on the theme of 'the Church' at the present time that might unexpectedly reduce tension and aid relaxation.[53] St Thomas was able to combine his very unambiguous partisanship for the form of the western Church, with the papacy at its head, with an equally unambiguous, almost Lutheran way of viewing all institutional aspects of the Church as a pure means of God's grace.[54]

On the basis of such insights there can even be a partial upward revaluation of further developments in Thomist writing on St Thomas's ecclesiology. Not only have the researches of Ulrich Horst brought to light the surprising differences in the ecclesiological positions even among the most 'papalistic' opponents of Luther and the Thomist defenders of papal primacy at the First Vatican Council.[55] After his research, also Thomist writers like Melchior Cano can be considered key spokesmen in theological demand for a proper self-restraint on clerical teaching with regard to interventions in theological discourse.[56]

As is well known, in the last two decades, even Protestant theology has developed a surprising interest in the notion and the matter of founda-

---

[51] F. Schüssler Fiorenza, *Foundational Theology: Jesus and the Church* (New York: Crossroad, 1992) [German title: *Fundamentale Theologie: Zur Kritik theologischer Begründungsverfahren* (Mainz: Matthias-Grünewald Verlag, 1992)].

[52] See, in particular, M. Seckler, 'Theologie als Glaubenswissenschaft', in W. Kern, H. J. Pottmeyer and M. Seckler (eds.), *Handbuch der Fundamentaltheologie*, 4 vols. (Tübingen: Francke Verlag, 2000), vol. 4, pp. 132–84; see also M. Seckler, 'Theologien. Eine Grundidee in dreifacher Ausgestaltung: Zur Theorie der Theologie und zur Kritik der monokausalen Theologiebegründung', *Theologische Quartalschrift* 163 (1983), pp. 241–64.

[53] See J. G. J. van den Eijnden, *Poverty on the Way to God* (Leuven: Peeters, 1994).

[54] See on this the work of G. Sabra, *Thomas Aquinas' Vision of the Church* (Mainz: Matthias-Grünewald Verlag, 1987).

[55] See U. Horst, *Evangelische Armut und Kirche* (Berlin: Akademie-Verlag, 1992).

[56] See M. Seckler, 'Die ekklesiologische Bedeutung des Systems der "loci theologici", Erkenntnistheoretische Katholizität und strukturale Weisheit', in W. Baier, S. O. Horn et al. (eds.), *Weisheit Gottes, Weisheit der Welt: Festschrift für Joseph Kardinal Ratzinger zum 60. Geburtstag*, 2 vols. (Sankt Ottilien: EOS Verlag, 1987), vol. 1, pp. 37–51.

tional theology.[57] However, Protestant theology in no way sets itself the same goals as Catholic theology. Thomas Aquinas again comes unavoidably more clearly into the picture than before. The more so as a newly thought-through foundational theology, whether Catholic or Protestant, has today inevitably to face the question of the scientific status of theology, and so must address the way the understanding of theology has been developed in the tradition of Christian theological history. St Thomas is then once again so to speak the first port of call.[58]

St Thomas as a traditional court of appeal

What now follows, can only be a few snapshots of current theological debate. Where Aquinas scholarship takes its principal concerns from current interest, contemporary theology grasps the current problems where appropriate, preferably with reference back to St Thomas, and, in doing so, doubles the number of focus areas of Aquinas research. Such a process is only natural. We are used to it in the area of biblical studies. Numerous publications of recent years show how exegesis addresses itself to current discussion topics from its own specialist base, and how, conversely, current discussion asks anew about the contributions of biblical evidence.[59] This is almost the way it is with regard to St Thomas – but only, almost!

An especially revealing example is the eschatological discussion carried on for the last two decades with the new, central question about the relation between the resurrection of the dead and the immortality of the soul. Where some fix firmly on St Thomas's notion of the immortality of the soul, others, in favour of continuing reflections on bodily raising from the dead, stress the paradox that never escaped St Thomas, that a soul which is essentially linked to *its* body can also be perfectly happy without this body. Another example is the debate, now somewhat subsided, about how we are to understand the Eucharist and more particularly the real presence of the body and blood of Christ in the eucharistic offerings. Some lay emphasis on the fact that the Council of Trent in its Decree on the Eucharist fully adopted St Thomas's doctrine of transubstantiation, so that a Catholic theologian is not allowed the slightest doubt over this doctrine. All 'inclinations to duck the issue' are to be

---

[57] For an analysis see M. Seckler, 'Evangelische Fundamentaltheologie: Erwägungen zu einem Novum aus katholischer Sicht', *Theologische Quartalschrift* 155 (1975), pp. 281–99.

[58] See W. Pannenberg, *Wissenschaftstheorie und Theologie* (Frankfurt: Suhrkamp Verlag, 1973), pp. 226–30 [ET: *Theology and the Philosophy of Science* (London: Darton, Longman & Todd, 1976)].

[59] An especially fine example: N. Lohfink, *Unsere großen Wörter: Das Alte Testament zu Themen dieser Jahre* (Freiburg: Herder, 1977).

nipped in the bud. Others point out that this doctrine had totally opposing thrusts in the thirteenth and sixteenth centuries; in the thirteenth
century guarding against notions of a solid material manifestation of
Christ's presence in the form of the Eucharist, in the sixteenth century
against the fear of a crass and rationally conceived symbolism.[60]

It is self-evident that no theological doctrine about God can today
avoid taking up a position on St Thomas's 'proofs of God's existence'.
Once again, some insist on their indispensable significance and their
strictness of thought. Others however, precisely in the case of the proofs
of God's existence, appeal to St Thomas in setting forth how far reason
in and of itself can be sure of God's reality and how far not. In concurring
with or contradicting these views, Aquinas takes on the role of a court of
last instance in the context of the newly-launched debate on so-called
'natural theology', a debate which is also occurring in Protestant theology.

St Thomas seems to enter the discussion anew most vigorously in the
area of theological ethics, at any event in the question about the basis of
a theological ethic, or more specifically, the rationale for ethical norms
derived from faith. A theological ethic, which is included in a discussion
on the extra-theological bases for ethics, is seeking with renewed effort
corresponding approaches in Thomas Aquinas. What Aquinas scholarship has produced, recent moral theology has made its own.[61] For
'natural law' is understood as the God-given autonomy of Man, which
he has to develop through reason and experience in the light of his religious self-understanding, literally in order to 'invent' ethical norms.

What holds in the first instance for the rather philosophical problem of
the basis of norms has its complement in the area of the specifically theological grounding of ethics. In very concrete terms that means that, since
Catholic moral theology, taking its initial impulse from the Bible, re-
discovered 'Christian free will' as a basic concept of theological ethics, it
has also discovered it in Aquinas's doctrine of the 'new law'. This was a
key testimony from tradition, which was welcomed all the more enthusiastically because it was long neglected. Its weight grew not least after
research contributions from *Protestant* theology. It allowed the underlying suspicion of a 'legalistic treatment of the Gospel' to be dispelled, at
least as far as St Thomas is concerned. Thus St Thomas can again be
called on as an advocate for the 'freedom of a Christian'.[62]

---

[60] See amongst others, H. Jorissen, *Die Entfaltung der Transsubstantiationslehre
bis zum Beginn der Hochscholastik* (Münster: Aschendorffsche Verlagsbuch-
handlung, 1965).

[61] See the references in notes 39 and 40.

[62] See the corresponding systematic evaluations in the references cited in the notes
39 and 40; see also Oeing-Hanhoff, *Thomas von Aquin 1274/1974*.

Just as conversely Aquinas scholarship is occupied anew, not only on ecumenical but on the basis of medieval studies, with the issue of 'law and freedom', Law and Grace.[63]

Not so extensive, it appears, is recourse to St Thomas in the case of the treatment of material questions in ethics. That is not very surprising. If the findings of recent Aquinas scholarship are correct, that it is precisely St Thomas's view that 'Natural Law' has substantive ethical implications only in connection with divine law, but otherwise depends on Man's capacity for ethical discovery in the context of reason and experience, then the change of experiences and reasoned insights in the meantime necessarily means a substantive change in judgements on specific ethical questions. Thus there is no contradiction when the enormously increased significance of St Thomas in his doctrine of the ethical principles of human action goes hand in hand with increasing retreat from many of his specific ethical statements. It is most noticeable of course in the area of sexual and conjugal ethics. Some of the positions he adopts there are bound to strike us as strange – and that admittedly often. But they are nevertheless 'more reasonable' and so to speak 'less inhibited' than some Thomist scholastic answers derived from them, and above all the concrete ethical information also does not obviously appear to be at all a *necessary* conclusion from the basic ethical approach.[64]

What have proved most fruitful are a great number of individual ethical statements from the area of St Thomas's social and state ethics; and this precisely when the validity of Thomist thinking on Natural Law was no longer unchallenged.[65] At this point the influence of Aquinas has moved so to speak seamlessly, from Thomist scholasticism to a new topicality based on a better understanding of St Thomas himself in historical terms.

---

[63] See L. Elders and K. Hedwig (eds.), *Lex et libertas: Freedom and Law according to St. Thomas Aquinas: Proceedings of the Fourth Symposium on St Thomas Aquinas' Philosophy* (Vatican: Libreria Editrice Vaticana, 1987); O.-H. Pesch, 'Gesetz und Gnade', in F. Böckle (ed.), *Christicher Glaube in moderner Gesellschaft*, vol. 13, pp. 7–77; O.-H. Pesch, 'Begriff und Bedeutung des Gesetzes in der katholischen Theologie', in *Jahrbuch für biblische Theologie* 4 (1989), pp. 171–214.

[64] For a considered verdict see the essays, still readable today, of J. Pieper, *Das Viergespann: Klugheit, Gerechtigkeit, Tapferkeit, Maß* (Munich: Kösel Verlag, 1964 (1991)), on the four cardinal virtues. An example of the tenuous link between general principle and specific statement already alluded to is the position taken on involuntary nocturnal pollution: on the one hand, it is no sin, on the other, it is 'indecent' to take communion without having first confessed; see *ST* III, Q. 80, art. 7.

[65] The sixth, fully-revised post-war edition of the *Staatslexikon* by Hand Peters, published in 8 volumes and 3 supplementary volumes (Freiburg im Breisgau: Herder, 1957–), aimed to be, according to the editor's preface to the first volume, a 'defence of the notion of natural law (*Stauwerk der Naturrechtsidee*), as before it, Eberhard Welty's *Herders Sozialkatechismus* (incomplete), 3 vols. (Freiburg im Breisgau: Herder, 1951–8), vol. 1, pp. 161–215. On the situation today, see the references in note 39.

A final 'snapshot' in this regard. There is much exotic irony in this new presence of St Thomas in contemporary theology, as when Ludger Oeing-Hanhoff, for example, calling on the authority of St Thomas, speaks of a major settlement with 'political theology'.[66] But a little later Clodovis Boff writes an essay on Thomas Aquinas as a 'theologian of liberation'.[67]

As we pass on to the next section, let us note the amazing and highly pleasing fact that in the meantime, for more than two decades, biblical exegesis has also shown a leading interest in St Thomas. For a long time now there has been no doubt among experts that there is no basis for feelings of superiority on the part of Bible scholars towards St Thomas's exegetic writings. Not only did he strive with rare intensity for accurate, even historically accurate information, as far as that was attainable in his time, but without the benefit of the methods and means available to us today. But he hit on the right solution in interpreting individual biblical texts and arrived at judgements which have not been superseded to this day.

Beyond this, however, today's exegetic scholars are interested not only in interpretational history (*Auslegungsgeschichte*) and St Thomas's place in it, but also in what today is called the history of the effects (*Wirkungsgeschichte*) of certain biblical concepts and statements, which is not simply identical with interpretational history. One example of the re-linking of exegesis to attempts at solutions that St Thomas had already arrived at is the discussion on the 'Imminent Second Coming – Resurrection – Immortality'. Another is the – as yet incomplete but very extensive – project of the 'Protestant–Catholic Commentary on the New Testament', which the exemplary account of the history of effects of certain basic ideas in the Bible, such as the concept of 'justice' or 'preordination', has made a methodological principle of biblical commentary.

St Thomas and the ecumenical debate

The conditions have already been outlined under which St Thomas Aquinas became, at a certain point in the history of Aquinas research, a partner in debate rather than being seen as an enemy by Protestant theology. In this way, at least at the cutting edge of scholarship, the ban of excommunication declared against St Thomas by the verdict of Luther and the figures of the Reformation was lifted.[68] Protestant Aquinas

---

[66] Oeing-Hanhoff, *Thomas von Aquin 1274/1974*.

[67] C. Boff, 'Thomas von Aquin und die "Theologie der Befreiung". Brief an einen jungen Theologen', *Wort und Antwort* 26 (1985), pp. 33–40.

[68] For the history of the 'imposing' of this 'ban' see Pesch, *Martin Luther, Thomas von Aquin und die reformatorische Kritik an der Scholastik* (note 14 above).

research has existed for more than forty years, as well as Catholic Aquinas research which aims at bringing about precisely that specialist debate with Protestant theology that was impossible in the sixteenth century because of a whole chain of adverse factors of theological history and Church politics.

It is clear that this ecumenical discussion about St Thomas is not so very much concerned with typically intra-Thomist issues.[69] Protestant and ecumenical Aquinas scholarship understandably especially tackles, and does so critically where appropriate, those issues in particular in the Protestant–Catholic debate that have yet to be resolved or definitively settled. Those issues are: the doctrine of justification and grace, the notion of faith, hope and charity, the doctrine of the law, and more generally the doctrine of the bases of human action in God's grace, the question of 'natural theology' or of the 'natural knowledge of God', the doctrine of the sacraments, and last but not least the doctrine of the Church.

A case study: the doctrine of the 'Names of God'

It seems useful at this point to interrupt this account to demonstrate by way of a specialist issue how Aquinas's contribution to contemporary theological thought 'operates' in practice. In this case I choose an issue by way of an example that has a theological potential for debates that could become more pressing in the near future than they are at the present time. I choose the divine names for a didactic purpose.[70] In this connection St Thomas is deeply rooted in the tradition of so-called 'apophatic' or 'negative' theology, which was not begun by, but was passed on as a whole to the Middle Ages with historically important consequences, by that Neoplatonist theologian whose true identity has never been divined behind his pseudonym of Pseudo-Dionysius (the Areopagite).[71]

---

[69] Apart from the theology of history, points of interest were especially clarification in the area of the doctrine of justification and grace and the doctrine of the sacraments. References and literature in Pesch, *Theologie der Rechtfertigung*.

[70] *ST* Ia, Q. 13.

[71] The unknown theologian, as is well known, hides behind the name of the Dionysius whom Paul, according to Acts 17.34 converted on the Areopagus. The authority of the supposed follower of Paul drew him to the attention of medieval theologians and forced the Aristotelian St Thomas to make sense of the Neoplatonism of the pseudo-Dionysius. On this matter see J. Hochstaffl, *Negative Theologie: Ein Versuch zur Vermittlung des patristischen Begriffs* (Munich: Kösel Verlag, 1976). The first part of the book (pp. 13–156) provides a thorough history of the subject, pp. 120–51 covering Pseudo-Dionysius. Thomas provided a commentary on the book showing respect for the follower of the apostle: *Expositio super librum Dionysii De divinis nominibas*. For more detail see the biographies by J. A. Weisheipl, *Friar Thomas d'Aquino: His Life, Thought and Works* (New York: Doubleday, 1974) and Torrell, *Initiation à saint Thomas d'Aquin*.

The question here appears to be very straightforward. What does it mean when I apply a 'name' to God? For example, when I say: 'God is the living God', or 'God is being', or 'God is good'? Or even, God is the 'Lord', God is 'Father'? Modern theology would hardly hesitate to say: here God is brought demonstratively to our gaze in a picture or a corresponding pictorial concept which we know from experience of ourselves and our world. All the 'names' that we give God are metaphors. It seems to us today simply a truism that we can only talk of God in pictorial terms and sense his reality through our pictures. But aren't there any differences here at all? Is it one and the same way of talking about God when I say, God is 'king', God is a 'rock', *ein feste Burg*' or whether I say, 'God lives', God has power', 'God is wise'? At this point St Thomas insists on a precise and fundamental distinction. Not all of our 'names for God' are metaphors. There is an 'actual' and 'substantive' way of talking about God characterised by the exclusion of all pictorial elements. It is exactly this that is the subject of the thirteenth question in the first part of the *Summa Theologiae*. We will do best to explain this by an example that St Thomas himself develops, in the sentence 'God lives' or 'God is life'.

'Life' is a reality that we encounter in the world of our experience, theologically speaking, in creation. St Thomas refers to it as a 'perfection'. All perfections of creatures however must somehow pre-exist in God, just as effects reside in causes. And so God must somehow encompass in himself the perfection of 'life', at least in the sense that God cannot be counted among those things that are lifeless, and that it lies in his creative power to create life. But the sentence, 'God lives' *not only* states that God is not lifeless, and also not just that God is the creator of life. Technically speaking, 'God lives' is not only a negative and also not only a relative statement. The sentence claims rather to say something *substantialiter* about God, and means that God (himself) lives (in a real sense).[72] Thus, if such a sentence is actually to say something of God's reality, then two conditions need to be met.

First: the objective meaning, the *significatum*, of the spoken name of God, may not only incorporate nothing of a material nature, but no imperfection whatever. In other words, it must contain an 'absolute perfection'.[73] Certainly all the names of God taken from creation and the concepts associated with them can only 'represent' the perfection of God in the same way that creatures 'represent' God, that is, in an incomplete way, as the 'origin behind whose form effects remain'.[74] But there are

---

[72] *ST* Ia, Q. 13, art. 2; see *In I Sent*, Ds. 2, art. 2; *SCG* I, Ch. 31; *QDP*, Q. 7, art. 5.
[73] *ST* Ia, Q. 13, art. 3, ad. 1.
[74] *ST* Ia, Q. 13, art 2, contra.

names whose meaning, as is obvious, not only have reality simply in the difference between created beings and God, but also include this difference, this incomplete separation from God, as something expressly included in the meaning at the same time. Examples are all the names of material things and generally of all that contains the structure of possibility and reality, potential and act; that is, of all yet unattained reality and thus of imperfection. Such names cannot in terms of their content 'actually' (*proprie*) denote the nature of God, but only do so in a 'figurative' sense (*metaphorice*).[75] For example, when God is called a 'rock' or a 'lion'. The thought is of pressing importance for St Thomas because of the development of his thought on the simplicity and perfection of God.[76] Other names are also formed from the incomplete realities of created beings, but *describe* their content regardless of the fact that their meaning is thus an 'absolute perfection'. Only such names can thus be uttered in a real sense about the nature of God.[77] If one understands the meaning of 'life' on the highest level at which it occurs in the created world, that is as spiritual life, then the word 'life' meets the condition laid down for an appropriate word for God.[78]

Second: if I speak of 'life' in connection with God, I must, since God was not created, disregard the fact that this name, even if its content is an 'absolute perfection' in the sense described, essentially merely signifies something 'created', in this case created life. For our power of apprehension only allows statements according to the way in which we apprehend. It recognises only what is created, and this only in a finite, created way. This means that we can only posit life *proprie* in connection with God with regard to the meaning content itself (*id quod significat nomen*), not according to the form of its signification (*modus significandi*).[79] Every 'real' statement about God's nature must therefore disregard the fact that it can only describe God in a created way.

Unlike the first condition, the second cannot be realised. Created intellect can, at the ultimate peak of its finite power of comprehension, nevertheless, through methodical abstraction, form the concept of an 'absolute perfection', free of finite limits. But it cannot grasp such a pure perfection in concrete terms, for this would mean to grasp God in his infinity.[80] Even in a statement that 'substantively' and 'really' holds for God, God is not 'grasped'.[81] He is only 'signified', 'meant', 'encountered', 'represented',

---

[75] *ST* Ia, Q. 13, art. 3, ad 1 and ad 3; *QDP*, Q. 7, art. 5, ad 8.
[76] *ST* Ia, Q. 13, arts. 3 and 4.
[77] See the places cited in note 75.
[78] *ST* Ia, Q. 18, art. 3; *SCG* I, Chs. 97–8.
[79] *ST* Ia, Q. 13, art 3, contra.; *QDP*, Q. 7, art. 5, ad 2.
[80] *ST* Ia, Q. 12, art. 7.
[81] *ST* Ia, Q. 13, art 2, ad 3; *QDP*, Q. 7, art. 5, contra; ad 1; ad 6; ad. 9; ad 14.

through the medium of an abstractly-conceived 'absolute perfection', which is only realised in concrete terms in the finite nature of created beings. Forced by a metaphysical analysis of created life leading to the existence of God, I am *obliged* to say in our example: 'God lives, God is life.' And I know for sure that in doing so, I am not making just a negative or a relative statement, let alone merely a metaphorical one, but am referring to and describing God *positively in himself (substantialiter)*. And yet in doing so, I have *not* grasped precisely the actual divine essence, namely the uncreated, *unlimited* way that what is said in my statement really is in God.[82]

The sentence 'God lives' thus implies an unreal hypothetical statement. If I *were* able to grasp what 'life' beyond created existence and the apprehension of created intellect was, then my statement 'God lives' would not only have touched on God, but brought him within my conceptual grasp. Since I *cannot* do this, I have only touched on him by way of description, and grasped him only in so far as he is depicted in created perfection, and his divine other nature remains hidden from view.

So much for the example. What does it mean, and the conception of the 'name of God' which lies behind it, for contemporary theology and in contemporary theology? First of all, it is clear that we have arrived at the heart of the problem of theological 'analogy'.[83] 'Life' is ascribed to God *and* to created life. But since God and created life are infinitely different, this can only mean something in which regard the two are 'simply different' (*simpliciter diversum*), and which therefore precludes any univocation. And yet created life 'resembles' the divine, *secundum quid idem*, namely in the form of a 'representation' of the cause by the effect, so that we can exclude the idea of a simple equivocation. But what entitles me to suppose that in this way I have *really* grasped something of the nature of God; that I have actually touched on something of the *reality* of God through my statement? How do I know about the 'similarity' between my life and God's? Is this talk of God by way of analogy not a typical case of the intellectual arrogance of Man, who presumes to derive God by thinking about his own experience of the world?

This is the jumping-off point for the sharply critical Protestant attack on the Catholic doctrine of God, and indirectly on St Thomas. This attack was led, as is well known, by Karl Barth, accusing the Catholic doctrine of what it calls *analogia entis*, the 'analogy of being'. In truth however, the only real possibility for us to make statements about God from our experience of the world is based on the God who cannot be conceived by human intellect and who has deigned to become Man through

---

[82] *ST* Ia, Q. 13, art. 4; *QDP*, Q. 7, art. 6; *SCG* I, Ch. 35.
[83] *ST* Ia, Q. 13, art. 5; *QDP*, Q. 7, art. 7; *SCG* I, Chs. 32–4.

Jesus Christ. By this God made the reality of the world a way to know-ledge of God: *analogia fidei*, 'analogy of faith', in place of *analogia entis*.

Protestant criticism is right on this point. For the decisive characteris-tic of *this*, the *theological* analogy – in which God is thus the subject of an analogical statement, distinguishing it from all other cases of analogy – resides in the fact that the 'similarity' between God and created beings, anchored in the analogous name 'life', is not established by a sort of com-parison between the patterns of behaviour of God and created beings resulting in a proportionate correspondence. Something similar happens in the terrestrial analogies of the phenomenon of life. When we call mental acts 'life', it is because we have first compared them with the phenomenon of life in the independent movements of animals and have established a resemblance which justifies the figurative transfer of the name of 'life' to mental acts, and so makes possible a positive recognition of mental life.[84] It is precisely this comparison as a basis and justification of the analogical statement that does not apply to our analogical state-ments about God. This is for the simple reason that the two poles on which the comparison should rest do not fall within our empirical knowledge, but in this case only one does so, namely the created life of experience.

Protestant criticism has, directly or indirectly, caused Aquinas research to look again with a sharper eye at St Thomas, and once more to put in question the relevant supposedly self-evident truths of Thomist scholasti-cism. The conclusion has been that St Thomas knew very well that in making statements about God by analogy, we do not compare God and created being from a neutral standpoint and then establish similarities. All the possible ways of giving God a 'name' reside in the fact that we as created beings have a 'proportionate' relationship to God.[85] We can only name him *on the basis of this*. This 'proportion' is the 'relation' of the created to the Creator. Just that 'relation', which is not the only meaning content of our discourse about God, is nevertheless its sole basis. One may always see this as problematic on other theological grounds, but it is not mere *analogia entis* in the sense that has been criticised. Talk of God occurs in St Thomas on the basis of an *analogia fidei*, but it is not, as in Karl Barth, founded in Christology, but in belief in creation which – and we recall here the first stage in the modern view of St Thomas – always determines St Thomas's philosophising like a 'hidden key signature' (Josef Pieper).

Second, this leads us directly to the second consequence for contempo-rary theology. Even with the analogy of faith based on belief in the creation, it remains the case that a finite intellect is always bound to

---

[84] See the analyses in *ST* Ia, Q. 18, art. 3; *SCG* IV, Ch. 11.
[85] See the places cited in note 83.

doubt that it can ever gain a view of God with its naming of God by analogy. To stay with the same example, 'God lives' thus now means that the reality of 'life' as a property of created beings affords a notion of what 'life' means in God – in so far, that is, as it refers to God as Creator and the embodiment of itself in the highest purity and actuality – so that the word 'life' touches on something in God which is not touched on by any other word from the same perspective. At the same time, we must add the thought that this 'life' is so different in God from what life in created beings is able to 'represent' that I have basically grasped nothing of God's life other than that it is actually life. The dissimilarity is greater than the similarity because the intellect of a created being cannot, at the critical point, overcome the ever greater dissimilarity of our names of God from the reality of God. St Thomas's thinking by analogy thus entails a clear 'agnostic element'. It is an element of which he is aware, and one which incidentally is clearly linked to important religious texts from the time directly preceding his.[86]

This element was, it must be admitted, hardly adequately heeded in scholasticism or in the old Aquinas scholarship, although theological thought is protected against radical agnosticism because it knows that its statements from analogy 'do not simply lead to just darkness and name-lessness, just because of an objective similarity with what is experienced applies also to that which is not experienced'.[87] On the other hand, the similarity is so fundamentally bound up with dissimilarity and based on the transcendental dependence of the created from the Creator, the concept formed from the life of created beings is such a radically alien idea for the life of God that, as has been shown, it can hardly be justified to talk of *understanding* by analogy, still less of *statements* from analogy about the 'name' of God.

Within Christian theological circles it is questionable whether, considering the above, the sharp distinction between analogy and metaphor can in fact be any further sustained, since on close examination statements about God based on analogical reasoning have a status not superior to that of a higher-order metaphor. From an external perspective on Christian theology, however, the question here is: what theological potential does the doctrine of the divine names in Thomas Aquinas's work hold for inter-religious dialogue? This goes especially for dialogue

---

[86] See the statements of the Fourth Lateran Council (1215) in Denzinger-Schönmetzer §806.

[87] Karl Rahner, 'Was ist eine dogmatische Aussage?', in *Schriften zur Theologie*, vol. 5 (Einsiedeln: Benziger, 1961), pp. 54–81, p. 59; see also pp. 72–4 [ET: 'What is a Dogmatic Statement?' *Theological Investigations*, vol. 5 (London: Darton, Longman & Todd, 1966), pp. 42–66]. Without formally invoking St Thomas, Rahner is here formulating the doctrine of *ST* Ia, Q. 13.

with those religions – also at the cutting edge of their theological reflections – possibly even more basically permeated by the notion of the unutterability of God, even if only because they are not, like Christianity, literally shaped in their thinking by the 'picture book God' of the Bible (Helmut Thielicke).[88] We now leave this case study and return to our overview, concluding it with two short but necessary pieces of supplementary material.

St Thomas in student 'set texts'

It is not very surprising, although it is very regrettable, that there is not always enough evidence of these developments in the literature of the so-called 'set books'. It is helpful when eminent theologians of today use their knowledge and expository skills to help today's students of theology avoid an aimless journey through the seemingly infinite ocean of books and essays being produced, and provide them, as it were, with bearings so that they can reach a goal, even if only that of passing exams. It is all the more important that these set texts, from which students of theology today are probably getting their first impressions of theology and theologians of past and present, do not prolong for further decades the state of knowledge of the day before yesterday, allowing only a few of them to reach the goal of better knowledge.

If ecumenical theology is not to be, and remain, the hobby-horse of a few rather than an indispensable element of all contemporary theological thinking, then extreme care must be exercised in the area which has been marked by hundreds of years of misunderstanding. Otherwise one day, a half century of the most honest and intelligent ecumenical efforts at clarification and the dismantling of hostile views in the theology of both churches could prove to have been in vain. The 'textbooks' and 'introductions' used hitherto have not always been the happiest examples.[89] Incidentally, those from the Catholic side do not always agree in their expositions of Protestant theology![90] Hence an urgent warning and

---

[88] It therefore needs no further explanation why the arguments of *ST* Ia, Q. 13 gained in importance following the declaration *Dominus Iesus* of the Congregation for the Doctrine of the Faith of 6 August 2000.

[89] One thinks here of the sections on St Thomas in G. Müller, *Die Rechtfertigungslehre: Geschichte und Probleme* (Gütersloh: Gütersloher Verlagshaus, 1977); E. Mühlenberg, *Epochen der Kirchengeschichte* (Heidelberg: Quelle und Meyer, 1980); V. Subilia, *Die Rechtfertigung aus Glauben: Gestalt und Wirkung vom Neuen Testament bis heute* (Göttingen: Vandhoeck & Ruprecht, 1981). Considerably better because it is informative on the state of the debate is K. Beyschlag, *Grundriß der Dogmengeschichte II/2; Die abendländische Epoche* (Darmstadt: Wissenschaftliche Gesellschaft, 2000), pp. 247–77, despite the sometimes unfair and misguided criticism.

[90] For example, in the otherwise sympathetic book by G. Greshake, *Geschenkte*

request here. Writers of such textbooks should always take account of the current state of knowledge, even when not working from the primary sources, which is not always possible because of the great breadth of the material. Specifically, treatment of the themes must be informed by the most up-to-date specialist literature.

St Thomas in the new hourly prayer

As is well known, the Constitution on the Liturgy of the Second Vatican Council set in train a comprehensive reform of the liturgy, which had hardly changed in centuries. Those charged with the responsibility carried this through following the Council with surprising speed as regards the celebration of the Eucharist and the administration of the sacraments.

There is no disagreement that this was the quickest change.[91] At the same time, with worldwide co-operation, they undertook a reform of the hourly prayer used collectively in monasteries, by holders of clerical office, following the good old custom and duty in praying daily at various times. Until the reform of the liturgy, St Thomas hardly appeared in the texts, except for the office of *Corpus Christi* which he had written.[92] It was generally taken as agreed that only prayers and hymns of the old Church and readings from the Church Fathers should, along with the psalms, form the textual basis of hourly prayers. This restriction is now lifted. In this connection, in the middle years of the 1960s, the Institute for Liturgical Studies of the Theological Faculty of the University of Munich was given, among other things, the task of compiling proposals for readings from the works of St Thomas for the new prayer book.

From this point, I can give an almost autobiographical account of the rest of this review. The request came to me to propose and edit texts of St Thomas. This was done, and a large number of texts of St Thomas – I seem to recall it was about thirty – were sent as Munich's proposal to Rome. There were not only texts from the few spiritual writings of St Thomas in a narrow sense, but also from commentaries and even from 'scholastic' systematic works. The responsible authorities in the Roman Curia sent thanks by way of a letter of praise to the Seminar for Liturgical

---

Freiheit: Einführung in die Gnadenlehre (Freiburg: Herder, 1992 (1977)), pp. 73–5; see the comprehensive study by A. B. Hasler, *Luther in der katholischen Dogmatik: Darstellung seiner Rechtfertigungslehre in den katholischen Dogmatikbüchern* (Munich: Max Hüber Verlag, 1968).

[91] See O.-H. Pesch, *Das Zweite Vatikanische Konzil: Vorgeschichte – Verlauf – Ergebnisse – Nachgeschichte* (Würzburg: Echter Verlag, 2001), pp. 105–31.

[92] The work is now held (once more) to be a genuine work of St Thomas following a period when there was some doubt. See Weisheipl, *Friar Thomas d'Aquino*, p. 348; Torrell, *L'Initiation à saint Thomas d'Aquin*, pp. 189–99.

Studies, who informed me. A few weeks later, I spoke with the director of the Seminar *viva voce*. In this regard, if one looks at the index in the edition of the new hourly prayer, one discovers to one's joy that a considerable, if not a great number of texts by St Thomas were accepted as reading material, though, unfortunately in my view, fewer from his lesser-known biblical commentaries than from the better-known 'classical' texts, which are in any case available in translations into a number of languages. But however this may be, the new hourly prayer is testimony to the presence of St Thomas in the theology of our time.

Summary: sceptical optimism

Given how many positive things can be listed, our review here could be in danger of giving too rosy a picture. Hence then, in conclusion, I suggest that what we have been looking at is the leading edge of a *movement* in full flow and, at least in one case study, at an insight into untapped theological potential. Nothing damps excessive optimism more clearly than a look at the volumes of the *Rassegna di letterattura tomistica*.[93] Beside a report of what is happening at the cutting edge of international Aquinas scholarship, we find there in at least equal parts a Thomistic literature in the principal languages which poses the questions of modern theology to Thomas in the manner of the first decades of the twentieth century and finds in him the old answers, holding these to be valid for all times, proceeding to heap condemnation on the attempts of modern theology to find solutions.[94]

The debate with such 'actuality' of St Thomas must not be throttled by decree in St Thomas's name, but carried on in an honest way. The friends of St Thomas, especially also those of the newly-discovered Thomas of recent Aquinas research – and meanwhile, let it be noted, the female friends of St Thomas – have no reason, looking on their situation in this debate, to lose courage.[95] And thus we can, and may, end our reflections with the conclusion – that should have been apparent for some time – that anyone who knows a little of St Thomas is never safe from making surprising discoveries.[96]

[Translation by Colin Berry, amended]

---

[93] See further note 32 above.
[94] See also Berger, 'S. Thoma praesertium magistro'.
[95] See L. Maidl, *Desiderii interpres: Genese und Grundstruktur der Gebets-theologie des Thomas von Aquin* (Paderborn: F. Schöningh, 1994); L. Maidl and O.-H. Pesch, *Thomas von Aquin: Gestalt – Begegnung – Gebet* (Freiburg: Herder, 1994); see also note 44.
[96] *Deutsche Thomas-Ausgabe*, vol. 13: *Das Gesetz*, p. 743 (see note 39 above).

Philosophy as the Handmaid of Theology: Aquinas on Christ's Causality

PHILIP L. REYNOLDS

Like all scholastic theologians, Thomas Aquinas brought to the exercise of 'faith seeking understanding' expertise in the liberal arts and especially in Aristotelian philosophy. Theologians regarded the liberal arts and the philosophical disciplines as handmaids of theology.[1] Thomas and his mentor, Albert, stand out from other thirteenth-century theologians in the extent of their work on philosophy, and Thomas surpasses Albert in philosophical acumen. Nevertheless, he might have been disappointed to know that the twentieth century would place him in the canon of great philosophers. The schoolmen usually reserved the term 'philosophers' for ancient pagans, although they placed the Muslim sages in the same class.[2] To call Thomas a scholar of philosophy would have implied that he was one of the masters of arts, whose profession in the mid-thirteenth century was still humble as measured against the prowess of the masters of advanced subjects – medicine, law and theology.

Pope Leo's Encyclical of 1879, *Aeterni Patris*, was partly responsible for the rebirth of Thomas as a philosopher.[3] Leo found in Thomas a species of philosophy that was salutary for Catholic clergy and religious. The term 'scholasticism' came to signify a Thomistic way of doing

---

[1] 'misit ancillas suas vocare ad arcem', *ST* Ia, Q. 1, art. 5, sed contra (4b). Prov. 9.3. Editions cited: *ST*, cura et studio Instituti Studiorum Medievalium Ottaviensis, 5 vols. (Ottawa: Collège Dominicain, 1941–5); *Scriptum super Sententiis*, ed. P. Mandonnet and M. F. Moos, 4 vols. (Paris, 1933–47); *Quaestiones disputatae de potentia*, in *Quaestiones disputatae*, vol. 2, ed. P. Bazzi et al. (Turin: Marietti, 1965); *Quaestiones disputatae de veritate*, in *Opera omnia*, Leonine edn (Rome, 1882–), vol. 22. Since the Mandonnet/Moos edn of the *Scriptum super Sententiis* only goes up to Book IV, dist. 22, I use the Parma edn of the *Opera omnia*, vol. 7 (1857), thereafter.

[2] On the scholastics' use of the term *philosophi*, see M.-D. Chenu, 'Les "philosophes" dans la philosophie chrétienne médiévale', *Revue des sciences philosophiques et théologiques* 26 (1937), pp. 27–40.

[3] See Nicholas Lobkowicz, 'What happened to Thomism? From *Aeterni Patris* to *Vaticanum Secundum*', *American Catholic Philosophical Quarterly* 69 (1995), pp. 397–423.

philosophy that was both a preamble to theology and a discipline in its own right. Whereas Thomas and his colleagues had daringly appropriated philosophy from pagans and infidels, the scholastic philosophy of modern Catholicism was a home-grown product that protected Catholics from infidels. The less protective neo-Thomist movements that began to emerge in the 1930s were mainly philosophical. The Thomistic philosophy (both exegetical and constructive) that is still alive today, especially in the philosophy departments of American Catholic universities, is a descendant of neo-Scholasticism, although it usually lives peacefully with other philosophies. (In 1990, the journal *New Scholasticism* changed its name to *American Catholic Philosophical Quarterly*.)

Thomas the theologian has all but fallen silent today, but his shadow fell over much Catholic theology during the first half of the twentieth century, when there was a strong tradition of Thomistic theology among French Dominicans. The interests of some Thomistic philosophers (such as Bernard Lonergan, who belonged to the Louvain philosophical tradition) extended to a kind of philosophical theology. During the middle third of the twentieth century, chiefly in France, a distinct movement of Thomistic theological scholarship emerged. Its proponents emphasised context and historical method. Scholars such as Marie-Dominique Chenu, Ghislain Lafont and Michel Corbin meticulously analysed the architecture, methods, vocabulary and development of Thomas's theology. Walter H. Principe was a latter-day exponent of this tradition, as is Jean-Pierre Torrell. This movement was never as extensive as philosophical Thomism. That Thomistic scholarship has tended to develop along separate tracks, one philosophical and the other theological, is an irony of history.

Neither movement, it seems to me, gets to grips with the relationship between philosophy and theology in Thomas's own work. On the one hand, philosophical Thomists have depicted the relationship between philosophy and theology in grandly abstract terms. Moreover, they have usually been content to regard theology uncritically as a larger environment, somewhat as a monk might find the cloister an environment conducive to contemplation. On the other hand, theological Thomism of the sort that Chenu initiated, while closely allied to trends in constructive theology, has been descriptive rather than analytical or critical, since its proponents did not focus on the logic of argument. In this essay, I shall focus on a conspicuous example of the intrusion of philosophical concepts and vocabulary into the realm of faith: Thomas's doctrine that Christ is an efficient cause of salvation and of the final resurrection.

The doctrine of Christ's saving work, which by definition is at the very centre of Christianity, is the part of Christian doctrine that is the most refractory to rational analysis and furthest from philosophy: as St Paul observed, it seemed folly to the Greeks.[4] Thomas's aim is to show that although God could have saved us in other ways, the Incarnation was the most fitting way.[5] He does not try to achieve this end through any unified theory of the atonement. Instead, he tests and approves of several explanations and uses several more as occasions arise without trying to co-ordinate them and without leaning heavily on any of them. There is some justice in Adolf Harnack's complaint that Thomas's account of the atonement is *multa, non multum* (many things that do not amount to much).[6] But Thomas's pluralism may have been a reaction to the adventures of Anselm and Abelard.

In the *Cur Deus homo*, written in the 1090s, Anselm tried to prove that the incarnation and sacrifice of Christ would necessarily happen at some point in history. He presupposed nothing except certain general (and mainly tacit) premises about our fallenness and God's intentions, premises to which even infidels (i.e., Jews and Muslims) would consent. The work is a good example of non-philosophical rationalism. The core of Anselm's demonstration is the satisfaction theory: a judicial account of the atonement based on a calculus of honour and dishonour. The schoolmen seem not to have regarded Anselm's theory with much enthusiasm, although its influence is clear, and thirteenth-century theologians (shifting from analogies of honour, injury and blood-price to analogies of wealth and banking) recast the theory in terms of merit. But when Abelard, commenting on Romans in the 1130s, tries to explain how Christians are justified by Christ's blood,[7] he makes no explicit reference to Anselm's theory. Instead, having rejected old theories about Christ's rescuing humankind from the Devil, Abelard proposes that Christians are justified by their loving response to Christ's self-giving love.[8] Bernard of Clairvaux complained to the Pope about Abelard's theory in a letter full of marvellous rhetoric and invective,[9] and a local synod at Sens in 1141 condemned Abelard for teaching that Christ had not become incarnate to save us from the Devil's yoke.[10] Bernard had no objection to

---

[4] 1 Corinthians 1.23.

[5] *ST* IIIa, Q. 1, art. 2, resp. (2415–16).

[6] Adolf von Harnack, *Lehrbuch der Dogmengeschichte*, vol. 3, 4th edn (Tübingen: Mohr, 1932), p. 540.

[7] Romans 3.25–26.

[8] Abelard, *Commentaria in epistolam Pauli ad Romanos*, II, Rom. 3:25–26, in E. M. Buytaert (ed.), *Corpus Christianorum Continuatio Medievalis* 11 (Turnhout, 1969), pp. 113–18.

[9] Bernard of Clairvaux, *Epistola 190 (Ad Innocentium Papam)*, in *S. Bernardi Opera*, ed. J. LeClercq and H. Rochais (Rome, 1957–77), vol. 8: see sections VI.15 (pp. 28–30), VIII.21 (p. 35), and IX.24–25 (pp. 37–8).

[10] Cf. *Capitula Haeresum Petri Abaelardi*, 4, in E. M. Buytaert (ed.), *Corpus Christianorum Continuatio Medievalis* 12 (Turnhout, 1969), p. 474: 'Quod Christus non assumpsit carnem, ut nos a iugo diaboli liberaret.'

Abelard's theory in itself, only to the implication that this was the chief way in which Christ saved. It seemed to Bernard that a subjective theory such as Abelard's would be like something painted on air unless it was based on an objective foundation. Bernard's thought was closely tied to the sacraments. On Abelard's theory, how would Christ's sacrifice save babies when they are baptised? It is one thing to learn from Christ's example and to respond lovingly, Bernard argues, and quite another to eat his flesh and drink his blood.

Most of Thomas's themes are traditional: merit, satisfaction, deification, sacrifice and so on. Response theories are plentiful too.[11] But the theme of efficient causality stands out as novel and unusual. Of all the themes, it has the least to do with narrative: with a sense of story, history, drama, kinship and honour. Along with the doctrine that the sacraments are 'physical' causes of grace, it has been a cornerstone of Dominican theology, and like transubstantiation and the doctrine that all seven sacraments confer grace *ex opere operato*, it seems to epitomise the realistic mood of traditional Catholicism. Causal explanations of any sort have all but disappeared from theology – even Catholic theology – over the last 30 years,[12] but for those with an abiding interest in Thomas, the topic is worth revisiting. What would Christ's being an efficient cause entail?

Since my interpretation of Thomas's position is markedly different from that which has prevailed in Thomistic scholarship, I begin with an historical review of some twentieth-century interpretations of the causality of Christ in Thomas's work.

---

[11] At least eight of the ten reasons for the fittingness of the incarnation as the means of salvation in *ST* IIIa, Q. 1, art. 2, resp., entail affective response or example. The tenth reason is Anselm's satisfaction theory, although the cited *auctoritas* is from Pope Leo I.

[12] Cf. Liam G. Walsh OP, 'The divine and the human in St. Thomas's theology of the sacraments', in C. J. Pinto de Oliveira (ed.), *Ordo Sapientiae et Amoris: image et message de saint Thomas d'Aquin* (Fribourg: Éditions Universitaires, 1993), pp. 321–52, at p. 324: Walsh takes as his point of departure the critique of L.-M. Chauvet, according to whom 'the pervasive flaw in the sacramental theology of Thomas is its appeal to causality', which Chauvet regards as an instance of the same 'onto-theology' that Heidegger criticised in Greek philosophy. See Louis-Marie Chauvet, *Symbole et Sacrement: Un relecture sacramentelle de l'existence chrétienne* (Paris: Les Éditions du Cerf, 1987) [ET: *Symbol and Sacrament: A Sacramental Reinterpretation of Christian Existence*, trans. Patrick Madigan SJ and Madeleine Beaumont (Collegeville, MN: The Liturgical Press, 1995)].

Thomistic scholarship

The Thomists' doctrine that the sacraments are 'physical' causes of grace has conditioned how scholars have construed Thomas on the efficient causality of Christ. In the twelfth century, Parisian theologians such as Hugh of St Victor and Peter Lombard established that the sacraments proper (that is, the sacraments of the New Covenant) conferred or caused the grace that they signified.[13] Their successors in the thirteenth-century faculty of theology struggled to explain how that could be. The focus of discussion was an objection that presupposed a hierarchical concept of causality: since an effect is never superior to its cause, a material cause cannot have a spiritual effect;[14] but grace is a quality of the soul; therefore the sacramental elements (such as the water of baptism) cannot cause grace. According to one solution, which Bonaventure found plausible, the sacraments are occasional (*sine qua non*) causes of grace: the sacraments themselves have no causal power, but God invariably uses the occasion of their conferral (if there are no obstacles) to bestow grace directly.[15] Thomas rejected this solution on the grounds that an occasional cause is not a cause at all. If the sacraments of the New Covenant are merely occasions of grace, they are nothing more than signs, and it is their being more than signs that distinguishes them from the sacraments of the Old Covenant, such as circumcision. Thomas obviated the objection by arguing that the sacraments were instrumental efficient causes. In instrumental causality, the nobility of the effect tallies with that of the principal agent and not with that of the instrument: mere saws and adzes can be the instruments through which a craftsman (the principal agent) produces a work of human art, such as a bed or a table.[16]

Thomas is content to rebut the standard objection. He says next to nothing about how God uses the sacraments or what they contribute as

---

[13] Peter Lombard, *Sent*, IV, Ds. 1, ch. 4 (Grottaferrata edn, vol. 2 [1981], p. 233, n. 2): 'Sacramentum enim proprie dicitur, quod ita signum est gratiae Dei . . . ut ipsius imaginem gerat et causa exsistat'. Cf. Hugh of St Victor, *De sacramentis Christianae fidei*, I, p. 9, c. 2 (*PL* 176: 317D); and *Summa sententiarum*, tr. 4, c. 1 (*PL* 176: 117B).

[14] Cf. *Auctoritates Aristotelis* [=Johannes de Fonte OFM, *Parvi flores*], 6, De anima III, n. 150, ed. Jacqueline Hamesse (Louvain and Paris: Philosophes Médiévaux, vol. 17, 1974), p. 187: 'Agens est nobilius et honorabilius passo et forma materia.' Cf. Aristotle, *De anima* 430a10–19. See also Augustine, *De Genesi ad litteram* XII.16 (*CSEL* 28.1, pp. 401–2).

[15] Bonaventure, *in IV Sent*, Ds. 1, p. 1, art. 1, q. 4 (*Opera omnia*, Quaracchi edn, vol. 4 [1889], pp. 19–24).

[16] *in IV Sent*, Ds. 1, Q. 1, art. 4, quᵃ 1, resp. (4:31); *QDV*, Q. 27, art. 4 (Leonine edn, vol. 22, pp. 801–7). *ST* IIIa, Q. 62, art. 1 (2821–2822); *ST* IaIIae, Q. 112, art. 1, ad 2 (1374). Thomas explicitly links the instrumentality of the sacraments to that of Christ's humanity in the last of these texts.

instruments. During the Reformation period, some theologians insisted that the sacraments were physical causes of grace. The terminology is probably due to Cardinal Cajetan.[17] The doctrine reflects controversies of the period, especially the Thomists' opposition to the competing theory of 'moral causality'. The moral theory attributes a value to the sacraments deriving from Christ's acts and merits, a value that, as it were, induces God to bestow grace. On this view, although the sacraments are not really efficient causes, they are truly causes of grace rather than mere occasions for it.

For its opponents, the physical theory was rash and superfluous. For some Thomists, it became a shibboleth distinguishing them from other traditions, including the Franciscans. Thus Joseph Pohle counts among the proponents of the physical theory 'almost the entire Thomist school' as well as Suárez, Bellarmine and others. He includes the Scotists and Melchior Cano among those who defended the moral theory instead.[18] Pohle himself (a proponent of the moral theory) argues that the physical theory is unintelligible, but he adds that its unintelligibility alone would not make it false.[19]

It is easier to say what physical causality is not than what it is, for proponents of the theory insisted that God used the sacraments in a unique and unparalleled way that one could not fully understand. The sacrament was supposed to be a cause of grace ontologically, as a thing or nature rather than as a sign: a pen is a sign of writing, but its function as a writing instrument does not depend on its significance.[20] Some Thomists during the first third of the twentieth century attempted not only to defend the physical theory on grounds of Scripture and tradition but to articulate it philosophically, taking Thomas as their point of departure.[21] The usual idea seems to be that a causal influence passes

---

[17] See Bernard Leeming, *Principles of Sacramental Theology*, 2nd edn (London: Longmans / Westminster, MD: Newman Press, 1960), pp. 334–5.

[18] Joseph Pohle, *The Sacraments: A Dogmatic Treatise*, vol. 1, trans. A. Preuss (St. Louis: Herder, 1915), p. 152.

[19] Pohle, *The Sacraments*, p. 154.

[20] Leeming, *Principles of Sacramental Theology*, p. 336. See also L. G. Walsh OP, 'The divine and human in St. Thomas's theology of the sacraments', in C. J. Pinto de Oliveira (ed.), *Ordo Sapientiae et Amoris: image et message de saint Thomas d'Aquin* (Fribourg: Éditions Universitaires, 1993), p. 336: 'Most Thomists, under the influence of Cajetan, have interpreted the instrumental efficiency of the sacraments as a kind of physical instrumentality . . . The insistence on physical instrumental causality has meant that Thomists have had to struggle somewhat to state the relationship of the instrumental efficiency of the sacraments to their formal status as signs.'

[21] C. Spicq, 'Les sacrements sont cause instrumentale perfective de la grace', *Divus Thomas* (Piacenza) 32 (1929), pp. 337–56; C. V. Héris, *The Mystery of Christ: Our Head, Priest and King*, trans. D. Fahey (Cork and Liverpool: Mercier Press, 1950), pp. 140–2 (see also pp. 81–9). The first French edn of Héris's book (*Le mystère du*

through the very being of the sacramental element. Although what one can achieve through an instrument is normally limited by the instrument's natural powers (since the result of instrumental causality is supposed to be 'proportionate' to the instrument, as well as to the principal agent), God can use any creature to achieve any result, as C. V. Héris explains:

> there is nothing which God cannot produce with any created instrument whatever. God acts on the being of the instrument, and not on its external form. It is as being, and not because it is such a being, that God deigns to make use of it. In this respect, there is a proportion between the instrument elevated by Divine Power and everything that can be produced in the order of being. If the artist can elevate his instrument and make it capable of effects that bear the stamp of his intelligence and his genius, how much more readily can the Divine Omnipotence utilise things and make use of them to produce works that surpass the power of every creature.[22]

Like the doctrine of transubstantiation, the physical theory is at once religiously primitive and philosophically sophisticated: an attempt to save the immediacy of New Testament belief in philosophical terms. Just as the woman with an issue of blood believed that she would be healed by touching Jesus' garment, and Jesus felt a saving power (*virtus*) go out of him into the woman,[23] so the pious Christian believes that the sacraments are conduits of saving power.

Thomist theologians assumed that Christ's humanity was an instrument of grace in much the same way as the sacraments were. In 1905, writing in the *Revue thomiste*, Édouard Hugon includes under instrumental causality miracles, grace and all the gifts that flow from the Incarnation. Hugon considers four interpretations of the manner of this instrumentality: (i) that Christ's humanity is only a moral cause; (ii) that it is a physical instrument, but only of the miracles that Christ performed during his lifetime; (iii) that it is the physical instrument of all Christ's

---

Christ) was published in 1928 (Paris: Éditions de la Revue des Jeunes). Robert Reginald Masterson, 'Sacramental graces: modes of sanctifying grace', *The Thomist* 18 (1955), pp. 311–72. See also Masterson's article 'Instrumental causality' in the *New Catholic Encyclopaedia*, where he ascribes his own theory of sacramental causality to 'many theologians' (p. 550b). For references to Hugon, see the notes to Masterson's paper in *The Thomist*. Masterson's theory departs from older ones because he regards the signification of the sacrament, construed as an artificial form, as the instrumental means.

[22] Héris, *Mystery of Christ*, p. 84.
[23] Mark 5.27–30; Matthew 9.20.

supernatural effects, including those subsequent to his earthly life; and (iv) that it was the physical instrument of supernatural effects even before the Incarnation. Having dismissed the fourth hypothesis as manifestly impossible, Hugon defends the third, chiefly on the grounds that moral theories alone cannot fully do justice to Scripture and tradition.[24]

Theologians writing in the *Revue thomiste* during the 1920s and 1930s defend the general theory and present it as something which, while not strictly dogmatic, is an indispensable pillar of the faith.[25] Héris first outlines his theory of instrumental causality in treating Christ's saving work and subsequently applies it to the sacraments.[26] Spicq remarks that the evolution of Thomas's treatment of the causality of Christ as head of the Church confirms his treatment of sacramental causality, since the former topic is 'parallel, in our view, if not identical' to the latter.[27]

Nicholas Crotty, writing in *The Thomist* in 1962, focuses on the historical development of Thomas's teaching regarding the causality of the resurrection. Crotty takes issue with Holtz, who, in an article published a decade earlier, used Thomas's commentary on the *Sentences* to interpret the *Summa Theologiae*. According to Holtz, Thomas's understanding of how Christ's resurrection caused the resurrection of others did not change significantly. Crotty argues that while Thomas does treat Christ's resurrection as an instrumental cause in the *Scriptum*, careful attention to Thomas's analysis of this causality shows that it is not true efficient instrumental causality; and that Thomas attributes true instrumental efficiency to Christ's resurrection in the *Summa Theologiae*.[28]

Bernard Catão comes to similar conclusions in an historical study of Thomas's soteriology published in 1963.[29] While emphasising that there is no single focal theory in Thomas's treatment of Christ's saving work,

---

[24] Édouard Hugon, 'La causalité instrumentale de l'humanité sainte de Jésus', *Revue thomiste* 13 (1905), pp. 44–68, at pp. 44–6.

[25] M.-Benoît Lavaud, 'Saint Thomas et la causalité physique instrumentale de la sainte humanité et des sacrements: à propos d'un livre récent', *Revue thomiste* 32 (1927), pp. 292–316; M.-Benoît Lavaud, 'La thèse thomiste de la causalité de la sainte humanité et des sacrements: se heurte-t-elle à d'insurmontables difficultés?' *Revue thomiste* 32 (1927), pp. 405ff.; Humbert Bouëssé, 'La causalité efficiente instrumentale de l'humanité de Christ et des sacrements chrétiens', *Revue thomiste* 39 (1934), pp. 370–93; Humbert Bouëssé, 'La causalité efficiente instrumentale et la causalité méritoire de la sainte humanité du Christ', *Revue thomiste* 44 (1938), pp. 256–98.

[26] Héris, *The Mystery of Christ*, pp. 79–89.

[27] Thus Spicq, 'Les sacrements', p. 340: 'question parallèle disons-nous, sinon identique'.

[28] Nicholas Crotty CP, 'The redemptive role of Christ's resurrection', *Thomist* 25 (1962), pp. 54–106; F. Holtz, 'La valeur sotériologique de la résurrection du Christ selon saint Thomas', *Ephemerides theologicae Lovanienses* 19 (1953), pp. 608–45.

[29] Bernard Catão OP, *Salut et rédemption chez s. Thomas d'Aquin: L'acte sauveur du Christ* (Paris: Aubier, 1964).

Catão argues that by the time Thomas composed the *Summa contra Gentiles* (completed by 1265) and disputed the questions *De potentia* (1265–6), he attributed 'true instrumental efficiency' and 'a real instrumental power' to the humanity of Christ. Catão says that in Thomas's mature work, the meritorious and instrumental aspects of the atonement are 'properly distinct' and the objects of 'two complementary points of view'.[30] Romanus Cessario, in an historical reconstruction of Thomas's soteriology, focuses on satisfaction as Thomas's focal theme but mentions instrumental causality in passing, observing that the theme is not 'peripheral' but rather 'an essential element of the synthesis' and the means by which Thomas 'introduced into western theology the richly suggestive intuition of the Greek Fathers that the very union of God with human nature brought redemption to all that is human'. Cessario concludes: 'Aquinas seems to have put great emphasis on this element of his explanatory scheme.'[31]

There is general agreement among scholars of Aquinas, first, that in his *Scriptum super libros Sententiarum* (based on his teaching as a sententiary bachelor of theology in Paris, 1252–4), the instrumentality of Christ's humanity, because it is merely dispositive or meritorious, is not true efficient instrumental causality; and second, that Thomas attributes true efficient instrumental causality to Christ's humanity in the Tertia Pars of the *Summa Theologiae* (1271–3). As Jean-Pierre Torrell observes, scholars do not always agree about the intervening phases, but hardly anyone contests that such a development occurred.[32] The true instrumental efficient causality that such scholars envisage is, as far as I can see, the same as the Thomists' physical causality, although Torrell notes that such language is not Thomas's and prefers to characterise the efficiency of Christ's humanity as 'real and intrinsic'.[33]

---

[30] Catão, *Salut et rédemption*, pp. 142–3. Cf. Bouëssé, 'La causalité efficiente instrumentale', pp. 260–1: 'En ce qui concerne saint Thomas, il est certain que loin d'identifier dans le Christ la causalité efficiente instrumentale et la causalité méritoire, il les distingue expressément.' But the passages of the *Summa Theologiae* that Bouëssé cites (p. 261, n. 1) hardly support his thesis.

[31] Romanus Cessario OP, *The Godly Image: Christ and Salvation in Catholic Thought from St. Anselm to Aquinas* (Petersham, MA: St. Bede's Publications, 1990), pp. 160–1.

[32] J.-P. Torrell OP, 'La causalité salvifique de la résurrection du Christ selon saint Thomas', *Revue thomiste* 96 (1996), pp. 179–208, at p. 180: 'Entre le commentaire des *Sentences*, où il n'accorde a l'humanité du Christ qu'une causalité dispositive à l'égard de notre salut, et la *Somme de théologie*, où il lui reconnaît une véritable causalité efficiente instrumentale, sa pensée a connu diverses étapes . . . Les auteurs ne sont pas toujours d'accord sur le moment où les situer . . . mais le simple fait de cette maturation n'est guère contesté . . .'.

[33] Torrell, 'La causalité salvifique', p. 191: 'réelle et intrinsèque'.

Efficient, dispositive and instrumental causality

Since this essay concerns Thomas's appropriation of the philosophers' concept of efficient causality, it behoves us to consider what the latter entails. Following Aristotle, the schoolmen construe efficient causality typically as the self-replication of forms: through its own form, an agent that is actually X brings something else that is potentially X into actuality, educing specifically the same form or its inferior likeness from the matter of the patient. For example, the essential form of fire results in the fire's heat (a 'proper accident'), through which the fire actualises the potential heat in a pan of water placed upon it. The actuality in the patient is the final cause of the agent.[34] Whether the active form be the heat in a fire or the idea of a house in the mind of a builder, the analysis is essentially the same:

> The proximate end of every agent is to induce its likeness in another, as the end of a fire that heats is to induce a likeness of its own heat in the patient, and the end of a builder is to induce a likeness of his art in matter.[35]

But to influence its patient, the agent must be present to it. Whether the presence or 'touch' of a purely spiritual agent, such as God, is prior to its causal influence or rather a consequence of it is a moot point,[36] but a prior presence of some sort does seem to be required among corporeal agents. Thus an active form has no effect until it is applied to a patient. Without the locomotion of the celestial bodies, which in turn engenders constant rearrangement of the sublunary bodies, the natural world would be static.[37] Needless to say, the basic paradigm of efficient causality needs be stretched and qualified to fit many quite ordinary cases of efficient causality, such as sensory perception, momentum, magnetism and the apparently remote influence of the stars, let alone creation *ex*

---

[34] *ST* IaIIae, Q. 1, art. 2 resp. (712).

[35] *ST* IIaIIae, Q. 123, art. 7, resp. (2047b): 'Finis autem proximus uniuscuiusque agentis est ut similitudinem suae formae in alterum inducat; sicut finis ignis calefacientis est ut inducat similitudinem sui caloris in patiente, et finis aedificatoris est ut inducat similitudinem suae artis in materia.'

[36] See Philip L. Reynolds, 'The essence, power and presence of God', in Haijo Jan Westra (ed.), *From Athens to Chartres: Studies in Honour of Edouard Jeauneau* (Leiden: Brill, 1992), pp. 351–80; A. Fuerst, *The Omnipresence of God in Selected Writings between 1220-1270* (Washington, DC: Catholic University of America Press, 1951), pp. 203–4; and Stanislaus J. Grabowski, *The All-Present God: A Study in St. Augustine* (St. Louis and London: Herder, 1954), pp. 176–8.

[37] *ST* IaIIae, Q. 109, art. 1, resp. (1352a): 'quantumcumque ignis habeat calorem perfectum, non alteraret nisi per motionem corporis caelestis'.

nihilo. As we shall see, Thomas is at pains to show how Christ's resurrection touches the much later resurrection of others.

In dispositive causality, a secondary cause merely disposes something to receive a direct causal influence from elsewhere, usually from a superior source (which may also be the ultimate source of the disposition). For example, the 'character' conferred in baptism disposes the subject to receive grace directly from God.[38] In instrumental causality, the instrument is the means used by the principal agent, as a carpenter uses an adze: the power of the principal agent subsumes that of the instrument and works through it. Both models can serve to explain how a cause may have an effect superior to itself. Dondaine argues that the dispositive model comes from Avicenna, according to whom the sublunary efficient causes of generation merely prepare matter to receive forms from the superior giver of forms (*dator formarum*) in the sphere of the moon. Dondaine suggests that Thomas abandoned this explanatory model in favour of ones he owed to Aristotle and Averroes, such as that of efficient instrumental causality.[39] But although it does seem that Thomas abandoned dispositive models in favour of instrumental ones at some point in his career, his motives are not clear. Thomas is at pains to distinguish between dispositive and instrumental causality when he discusses sacramental grace in his sententiary commentary,[40] but throughout his career he uses the term *disponens* in a loose way to characterise all secondary causes, including instrumental ones.[41] Thomas seems to lose interest in the very distinction between dispositive and instrumental causality, as well as in dispositive causality *per se*.

Thomas provides a general analysis of instrumental causality when he discusses both the sacraments and the divine and human 'operations' of Christ (although not when he discusses the saving work of Christ).[42] The crux of his account is that because an instrument moves only inasmuch as it is itself moved by the primary agent, the instrument (as moved) may produce an effect that transcends itself.[43] Thomas takes as examples of

---

[38] *In IV Sent*, Ds. 1, Q. 1, art. 4, quᵃ 1, resp. (4:32, n. 128): 'Ad ultimum autem effectum quod est gratia, non pertingunt etiam instrumentaliter, nisi dispositive . . .'. Cf. *in IV Sent*, Ds. 18, Q. 1, art. 3, quᵃ 1, resp. (4:942, n. 80): 'baptismus non agit ut principale agens, sed ut instrumentum, non quidem pertingens ad ipsam gratiae susceptionem causandam etiam instrumentaliter, sed disponens ad gratiam, per quam fit remissio culpae.'

[39] H.-F. Dondaine,'A propos d'Avicenne et de saint Thomas: de la causalité dispositive à la causalité instrumentale', *Revue thomiste* 51 (1951), pp. 441–53.

[40] *In IV Sent*, Ds. 5, Q. 1, art. 2, resp. (4:203–4, nn. 26–8).

[41] Cf. *in III Sent*, Ds. 13, Q. 3, art. 1, resp. (3:418, n. 122); *QDP*, Q. 3, art. 4, ad 8 (*QQ disp.*, vol. 2, 48a); *ST* Ia, Q. 45, art. 5, resp. (288a).

[42] On the instrumentality of Christ's *operatio* as a human being, see Aquinas, *ST* IIIa, Q. 19, art. 1, resp. (2551b–52a).

[43] Thomas seems to imply that a cause's being *movens motum* is a sufficient

instrumental causality the craftsman using a tool, such as a saw or an adze, to make a piece of furniture, such as a bench or a table.[44] He also cites the way the nutritive soul uses heat, which naturally dissolves and consumes material, to digest food and to convert it into flesh.[45]

An instrument's power in relation to the principal effect is transient and imperfect, since it passes through the instrument and does not belong to it. The corresponding power of the principal agent is permanent and complete.[46] Thomas calls the transient power in the instrument a *motus* because a motion is by definition indefinite, being no longer that but not yet this.[47] The form from which the influence proceeds is in the principal agent and not in the instrument. The principal cause, on the contrary, acts through itself (*per se*), that is,

> through some form inherent in itself as a completed nature, whether it has this form from itself or from another, and whether naturally or violently. It is in this manner that the sun and the moon are said to illumine, and that fire, red-hot iron and hot water are said to heat.[48]

Thomas does not explain how the sacraments are instrumental causes, and it is not easy to see how his model applies. In the standard examples, the immediate result of instrumental causality is a single effect that can be construed in two ways: as a result that is proportionate to the instrument, and as a result that is proportionate to the principal agent. For example, one attributes the power to cut wood to the adze or the saw (although the tool cannot move itself), and one attributes to the carpenter the power to use the tool to cut wood in a certain way: the secondary causality, with its effect, is subsumed under the primary one. The result is not cut wood *and* a bench but a bench fashioned from wood. Thus Thomas says that the operation proper to a saw is to cut, while the operation of the carpenter is to cut accurately and thereby produce an artificial form.[49]

---

condition for instrumental causality – see *QDV*, Q. 27, art. 4, resp. (805a): 'Haec enim est ratio instrumenti in quantum est instrumentum, ut moveat motum' – but this condition should apply equally to any intermediate cause in an essentially ordered sequence.

[44] *In IV Sent*, Ds. 1, Q. 1, art. 4, quª 1, resp. (4:32–33, n. 129); *ST* IIIa, Q. 19, art. 1, resp. (2551b); and IIIa, Q. 62, art. 1, ad 2 (2822).

[45] *In IV Sent*, Ds. 1, Q. 1, art. 4, quª 1, resp. (4:32, n. 125); *QDP*, Q. 3, art. 4, resp. (46b).

[46] *QDV*, Q. 27, art. 4, ad 4 (806).

[47] *In IV Sent*, Ds. 1, Q. 1, art. 4, quª 2, resp. (4:34, n. 141).

[48] *QDV*, Q. 27, art. 4, resp. (805a).

[49] *QDV*, Q. 27, art. 4, resp. (805a, ll. 294–300): 'serra habeat aliquam actionem quae sibi competit secundum propriam formam, ut dividere, tamen aliquem effectum habet qui sibi non competit nisi in quantum est mota ab artifice, scilicet facere rectam incisionem et convenientem formae artis'.

Fire heats; the smith uses fire to heat iron.[50] It is true that one can use a corporeal instrument, such as the vocal apparatus or a pen, to produce a purely incorporeal entity, such as a mental conception. Thomas sometimes uses examples of this sort to illustrate how the sacraments cause grace.[51] But it is not clear that written or spoken words are efficient causes of the ideas that they communicate.[52] Moreover, the mental conception is a secondary result that presupposes the encoding of the idea in matter (as in the written or spoken word). Proponents of the physical theory envisage a quite different model, in which the spiritual effect is independent of any corporeal effect.

Thomas argues in the *Summa Theologiae* that Christ as a human being is an instrumental cause of grace,[53] that the Passion of Christ is an instrumental cause of our salvation,[54] and that Christ's resurrection is a 'quasi-instrumental' cause of the general resurrection.[55] Thomas reasons that because 'nothing can act beyond its species, since a cause must always be more powerful than its effect', Christ's humanity must be an instrumental rather than a principal cause of grace.[56] Since grace is a participation in the divine nature, it transcends everything created. Strictly, therefore, God alone is the efficient cause of grace.[57] But Christ in his human nature causes grace instrumentally. Here Thomas appeals to a favourite maxim from John Damascene:

> the humanity of Christ is like a certain instrument of his divinity, as Damascene says . . . Now an instrument does not perform the action of the principal agent by its own power, but by the power of the principal agent. And therefore the humanity of Christ does not cause grace by its own power, but by the power of the divinity to which it is joined, by virtue of which the human actions of Christ are saving.[58]

---

[50] *ST* IIIa, Q. 19, art. 1, resp. (2552a): 'calefacere est propria operatio ignis; non autem fabri, nisi quatenus utitur igne ad calefaciendum ferrum',

[51] *ST* IIIa, Q. 62, art. 4, ad 1 (2825a).

[52] Cf. Bonaventure, *in IV Sent*, Ds. 1, p. 1, a. 1, q. 4, arg. 4 & ad 4 (*Opera omnia*, vol. 4 [Quaracchi, 1889], pp. 19a, 22a): Bonaventure argues that a conventional sign is not an efficient cause of the cognition and emotional responses that follow in the soul of the recipient.

[53] *ST* IIIa, Q. 8, art. 1, ad 1 (2479a).

[54] *ST* IIIa, Q. 48, art. 6, resp. (2739).

[55] *ST* IIIa, Q. 56, art. 1, ad 2 (2787b).

[56] *ST* IaIIae, Q. 112, art. 2, resp. (1374a): 'Dicendum quod nulla res potest agere ultra suam speciem, quia semper oportet quod causa potior sit effectu.'

[57] *ST* IaIIae, Q. 112, art. 2, resp. (1374a): 'Et ideo impossibile est quod aliqua creatura gratiam causet. Sic enim necesse est quod solus Deus deificet communicando consortium divinae naturae per quandam similitudinis participationem, sicut impossibile est quod aliquid igniat nisi solus ignis.'

[58] *ST* IaIIae, Q. 112, art. 2, ad 1: 'Dicendum quod humanitas Christi est sicut "quoddam organum divinitatis eius," ut Damascenus dicit, in III libro. Instrumentum

Although Thomas is merely rebutting an objection here, the approach is typically abstract. He says nothing specific about the subordinate power that the instrument contributes.

The causality of Christ's life and Passion

Throughout his career, from the *Scriptum super libros Sententiarum* to the *Summa Theologiae*, Thomas maintains that while God alone is the author of grace and salvation, Christ's humanity is the instrument of his divinity. As a human being, Christ is the minister of grace; as God, he is the author of grace.[59] For as John of Damascus explained, the humanity of Christ is as it were the instrument of his divinity, just as the body is the instrument of the soul. When Christ cured a leper,[60] he did so by the power of his divine nature, and yet his touch was the means by which the divinity acted.[61] In the *Scriptum*, Thomas applies this general principle to merit: because Christ was also God, all his human actions participated in a supernatural power, and therefore his human actions, unlike those of any merely human being, were meritorious for all and not only for himself.[62]

Thomas's interpretation of John Damascene's maxim seems to have changed at some point in his career. In the *Scriptum*, Thomas argues that the humanity of Christ is a disposing rather than a strictly efficient-instrumental cause, and that Christ disposes us for grace by meriting on our behalf: Christ 'gives grace efficiently inasmuch as he is God, and through merit inasmuch as he is human'.[63] Just as a created nature is the disposing medium through which God prepares a human foetus to receive its soul directly, so Christ-as-man disposes the soul for grace; and

---

autem non agit actionem agentis principalis propria virtute, sed virtute principalis agentis. Et ideo humanitas Christi non causat gratiam propria virtute, sed virtute divinitatis adunctae, ex qua actiones humanitatis Christi sunt salutares.'

[59] *In III Sent*, Ds. 13, Q. 2, art. 1, ad 1 (3:408, n. 77).

[60] Matthew 8.3.

[61] John of Damascus, *De fide orthodoxa* III.15 (ed. Buytaert [1955], 59.5, pp. 230–1); and III.19 (63.2, pp. 257–8). Thomas applies Damascene's *auctoritas* as follows: to the reception by others of Christ's merits (*in III Sent*, Ds. 18, Q. 1., art. 6, quᵃ 1, resp. [3:576, n. 117]); to the resurrection (*in IV Sent*, Ds. 43, Q. 1, art. 2, quᵃ 1, resp. [Parma edn, vol. 7, p. 1061a]; *in IV Sent*, Ds. 48, expos. textus [ibid., 1179a]); to the spiritual resurrection (*QDV*, Q. 27, art. 3, ad 7 [799a]); to the grace of Christ as head (*QDV*, Q. 29, art. 4, resp. [859a]); to Christ's humanity as the source of grace (*ST* IaIIae, Q. 112, art. 1, ad 1 [1374a]); and to the sacraments (*QDV*, Q. 27, art. 4, resp. [805b]).

[62] *In III Sent*, Ds. 18, Q. 1, art. 6, quᵃ 1, resp. (3:576, n. 117).

[63] *In I Sent*, Ds. 16, Q. 1, art. 3, resp. (1:376): 'Ipse etiam [Christus] gratiam dedit, inquantum Deus, effective, et inquantum homo, per modum meriti.'

just as God himself makes each soul, so also, as the principal cause of grace, God immediately informs the well-disposed soul with grace. Christ in his humanity disposes us for grace in three ways: through our belief in him, which justifies us; by satisfying for our sins; and by making human nature more acceptable to God.[64] Likewise, Christ prepares human beings for the grace of headship (making them members of his body) by meriting on their behalf.[65] When Thomas considers the efficiency of the Passion in the *Scriptum*, he argues that God is the principal cause of salvation, Christ-as-man is the disposing cause, and the sacraments are instrumental causes.[66] A disposing cause disposes matter to receive a form. In this case, the members of the Church are the matter in which Christ, through merit, engenders a disposition for grace.[67] Here Thomas regards Christ's humanity as a moral cause.

Scholars maintain that by the time Thomas writes the *Summa Theologiae*, he attributes true instrumental efficiency to Christ's humanity and distinguishes this from its meritorious causality. But one may as readily construe the position of Thomas's later works as one of reticence and economy as one involving a different causal theory. Thomas does not explain how Christ's human nature is an instrument of the divine nature in the *Summa Theologiae*. He no longer analyses this instrumentality, as he did in the *Scriptum*, as meritorious and dispositive, but neither does he analyse it in any other way. Thomas's last accounts of this efficiency are so spare as to be consistent with any kind of ministerial causality whatsoever. Moreover, even in the *Scriptum* Thomas sometimes regards Christ's humanity, when no further analysis is required, simply as a quasi-physical conduit of saving power.[68]

In Question 48 of the Tertia Pars, Thomas devotes a series of articles to the means by which Christ's Passion causes salvation, asking in turn whether the Passion saves by merit, by satisfaction, by sacrifice, by

---

[64] *In III Sent*, Ds. 13, Q. 2, art. 1, ad 3 (3:409, n. 80).

[65] *In III Sent*, Ds. 18, Q. 1, art. 6, quᵃ 1, sed contra (3:574, n. 109): 'Christus, secundum quod homo, est caput nostrum. Ergo nobis aliquid influit. Sed nonnisi meritorie. Ergo Christus nobis aliquid meruit.'

[66] i.e., the sacraments are instrumental causes of something (such as the baptismal character) that in turn disposes the subject for grace, so that they are instrumental causes of the disposition and dispositive causes of the grace: see *in IV Sent*, Ds. 1, Q. 1, art. 4, quᵃ 1, resp. (4:31–2, n. 123); and *in IV Sent*, Ds. 18, Q. 1, art. 3, quᵃ 1, resp. (4:942–3, n. 80).

[67] *In III Sent*, Ds. 19, Q. 1, art. 1, quᵃ 1, resp. (3:587, n. 21): 'Alio modo dicitur efficiens, disponens materiam ad recipiendum formam. Et sic dicitur peccatum delere ille qui meretur peccati deletionem.'

[68] e.g., *in III Sent*, Ds. 19, Q. 1, art. 1, quᵃ 1, ad 1 (3:588, n. 24): 'Et ideo quamvis passio esset ejus secundum quod homo, tamen per passionem peccata delevit, sicut per tactum corporalem leprosum mundavit.'

redemption, and by efficient causality. Thomas answers affirmatively in each case. Thomas's entire response to the last question is as follows:

> There are two sorts of efficient cause, namely, the principal and the instrumental. Now the principal efficient cause of human salvation is God. But since Christ's humanity is the instrument of his divinity, as stated above, it follows that all Christ's actions and sufferings work instrumentally for human salvation in virtue of His Godhead. It is in this way that Christ's Passion causes human salvation efficiently.[69]

Thomas does not say what the proper operation of the instrument is. It is all too easy to overlook the simple logic of the argument: inasmuch as God, the efficient cause of our salvation, uses the humanity of Christ and the Passion as instruments, these are instrumental efficient causes. This modest interpretation is confirmed when Thomas sums up the results of Question 48 at the end of the final article. Which mode of causality one attributes to the Passion – whether it is by merit or by sacrifice and so on – depends upon to what one relates the Passion. The Passion is an efficient cause inasmuch as it is related to Christ's divinity.[70]

It is true that in the _Summa Theologiae_, Thomas does not reduce the instrumentality of Christ's humanity to dispositive or meritorious causality. On the contrary, he places merit and instrumentality side by side, as when he says: 'by the power of his divinity, his [human] actions were saving for us, namely, by causing grace in us through merit and through a certain efficiency'.[71] But as the summary at the end of question 48 shows, the different means are distinguished not so much as separate modes of causality but as points of view. Moreover, although Thomas reviews each of the five explanations on its own to test its validity, he makes no attempt either to integrate them or to establish their mutual distinctness. Satisfaction and redemption receive separate treatments, but satisfaction appears in Thomas's account of how the Passion redeems.[72] It would be perfectly consistent with Thomas's position in Question 48 to maintain that the efficiency of Christ's Passion consists in

---

[69] _ST_ IIIa, Q. 48, art. 6, resp. (2739a): 'Respondeo dicendum quod duplex est efficiens: principale, et instrumentale. Efficiens quidem principale humanae salutis est Deus. Quia vero humanitas Christi est divinitatis instrumentum, ut supra dictum est, ex consequenti omnes actiones et passiones Christi instrumentaliter operantur in virtute divinitatis ad salutem humanam. Et secundum hoc passio Christi efficienter causat salutem humanam.'

[70] _ST_ IIIa, Q. 48, art. 6, ad 3 (2739b): 'passio Christi, secundum quod comparatur ad divinitatem eius, agit per modum efficientiae.'

[71] _ST_ IIIa, Q. 8, art. 1, ad 1 (2479a): 'actiones ipsius . . . fuerunt nobis salutiferae, utpote gratiam in nobis causantes et per meritum et per efficientiam quandam.'

[72] _ST_ IIIa, Q. 48, art. 4, resp. (2737b).

one or more of the other means, such as merit. Thomas does not make the reduction himself: perhaps efficient causality includes something not covered elsewhere. But there are no good grounds for concluding that Thomas regards efficient causality as a means 'properly distinct' from the others.

The order of causality

In working out the implications of regarding Christ as an instrumental efficient cause, Thomas is concerned with the order implied by the model. The conceptual map of efficient causality implies priority and subordination: the subordination of effect to cause, the mediation of proximate causes between principal causes and effects, and the prior status of that member of a genus which possesses a form naturally and educes it adventitiously in others (such as the priority of fire in relation to other hot things). In Thomas's view, these patterns of order apply as well to grace as to nature, for 'the work of grace is no less orderly than the work of nature'.[73] God might move the sublunary world directly but chooses to do so by means of the heavens; likewise, God might have raised us from the dead without raising Christ first but chose not to.[74] A conviction that salvation and resurrection should imitate the order apparent in natural causes may have been Thomas's chief reason for regarding the God-man as an efficient instrumental cause.

   Dealing with the standard questions as to the timing of the Incarnation in the *Summa Theologiae* – would it not more fittingly have occurred at the beginning of the world's history or at the end rather than in the middle? – Thomas considers two sorts of causal order. On the one hand, there is a due order in the promotion of the good (*ordo promotionis*), according to which the less perfect precedes the more perfect, and the natural precedes the spiritual. (Here Thomas cites 1 Cor. 15.46–47.)[75] But there is another order, whereby nature runs downwards, from perfection to imperfection.[76] Imperfection comes before perfection in one and the same subject. Perfection precedes imperfection, even in time, when we compare different subjects, especially when one is the efficient cause of the other.[77] By putting these two principles together, Thomas

---

[73] *ST* IIIa, Q. 1, art. 5, arg. 3 (2420a): 'Opus gratiae non est minus ordinatum quam opus naturae.'
   [74] *In IV Sent*, Ds. 43, Q. 1, art. 2, quᵃ 1, ad 2 (Parma edn, vol. 7 [1857], p. 1061a).
   [75] *In IV Sent*, Ds. 43, Q. 1, art. 2, quᵃ 1, ad 2, resp. (2420b).
   [76] *In IV Sent*, Ds. 43, Q. 1, art. 2, quᵃ 1, ad 2, arg. 3 (2420a).
   [77] *In IV Sent*, Ds. 43, Q. 1, art. 2, quᵃ 1, ad 3 (2421b); and *ST* IIIa, Q. 1, art. 6, resp. (2422). This is a puzzling observation, because cause and effect are simultaneous when they are essentially ordered (as equivocal causes usually are).

can show that the Incarnation should have happened neither at the beginning nor at the end of history but in the middle, since both principles apply. On the one hand, the imperfection of human nature should precede its perfection; indeed, its glorification will not occur until the end of history. Hence it was not fitting (*non decuit*) for the Incarnation, as a perfecting of human nature, to happen at the beginning. On the other hand, inasmuch as Christ's Incarnation was to be the efficient cause of our salvation, it ought to occur before our salvation, and therefore it should not have been postponed until the end of history.[78] This entire argument proceeds at the level of fittingness (*convenientia*). Thomas is not proposing a naturalistic or mechanical account of salvation.

The causality of Christ's resurrection

Thomas maintains that Christ's resurrection is in some way the efficient cause of our corporeal resurrection. The source of the idea is 1 Corinthians, where Paul argues that Christ's resurrection is a necessary condition and the origin of our resurrection: 'Christ has been raised from the dead, the first fruits [*primitiae*] of those who sleep.'[79] Already in the *Scriptum*, Thomas couples this principle with a maxim attributed to Aristotle: 'that which is first in any order (*genus*) is the cause of what comes after it.'[80] Here too he applies Damascene's idea that Christ's humanity was as it were the instrument (*organum*) of his divinity.[81]

Thomas's treatment of the causes of resurrection is necessarily complicated. He regards Christ's resurrection as both an exemplar cause and an efficient instrumental cause of the resurrection of others. He tries to explain in what sense Christ's resurrection is the cause of the general resurrection and in what sense it is the cause only of the resurrection of the blessed. He has to compare the causality of the bodily resurrection with that of spiritual resurrection (*resurrectio animarum*). It must suffice here to consider Thomas's treatment of one question alone: how is the resurrection of Christ an efficient cause of the general resurrection? Christ's resurrection is clearly not a meritorious cause, in Thomas's view, since one achieves merit or demerit only while one is still a wayfarer (*viator*).

---

[78] *ST* IIIa, Q. 1, art. 6, resp. (2422).

[79] 1 Cor. 15.20. Cf. *ST* Ia, Q. 1, art. 8, resp. (7b), where Thomas cites 1 Cor. 15.12–20 to illustrate how theology, as a subalternated science, proceeds *a priori* through deduction from principles held by faith. Note that inasmuch as theology is logically posterior to the *articuli fidei*, it cannot explain them.

[80] *In IV Sent*, Ds. 43, Q. 1, art. 2, qu^a 1, sed contra (Parma edn, vol. 7 [1857], p. 1060a).

[81] *In IV Sent*, Ds. 43, Q. 1, art. 2, qu^a 1, resp. (1061a).

Thomas provides a careful analysis of the efficiency of Christ's resurrection in his commentary on Peter Lombard's *Sentences*. Although God is not tied to any secondary causes and can produce any effect immediately, he may use secondary causes if he wishes. Thus God might cause the motions of our sublunary world directly, but in fact God uses the motion of the heavenly bodies as a means.[82] Because Christ was nearer to God than any other human being, his resurrection was the cause of all other resurrections.[83]

To explain how Christ's resurrection is an efficient cause, Thomas distinguishes both between primary and proximate (intermediary) causes and between equivocal and univocal causes. A univocal cause replicates its form in a recipient (e.g., a human being begets another human being), while an equivocal cause produces an inferior likeness of itself (e.g., the heat of the sun generates terrestrial heat). Christ is the primary, equivocal cause of our resurrection inasmuch as he is God. As the God-man who rose from the dead (*Deus et homo resurgens*), Christ is the proximate, univocal cause of our resurrection. Now an efficient cause can produce its own likeness in the patient in two ways. The form in the agent may itself educe a like form in the patient. For example, it is the heat in fire that causes something else to be hot. But in other cases, the true source of generation in the patient is not in the agent but in the principles that produced the agent. For example, when a white man begets a white child, we regard the father's whiteness as the cause of the child's whiteness, but what really happens is that certain principles involved in sexual generation cause whiteness both in the father and in the child. Christ's resurrection is the cause of our resurrection in the latter sense, for what causes his resurrection is his divinity, which Christ possesses as God, and the same power is the cause of our resurrection.[84]

Since the God-man, through rising from the dead, is in some sense the univocal cause of our resurrection, the resurrection itself, by virtue of the conjoined divinity, is as it were the instrumental cause (*causa quasi instrumentalis*) of our resurrection. Here Thomas cites Damascene again, according to whom Christ's flesh was an instrument of his divinity. But although Thomas has established that God is the cause both of Christ's resurrection and of our resurrection, he still needs to show that God caused our resurrection precisely through causing Christ's resurrection. Thomas argues that the divinity of Christ mediates between Christ's resurrection and our resurrection inasmuch as the divine power 'will make our resurrection in the likeness of Christ's resurrection'.[85] His

---

[82] *In IV Sent*, Ds. 43, Q. 1, art. 2, qu^a 1, ad 2 (1061a).
[83] *In IV Sent*, Ds. 43, Q. 1, art. 2, qu^a 1, ad 3 (1061b).
[84] *In IV Sent*, Ds. 43, Q. 1, art. 2, qu^a 1, resp. (1061a).
[85] *In IV Sent*, Ds. 43, Q. 1, art. 2, qu^a 1, ad 1.

reasoning seems to be that since God causes both Christ's resurrection and our resurrection, and since God ordains that Christ's resurrection shall be the exemplar for our resurrection, Christ's resurrection is *ipso facto* the proximate, univocal cause of ours.[86] What is interesting about this sometimes tortuous argument is that Thomas constructs, piece by piece, a complex account of the causality of the resurrection that approximates to efficient instrumental causality without quite amounting to it.

Although Thomas aims to show that the causality of Christ's resurrection matches models derived from natural efficient causes, he does not expect the fit to be exact. In the *Scriptum*, Thomas considers the objection that causes must be simultaneous with their effects, whereas Christ's resurrection precedes the resurrection of the others. He replies that Christ's resurrection does not directly cause the resurrection of others: rather, it does so through the mediation of the divine power, which uses Christ's resurrection as an exemplar. The divine power is in turn mediated by the divine will, so that the effect arises only when God wills and need not be immediate. Among the various elements in this analysis, God's will, Thomas says, is the cause nearest to the effect (*propinquissima effectui*).[87] Likewise, in the *Summa Theologiae*, replying to the objection that causes must be in contact with their effects, Thomas argues that the power of God, which is present always and everywhere, fulfils what the concept of efficiency requires.[88] But among physical causes it is precisely the instrument, rather than power that flows through it, that establishes contact.

Crotty correctly argues that the causality which Thomas attributes to Christ's resurrection in the *Scriptum* is not strictly efficient instrumental causality. But Crotty also reasons that Thomas's view changed significantly, and that in later works Thomas regards Christ's resurrection as an efficient instrumental cause in a strict sense. I do not see any positive evidence for this interpretation. Even in the commentary on the *Sentences*, Thomas sometimes treats Christ's resurrection in relation to ours simply as an instrumental efficient cause, without further analysis.[89] Thomas does not offer any analysis of the causality of Christ's resurrection in the *Summa Theologiae*, where he maintains merely that God is the primary cause of our resurrection while the resurrection of Christ is

---

[86] *In IV Sent*, Ds. 43, Q. 1, art. 2, quᵃ 1, ad 2: 'secundum ordinem quem rebus humanis divina providentia praefixit, resurrectio Christi est causa nostrae resurrectionis'.

[87] *In IV Sent*, Ds. 43, Q. 1, art. 2, quᵃ 1, ad 1 (1061a). See also *ST* IIIa, Q. 56, art. 1, ad 1 (2787a–b).

[88] *ST* IIIa, Q. 56, art. 1, ad 3 (2787b): 'et talis contactus virtualis sufficit ad rationem huius efficientiae'.

[89] *In IV Sent*, Ds. 48, expos. textus (Parma edn, p. 1179a).

the secondary, quasi-instrumental cause. God's power is not limited to this means, yet God chooses to act through it.[90] To show that God's choice of means is reasonable, Thomas points out that in the 'divinely instituted natural order of things', a cause acts first on things nearest to it and thereby on things further away. For example, fire first heats the air adjacent to it and thereby heats bodies that are further away. Again, according to Dionysius, God first illumines the spirits that are nearest to him and thereby illumines those that are further away.[91] But Thomas said as much in the *Scriptum*. There is no analysis of the cause in the *Summa*, as there was in the *Scriptum*. Regarding the question of how Christ's resurrection causes, Thomas remains silent. Here too, one may as readily interpret Thomas's mature position as the result of economy and reticence as of a theoretical advance.

The causality of Christ as head of the Church

Thomas maintains that Christ bestows grace in two ways: 'authorially' (*auctoritative*) as God, and instrumentally (*instrumentaliter*) as a human being.[92] As well as arguing that Christ's humanity is an instrumental cause of grace and salvation, Thomas argues that as head of the Church, Christ is the source of the grace that flows from the head to the members. As a human being, Christ received a certain 'fullness' (*plenitudo*) of grace, a fullness that is extensive (inasmuch as all varieties of grace pre-exist in Christ) as well as intensive.[93] Because of its fullness, Christ's habitual grace (which he possesses as an individual human being) over-flows ('redounds') into the Church. Contrariwise, because grace comes to all the faithful from Christ, he himself must enjoy fullness of grace. The language that medieval theologians use to characterise this bestowing of grace is strikingly corporeal: they say Christ's habitual grace overflows (*redundat*) and that it flows (*influit*) into the Church; they characterise the grace as an influx from the head (*influentia capitis*). The term *influentia* and its cognates describe efficient causality.[94]

---

[90] *ST* IIIa, Q. 56, art. 1, ad 2 (2787b).
[91] *ST* IIIa, Q. 56, art. 1, resp. (2787a).
[92] *ST* IIIa, Q. 8, art. 1, ad 1 (2479a).
[93] Cf. John 1.16: 'from his fullness we have all received'.
[94] *QDV*, Q. 29, art. 4, resp. (858b, ll. 141–2): 'ratione causalitatis, nam caput influit omnibus membris sensum et motum'. This use of the verb *influere* derives from the Neoplatonic notion of emanation, probably via Arabic (*afâdat*). Bernard Catão (*Salut et rédemption* [1964], p. 99) finds this language overly material and prefers metaphors of light: thus Thomas's *influentia* becomes a *rayonnement* ('radiance'). See pp. 97–100 on the notion of the *influentia* of grace.

Thomas's treatment of Christ as head of the Church is dependent on that of the *Summa fratris Alexandri,* a work produced by several masters of the Franciscan studium in Paris.[95] The author's extension of the term 'head' from its natural setting to its mystical one involves a detailed analysis of the relational concept (*ratio*) of headship. The author notes three metaphorical notions of headship: a thing may be called a head as a king is head of a kingdom, or as the noblest member of a genus is head of the other members (e.g., the lion is head of the beasts), or as a father is head of his family. Furthermore, all five senses are present in the head, but not in the rest of the body. Christ can certainly be called head of the Church 'according to the aforesaid metaphors', that is, as one who governs a kingdom as a king, as he who is the noblest of his kind, as he who presides like a father over the Church, and as the one in whom there is fullness of grace.[96] But when construed not metaphorically but literally, the relationship of being head of something pertains rather to the sensory and motor 'influences' that flow from the head into the body, whereby the head mediates between soul and body. These relationships are replicated in the human Christ, who is the means whereby the grace of the Holy Spirit flows into the Church. Just as the sensory and motor powers flow into the body via nerves from the natural head, so likewise the gifts of faith and love flow into the Church from Christ, whose influence is not corporeal but spiritual.[97] The author explicates another feature of headship in the following article: head and body must share a common nature. Therefore God may be said to be head of the Church in a broad sense (*communiter*), but only the God-man is head in the strict sense (*proprie*).[98]

Thomas reminds the reader that in calling Christ 'head', we are transferring a term from its primary sense to a secondary one: 'just as the entire Church is said to be one mystical body because of a likeness to the

---

[95] On the authorship of this work, see V. Doucet's separate *prolegomena* to vol. 3 of the Quaracchi edn; or V. Doucet, 'The history of the problem of the authenticity of the *Summa*', *Franciscan Studies* 7 (1947), pp. 26–41, 274–312. John of La Rochelle seems to have been responsible for much of Books I and III. The reason for the work's being ascribed, even during the thirteenth century, to Alexander of Hales is unclear; he may have initiated or directed the project.
[96] *Summa fratris Alexandri* IIIa, n. 102, arg. 1–4 & resp. (Quaracchi edn, vol. 4 [1958], pp. 148–9).
[97] *Summa fratris Alexandri* IIIa, n. 102, arg. 1–4 & resp., p. 149a: 'tamen propria ratione dicitur caput per rationem influentiae, ut, sicut ab ipso capite est influentia sensus et motus secundum diversas partes eius – quia ab anteriori parte capitis fluunt nervi, per quos fluit sensus ad membra, a posteriori vero parte fluunt nervi, per quos fluit motus ab anima ad singula membra – similiter Christus in Ecclesia influit sensum et motum spiritualiter. Sensum influit per fidem, motum vero per amorem: influit enim sensum fidei et motum amoris, et illa ratione proprie dicitur caput Ecclesiae.'
[98] *Summa fratris Alexandri* IIIa, n. 102, arg. 1–4 & resp., n. 103 (p. 150).

natural human body . . . so also Christ is said to be head of the Church because of a likeness to the human head'.[99] Thomas follows the method of the *Summa fratris Alexandri* closely, although he is less interested in the idea of sensory and motor influence (*sensus et motus*), and he assumes that the usage is metaphorical. In the *Summa Theologiae*, replying to an objection based on a dissimilarity between Christ's relationship to the Church and human headship, Thomas remarks: 'one should not expect to find likeness in every respect in metaphorical expressions, for in that case one would not have a likeness but the thing itself'.[100] Nevertheless, he expects to find an exact match in certain respects, for having listed the conditions that comprise the *ratio* (concept, notion, account, definition) of natural headship, he finds them all replicated analogously in Christ and the Church. Thomas posits several features which together suffice for the *ratio* of headship.

In his commentary on the *Sentences*, Thomas begins with the premise that Christ is said to be head of the Church by virtue of a likeness to a natural head. He finds four salient features of natural headship: (i) the head's superiority, excellence and pre-eminent dignity in relation to the body; (ii) its causal influence of vivifying powers, including the sensory and motor powers; (iii) its directing of the body's activity; and (iv) its conformity with the body in a common nature. Each of the first three features is the basis of a commonplace metaphor: (i) the most perfect member of a genus is said to be the head of others (e.g., the lion is head of the beasts); (ii) any source may be called a head, such as the source of river and a chapter heading (*caput*) in a book; (iii) and every ruler, such as a king, a lord or a pontiff, is called the head of his people. Christ-as-God is head of the Church in these three senses and therefore may be called head broadly speaking (*communiter loquendo*). But as a human being, Christ is head in the fourth sense as well. Conformity in a common nature completes in Christ what the concept of being a head entails.[101]

Thomas presents a more complex version of this inquiry in his disputed questions *On Truth*. He begins his response by pointing out that one applies the term 'head' to Christ, our spiritual head, by metaphorical

---

[99] *ST* IIIa, Q. 8, art. 1, resp. (2478b): 'sicut tota Ecclesia dicitur unum corpus mysticum per similitudinem ad naturale corpus hominis . . . ita Christus dicitur caput Ecclesiae secundum similitudinem humani capitis'. Following the Berengarian controversy, theologians transferred the term *corpus mysticum*, which had formerly signified the Eucharist, to the Church, while the Eucharist became *verum corpus*.

[100] *ST* IIIa, Q. 8, art. 1, ad 2 (2479a): 'in metaphoricis locutionibus non oportet attendi similitudinem quantum ad omnia; sic enim non esset similitudo, sed rei veritas'.

[101] *In III Sent*, Ds. 13, Q. 2, art. 1, resp. (3:408, n. 75): 'Sed quarta conditio convenit Christo secundum humanam naturam tantum, et haec complet in ipso rationem capitis.'

transference (*per transumptionem*) from the natural head. Through considering the natural head, Thomas comes up with six conditions, three of which involve conformity and three distinction. These conditions work in pairs, so that each pair produces a double condition, which, taken in itself, is the basis of a commonplace metaphor. First, there is conformity through a common nature with a distinction whereby one member is eminent. Thus the lion is called head of the beasts, and a capital city is called head of a kingdom. Second, there is conformity in a common goal in respect of which one member governs (and is thereby distinguished from) the others. Thus a ruler is called head of his people. Third, there is the conformity of continuity (since the head is joined to the body) coupled with causal influence. Thus a river's source is called its head. What distinguishes Christ's headship is that as a human being, he is head in all three ways.[102] Whatever conditions are entailed by the concept of natural headship suffice to establish spiritual headship too.[103]

Thomas uses ideas from the natural philosophy of heat and of light to illustrate how there is a fullness of grace in Christ that flows over into the Church. In his commentary on the *Sentences*, he points out that there are three ways in which something may possess corporeal light. First, a thing may glow without illuminating other things, such as rotting oak wood, carbuncles and certain worms. Second, a thing may not only shine but also illumine other things, such as a candle. Third, a thing may not only illumine other things but be the source of all light, by bestowing on others not only light but also the power to illumine. Such is the sun, and such also is the grace of Christ, for Christ not only possesses grace and is the source of grace: he so graces others that they in turn become ministers of grace.[104]

This line of thought leads Thomas to regard the human Christ as the source of grace and even as the primary efficient cause of grace, albeit one subordinate to the power of Christ's divinity, somewhat in the manner that any natural efficient cause derives its causal power from God. In the *De veritate*, Thomas distinguishes the power of Christ's humanity from the power of other ministers by saying that Christ's power vis-à-vis grace was his own:

> the other ministers of the Church neither dispose for nor bring about the spiritual life as from their own power, but only as from the power

---

[102] *QDV*, Q. 29, art. 4, resp. (859a, ll. 173–5): 'Et istis tribus modis Christus secundum humanam naturam dicitur esse ecclesiae caput.' But Thomas concludes (859b) that it is better to say that Christ as a whole (*totus Christus*) is head, that is, in both natures at once.

[103] *QDV*, Q. 29, art. 4, resp. (859a): 'Et hoc ad rationem capitis sufficere videtur.'

[104] *In III Sent*, Ds. 13, Q. 1, art. 2, quᵃ 1, resp. (3:400–1, n. 35).

of another, but Christ does so by his own power. Hence Christ was able to bestow the effects of the sacraments through himself, because the entire efficacy of the sacraments was in him originally. Others who are ministers in the Church cannot do this, and therefore they cannot be called head, except perhaps because they govern, as any ruler is said to be a head.[105]

A series of questions on the grace of Christ in the *Summa Theologiae* develops this idea of the human Christ as the source of grace. Here Thomas takes analogies from natural philosophy pertaining to fire, heat, sun and light. Christ, Thomas argues, possesses habitual grace in such a way that his grace flows into the Church. Christ's human soul possesses habitual grace and possesses it to the highest degree, for he was 'full of grace and truth'.[106] This is because the cause of grace in the human soul is the presence of God, just as the cause of light in air is the presence of the sun, and there can be no greater presence of God than the union of natures in Christ.[107] Christ had fullness of grace intensively because the nearer something receptive to an influence is to the source of that influence, the more it receives. Moreover, to fulfil his role as mediator, Christ had to possess grace not only for himself but for others too, 'just as fire, which is the cause of heat in all hot things, is hot to the maximum extent'. Christ had fullness of grace extensively as well as intensively, because all kinds of grace came from him, just as all the powers of generation pre-exist in the sun, from which they derive. Within the order (*genus*) of those who have grace, Christ is 'a certain universal principle'.[108]

Thomas has in mind here a maxim derived from a passage in Aristotle's *Metaphysics*: 'That which is first in any genus is the cause of the things that come after it.'[109] The maxim describes the causal relationship between something that possesses a certain quality essentially and

---

[105] *QDV*, Q. 29, art. 4, ad 2 (859–60): 'alii ministri Ecclesiae non disponunt nec operantur ad spiritualem vitam quasi ex propria virtute, sed virtute aliena, Christus autem virtute propria. Et inde est quod Christus poterat per se ipsum effectum sacramentorum praebere, quia tota efficacia sacramentorum in eo originaliter erat; non autem hoc possunt alii qui sunt Ecclesiae ministri, unde non possunt dici caput nisi forte ratione gubernationis, sicut quilibet princeps dicitur caput'.

[106] John 1.14.

[107] *ST* IIIa, Q. 7, art. 13, resp. (2477b).

[108] *ST* IIIa, Q. 7, art. 9, resp. (2473a). See also IIIa, Q. 7, art. 8, resp. (2472a).

[109] The typical maxim is thus: 'Illud quod est primum in quolibet genere est causa omnium quae post sunt.' Cf. Aristotle, *Metaphysics* II, 993b24–25. See V. de Couesnongle, 'La causalité du maximum: l'utilisation par saint Thomas d'un passage d'Aristote', *Revue des Sciences philosophiques et théologiques* 38 (1954), pp. 433–4; 'La causalité du maximum: pourquoi saint Thomas a-t-il mal cité Aristote', *Revue des Sciences philosophiques et théologiques* 38 (1954), pp. 658–80.

other things that possess it through participation. For example, fire is essentially hot while other things are hot by participation. As a human being, Christ is the first in the genus of those who have grace. The closer another member of the genus approaches the first, the more that member receives grace. Therefore the Virgin Mary receives more from Christ's fullness than anyone else.[110]

The grace of Christ was always perfect and could never increase, for not only did Christ possess as much grace as the human soul is capable of possessing, but his grace is the source of all other grace. To explain the difference between these two kinds of maximum, Thomas points out that the form of heat may be maximum either relative to a subject or in respect of the form itself. For example, some air might be as hot as air can be, although something else is hotter. But nothing can be hotter than fire because fire is the source of heat in other things. Hence the heat of fire is maximum not only relative to its subject (*ex parte subiecti*) but also in relation to the very form of heat (*ex parte formae*).[111] Since what limits anything is the capacity of a recipient, a form is infinitely present in the source. For example, inasmuch as the sun does not receive or participate light in some measure but rather possesses whatever pertains to the nature of light, its light is infinite. Likewise, although Christ's habitual grace is finite as a quality in a created substance, it is infinite inasmuch as it is the source of all other grace, as the sun is the source of all light.[112] The pattern that emerges from this analysis reminds Thomas of the angelic hierarchy (as interpreted by Dionysius), for the angels, being nearer to God, receive more of the light of illumination than we do and pass that light on to us.[113]

In regarding Christ as the unlimited source of grace, Thomas is going against his own account of instrumental causality, according to which the instrumental power does not come from any form in the instrument, whether inherent or contingent. As he says later in the *Summa* when discussing the sacraments: 'there are two kinds of agent cause: principal and instrumental. A principal cause works by the power of its own form, to which the effect is assimilated, as fire heats by its own heat. In this way, only God can cause grace.'[114] But the grace that Christ bestows upon the

[110] *ST* IIIa, Q. 27, art. 5, resp. (2593b).
[111] *ST* IIIa, Q. 7, art. 12, resp. (2476a).
[112] *ST* IIIa, Q. 7, art. 11, resp. (2475a).
[113] See *ST* IIIa, Q. 27, art. 5, resp., on Mary (2593b); and IIIa, Q. 56, art. 1, resp., on the resurrection (2787a).
[114] *ST* IIIa, Q. 62, art. 1, resp. (2822a). See also *QDV*, Q. 27, art. 4, resp. (805a). Thomas emphasises that the instrumental power does not come from any form in the instrument in two contexts: the sacraments (see above), and the two 'operations' (divine and human) of Christ (see *ST* IIIa, Q. 19, art. 1, resp. [2551b–52a]).

faithful as their head is only conceptually different from the habitual grace of Christ as an individual human being, since 'the heat by which a fire is hot is the same as that by which it heats'.[115] The grace of Christ is even 'a certain natural property' (*quaedam proprietas naturalis*), for as Augustine says, 'grace is in a certain way natural to Christ-as-man'.[116] Hence Christ as a human being is in some sense the principal cause of grace, although (unlike God) he is only the univocal cause.[117]

While the sense of cosmic order and fittingness entailed by Thomas's treatment of *influentia capitis* is impressive, his intentions are unclear. Does he mean to posit a physical influence whereby Christ's grace, exactly like light or heat, replicates itself directly as a form in the souls of others? Or is the model a metaphor for summarising the work of merit, satisfaction, example and so on? Thomas provides us with no way to answer that question definitively.

Conclusion

While Thomas's treatment of the instrumental causality of Christ in his early work is certainly different from that in his late work, I do not see in this development, as others have done, a shift to a definite notion of a distinct, quasi-physical efficient causality. Whereas in his early work Thomas painstakingly constructs models of instrumentality that approximate to but fall short of efficient instrumental causality, in his late work he simply affirms that Christ is an efficient instrumental cause and leaves it at that. His mature account is so spare as to be consistent with any theory as to how Christ's humanity is the instrument of his divinity. Thus his appeal to efficient causality seems to be rather descriptive than explanatory: Thomas merely shows that the causality of Christ's humanity fulfils the criteria for instrumental efficient causes and for their ordination (for example, it does not contravene the principle that a cause must be superior or prior to its effect).

All of Thomas's discussions around this topic depend, in one way or another, on analogical reasoning. The scholastics use the term *analogia* to signify modes of name-sharing that are in some sense a mean between univocity and equivocity, as when one calls both an animal and a diet 'healthy'. But what I have in mind here is the older sense of *analogia*, as

---

[115] *ST* IIIa, Q. 8, art. 5, resp. (2483a): 'oportet quod idem sit actus quo aliquid est actu, et quo agit, sicut idem est calor quo ignis est calidus, et quo calefacit.'

[116] *ST* IIIa, Q. 7, art. 13, ad 2 (2478a). Cf. Augustine, *Enchiridion* 12, 40 (*Corpus Christianorum Series Latina* 46, p. 72, ll. 58–60).

[117] *In III Sent*, Ds. 13, Q. 2, art. 1, resp. (3:408, n. 75): 'Christus secundum humanam naturam . . . est principium quasi univocum'.

in Aristotle, according to whom an analogy is an equivalence of relationships, such that A is to B as C is to D.[118] Analogy accounted for metaphors, such as calling old age the twilight of life and twilight the old age of a day. But it was useful too in natural philosophy, for extremely unlike things, even things which belonged to no common genus, might be analogous. Hence Aristotle said that two things might be the same numerically, specifically, generically, or only by analogy.[119]

To construe Christ's humanity as an efficient instrumental cause, Thomas's point of departure is a causal model that characterises a certain relationship. Although in principle abstract and universal, the model is exemplified by instances drawn both from everyday life and from natural philosophy: the sun and sunlight, fire and heat, the carpenter and his adze, and so on. The use of a small stock of examples is a salient feature of scholastic thought. Most of the examples in this case involve archetypes hallowed by long tradition and by a kind of natural piety, such as the Craftsman and the Sun. The causal model, as embodied in the examples, constitutes the paradigm against which one can match the thing that one is trying to explicate or illumine. But the rules of such reasoning are far from clear. What does matching something to the paradigm achieve? What counts as a salient feature and what counts as only an insignificant feature? Once one has made a match and transferred the name from the paradigm to the thing that one aims to illumine, how does one know whether the second application of the name is metaphorical or literal? Why is calling Christ an efficient cause of salvation or resurrection less metaphorical than calling him head of the Church? What else, beyond permission to use a name, does the match imply? While talk of an influx of grace from Christ as head sounds like a causal explanation, the analysis of such usage in the *Summa fratris Alexandri* indicates that what one means by calling Christ head is simply that Christians are united with the God-man through faith and charity.

As far as I know, the scholastics themselves did not codify the rules of analogical reasoning. Consider the following analogical syllogism, designed to show that the soul is present in its entirety in every part of the body:

Augustine says that just as God is in the macrocosm, so is the soul present in the microcosm. But God is present in the macrocosm in such a

---

[118] See M. D. Philippe, '*Analogon* and *analogia* in the philosophy of Aristotle', *The Thomist* 33 (1969), pp. 1–74; and Joseph Owens, *The Doctrine of Being in the Aristotelian Metaphysics*, 3rd edn (Toronto: Pontifical Institute of Mediaeval Studies, 1978), pp. 123–5. For Plato's similar use of the concept, see *Timaeus* 29c and *Republic* 533e–34a.

[119] Aristotle, *Metaphysics* V, 1016b31–1017a3. See also *De partibus animalium* 645b27–8 and 645b3–8.

way that he is entire in every part of it. Therefore the soul is present in the same way in the microcosm, that is, in the body.[120]

The major of the syllogism states the analogy: A is to B as C is to D. The minor specifies that the relationship between C and D is X–Y. The conclusion infers that the relationship between A and B must be X–Y also. The argument is demonstrative only if the major premise is taken to mean that the two pairs are related in the same way in every respect; but then the major would be false. The argument presupposes something about what is salient in this case, but what one can presuppose without making the argument circular and tautologous is not obvious. The major has the structure of metaphor, and as Thomas notes, 'one should not expect to find likeness in every respect in metaphorical expressions, for in that case one would not have a likeness but the thing itself'.[121]

Scholars have often noted how Thomas uses qualifiers such as *quasi*, *quoddam* and *quodammodo* when he draws on analogies in theology, but they have not considered the logic of this reserve.[122] To what would one commit one's self by affirming that the resurrection is in some sense like an instrumental cause? How does the affirmation add to our understanding? Does it explain anything? Thomas's doctrine that the God-man is an efficient instrumental cause of salvation and resurrection, and even in some sense the principal cause of grace in the Church, may add something to the more familiar themes of redemption, merit and so on, but what it adds is not obvious. And absent a clear understanding of the rules and results of analogical reasoning, there seems to be no way to determine what it adds.

---

[120] Bonaventure, *in I Sent*, Ds. 8, p. 2, art. 1, Q. 3, arg. 1 (Quaracchi edn, vol. 1 [1882], p. 170a): 'Augustinus dicit, quod sicut Deus est in maiori mundo, sic anima in minori; sed Deus est in maiori, quod in qualibet parte totus: ergo anima sic est in minori, scilicet in corpore.' The *auctoritas* is from the ps.-Augustinian *De spiritu et anima*, c. 13.

[121] *ST* IIIa, Q. 8, art. 1, ad 2 (2479a): 'in metaphoricis locutionibus non oportet attendi similitudinem quantum ad omnia; sic enim non esset similitudo, sed rei veritas.' Cf. *ST* IIIa, Q. 48, art. 3, ad 1 (2736b), on Christ as a sacrifice: 'licet veritas respondeat figurae quantum ad aliquid, non tamen quantum ad omnia, quia oportet quod veritas figuram excedat.' Likewise, *in IV Sent*, Ds. 44, Q. 1, art, 1, quᵃ 1, ad 1 (Parma edn, p. 1073b): 'similitudo non currit per omnia, sed quantum ad aliquid'.

[122] *ST* IIIa, Q. 56, art. 1, ad 2 (2787b): 'resurrectio autem Christi est causa secundaria, et quasi instrumentalis.' *ST* IIIa, Q. 56, art. 1, ad 3: 'humanitas Christi, secundum quam resurrexit, est quoddamodo instrumentum divinitatis ipsius.' *ST* IIIa, Q. 48, art. 4, ad 2 (2737b): 'Quia igitur passio Christi fuit sufficiens et superabundans satisfactio . . . fuit quasi quoddam pretium per quod liberati sumus'.

Aquinas and Platonism[1]

FRAN O'ROURKE

One is unlikely to find far-reaching agreement between Bertrand Russell
and Etienne Gilson: the former a brilliant logician, the latter a brilliant
historian of medieval philosophy. They are unanimous, however, in their
historical characterisation of Thomas Aquinas. In his *History of Western
Philosophy*, published in 1945, Russell wrote:

> Aquinas, unlike his predecessors, had a really competent knowledge
> of Aristotle . . . Until his time, men's notions had been obscured by
> Neoplatonic accretions. He, however, followed the genuine Aristotle,
> and disliked Platonism, even as it appears in Saint Augustine. He
> succeeded in persuading the Church that Aristotle's system was to be
> preferred to Plato's as the basis of Christian philosophy, and that
> Mohammedans and Christian Averroists had misinterpreted Aris-
> totle.[2]

Is it possible that Russell was influenced, even indirectly, by the authoritative judgement of Etienne Gilson, expressed some twenty years
previously? Gilson pronounced that

> Aquinas was obliged to choose, once and for all, between the only two
> pure philosophies which can exist, that of Plato and that of Aristotle.
> Reduced to their bare essences, these metaphysics are rigorously anti-
> nomical; one cannot be for the one without being against all those who
> are with the other, and that is why Saint Thomas remains with Aris-
> totle against all those who are counted on the side of Plato . . . As a
> philosophy, therefore, Thomism was born out of a pure philosophical

[1] This essay is dedicated to W. Norris Clarke SJ in gratitude and admiration. I
express my profound gratitude to the Alexander S. Onassis Foundation, Athens, and
University College Dublin, for research fellowships which allowed me to research
and write this article in Athens during Spring 2002. I thank Gorazd Kocijancic, David
Burrell and Wayne Hankey for helpful criticisms and suggestions.
[2] Bertrand Russell, *A History of Western Philosophy* (New York: Simon &
Schuster, 1945), p. 453.

option to choose against the philosophy of Plato, in favour of that of Aristotle.[3]

During the decade preceding publication of Russell's *History*, a number of scholars had engaged in studies which would prove conclusively that the view of Aquinas as strict Aristotelian was no longer tenable.[4]

---

[3] Etienne Gilson, 'Pourquoi Saint Thomas a critiqué Saint Augustin', *Archives d'histoire doctrinale et littéraire du moyen age* 1, 1926–7, p. 126. More balanced is Werner Beierwaltes' view that 'Platonism' and 'Aristotelianism' compete productively in Aquinas; see '*Primum est dives per se*: Meister Eckhart und der Liber de Causis', in E. P. Bos and P. A. Meijer (eds.), *On Proclus and his Influence in Medieval Philosophy* (Leiden: Brill, 1992), p. 143.

[4] The pioneering studies were those of Cornelio Fabro, *La nozione metafisica di partecipazione secondo S. Tomaso d'Aquino* (Milan: Vita e Pensiero, 1939) and L.-B. Geiger, *La participation dans la philosophie de S. Thomas d'Aquin* (Paris: Vrin, 1942). Fabro published an expanded edition of his original study in 1950 (Turin: Società Editrice Internazionale); his monumental *Participation et causalité selon S. Thomas d'Aquin* appeared in 1961 (Publications Universitaires de Louvain). Worthy of mention is Arthur Little, *The Platonic Heritage of Thomism* (Dublin: Golden Eagle Books, 1950). R. J. Henle's work, *Saint Thomas and Platonism: A Study of the Plato and Platonici Texts in the Writings of Saint Thomas* (The Hague: Martinus Nijhoff, 1956) is an indispensable research tool for the comparison of Aquinas with Plato; unfortunately Henle examines only those texts in which Aquinas refers explicitly to Plato or the *Platonici*, neglecting the Platonism which is implicit in much of Aquinas's reflection; consequently he minimises Aquinas's Platonist influence (see Norris Clarke's review, noted below). More recent studies (noting only a selection) to examine the Platonic and Neoplatonic character of Aquinas's philosophy are: Klaus Kremer, *Die Neuplatonische Seinsphilosophie und ihre Wirkung auf Thomas von Aquin* (Leiden: Brill, 1966, 2nd edn 1971); Pierre Faucon, *Aspects néoplatoniciens de la doctrine de saint Thomas d'Aquin* (Paris: Honoré Champion, 1975); Edward Booth, *Aristotelian Aporetic Ontology in Islamic and Christian Thinkers* (Cambridge: Cambridge University Press, 1983); W. J. Hankey, *God in Himself: Aquinas' Doctrine of God as Expounded in the ST* (Oxford: Oxford University Press, 1987; Hankey has also published a large number of important articles which provide comprehensive and valuable bibliographical information); Fran O'Rourke, *Pseudo-Dionysius and the Metaphysics of Aquinas* (Leiden: Brill, 1992); Vivian Boland, *Ideas in God According to Saint Thomas Aquinas: Sources and Synthesis* (Leiden: Brill, 1996). The most recent work of major importance is Rudi A. te Velde's outstanding *Participation and Substantiality in Thomas Aquinas* (Leiden: Brill, 1995). A valuable tool for the examination of Aquinas's Neoplatonist influence is the recent English translation of the *Commentary on the Book of Causes* by Vincent A. Guagliardo OP, Charles R. Hess OP and Richard C. Taylor (Washington, DC: Catholic University of America Press, 1966), with its excellent introduction and annotations. Worthy of special mention are the many writings, over the past half century, of W. Norris Clarke SJ. Particularly relevant are 'The Limitation of Act by Potency in St Thomas: Aristotelianism or Neoplatonism?' and 'The Meaning of Participation in St. Thomas', initially published in 1952 and now available in *Explorations in Metaphysics* (Notre Dame, IN: University of Notre Dame Press, 1994). An excellent summary of Aquinas's participation metaphysics may be found in part II of *The Philosophical Approach to God* (Winston-Salem, NC: Wake Forest University, 1979). Of great importance to the discussion of Aquinas and Plato are his

Conclusive perhaps, but not coercive, since even Gilson himself never fully accepted their results. Half a century later a well-known author still referred to Aquinas as 'the leading christian Aristotelian of the Middle Ages', declaring:

> Thomas of Aquino wove, by his teaching and writings, the greatest of all the medieval tapestries of christian intellectual vision, its warp from Aristotelian theory, with its own characteristic value implications, shot through with the woof of christian traditions and symbols, laden with commitment to the final values of worship.[5]

More recently, in the first year of the new millennium, a course on St Thomas was offered at a historic German university, based upon Josef Gredt's manual, *Elementa philosophiae aristotelico-thomisticae*.[6] With such exceptions, however, Aquinas's substantial debt to the Platonic tradition has been widely acknowledged.

The presence of Platonist elements in the work of Thomas Aquinas is multifaceted and profound. Assessment of his debt to the Platonic heritage, however, is problematic; there is no clear evidence that he made use of any of the three works of Plato available to the Latin West in the thirteenth century.[7] His knowledge of Platonism derived from a complex tradition of commentators and followers who in varying degrees had themselves modified original sources. Plato's doctrines were gradually and significantly transformed in turn by Plotinus, Augustine, Proclus, Pseudo-Dionysius and the writer of the *Liber de Causis*, to name the most important.[8] Aquinas's debt to Aristotle is also a case of refracted Platonism; the Stagirite retained inspiration from his days at the Academy and remained profoundly Platonist in many respects. This brought a unique problem. Having at his disposal the newly translated works of Aristotle,

---

perceptive and critical reviews of Arthur Little, 'The Platonic Heritage of Thomism', *Review of Metaphysics* 8 (1954), pp. 105–24, and of Robert J. Henle, 'St Thomas and Platonism', *Thought* 32 (1957), pp. 437–43. These reviews, unfortunately, have not received the attention they deserve.

[5] Frederick Ferré, *Being and Value: Toward a Constructive Postmodern Metaphysics* (Albany, NY: SUNY Press, 1996), pp. 94, 98.

[6] Josef Gredt OSB, *Elementa philosophiae aristotelico-thomisticae* (Freiburg im Breisgau: Herder, 1937).

[7] Henle, *Saint Thomas and Platonism*, p. xxi. See James A. Weisheipl, 'Thomas' Evaluation of Plato and Aristotle', *New Scholasticism* 48 (1974), pp. 101–3.

[8] For an excellent account of the Platonist influences on Aquinas, see Wayne J. Hankey's comprehensive entry, 'Aquinas and the Platonists', in Stephen Gersh and Maarten J. F. M. Hoenen (eds.), *The Platonic Tradition in the Middle Ages: A Doxographic Approach* (Berlin: De Gruyter, 2002), pp. 279–324. I am most grateful to Professor Hankey for generously providing me with a copy of his manuscript, from which I have greatly benefited. In light of his approach, I have chosen here to adopt a speculative rather than historical approach.

Aquinas had direct access both to Plato's best pupil and his keenest critic; he perceived thus a Plato critically filtered through the eyes of the one who knew him best, but painted with the darker hues of the pupil's palette. Thus Aquinas could only with difficulty discern the real Plato.

No amount of *Quellenforschung* will explain the personal genius of a great thinker. There remains an inexplicable element – the ἕτερόν τι, by which Aristotle explains the difference between living and inanimate: the 'something else' which animates the vision of an original thinker and inspires his written *oeuvre*. It is a grace of nature, and Plato and Aquinas alike were gifted. They had the same searching approach to the world – even though the world of each was different. Great minds have like visions and think equally great thoughts, though never the same. Regardless of the differences separating them, Plato and Aquinas have many philosophical attitudes in common. It is not always a case of historical influence, but frequently a viewpoint attained independently by Aquinas. The Platonism of St Thomas was unreflected rather than conscious. Prescinding for the most part from the question of putative influence, I wish in the following reflections to explore some of the affinities binding Plato and Aquinas across a millennium and half. In accord with the title of the present volume, I propose to contemplate Aquinas as a Platonist, without negating – this should be stressed – the many other defining elements of the Thomist synthesis.[9]

Etienne Gilson's judgement of Aquinas is correct inasmuch as there are irreconcilable inconsistencies between Plato's starting-point and that proposed by Aristotle; Aquinas indeed made a philosophical option for the method of Aristotle. He could never declare with Cicero that he would rather err with Plato than hear the truth from others.[10] Aquinas was an unwitting, avowed, but critical Platonist. His genius was to discern truth subtly even alongside error. The key to his approach is the distinction between a Platonic *positio* or conclusion, and the *via*, *ratio* or methodic principle by which such a conclusion is attained; rejecting the latter he frequently adopted the former, attained more securely – sometimes, but not always – under the guidance of Aristotle.[11] (Conversely, a

---

[9] I limit my remarks to Plato's influence in Aquinas's metaphysics and theory of knowledge; one should not overlook his role in the formation of Aquinas's ethics, especially the doctrine of the cardinal virtues, so-called by St Ambrose, but first canonised by Plato – articulating, it appears, a view already crystallised in Greek culture, a fact unknown to Aquinas.

[10] Cicero, *Tusculanae Disputationes* 1, 39: 'A. Errare mehercule malo cum Platone, quem tu quanti facias scio et quem ex tuo ore admiror, quam cum istis vera sentire. M. Macte virtute! ego enim ipse cum eodem isto non invitus erraverim.'

[11] Henle's work, *Saint Thomas and Platonism*, has documented the important distinction between the *viae* and the *positiones* of Plato and their place in Aquinas's system. See Clarke's important review in *Thought* 32 (1957), pp. 437–43.

position attained with the help of Aristotle might well rest more profoundly upon a Platonist intuition.) Aquinas was critical of Plato's style, accusing him of having a bad method of teaching, speaking figuratively and through symbols, 'intending by his words something other than what the words themselves signify'.[12] Aquinas follows, *grosso modo*, Aristotle's explanation of the scope and nature of knowledge, yet many of his deepest metaphysical intuitions are unmistakenly Platonist. Before considering what unites Aquinas with Plato, it will be helpful to review briefly his critique of Plato's approach to knowledge. Here too we notice his skill at detecting truth even in alien doctrines, absorbing elements and applying them appropriately and analogously within his own system.

Knowledge

Aquinas notes that Plato adopted the Presocratic principle of similitude between knower and known: 'like is known by like'. The Presocratics presumed that this likeness was materialistic; Aquinas praises Plato for recognising it as immaterial.[13] In correcting the materialism of the Presocratics, however, he took the error to its opposite extreme, explaining every aspect of cognition as exclusively immaterial, including the very being of the object itself: the real is the ideal. 'Plato, having observed that the intellectual soul has an immaterial nature, and an immaterial mode of knowledge, held that the forms of things known subsist immaterially.'[14] He failed to distinguish between the real and cognitive orders. Aquinas notes the confusion: 'What is a principle of knowledge is not necessarily a principle of existence, as Plato thought.'[15] He explains:

> It does not follow that, because science is about universals, universals are subsistent of themselves outside the soul, as Plato maintained. For, although true knowledge requires that knowledge correspond to

---

[12] *In I DA*, viii: 'Plato habuit malum modum docendi; omnia enim figurate dicit et per symbola, intendens aliud per verba, quam sonent ipsa verba.'

[13] *DSS*, I, 4 [ET: ed. and trans. Francis J. Lescoe (West Hartford, CT: St Joseph College, 1963), p. 38].

[14] *ST* Ia, Q. 84, art. 2: 'Plato enim, quia perspexit intellectualem animam immaterialem esse et immaterialiter cognoscere, posuit formas rerum cognitarum immaterialiter subsistere.' Ia, Q. 84, art. 1: 'Videtur autem in hoc Plato deviasse a veritate, quia, cum aestimaret omnem cognitionem per modum alicuius similitudinis esse, credidit quod forma cogniti ex necessitate sit in cognoscente eo modo quo est in cognito.' See Ia, Q. 76, art. 2, ad 4.

[15] *ST* Ia, Q. 85, art. 3, ad 4: 'Non autem est necesse quod omne quod est principium cognoscendi, sit principium essendi, ut Plato existimavit.'

things, it is not necessary that knowledge and thing should have the same mode of being.[16]

As Aquinas portrays it, Plato needed to accommodate two aspects of knowledge: its assimilation to the object, and its stability. He concluded that since knowledge is an immaterial activity, its object must likewise be immaterial, and because it requires fixity, its object must be immutable in itself. Plato is reacting against the Presocratic view that, since everything in the world is in continual flux, there can be no knowledge of truth.[17] What is in a continual state of flux cannot be known with any certainty. Plato thus posited the separate unchanging 'ideas', by participation of which all singular and sensible things are said to be either a man, or a horse, or the like. Science refers not to sensible bodies, but to those immaterial and separate substances: thus the soul does not understand corporeal, but the separate species. Aquinas rejects Plato's theory of subsistent ideas as useless: if knowledge is only of immaterial, immovable, essences, there can be no scientific knowledge of matter and movement; it is ridiculous (*derisibile*), he declares, to seek the substance of things outside them.[18]

There is an alternative: 'Aristotle proceeded along another way. For first he showed in many ways that there is something stable in sensible things.'[19] Aquinas states their distinct approaches:

> Some, in order to investigate the truths of nature, have taken as their starting point intelligible essences (*ex rationibus intelligibilibus*), and this was the characteristic of the Platonists; whereas some began with sensible things (*ex rebus sensibilibus*), and this was characteristic of Aristotle.[20]

---

[16] *SCG*, Bk 2, Ch. 75: 'Nec tamen oportet quod, quia scientiae sunt de universalibus, quod universalia sint extra animam per se subsistentia, sicut Plato posuit. Quamvis enim ad veritatem cognitionis necesse sit ut cognitio rei respondeat, non tamen oportet ut idem sit modus cognitionis et rei.'

[17] *ST* Ia, Q. 84, art. 1: 'Primi philosophi qui de naturis rerum inquisiverunt, putaverunt nihil esse in mundo praeter corpus. Et quia videbant omnia corpora mobilia esse, et putabant ea in continuo fluxu esse, aestimaverunt quod nulla certitudo de rerum veritate haberi posset a nobis.'

[18] *ST* Ia, Q. 84, art. 1: 'Derisibile videtur ut, dum rerum quae nobis manifestae sunt notitiam quaerimus, alia entia in medium afferamus, quae non possunt esse earum substantiae, cum ab eis differant secundum esse.'

[19] *QDSC*, art. 10, ad 8: 'Aristoteles autem per aliam viam processit. Primo enim, multipliciter ostendit in sensibilibus esse aliquid stabile.' [ET: *On Spiritual Creatures*, trans. Mary C. Fitzpatrick (Milwaukee, WI: Marquette University Press, 1949), p. 122.]

[20] *QDSC*, art. 3: 'Quidam ad inquirendam veritatem de natura rerum, processerunt ex rationibus intelligibilibus, et hoc fuit proprium Platonicorum; quidam vero ex rebus sensibilibus, et hoc fuit proprium philosophiae Aristotelis.' [p. 47]; See art. 9, ad 6; *ST* Ia, Q. 85, art. 3, ad 1.

It is not the existence of separate substances, free from matter, that Aquinas rejects – these he affirms himself – but rather Plato's ground for affirming them, what he calls the 'root of his position' (*positionis radix*), which, he says, 'is found to be without efficacy, for it is not necessary that what the intellect understands separately should have a separate existence (*esse*) in reality'. Aristotle also affirms the existence of separate substances, but 'follows a more manifest and surer way (*manifestiori et certiori via*), namely, by way of motion'.[21]

Plato and Aristotle agree that intellect only knows what is intelligible. They both reject the materialism of the Presocratics, but assign different immaterial causes of knowledge: 'Plato ascribed the cause of our knowledge to ideas, Aristotle to the active intellect.'[22] For Plato intelligible objects exist prior to cognition, as separate, self-subsisting, spiritual realities in themselves; knowledge is effected when the intellect somehow participates in them. According to Aristotle, the intelligible is not given *a priori*, but is latent in the objects of sense and is actualised by intellect itself through the mental activity of abstraction. The sensible cannot enter as such into the intellect; the role of the active intellect is to raise the intelligible content to the immaterial level required for intellection.[23] For Aristotle, the agent intellect illuminates the essence of the individual, disengaging it from its individualising characteristics and providing a concept which is immaterial and universal.[24] According to Plato, the mind is illuminated by the separated intelligible substances themselves;

---

[21] *DSS* 2, no. 8, p. 43: 'Huius autem positionis radix invenitur efficaciam non habere. Non enim necesse est ea quae intellectus separatim intelligit separatim esse habeant in rerum natura . . . Et ideo Aristoteles manifestiori et certiori via processit ad investigandum substantias a materia separatas, scilicet per viam motus.'

[22] *SCG*, Bk 3, Ch. 84: 'Omnes autem sequentes philosophi, intellectum a sensu discernentes, causam nostrae scientiae non aliquibus corporibus, sed rebus immaterialibus attribuerunt, sicut Plato posuit causam nostrae scientiae esse ideas; Aristoteles autem intellectum agentem.'

[23] *ST* Ia, Q. 79, art. 3: 'Posuit enim Plato formas rerum naturalium sine materia subsistere, et per consequens eas intelligibiles esse: quia ex hoc est aliquid intelligibile actu, quod est immateriale . . . Sed quia Aristoteles non posuit formas rerum naturalium subsistere sine materia; formae autem in materia existentes non sunt intelligibiles actu. Sequebatur quod naturae seu formae rerum sensibilium, quas intelligimus, non essent intelligibiles actu. Nihil autem reducere de potentia in actum, nisi per aliquod ens actu, sicut sensus fit in actu per sensibile in actu. Oportebat igitur ponere aliquam virtutem ex parte intellectus, quae faceret intelligibilia in actu, per abstractionem specierum a conditionibus materialibus. Et haec est necessitas ponendi intellectum agentem.' See *QDSC*, art. 9: 'Sed quia Aristoteles posuit ea non subsistere nisi in sensibilibus, quae non sunt intelligibilia actu, necesse habuit ponere aliquam virtutem quae faceret intelligibilia in potentia esse intelligibilia actu, abstrahendo species rerum a materia et conditionibus individuantibus; et haec virtus vocatur intellectus agens.'

[24] *ST* Ia, Q. 84: 'Dicendum est ergo quod anima per intellectum cognoscit corpora cognitione immateriali, universali et necessaria.'

for Aristotle and Aquinas, it is the mind which actualises and illuminates the potential intelligibility latent in material beings, thus assimilating the object to itself and making possible a knowledge which is stable and necessary.

Because Plato failed to grasp the nature of abstraction he believed that whatever is abstract in mind is also abstract in reality, hence the existence of separate universal essences.[25] 'The Platonists posited an order of intelligible beings beyond the order of intellects, since the intellect understands only by participation of the intelligible; and they maintain that which participates is below what it participates.'[26] Aquinas concedes counterfactually that there would be no need for the agent intellect if such intelligible universals really existed outside the soul.[27] But such is not our experience; man is both body and soul:

> Plato, considering only the immateriality of the human intellect, and not its being in a way united to the body, held that the objects of the intellect are separate ideas; and that we understand not by abstraction, but by participating things abstract.[28]

Aquinas finds fundamental fault with Plato's view of human nature: man is not a unity composed of body and soul, but 'a soul using a body (*anima utens corpore*), so that he is understood to be in a body in somewhat the same way as a sailor in a ship (*sicut nauta in navi*)'.[29]

While he rejects Plato's exaggerated immaterialism, Aquinas adapts to his purposes the Platonic noetic of superior illumination. He deftly harmonises the twin interpretations of Plato and Aristotle of knowledge as a lighting process, either infused from a higher source or as a sponta-

---

[25] *ST* Ia, Q. 85, art. 1, ad 2: 'Et quia Plato non consideravit quod dictum est de duplici modo abstractionis, omnia quae diximus abstrahi per intellectum, posuit abstracta esse secundum rem.'

[26] *ST* Ia, Q. 87, art. 1: 'Sic enim Platonici posuerunt ordinem entium intelligibilium supra ordinem intellectuum, quia intellectus non intelligit nisi per participationem intelligibilis; participans autem est infra participatum, secundum eos.'

[27] *QDSC*, art. 9: 'Et similiter non esset necesse ponere intellectum agentem, si universalia quae sunt intelligibilia actu, per se subsisterent extra animam, sicut proposuit Plato' [p. 102]; see art. 10 [pp. 114–24].

[28] *ST* Ia, Q. 85, art. 1: 'Plato autem, attendens solum ad immaterialitatem intellectus humani, non autem ad hoc quod est corpori quodammodo unitus, posuit objectum intellectus ideas separatas; et quod intelligimus, non abstrahendo quidem, sed magis abstracta participando.'

[29] *QDSC*, art. 2: 'Unde dicebat ut dictus Gregorius refert, quod homo non est aliquid compositum ex anima et corpore, sed est anima utens corpore, ut intelligatur esse in corpore quodammodo sicut nauta in navi' [p. 35]. Cf. *ST* Ia, Q. 75, art. 4. The soul, Plato also states, is united to the body as a motor (*ut motor*). Cf. Ia, Q. 76, art. 3; Ia, Q. 76, art. 7.

neous personal activity; he combines the motif of *lumen naturale* with that of transcendent light. Whichever model is proposed, it requires also the other, he argues, in order to be complete; the superior light must act through an individual agent, and the lighting faculty of the individual participates in a higher source. Emphasising that knowledge is the act of an individual soul, he states: 'No action belongs to anything except through some principle formally inherent therein; therefore the power which is the principle of this action must be something in the soul.'[30] Thus, even if Plato is correct in presupposing a separate intellect, the human soul still needs a faculty which acts individually in the concrete, although it participates in the superior intellect. And while Aristotle is correct in attributing to the soul a power which illuminates the phantasms of sense, this faculty is dependent upon a higher intellect.[31] The light imagery of both converges: Aristotle compared the active intellect to the light received into the air; Plato likened the separate intellect which illuminates the soul to the sun, the source of light itself. For Aquinas God is himself the 'separate intellect', as it were the spiritual sun from which the human soul receives its intellectual light. In the words of the Psalm: 'The light of your countenance, O Lord, is signed upon us.'[32] God's light is stamped upon the soul, but the soul acts with autonomy. The *lumen naturale* is participated light, but is also individual and personal; both motifs are inseparable. God is the ultimate source, therefore, of both subjective knowledge and objective knowability; he infuses reality with its intelligibility, and the knower with the personal power of intellection. We are close to the symbolism of *Republic* VI.

Aquinas is also able to explain cognition in terms both of Platonist participation and of Aristotelian causality. Knowledge is intellectual, but imperfectly so, that is, it participates in the power of intellect; on the other hand, it acquires knowledge progressively, moving from potency to act. According to Plato, whatever is imperfect requires the pre-existence

---

[30] *ST* Ia, Q. 79, art. 4: 'Nulla autem actio convenit alicui rei, nisi per aliquod principium formaliter ei inhaerens . . . Oportet igitur virtutem quae est principium huius actionis, esse aliquid in anima.'

[31] Boland (*Ideas in God*, p. 328) remarks: '[H]uman intellectual activity involves a kind of illumination or enlightenment because it is, ultimately, a participation in divine intelligence. For Saint Thomas this is especially clear in the functioning of the *intellectus agens* which he understands, not as an occasional or adventitious gift from God, but as an enduring capacity within human nature for appropriate intellectual activity.'

[32] *ST* Ia, Q. 79, art. 4: 'Et ideo Aristoteles comparavit intellectum agentem lumini, quod est aliquid receptum in aere. Plato autem intellectum separatum imprimentem in animas nostras, comparavit soli . . . Sed intellectus separatus, secundum nostrae fidei documenta, est ipse Deus, qui est creator animae, et in quo solo beatificatur . . . Unde ab ipso anima humana lumen intellectuale participat, secundum illud Psalmi 4: "Signatum est super nos lumen vultus tui, Domine." '

of essential perfection; and according to Aristotle, whatever is mobile depends on something immobile. Appealing to both principles, Aquinas concludes that above the intellectual soul of man we must necessarily affirm a superior intellect.[33] Jacques Maritain suggests that the main difference between St Augustine and St Thomas in the philosophic and noetic order was the 'substitution of efficient causality, the dominant Aristotelian-Thomistic note, for participation, the dominant Augustinian note'.[34] This must be seen as referring, not to the metaphysics of being but to the metaphysics of cognition, that is, to the manner in which knowledge is effected: through an illuminative participation in subsistent truth, or the efficient causation of the agent intellect. Aquinas gives priority *quoad nos* to the latter, but grounds it ultimately in the former.

Being

Plato and Aquinas share a basic realism regarding the objectivity of knowledge. Notwithstanding a critical divergence of philosophic method, both are equally committed to the primacy of being *vis-à-vis* cognition. With his emphasis on the primacy of the act of existence, Aquinas's philosophy is a philosophy of being *par excellence*. Because he affirmed the primacy of the Good, Plato might be considered to have neglected the paramount importance of existence. However, his philosophy is in intention, I suggest, first and foremost a philosophy of being. Jacques Maritain declares that Plato, but not Aristotle, was blessed with the intuition of being.[35] Plato had, more than Aristotle, a powerful and profound sense of existence but, lacking the conceptual language to articulate its significance, was obliged to go beyond being to seek its ultimate foundation. He recognised diverse meanings of the verb 'to be', and had, I suggest, a conscious but inchoate awareness of existence in the radical sense.[36] He certainly had a strong sense of the actuality of being,

---

[33] *ST* Ia, Q. 79, art. 4: 'Supra animam intellectivam humanam necesse est ponere aliquem superiorem intellectum, a quo anima virtutem intelligendi obtineat. Semper enim quod participat aliquid, et quod est mobile, et quod est imperfectum, praeexigit ante se aliquid quod est per essentiam suam tale, et quod est immobile et perfectum.'

[34] Jacques Maritain, *Degrees of Knowledge* (London: Geoffrey Bles, 1959), p. 305.

[35] Jacques Maritain, *Man's Approach to God* (Latrobe, PA: The Archabbey Press, 1960), p. 4. Aristotle, in contrast, whom Maritain describes as his 'old master', and the 'grand head of the *philosophia perennis*', had the intuition of being only implicitly, not formally: 'it is still only present to thought in a blind or virtual fashion, not yet perceived in full light'. See 'Réflexions sur la nature blessée et l'intuition de l'être', *Revue thomiste* 68 (1968), p. 17.

[36] There has been lively debate whether or not Plato discerned the diverse senses of being (existence, identity and the copula); a detailed examination of the question lies beyond our present scope. A. E. Taylor, J. L. Ackrill and Stanley Rosen are represen-

without naming it as such: an acute awareness of 'realness' as what is most profound in all things. How else can one explain the phrase 'really existing essence' (οὐσία ὄντως οὖσα),[37] in which he enlists every grammatical trope of the verb 'to be', in order to convey the pre-eminently realistic character of 'true being without colour or shape', the fully essential and firmly existential character of the Form? Plato misidentifies the true locus of being and misinterprets the ontological density of ordinary reality, but has nonetheless a keen sense of the need for existential adequacy and vehemence. Moreover, what he ultimately affirms as the transcendent and infinite plenitude, the Good in itself, is, I suggest, an adumbration of Aquinas's *ipsum esse subsistens*, the self-subsisting plenitude of existence. In order to clarify the widespread agreement between Thomist and Platonist ontology, it will be worth expounding some elements from Plato's dialogues which, had he known them, would have found favour with Aquinas.

The question of being is central to Plato's philosophy: his thought is marked by a zeal for Being as the object and goal of all authentic thought and endeavour. While this is masked under the guise of the Good, if we

---

tative of those who believe he did; Michael Frede, G. E. L. Owen, W. G. Runciman and J. Malcolm of those who believe that he did not. See J. L. Ackrill, 'Plato and the Copula: *Sophist* 251–59', in Gregory Vlastos (ed.), *Plato: A Collection of Critical Essays* (Notre Dame, IN: University of Notre Dame Press, 1978), pp. 210–22; Stanley Rosen, *Plato's Sophist: The Drama of Original and Image* (New Haven, CT: Yale University Press, 1983), pp. 229–44; G. E. L. Owen, 'Plato on Not-Being', in *Plato: A Collection of Critical Essays*, pp. 223–67; M. Frede, *Prädikation und Existenzaussage* (Göttingen: Vandenhoeck & Ruprecht, 1967); W. G. Runciman, *Plato's Later Epistemology* (Cambridge: Cambridge University Press, 1962); J. Malcolm, 'Plato's Analysis of τὸ ὄν and τὸ υὴ ὄν in the *Sophist*', *Phronesis* 12 (1967), pp. 130–46. According to P. Shorey, Plato laid the foundations of logic by 'explicitly distinguishing the copula from the substantive *is*': *What Plato Said* (Chicago, IL: University of Chicago Press, 1933), p. 298. A. E. Taylor asserts that Plato clearly distinguished the 'logical' copula, or sign of assertion, from the existential sense of 'is': *Plato: The Man and his Work* (Cleveland, OH: Meridian Books, 1966), p. 392. Taylor states:

> Plato has certainly laid the ghost of Eleatic monism by making a beginning with the discovery of the principle, familiar to us in Aristotle's formulation, that τὸ ὄν πολλαχῶς λέγεται. He has definitely distinguished the 'is' of the copula from the 'is' which asserts 'actual existence' . . . He has further discriminated the existential sense of is from the sense in which 'is' means 'is the same as', 'is identical with'. Beyond this we can hardly say that he has gone. (Raymond Klibansky and Elizabeth Anscombe (eds.), *Plato: The 'Sophist' and the 'Statesman'* (London: Thomas Nelson, 1961), pp. 81–2)

See also I. M. Crombie, *An Examination of Plato's Doctrines*, 2 (London: Routledge & Kegan Paul, 1963), pp. 498–516; J. M. E. Moravcsik, 'Being and Meaning in the Sophist', *Acta Philosophica Fennica* 14 (1962), pp. 23–78.

[37] *Phaedrus* 247c.

look closely at the language, presuppositions, thrust and spirit of his thinking, we cannot but notice that it is imbued with a desire for *that-which-is*. Plato declares in the *Republic* that knowledge is related to being and knows it as it is.[38] The philosopher loves such knowledge as reveals the essence of permanent and unchanging reality and seeks such reality in its totality.[39] The philosopher, in contrast to the lover of opinion, seeks each true reality.[40] True philosophy is the turning away from darkness to light and the ascent to real being.[41] His gaze is fixed upon 'all time and all existence'. Habituated to thoughts of grandeur, his mind seeks integrity and wholeness in all things human and divine.[42] Such wholeness and permanence, untouched by multiplicity or change, is for Plato the mark of true being – pure being, τοῦ ὄντος εἰλικρινῶς.[43] Such being exists *more*, to a *fuller degree* than limited, changing reality.

Plato professes an axiomatic commitment to being as the ground of truth. Truth and being imply one another: truth reveals being, and being is the foundation of truth. Being is the ultimate value in knowledge and raises for Plato the basic question: 'Is it possible for one to attain "truth" who cannot even get as far as "being"?'[44] In evaluating sensation, Socrates even suggests that, 'since it is always of something which is' (τοῦ ὄντος ἀεί ἐστιν), perception must be infallible,[45] but concludes after analysis: 'Knowledge does not reside in sensations, but in our reflection upon them, since it is possible to apprehend *being and truth* (οὐσίας γὰρ καὶ ἀληθείας) by reflection but not by sensation.'[46] Knowledge is found not in perception, but in the soul, when it is engaged directly with beings (περὶ τὰ ὄντα).[47]

Plato provides a simple demonstration of the concept of being as fundamental and universal. In an analysis of cognition, he traces the limited and disparate grasp of the sense faculties back to the all-

---

[38] *Republic* 478a: ἐπιστήμη μέν γέ που ἐπὶ τῷ ὄντι, τὸ ὂν γνῶναι ὡς ἔχει;

[39] *Republic* 485ab: τοῦτο μὲν δὴ τῶν φιλοσόφων φύσεων πέρι ὡμολογήσθω ἡμῖν, ὅτι μαθήματός γε ἀεὶ ἐρῶσιν, ὃ ἂν αὐτοῖς δηλοῖ ἐκείνης τῆς οὐσίας τῆς ἀεὶ οὔσης καὶ μὴ πλανωμένης ὑπὸ γενέσεως καὶ φθορᾶς.

[40] *Republic* 480a: τοὺς αὐτὸ ἄρα ἕκαστον τὸ ὂν ἀσπαζομένους φιλοσόφους, ἀλλ' οὐ φιλοδόξους κλητέον;

[41] *Republic* 521c: ψυχῆς περιαγωγὴ ἐκ νυκτερινῆς τινος ἡμέρας εἰς ἀληθινήν, τοῦ ὄντος οὖσα ἐπάνοδος, ἣν δὴ φιλοσοφίαν ἀληθῆ φήσομεν εἶναι.

[42] *Republic* 486a: τοῦ ὅλου καὶ παντὸς ἀεὶ ἐπορέξεσθαι θείου τε καὶ ἀνθρωπίνου . . . μεγαλοπρέπεια καὶ θεωρία παντὸς μὲν χρόνου, πάσης δὲ οὐσίας.

[43] *Republic* 479d.

[44] *Theaetetus* 186c: οἷόν τε οὖν ἀληθείας τυχεῖν, ᾧ μηδὲ οὐσίας;

[45] *Theaetetus* 152c: αἴσθησις ἄρα τοῦ ὄντος ἀεί ἐστιν καὶ ἀψευδὲς ὡς ἐπιστήμη οὖσα.

[46] *Theaetetus* 186d: ἐν μὲν ἄρα τοῖς παθήμασιν οὐκ ἔνι ἐπιστήμη, ἐν δὲ τῷ περὶ ἐκείνων συλλογισμῷ· οὐσίας γὰρ καὶ ἀληθείας ἐνταῦθα μέν, ὡς ἔοικε, δυνατὸν ἅψασθαι, ἐκεῖ δὲ ἀδύνατον. See 186e: ᾧ γε, φαμέν, οὐ μέτεστιν ἀληθείας ἅψασθαι· οὐδὲ γὰρ οὐσίας.

[47] *Theaetetus* 187a: ὥστε μὴ ζητεῖν αὐτὴν ἐν αἰσθήσει τὸ παράπαν, ἀλλ' ἐν ἐκείνῳ τῷ ὀνόματι, ὅ τί ποτ' ἔχει ἡ ψυχή, ὅταν αὐτὴ καθ' αὑτὴν πραγματεύηται περὶ τὰ ὄντα.

embracing first affirmation of being, upon which all truth and knowledge are grounded. Each sense faculty is restricted to objects of its own domain; none perceives what is particular to another.[48] We have, nonetheless, a knowledge of objects which goes beyond sensation; the hardness of one thing and the softness of another are both attained through touch, but the sense of touch does not grasp their very existence: that each exists distinctly, but that existence nevertheless is common to both.[49] The various senses seize material aspects of bodies but cannot rise beyond these to apprehend their being, commonality or differences. Our knowledge, nevertheless, is more than the aggregate of disparate impressions; we know them in their unity and diversity. The soul apprehends the so-called κοινά, the common or universal features which characterise all objects of knowledge, the *universalia universalissima*: being and non-being, likeness and unlikeness, identity and difference, unity and plurality.[50] The apprehension of being provides the ultimate synthesis, expressing the fundamental unity which embraces all things. Being is the primary concept: 'With regard to sound and colour, have you not, to begin with, this thought which includes both at once – that they both exist?'[51] Being is also the most universal: 'Being (οὐσία). . . more than anything else, belongs to all things'.[52]

This appreciation of Being as the ground and goal of all knowledge becomes more explicit in the *Sophist*. The occasion of the dialogue is to reveal the true nature of the sophist, who parades falsity as truth. He is a maker of non-real images, mere semblances devoid of being. He seeks subterfuge in obscurity and falsehood. 'The sophist runs away into the darkness of not-being (εἰς τὴν τοῦ μὴ ὄντος σκοτεινότητα), feeling his way by practice, and is hard to discern on account of the darkness of the place.'[53] In contrast, 'the philosopher, always devoting himself through reflection to the idea of being, is also very difficult to see due to the brilliance of that region; for the eye of the vulgar soul cannot endure to gaze upon the divine'.[54] Being is the ultimate goal and horizon of the soul.

---

[48] *Theaetetus* 185a.

[49] *Theaetetus* 186b: τὴν δέ γε οὐσίαν καὶ ὅ τι ἐστὸν καὶ τὴν ἐναντιότητα πρὸς ἀλλήλω καὶ τὴν οὐσίαν αὖ τῆς ἐναντιότητος αὐτὴ ἡ ψυχὴ ἐπανιοῦσα καὶ συμβάλλουσα πρὸς ἄλληλα κρίνειν πειρᾶται ἡμῖν.

[50] *Theaetetus* 185cd: οὐσίαν λέγεις καὶ τὸ μὴ εἶναι, καὶ ὁμοιότητα καὶ ἀνομοιότητα, καὶ τὸ ταὐτόν τε καὶ τὸ ἕτερον . . . αὐτὴ δι᾽ αὑτῆς ἡ ψυχὴ τὰ κοινά μοι φαίνεται περὶ πάντων ἐπισκοπεῖν.

[51] *Theaetetus* 185a: περὶ δὴ φωνῆς καὶ περὶ χρόας πρῶτον μὲν αὐτὸ τοῦτο περὶ ἀμφοτέρων ἦ διανοεῖ, ὅτι ἀμφοτέρω ἐστόν;

[52] *Theaetetus* 186a: μάλιστα ἐπὶ πάντων παρέπεται.

[53] *Sophist* 254a.

[54] *Sophist* 254ab: ὁ δέ γε φιλόσοφος, τῇ τοῦ ὄντος ἀεὶ διὰ λογισμῶν προσκείμενος ἰδέα, διὰ τὸ λαμπρὸν αὖ τῆς χώρας οὐδαμῶς εὐπετὴς ὀφθῆναι· τὰ γὰρ τῆς τῶν πολλῶν ψυχῆς ὄμματα καρτερεῖν πρὸς τὸ θεῖον ἀφορῶντα ἀδύνατα.

It is radiant in its brilliance and merits the name 'divine'. Whereas the Idea of the Good is presented in the *Republic* as the greatest of all things to learn (μέγιστον μάθημα),[55] in the *Sophist* it is the Idea of Being which is affirmed as the object of 'the greatest science' (τῆς μεγίστης ἐπιστήμης).[56]

One of the most significant results of the contrasting analysis in the *Theaetetus*, of sensation which grasps particulars and of reflection which knows universal or common being, is that being may not be identified with any particular object of knowledge, since it is common to all. Being is what all sense data have in common but is itself distinct from whatever is sensed. Any datum of sense will exhibit existence, but will not reveal its fullness; what it discloses cannot be identified simply with being itself. For something to be sensible is for it to be; for something to be, is not necessarily for it to be sensible. This is brought out at length in the *Sophist*, where the Stranger judges the legacy of the φυσιολόγοι and arbitrates between the monists and the pluralists. Being is not to be equated with any of its determinants, but is a value which is variously participated. Being cannot be equated with cold, since its opposite would then be impossible; nor with sameness, else difference would not exist. An entity of which 'cold' is not affirmed, need not necessarily be affirmed as 'not cold'. It may lie outside the range of this mutually exclusive disjunctive: it may be non-material. Reality may not be equated with any one of its modes. Being may not be identified with its determinations – this is the golden rule to avoid all reductionism. Being is a universal value which is diversely participated, but may not be identified with any of its participants. In the language of Aquinas, it is disclosed through the judgement of negative separation (being *is*, but is not '*this*'), rather than grasped abstractively like other concepts.[57]

Being and sameness are among those γένη which 'pervade all and connect them so that they can blend'. Being and otherness are among those which 'traverse wholes and are responsible for division'.[58] 'Being and otherness traverse all things and interpenetrate so that the other partakes of being, and *is*, by reason of this participation, and yet *is not*

---

[55] *Republic* 505a: ἐπεὶ ὅτι γε ἡ τοῦ ἀγαθοῦ ἰδέα μέγιστον μάθημα.

[56] *Sophist* 253c–254a: τῆς μεγίστης ἐπιστήμης . . . τοῦ ὄντος ἰδέα.

[57] Aquinas deals briefly with the importance of the judgement of separation for metaphysical knowledge in *In BDT*, 5, 3. See the excellent pages by John F. Wippel in his monumental work, *The Metaphysical Thought of Thomas Aquinas* (Washington, DC: Catholic University of America Press, 2000), pp. 44–62. Cf. p. 49:

> Through separation one does not deny that beings of this or that kind also fall under being. On the contrary, by denying that being must be limited to any one of its actual or possible kinds, one opens the way for considering these, including the differences which are realised in each, within the realm of being, and as being.

[58] *Sophist* 253c: διὰ πάντων εἰ συνέχοντ' ἅττ' αὔτ' ἐστιν, ὥστε συμμίγνυσθαι δυνατὰ εἶναι, καὶ πάλιν ἐν ταῖς διαιρέσεσιν, εἰ δι' ὅλων ἕτερα τῆς διαιρέσεως αἴτια;

that of which it partakes, but other.'[59] Being is, therefore, the source of both unity and diversity, of sameness and difference. Being is what all things have in common, yet each is distinct because, while not identical with Being itself, it has being in its own limited way. The structure of unity and similarity is one of communion and participation. Being is not simply one among the endless forms or perfections of the universe but is the most fundamental of all, embracing all others as secondary and implicit. In affirming the existence of an individual, what is affirmed is at once the participation of the individual in existence, and simultaneously its non-identity with existence itself. The individual shares in existence, but is not itself identical with existence: it is not the fullness of being. Likewise to affirm an accidental mode of being is to affirm that the accident shares in the being of the object, but is not identical with it. Being is the presence which contains all things, but is contained by none.

In the *Sophist* Plato deals explicitly with the nature of being and gives the clearest statement on being in his entire works. He considers the universe of beings from a dynamic point of view, that is, how they interact and influence one another, and defines being as the 'power to act and be acted upon'.[60] He understood being, however, in terms of movement (κίνησις), and conceived life and even thought as motions. He correctly grasped that Being was not static and insisted that perfect being must contain life and knowledge. This involved him in the contradiction that perfect reality implied motion, which was anathema to his entire system.[61] Aristotle's theory of act, and the deeper meaning of actuality (ἐνέργεια / ἐντελέχεια) as the action or actualisation of a substance, already complete within itself, allowed Aquinas to overcome this problem: life and knowledge do not necessarily imply movement. Being, considered in itself as simple act and perfection, is the most fundamental activity of all; it has its end and fulfilment in itself and needs nothing else to act upon.[62]

Aquinas's philosophy of being is well known and needs only a brief outline; Being is primary, he holds, in two related respects. First, the concept of *ens* ('that-which-is') is the most universal and fundamental of all; it is presupposed by all other concepts and is implied in them. The concept of being is the *primum cognitum*; every other notion makes explicit a characteristic already silently affirmed in the universal assertion: 'reality is'. But more important than this mental concept of *ens* is the

---

[59] *Sophist* 259a: τό τε ὂν καὶ θάτερον διὰ πάντων καὶ δι' ἀλλήλων διεληλυθότα τὸ μὲν ἕτερον μετασχὸν τοῦ ὄντος ἔστι μὲν διὰ ταύτην τὴν μέθεξιν, οὐ μὴν ἐκεῖνό γε οὗ μετέσχεν ἀλλ' ἕτερον.

[60] *Sophist* 247de: δύναμιν εἴτ' εἰς τὸ ποιεῖν . . . εἴτ' εἰς τὸ παθεῖν.

[61] See *Sophist* 249d–250d.

[62] A separate problem is the need in finite beings for transitive action in order to fulfil themselves.

act by which beings in the first place exist, that is, are actualised and enacted, as opposed to the only alternative, which is nothingness. This is the meaning attached by Aquinas to the verbal infinitive 'to be' (*esse*). The act of being, however, is not simply a neutral function determining the option between existence or non-existence. It determines also the level of existential perfection enjoyed by an individual. It is not only the 'act of all acts', but also the 'perfection of all perfections'.[63] The act of being is a variable value which determines the status of the individual in the hierarchy of being. *Esse* is the first participation in divine goodness, containing virtually within itself all other perfections. The value scale of existence ultimately accounts for the hierarchy of reality: *gradus in ipso esse invenitur*.[64]

There is much in the *Theaetetus* and *Sophist* which anticipates Aquinas's teaching on being. Plato grasped the fundamental and universal character of being; in this he adumbrates Aquinas's doctrine. We cannot find in the dialogues anything exactly corresponding to Aquinas's view of existence as intensive perfection, yet there are some preparatory and kindred elements. Plato asserts that οὐσία, 'more than anything else, belongs to all things'. In the *Sophist*, Being is regarded as a kind of 'superform', in which all things participate. The participation of individuals in the fullness of essence, moreover, entails the intensive gradation of a received perfection; the reality of the individual – regarded formally or quidditatively – is virtually present in its archetype, not in the same concrete mode, but according to a higher, sublimated, presence, within the power of the εἶδος. The motif of the virtual or intensive presence of the positive value of individuals in the Form is adopted by Aquinas in his conception of being as the comprehensive value in which all specific perfections partake. Hence life and knowledge participate in the primary value and perfection of being. Aquinas's conception of being as comprehensive intensive perfection echoes the Platonist motif of the pre-eminent presence of effects in the cause. Aquinas transfers the relationship between participant and participated to the dependence of every secondary mode of being upon the perfection of being, and ultimately to the participation of all creatures in subsistent divine being (*ipsum esse subsistens*).

Plato's insight into being as the 'power to act or be acted upon' anticipates Aristotle's distinction between actuality and potency, which is central to many of Aquinas's doctrines, not only his metaphysics, but also his psychology, epistemology, ethics and theory of art. The definition of being as δύναμις prefigures to some extent Aquinas's notion of being as *virtus essendi*, the fundamental power whereby all things are present in

---

[63] *QDP* 7, 2, ad 9: 'Hoc quod dico esse est actualitas omnium actuum, et propter hoc est perfectio omnium perfectionum.'

[64] *ST* Ia, Q. 48, art. 2.

themselves and to the universe, according to varying degrees of perfection. Plato's insistence[65] that what is fully real must be endowed with life and intelligence becomes an important source for the Neoplatonic doctrine of the threefold levels of reality, adopted enthusiastically by Aquinas. It matures into his doctrine of the intensive fullness of existence: being according to its fullest meaning is alive and intelligent; life and intelligence are not added as extra perfections to existence, as from without, but flow from the individual's act of being, as modes of its actuality.[66]

Participation

It was to explain the various modes of existence exercised by different realities that Plato proposed his theory of participation. Wishing to describe the metaphysical realities and relations underlying human experience, Plato was obliged – as Parmenides and Heraclitus before him, and philosophers ever since – to turn to the inadequate vocabulary of physical reality. The analogy of part to whole seemed best to depict the relationship of limited, changing, individuals to their essence conceived as perfect and immutable. Participation indicates the dependent status of individuals which possess in limited measure the identity and perfection of a specific nature, but which do not exhaust its full reality. Plato also took from Pythagoras the model of imitation, but found in participation a more profound and comprehensive explanation.

The core principle of participation is stated in the *Republic*: 'Whenever a number of individuals have a common name, we assume them to have a corresponding idea or form.'[67] According to Plato, wherever there is a many there must be a one: if a multiplicity possesses a common perfection or quality, there must exist a single source which is itself the fullness of that perfection and the source for all others. 'We affirm an absolute beauty and an absolute good; likewise for all things which we affirm as many, we posit a single idea, assuming it to be a unity, which we call the essence of each.'[68] Plato's ideal forms are possessed not simply of a

---

[65] *Sophist* 248e–249a: τί δὲ πρὸς Διός; ὡς ἀληθῶς κίνησιν καὶ ζωὴν καὶ ψυχὴν καὶ φρόνησιν ἦ ῥᾳδίως πεισθησόμεθα τῷ παντελῶς ὄντι μὴ παρεῖναι, μηδὲ ζῆν αὐτὸ μηδὲ φρονεῖν, ἀλλὰ σεμνὸν καὶ ἅγιον, νοῦν οὐκ ἔχον, ἀκίνητον ἑστὸς εἶναι; See Pierre Hadot's classic study 'Être, vie, pensée chez Plotin et avant Plotin', in *Les sources de Plotin*, Entretiens sur l'Antiquité Classique 5 (Geneva: Vandoeuvres, 1960), pp. 105–41.

[66] For a detailed treatment, see O'Rourke, *Pseudo-Dionysius*, pp. 174–80.

[67] *Republic* 596a: εἶδος γάρ πού τι ἓν ἕκαστον εἰώθαμεν τίθεσθαι περὶ ἕκαστα τὰ πολλά. See also *Republic* 507b; *Meno* 72d; *Cratylus* 439cd–440b.

[68] *Republic* 507b: καὶ αὐτὸ δὴ καλὸν καὶ αὐτὸ ἀγαθὸν καὶ οὕτω περὶ πάντων, ἃ τότε ὡς πολλὰ ἐτίθεμεν, πάλιν αὖ κατ' ἰδέαν μίαν ἑκάστου ὡς μιᾶς οὔσης τιθέντες ὃ ἔστιν ἕκαστον προσαγορεύομεν.

mental reality, but of an existence more powerful and complete than that of physical objects. The relation of individuals to the universal is not one of mental association or abstraction, as for Aristotle, but of real dependence and causation.

Regarding the ontological status of the forms Plato states, in the case of equality, that it is 'not the equality of stick to stick and stone to stone, or anything else of the like, but something beyond all that and distinct from it' (παρὰ ταῦτα πάντα ἕτερόν τι).[69] Similarly with beauty itself, goodness, justice and holiness; likewise all those things which, as he puts it, are stamped with the seal of 'that which is' (περὶ ἁπάντων οἷς ἐπισφραγιζόμεθα τὸ ὃ ἔστι).[70] Marked with the indelible character of existence, these absolute forms are the only true realities. Εἶδος is the pure and perfect essence, free from change, defect and limitation. 'Beauty, goodness and the other forms have a most real actuality, existing to the fullest possible extent' (εἶναι ὡς οἷόν τε μάλιστα).[71]

It is the form in its fullness and independence which alone constitutes the ground and adequate cause for individuals. 'There is no other way by which anything comes to be than by participating in the proper essence of each thing in which it participates.'[72] As Plato states in the *Phaedo*, it is not its lovely colour or shape which makes a thing beautiful; 'nothing else makes it beautiful but the presence or communion of that absolute beauty'.[73] He does not know how this has come about, or how exactly it functions, but repeatedly insists that the principle 'beautiful things are beautiful through beauty'[74] is sure and secure (ἀσφαλέστατον).

---

[69] *Phaedo* 74a.

[70] *Phaedo* 75d.

[71] *Phaedo* 77a; see 78d. Clarke conveys well the importance of Plato's inspired intuition:

The breakthrough to discover the abiding presence of this transcendent dimension of reality, for the first time in the history of Western thought, must have been a powerful, almost intoxicating, experience for him, as though a veil had been pulled aside to reveal at last the splendor of the truly real, in comparison with which our changing world of sensible objects was only a shadowlike imperfect image. No modern neo-Kantian or analytic philosophy reinterpretation of the theory of ideas as merely conceptual or linguistic categories should be allowed to vitiate the strength of Plato's ontological commitment to the objective reality of ideas, however this be finally interpreted. (W. Norris Clarke, 'The Problem of the Reality and Multiplicity of Divine Ideas in Christian Neoplatonism', in Dominic J. O'Meara (ed.), *Neoplatonism and Christian Thought* (Albany, NY: SUNY Press, 1982), p. 110)

[72] *Phaedo* 101c: καὶ μέγα ἂν βοῴης ὅτι οὐκ οἶσθα ἄλλως πως ἕκαστον γιγνόμενον ἢ μετασχὸν τῆς ἰδίας οὐσίας ἑκάστου οὗ ἂν μετάσχῃ.

[73] *Phaedo* 100d: οὐκ ἄλλο τι ποιεῖ αὐτὸ καλὸν ἢ ἡ ἐκείνου τοῦ καλοῦ εἴτε παρουσία εἴτε κοινωνία.

[74] *Phaedo* 100de: ὅτι τῷ καλῷ πάντα τὰ καλὰ γίγνεται καλά . . . ὅτι τῷ καλῷ τὰ καλὰ καλά.

The words used by Plato for 'participation', μέθεξις, μετάληψις and κοινωνία, refer to the subtle and inscrutable relationship between individuals and the objective fullness of the perfection which they exemplify and share with others. The relation of multiple parts to a unique whole is a profound and illuminating analogy; yet eventually Plato becomes aware of its limitations, recognising the difficulties inherent in his own theory of participation. He registers in the *Parmenides* two critical difficulties: problems associated with the multiplication of what is shared by its participants, and the impropriety that there should be forms of realities which are in themselves imperfect, such as dirt, mud and hair: how can these exist in a state of perfection?

Aquinas has an accurate grasp of the theory of forms,[75] and recognises the difficulties implicit in Plato's participation. He notes that Plato establishes an order among the forms themselves, on the ground that according as something is simpler in the intellect, it is prior within the order of things:

> In accordance with the order of forms, the Platonists posited the order of separate substances; for example, there is a single separate substance, which is horse and the cause of all horses, whilst above this is separate life, or life itself, as they term it, which is the cause of all life, and above this again is that which they call being itself, which is the cause of all being.[76]

He recognises, however, that beyond being Plato places a higher principle:

> Now that which is first in the intellect is the one and the good; for he understands nothing who does not understand something one, and the one and the good follow upon one another. Hence Plato held that the first Idea of the One, which he called the One-in-Itself and the Good-in-Itself, was the first principle of things and this Idea he said was the highest good.[77]

---

[75] For a brief exposé see *ST* Ia, Q. 65, art. 4.

[76] *ST* Ia, Q. 65, art. 4: 'Et secundum ordinem formarum ponebant platonici ordinem substantiarum separatarum: puta quod una substantia separata est quae est equus, quae est causa omnium equorum; supra quam est quaedam vita separata, quam dicebant per se vitam et causam omnis vitae; et ulterius quandam quam nominabant ipsum esse, et causa omnis esse.'

[77] *DSS* 1, 5, p. 39: 'Id autem quod primo est in intellectu est unum et bonum. Nihil enim intelligit qui non intelligit unum; unum autem et bonum se consequuntur. Unde ipsam primam ideam unius quod nominabat secundum se unum et secundum se bonum, primum rerum principium esse ponebat et hanc summum bonum esse dicebat.'

All forms, therefore, participate in the One (*omnes species participant uno*).[78]

As Aquinas expounds it, Plato's theory provides the solution to two questions: the nature of knowledge and the origin of finite beings. The forms are the foundation of a twofold participation: they furnish a ground both for the certainty of truth and for the existence of individuals. The immaterial forms

> are participated both by our soul and by corporeal matter; by our soul, to the effect of knowledge thereof, and by corporeal matter to the effect of existence: so that, just as corporeal matter by participating the idea of a stone, becomes an individuating stone, so our intellect, by participating the idea of a stone, is made to understand a stone.[79]

Aquinas explains the analogous nature of participation in both cases:

> Plato held that the forms of things subsist of themselves apart from matter; and these he called ideas, by participation of which he said that our intellect knows all things: so that just as corporeal matter by participating the idea of a stone becomes a stone, so our intellect, by participating the same idea, has knowledge of a stone.[80]

As we have seen, Aquinas rejects Plato's theory of forms. Yet he embraces with approval the principle that when many individuals possess a common perfection, there must be a single causal source. Rejecting separate subsistent ideas as the formal causes which generate sensible things, he applies the principle of participation more radically to the universal and intimate perfection of being; the common perfection of existence requires a single creative cause.[81] He states this with clarity and

---

[78] *DSS* 1, 6, p. 40.

[79] *ST* Ia, Q. 84, art. 4: 'Has igitur formas separatas ponebat participari et ab anima nostra, et a materia corporali; ab anima quidem nostra ad cognoscendum, a materia vero corporali ad essendum; ut sicut materia corporalis per hoc quod participat ideam lapidis, fit hic lapis, ita intellectus noster per hoc quod participat ideam lapidis, fit intelligens lapidem.'

[80] *ST* Ia, Q. 84, art. 5: 'Posuit autem Plato formas rerum per se subsistere a materia separatas, quas "ideas" vocabat, per quarum participationem dicebat intellectum nostrum omnia cognoscere; ut sicut materia corporalis per participationem ideae lapidis fit lapis, ita intellectus noster per participationem eiusdem ideae cognosceret lapidem.'

[81] Clarke (*Thought* 32 (1957), p. 442), gives the following assessment in the context of his evaluation of Henle's verdict of the importance of Platonist participation for Aquinas:

> It seems most significant to me that in all his criticisms of the Platonic system the Angelic Doctor always studiously excludes from attack the principle itself that

brevity in the prologue to his Commentary on St John's Gospel, remarking that the Platonists attained knowledge of God through his dignity, based on the notion of participation: 'that which is something by participation is reduced to what is the same thing by essence, as to the first and highest'. Aquinas himself applies this principle to what is for him the most universal and fundamental value of existence:

> Since all things which exist participate in existence (*esse*) and are beings by participation, there must necessarily be at the summit of all things something which is existence by its essence, i.e., whose essence is its existence. And this is God, who is the most sufficient, the most eminent, and the most perfect cause of the whole of existence, from whom all things that are participate existence.[82]

This is a significant example of the distinction between *via* and *positio*. Aquinas applies the élan of Platonic principles to a new milieu, where existence is the primary ambient and element. Participation constitutes

---

> every many requires a one and the resulting laws of participation . . . Granted that St. Thomas differs specifically from the Platonists in operating the reduction to unity through efficient and not merely formal causality, it does not follow that Thomistic participation is really only a synthesis of the causalities already found in Aristotle. No Aristotelian causal theory can deliver that every 'many', precisely because it is 'many', requires one cause, nor determine the mode of possession of the common perfection in the cause and the participants, since there is no theory of the limitation of act by potency in Aristotle. Yet St. Thomas could find all this most explicit in the line of Proclus, the Pseudo-Dionysius, Boethius, the *Liber de causis*, etc., all stemming from Plotinus, and no matter how profoundly St. Thomas modified the Platonic 'many–one' principle, it seems to me impossible completely to 'de-Platonize' it.

See also pp. 440–1:

> There is one basic element of the *via Platonica* itself which St. Thomas considers sound and fruitful enough to be taken over and applied to the order of existence to explain the necessity of a unique First Cause and the relations of all other beings to it. This is the principle of participation, namely, that wherever there is a 'many', that is, many subjects possessing some common perfection, there must be a 'one', that is, one source or cause of this common property in all the participants, such that the common perfection is possessed by the source according to identity of essence and unlimited plenitude and by the participants according to varying modes of limitation and composition.

[82] *In Joh, Prologus*, n. 5: 'Quidam autem venerunt in cognitionem dei ex dignitate ipsius dei: et isti fuerunt Platonici. Consideraverunt enim quod omne illud quod est secundum participationem, reducitur ad aliquid quod sit illud per suam essentiam, sicut ad primum et ad summum . . . Cum ergo omnia quae sunt, participent esse, et sint per participationem entia, necesse est esse aliquid in cacumine omnium rerum, quod sit ipsum esse per suam essentiam, id est quod sua essentia sit suum esse: et hoc est deus, qui est sufficientissima, et dignissima, et perfectissima causa totius esse, a quo omnia quae sunt, participant esse.'

the central axis of Plato's dialectic: it is the foundation and coping-stone of his entire vision; it becomes the same for Aquinas. Plato and Aquinas share comparable principles, applied analogously within distinctive intellectual and existential environments. The ultimate metaphysical explanation of individual beings is best accounted for by each, however, through the act of participation, pointing ultimately to the existence of a unique transcendent plenitude of perfection, the source of all existence and intelligibility.

The notion of participation was unquestionably the most fruitful insight which Aquinas consciously adopted from Plato. The dual relation of participant–participated signifies the indwelling presence of spirit, the efficacy of non-material power, the relation of the individual to its universal essence, the cognisance of objects by consciousness, and the intimate and profound action of God as creative presence to each individual. The analogy of part to whole is capable of expressing the relationship between any metaphysical principle – of material or non-material being – and its wider context. L.-B. Geiger remarks that the terms *participatio*, *participare*, and their derivatives are to be found on almost every page of Aquinas's writings, claiming that 'almost all of his philosophical and theological theses are formulated with the aid of the vocabulary of participation'.[83]

Plato's principle of participation, introduced to solve a false problem, provided Aquinas with an ontological structure which he transformed and applied to his own original concept of existence. It is not participation as such which he criticises, but its use by Plato. For Aquinas, participation is the best explanation for the obvious paradox of limited perfection; being is the fundamental and primary perfection of all things, the universal value in which each individual participates according to its unique measure. Each individual captures the perfection of existence in the measure of its specific essence, placing a limitation to what in itself is infinite. But, how can the infinite be limited? As Norris Clarke explains,

Plato was unable to express the participation structure in terms of the limited reception by the participants of a perfection that exists in its source in a state of illimitation or infinity. This is the position that St. Thomas, following the whole Neoplatonic tradition, was to hold.[84]

Clarke remarks:

---

[83] Geiger, *La participation*, pp. 11, 13, note 1.
[84] Clarke, 'The Meaning of Participation in St. Thomas', in *Explorations in Metaphysics*, p. 90.

Although Plato had the genius to discover the doctrine of participation in general and the necessity of some principle of negation or imperfection in reality, his equally deep-rooted conception of perfection as distinct form, and hence of finite and infinite as correlatives of perfect and imperfect, prevented him from carrying through his analysis of participation to its more natural consequence, i.e., to expression in terms of a limitation of the higher by the lower.[85]

Aquinas adopted with enthusiasm the Platonist principle of participation in order to demonstrate the reality of a first cause. He adopts from Plato the axiom that wherever there is a 'many', there must be a 'one', that is, wherever there is a multiplicity sharing a common perfection, there must be a single plenary cause of that perfection. Aquinas's *Quarta Via*, which argues from the grades of being to the existence of God, is essentially Platonist. The existence of varying degrees of perfection merely adds an extra dimension to the phenomenon of the one and the many, of multiplicity and unity in the universe, lending added force to metaphysical reflection on the problem. Aquinas's reliance on Plato is more clearly evident in the simpler formulation in *De Potentia*, where he applies the argument of participation to both the diversity of being and the degrees of perfection. When something is common to all, he states firstly, it must be the effect of a single cause, since no individual can itself be the cause of what it shares with others. Beings are diverse, yet existence is common to all; hence they must come into being not by themselves, but by the action of a common single cause. He asserts: 'Seemingly this is Plato's argument, since he required every multitude to be preceded by unity not only as regards number but also in reality.'[86] Second, he states, whenever a perfection is participated by many beings in varying degrees, no individual with a limited measure can itself be the source of its own perfection; if it could cause it, it should not place a limit to its own perfection but would by necessity possess it to an infinite degree –

---

[85] Clarke, 'The Limitation of Act by Potency', in *Explorations in Metaphysics*, pp. 71–2.

[86] *QDP*, 3, 5: 'Oportet enim, si aliquid unum communiter in pluribus invenitur, quod ab aliqua una causa in illis causetur; non enim potest esse quod illud commune utrique ex se ipso conveniat, cum utrumque, secundum quod ipsum est, ab altero distinguatur; et diversitas causarum diversos effectus producit. Cum ergo esse inveniatur omnibus rebus commune, quae secundum illud quod sunt, ad invicem distinctae sunt, oportet quod de necessitate eis non ex se ipsis, sed ab aliqua una causa esse attribuatur. Et ista videtur ratio Platonis, qui voluit, quod ante omnem multitudinem esset aliqua unitas non solum in numeris, sed etiam in rerum naturis.' Cf. *ST* Ia, Q. 44, art. 1: 'Unde et Plato dixit quod necesse est ante omnem multitudinem ponere unitatem.'

and there would be no difference of degrees. It must be caused in those in which it exists imperfectly by the most perfect.[87]

One commentator has remarked: 'Thomas was more convinced than Plato that participation helped us to appreciate what is going on in the created universe.'[88] Participation for Aquinas, however, was not the participation in Plato's forms, but in the basic activity and perfection of existence. By bringing participation to bear on the most fundamental, intimate and universal perfection which all things have in common, Aquinas was able to affirm the existence of God who causes creatures by sharing his being, so that finite things may participate in the effect of creation.[89] Aquinas thus transforms participation by equating it with the efficient causality of creation.

Aquinas would agree with Plato's own objections to participation and the theory of forms, stated in the *Parmenides*. How can something be shared without losing its simplicity and fullness? Can there be forms of imperfect realities? Plato has no difficulty in affirming the reality of such separate forms as justice in itself, beauty, and goodness.[90] He hesitates, however, whether there can be separate forms of such realities as man, fire and water and rejects as outright absurd the existence of separate forms of such things as hair, mud or dirt.[91] This level of reality is, he declares, most ignoble and vile (ἀτιμότατόν τε καὶ φαυλότατον).

Plato's problem was largely solved by a distinction which was funda-

---

[87] See *QDP* 3, 5: 'Nam ea quae positive secundum magis et minus dicuntur, hoc habent ex accessu remotiori vel propinquiori ad aliquid unum: si enim unicuique eorum ex se ipso illud convenirent, non esset ratio cur perfectius in uno quam in alio inveniretur . . . Est autem ponere unum ens, quod est perfectissimum et verissimum ens.' While Aquinas attributes to Aristotle the argument that the lesser members of a genus are caused by what is primary and perfect, the argument finds its full power in the metaphysics of participation.

[88] Mary T. Clark (ed.), *An Aquinas Reader* (New York: Fordham University Press, 1988), p. 31. Fabro (*Participation et causalité*, p. 194) declares: 'Whatever may have been the obscurities, deviations and contradictions of Plato's thought and its developments within Platonism, it remains a fact that his fundamental intuition of participation has resisted all attacks, and is still conserved today – after modern thought and all its research into the dialectic of act and the subjectivity of being – as the sole formula capable of expressing the relation of parts to whole, finite to infinite, of beings to Being itself.'

[89] See Fabro, *Participation et causalité*, p. 193: 'One must recognise that if Aristotle has the merit of having discovered the knowledge of substance and of cause, it is Plato who has laid down the foundations of the transcendental structure of substance and of cause, and it is thanks to this doctrine that one can establish the relations of concrete dependence of the finite to the Infinite.'

[90] *Parmenides* 130b.

[91] *Parmenides* 130c.

mental for Aquinas: that between pure and impure perfections. Pure perfections connote no mark of limitation and may be found formally in God, and affirmed essentially of him. Impure perfections are contained virtually in God, that is, in his power, such that he is their cause, but in no way resembles them. Pure perfections have also the fullness which escapes the problems of participation. The sharing by a multiplicity in the fullness of a pure spiritual perfection does not shatter its unity. The realities of spirit, such as love, joy or knowledge may be shared without being divided; participation is not division. With material being, this is not the case; when shared, it loses its wholeness or entirety. At a yet higher level of independence or freedom than spiritual being from the restrictions of matter is the unbounded perfection of existence which, unlimited in itself since restricted by nothing, may be given or shared without diminishing the richness of its source.

Aquinas provides adequate solutions to the difficulties acknowledged by Plato in the *Parmenides*, with his application of participation to a newly conceived concept of existence, and with his distinction among essential forms (now transferred as perfections to the mind of God) between pure perfections, the names of which are applied properly to God, and those denoting imperfect modes of being which may only be affirmed symbolically of divine nature, or more adequately which are removed from God, but which have the merit of denoting his transcendence beyond the physical world.

The theory of ideas was a flawed solution to the problem of stable and universal knowledge. Following the example of Aristotle, Aquinas rejected Plato's ultrarealism; he denies that natural individuals participate formally in extramental, universal, essences which determine 'what' they are. For Aquinas, beings participate in the perfection of existence, not in a universal quiddity. Yet, a problem still remains: how to account for the similarity of essence throughout a diversity of individuals, that is, their resemblance in *what* they are. The theory of abstraction does not respond to this question, but to the problem how we grasp a diversity of similar individuals by means of a single concept. Aquinas finds a ready-made solution to the deeper problem in Augustine, following a tradition already established in Middle Platonism.

> Imbued with the doctrines of the Platonists (*qui doctrinis Platonicorum fuerat imbutus*), whenever he found anything contrary to faith, he substituted something better; thus for Platonic forms he substituted the reasons (*rationes*) of all creatures existing in the divine mind.[92]

---

[92] *ST* Ia, Q. 84, art. 5; cf. Ia, Q. 15; Ia, Q. 83; Ia, Q. 46; Ia, Q. 65, art. 4 ad 2. Augustine was drawing on a modification already established in Middle Platonism, as early as the first century BC; see Boland, *Ideas in God*, pp. 22–3.

Following Augustine, Aquinas adapted Plato's theory of universals *ante rem* to the only level where it could be true. Aristotle had dismissed the forms as birdlike 'twitterings' (τερετίσματα),[93] and explanations of participation as empty words and poetic metaphors.[94] It would be interesting to speculate how the *Thomas aristotelicus* of the handbook would interpret the fortunes of this fertile theory. The 'twitterings' are now the thoughts of God, and participation – analogy more than metaphor – is the universal principle and structure joining all things in the universe, both to one another and to their divine source.

The Divine Good

A point of fundamental difference between Aquinas and Plato – and the entire Neoplatonist tradition – is the relation of being and goodness in the definition of the divine principle. For Plato the Good is beyond being (ἐπέκεινα τῆς οὐσίας).[95] He attains the ground and unity of existence by transcending being and sacrificing the reality of sense objects; being is a participation in the Good. Influenced by Pseudo-Dionysius and the writer of the *Liber de Causis*, for whom being is the first created perfection, Aquinas arrived at an understanding of existence as the absolutely first of all perfections. Being is not only the first participation in a transcendent Good but is itself perfection unlimited: Being and the Good are identical. The excellence of Goodness, overstressed by Plato, is restored within the implicit meaning of Being, which on deeper reflection is revealed as primary. God is praised not primarily as Good, but as Being. His proper name is *Qui est*; he is described by Aquinas as the 'infinite ocean of substance' (*pelagus substantiae infinitum*),[96] in a phrase borrowed from John Damascene, but which echoes powerfully Plato's praise of the Good in the *Symposium* as 'the great ocean of beauty'.[97]

Despite Plato's assertion that Good is 'beyond being', we cannot conclude that it is therefore non-existent. The passage indicates rather the difficulty of conveying its supremacy and excellence. The Good is something most real in itself:

---

[93] *Posterior Analytics* I, 22, 4, 83a32-34.

[94] *Metaphysics* I, 991a 20–23: τὸ δὲ λέγειν παραδείγματα αὐτὰ εἶναι καὶ μετέχειν αὐτῶν τἆλλα κενολογεῖν ἐστι καὶ μεταφορὰς λέγειν ποιητικάς.

[95] *Republic* 509b: οὐκ οὐσίας ὄντος τοῦ ἀγαθοῦ, ἀλλ' ἔτι ἐπέκεινα τῆς οὐσίας πρεσβείᾳ καὶ δυνάμει ὑπερέχοντος.

[96] *ST* Ia, Q. 13, art. 11: 'Hoc nomen "qui est" nullum modum essendi determinat, sed se habet indeterminate ad omnes; et ideo nominat ipsum pelagus substantiae infinitum.' See *In I Sent*, 8, 1, 1 ad 4.

[97] *Symposium* 210d: τὸ πολὺ πέλαγος . . . τοῦ καλοῦ.

Every soul pursues it and does all that it does for its sake, with an intuition of its reality, yet baffled and unable to apprehend its nature adequately, or to attain to any stable belief about it as about other things.[98]

Most convincing are the phrases which describe the idea of the good as 'the brightest part of being' (τοῦ ὄντος τὸ φανότατον),[99] 'the most blessed part of being' (τὸ εὐδαιμονέστατον τοῦ ὄντος),[100] and 'what is best among things which are' (τὸ ἄριστον ἐν τοῖς οὖσι).[101] As the origin of being and perfection, the Good constitutes the fullness of ontological perfection.

Why did Plato situate the Good beyond Being? Is not an *au-delà de l'être* inconceivable and contradictory? Aquinas sought to understand the reasons why Plato gave priority to goodness over being. Plato was unaware of the distinction between actual being and potential being and therefore classified matter with non-being.[102] Through its power of attraction, however, goodness extends its causality to matter and may therefore be said to embrace non-being.[103] From the perspective of final causality, goodness has wider extension than being, comprehending not only what actually is, but also potential being. As Aquinas understands the Platonist view, matter is strictly speaking non-being, but through its predisposition towards the good, 'partakes something of the good'.[104]

For Aquinas, the good is what is desired; desirability is rooted in the act of existence – unless it exists nothing can be desired. Goodness and being are identical; what is potentially real is equally only potentially good. Because goodness adds to being an explicit reference to purpose and will, it has a certain conceptual primacy. Goodness however is

---

[98] *Republic* 505e: ὃ δὴ διώκει μὲν ἅπασα ψυχὴ καὶ τούτου ἕνεκα πάντα πράττει, ἀπομαντευομένη τι εἶναι, ἀποροῦσα δὲ καὶ οὐκ ἔχουσα λαβεῖν ἱκανῶς τί ποτ' ἐστὶν οὐδὲ πίστει χρήσασθαι μονίμῳ οἵᾳ καὶ περὶ τἆλλα.

[99] *Republic* 518c.

[100] *Republic* 526e.

[101] *Republic* 532c. See Werner Beierwaltes, *Lux intelligibilis: Untersuchung zur Lichtmetaphysik der Griechen* (Munich: doctoral thesis, 1957), pp. 46, 65; Matthias Baltes, 'Is the Idea of the Good in Plato's *Republic* Beyond Being?' in DIANOHMATA, *Kleine Schriften zu Platon und zum Platonismus* (Stuttgart: Teubner, 1999), p. 353.

[102] Aristotle's recognition of the metaphysical importance of matter, with the allied discovery of potency, merited high praise from Cajetan, who referred to him as 'divus Aristoteles, quia invenit materiam'.

[103] *QDM* I, 2: 'Et quia Platonici non distinguebant inter materiam et privationem, ordinantes materiam cum non ente, dicebant, quod bonum ad plura se extendit quam ens.' Cf. *QDV* 21; Aristotle, *Physics* I, 9, 191b35–192b4.

[104] *ST* Ia, Q. 5, art. 3, ad 3: 'Dicendum quod materia prima, sicut non est ens nisi in potentia, ita nec bonum nisi in potentia. Licet, secundum Platonicos, dici possit quod materia prima est non ens, propter privationem adiunctam. Sed tamen participat aliquid de bono, scilicet ipsum ordinem vel aptitudinem ad bonum.'

grounded in the deeper principle of being, not in existence as neutral observable fact, but in being as intrinsic power (*virtus essendi*) and actuality (*actus essendi*). Implicit in Aquinas's metaphysics are two notions of being, one logical, the other metaphysical. Goodness receives its radical explanation in a shift from the concept of being (*ens*), simply stating the fact that things exist, to the inner act of being (*esse*), which grounds the resources and perfection of each individual. *Bonum* exceeds *ens*, and attains its entire significance in *esse*, the act of all acts and perfection of all perfections. *Esse* is the existential abundance from which flows the self-diffusing activity of each individual, and which bestows every quality which makes it an object of desire.

Aquinas gives a plausible explanation for the primacy of το Ἀγαθὸν, but takes Plato's thought a stage further. W. K. C. Guthrie remarks on Plato:

> In his teleological world, if one knows that something *is*, or exists, there is always the further question, What is it *for*? What is the *good* of it? The good of a thing is the final explanation of its existence. But for Goodness itself there is no such further question.[105]

Aquinas can agree that in its explicit content the idea of goodness surpasses the primitive concept of being, which remains silent about purpose or finality. Etienne Gilson states:

> Precisely because it is essentially desirable, goodness is a final cause. Not only this, but it is both prime and ultimate in the order of purposiveness. Even being is only because it is for the sake of something, which is its final cause, its end. In the order of causality, then, goodness comes first, and it is in this sense that Platonism receives from Thomas Aquinas all the credit to which it is entitled.[106]

However, for Aquinas, there is no final goal which is extrinsic to the totality of the real; there is no separate Good. Divine subsistent being is the transcendent good from which all things emanate as efficient source, and the final cause which draws all creatures to itself. It is such because it is the unlimited and subsisting fullness of existence, containing to an infinite degree the perfections which are manifested in creatures. God is beyond being (*ens*) inasmuch as he is infinite being (*esse*) itself.[107]

---

[105] W. K. C. Guthrie, *History of Greek Philosophy*, vol. 4 (Cambridge: Cambridge University Press, 1975), p. 507.

[106] Etienne Gilson, *The Elements of Christian Philosophy* (New York: Mentor-Omega, 1963), p. 169.

[107] *In LDC* VI, ed. H. D. Saffrey (Fribourg: Louvain, 1954), p. 47: 'Sed secundum veritatem causa prima est supra ens inquantum est ipsum esse infinitum.'

As the origin of being, Plato's Good constitutes the fullness of onto-logical perfection. 'The nature of the Good is necessarily the most perfect of all things . . . and surpasses all others in sufficiency'.[108] This super-abundance of perfection is the ultimate reason for the generation of both the natural and ideal worlds. His doctrine of the diffusion of goodness is illustrated in the myth of the Demiurge told in the *Timaeus*, where Plato wishes to relate as a 'likely story' how the cosmos was engendered. It is, we are told, the work of a master artisan who fashions the natural world according to an eternal order. While the artisan is assumed to be divine, he cannot truly be called 'creator' in the strict sense or be identified with the Good. It is more likely, as Proclus concluded, that the demiurge is related to the sensible world as the One or the Good is to the whole of reality. Nevertheless in this myth Plato introduces to Greek philosophy the first real account of the formation of the cosmos through divine agency.

Aquinas praises both Plato and Aristotle for surpassing the limited perspective of earlier thinkers to investigate the origin of all things. 'Plato, Aristotle and their disciples attained to the study of universal being: and hence they alone posited a universal cause of things.'[109] Previous philosophers adverted to accidental external change, or recog-nised only the causality of corporeal principles, although admittedly Empedocles discovered formal causality. 'But beyond this mode of becoming, it is necessary according to the teaching of Plato and Aristotle, to posit a higher one (*ponere alium altiorem*).'[110] He further clarifies that although Plato and Aristotle supposed immaterial substances to have always existed, they did not deny they were caused in their being, or depart from the faith by holding them to be uncreated.[111] Aquinas thus attributes both to Plato and Aristotle the doctrine of a universal cause of the existence of all things ('universalem causam rerum, a qua omnia alia in esse prodirent'). In this sense he credits them with a doctrine of creation,[112] but clearly not the fully elaborated theory championed by himself.

---

[108] *Philebus* 20d.

[109] *QDP* 3, 5: 'Posteriores vero philosophi, ut Aristoteles et eorum sequaces, pervenerunt ad considerationem ipsius esse universalis; et ideo ipsi soli posuerunt aliquam universalem causam rerum, a qua omnia alia in esse prodirent.'

[110] *DSS* 9, no. 48, p. 86: 'Sed ultra hunc modum fiendi necesse est secundum sententiam Platonis et Aristotelis ponere alium altiorem'.

[111] *DSS* 9, no. 51, p. 90: 'Non ergo existimandum est quod Plato et Aristoteles propter hoc quod posuerunt substantias immateriales seu etiam coelestia corpora semper fuisse, eis subtraxerunt causam essendi. Non enim in hoc a sententia catholi-cae fidei deviarunt quod huiusmodi posuerunt increata, sed quia posuerunt ea semper fuisse, cuius contrarium fides catholica tenet.'

[112] See Mark Johnson, 'Aquinas's Changing Evaluation of Plato on Creation', *American Catholic Philosophical Quarterly* 46 (1992), pp. 81–8.

A. E. Taylor suggests that the idea of creation out of nothing was intelligible to Plato. God causes all things without any pre-existing material. He remarks: 'The language, perhaps, must not be unduly pressed, but it proves at least that the idea of "creation *ex nihilo*" was quite intelligible to Plato.'[113] In the *Sophist*, Plato defines the productive arts as those which bring into being something which did not previously exist (ἄγειν εἰς οὐσίαν).[114] He divides the productive arts into the divine and the human. The human arts produce things which did not exist, by combining or moulding given materials (περὶ τὸ σύνθετον καὶ πλαστόν). It is tantalising to speculate what meaning Aquinas would have attached to Plato's conception of divine production. It is worth quoting the Stranger's words in full:

> We said that every power is productive which causes things to come into being which did not exist before . . . There are all the animals, and all the plants that grow out of the earth from seeds and roots, and all the lifeless substances, fusible and infusible, that are formed within the earth. Shall we say that they came into being, not having been before, in any other way than through God's workmanship? Or, accepting the commonly expressed belief – that nature brings them forth from some self-acting cause, without creative intelligence. Or shall we say that they are created by reason and by divine knowledge that comes from God?[115]

In the *Timaeus* we encounter for the first time the motif of goodness as the origin and reason for creation. The fundamental tenet, central to the Neoplatonist and Christian traditions, of the diffusive nature of the good, provided Aquinas with the ultimate answer to the question: 'Why is there something rather than nothing?' This received its classical formulation in the *Timaeus*. To the question 'Why did the artisan of the universe shape it at all?', Plato replies: 'He was good, and what is good has no particle of envy in it; without envy, therefore, he wished all things to be as like himself as possible.'[116] Plato's view of reality might well be

---

[113] Taylor, *Plato*, p. 391.

[114] *Sophist* 219b.

[115] *Sophist* 265bc: ποιητικήν . . . πᾶσαν ἔφαμεν εἶναι δύναμιν ἥτις ἂν αἰτία γίγνηται τοῖς μὴ πρότερον οὖσιν ὕστερον γίγνεσθαι . . . ζῷα δὴ πάντα θνητὰ καὶ φυτὰ ὅσα τ' ἐπὶ γῆς ἐκ σπερμάτων καὶ ῥιζῶν φύεται καὶ ὅσα ἄψυχα ἐν γῇ ξυνίσταται σώματα τηκτὰ καὶ ἄτηκτα, μῶν ἄλλου τινὸς ἢ θεοῦ δημιουργοῦντος φήσομεν ὕστερον γίγνεσθαι πρότερον οὐκ ὄντα;

[116] *Timaeus* 29e–30a. The pagan philosopher and physician Galen favours the cosmology of the *Timaeus* over the belief of Moses that everything is arbitrarily possible to the will of God. 'Plato and the other Greeks who have treated correctly of natural principles' hold that 'some things are naturally impossible and God does not attempt these at all but chooses from among the possible what is best to be done': *De*

characterised as a metaphysical optimism. All things are the generous outpouring of all-perfect Goodness which, self-sufficient and superabundant, wishes to share its perfection. Goodness is generous; it is *generative*. This Platonic motif of the self-bestowal of goodness is crystallised in the medieval principle *bonum diffusivum sui*: goodness is diffusive of itself. This is the radical reason given by Aquinas for creation.[117]

Aquinas famously adopted from the Pseudo-Dionysius the doctrine of the *triplex via* for naming God, based upon the positive likeness of creatures to God, the deficiency of this likeness and the pre-eminent transcendence of God beyond creation. He could not have been aware that this triple doctrine had its origins in diverse dialogues of Plato. The earliest known formulation is found in the *Didaskalikos* of Alcinous, second century AD, who is reporting a long established tradition within Platonism.[118] The approach to God in positive analogous terms, through causality, is anticipated by the simile of the sun in the *Republic*.[119] The negative step through the removal of attributes is prefigured in the First Hypothesis of the *Parmenides*.[120] Finally, the purified affirmation of transcendent perfection has its antecedent in the ascent of the soul from beautiful things to the 'vast ocean of beauty' in the *Symposium*.

In the celebrated passage of the *Symposium* Plato's Diotima describes the ascent of the philosophic soul to the plenitude of divine suprasensual beauty.[121] In the reply to an objection in the Secunda Secundae there is a passage which has remarkable parallels. Aquinas refers to six steps whereby the soul rises by means of creatures to the contemplation of God. It is worth citing *in toto*:

---

usu partium II, XI, 14, ed. Helmreich (Leipzig: Teubner, 1909; repr. Amsterdam: Hakert, 1968), pp. 158–9 [ET: *On the Usefulness of the Parts of the Body*, trans. Margaret Tallmadge May (Ithaca, NY: Cornell University Press, 1968), p. 533].

[117] See O'Rourke, *Pseudo-Dionysius*, pp. 241–54.

[118] *Didaskalikos* X, H 165, pp. 16–34. See John Whittaker, *Alcinoos, Enseignement des doctrines de Platon* (Paris: Les Belles Lettres, 1990), pp. 24–5, 106–7; John Dillon, *The Middle Platonists* (Ithaca, NY: Cornell University Press, 1996), p. 284; John Dillon, *Alcinous: The Handbook of Platonism* (Oxford: Clarendon Press, 1993), pp. 18–19, 109–10; Werner Beierwaltes, *Platonismus im Christentum* (Frankfurt am Main: Klostermann, 1998), pp. 135–6; F. O'Rourke, 'Via Causalitatis; via negationis; via eminentiae', in *Historisches Wörterbuch der Philosophie*, vol. 11: *U–V* (Basel: Schwabe, 2001), cols. 1034–8.

[119] Pierre Aubenque, 'Néoplatonisme et analogie de l'être', in *Néoplatonisme: Mélanges offerts à Jean Trouillard* (Fontenay-aux-Roses: Ecole normale supérieure, 1981), p. 72: 'Le paradigme de l'analogie métaphysique n'est pas à chercher dans les analyses philosophico-linguistiques d'Aristote, mais dans le discours allégorique de la *République* platonicienne.'

[120] Plato's negative theology is likewise explicit in the *Timaeus* 28c, where he states that 'the father and maker of all this universe is past finding out, and even if we found him, to tell of him to all men would be impossible'.

[121] *Symposium* 210a–d.

For the first step consists in the mere consideration of sensible objects; the second step consists in going forward from sensible to intelligible objects; the third step is to judge of sensible objects according to intelligible things; the fourth is the absolute consideration of the intelligible objects to which one has attained by means of sensibles; the fifth is the contemplation of those intelligible objects that are unattainable by means of sensibles, but which reason is able to grasp; the sixth step is the consideration of such intelligible things as reason can neither discover nor grasp, which pertain to the sublime contemplation of divine truth, wherein contemplation is ultimately perfected.[122]

On the lasting significance of Plato and his unique legacy, Gerard Manley Hopkins remarked:

There have been in all history a few, a very few men, whom common repute, even where it did not trust them, has treated as having had something happen to them that does not happen to other men, as having *seen something*, whatever that really was. Plato is the most famous of these... Human nature in these men saw something, got a shock; wavers in opinion, looking back, whether there was anything in it or no; but is in a tremble ever since.[123]

Plato occupies a singular place in the spiritual history of humanity, challenging mankind to confront the transcendent mystery of reality. He bequeathed to mankind for evermore an abiding sense of self-awareness in the face of what is most great and magnificent. Aquinas was profoundly attuned to the mystery glimpsed by Plato. Had he been familiar with the dialogues, he would have seen how much they had in common. There is between them a latent but profound metaphysical sympathy, an underlying congeniality regarding what is sublime and significant in human life. Fundamental for each is that the world of experience is insufficient in itself, and therefore dependent on an absolute principle;

---

[122] *ST* IIaIIae, Q. 180, art. 4, ad 3: 'Per illa sex designantur gradus quibus per creaturas in dei contemplationem ascenditur. Nam in primo gradu ponitur perceptio ipsorum sensibilium; in secundo vero gradu ponitur progressus a sensibilibus ad intelligibilia; in tertio vero gradu ponitur diiudicatio sensibilium secundum intelligibilia; in quarto vero gradu ponitur absoluta consideratio intelligibilium in quae per sensibilia pervenitur; in quinto vero gradu ponitur contemplatio intelligibilium quae per sensibilia inveniri non possunt, sed per rationem capi possunt; in sexto gradu ponitur consideratio intelligibilium quae ratio nec invenire nec capere potest, quae scilicet pertinent ad sublimem contemplationem divinae veritatis, in qua finaliter contemplatio perficitur.'
[123] John Pick (ed.), *A Hopkins Reader* (New York: Image Books, 1966), p. 224 (emphasis in original).

equally central for both thinkers is man's transcendent destiny, although their attitudes differ. Plato, in the words of Ps.-Justin, has 'the air of one who has descended from above, and has accurately seen all that is in heaven';[124] for him man is a creature not of earth but of heaven (φυτὸν οὐκ ἔγγειον, ἀλλ᾽ οὐράνιον).[125] With Aquinas, man walks the earth in the promise and hope of beatitude, a *viator* travelling towards the transcendent mystery. For St Thomas, 'the most wonderful thing of all is that earthly and corruptible man may be promoted to the possession of spiritual and heavenly things'.[126]

Aquinas's philosophy was an original and creative synthesis of elements from all traditions; a thinker of vast erudition, he had at immediate recall to memory all the relevant literature available in his time: philosophical, theological, scriptural and secular. Vigorously active 'in the quick forge and working-house of thought', he took truth from every quarter. Aristotle remained the master *philosophus*, the guide on the path of safe discovery. But on occasion Aquinas recognised that although Aristotle's position is more certain (*certior*), it appears less satisfactory (*minus sufficiens*) than that of Plato.[127] Although secure it does not always lead to the depths of Plato's wisdom. Precisely because he emulated Aristotle, Aquinas could embrace the truth of others with greater certainty. Inspired frequently – sometimes consciously, sometimes unwittingly – by truths first disclosed by Plato, we can say with Aquinas: *amica veritas, ergo amicus Plato.*

---

[124] See Christoph Riedweg (ed.), *Ps.-Justin (Markell von Ankara?), Ad Graecos de vera religione (bisher 'Cohortatio ad Graecos')* (Basel: Friedrich Reinhardt, 1994), 5, 2: Πλάτων μὲν γὰρ, ὡς ἄνωθεν κατεληλυθὼς, καὶ τὰ ἐν οὐρανοῖς ἅπαντα ἀκριβῶς ἑωρακὼς.

[125] *Timaeus* 90a.

[126] *Expositio super Job ad litteram*, 37: 'Hoc autem est inter omnia maxime admirandum quod homo terrenus et corruptibilis ad spiritualium vel caelestium possessionem promoveatur.'

[127] *DSS* 2, no. 11, p. 46: 'Haec autem positio Aristotelis positio certior quidem videtur esse eo quod non multum recedit ab his quae sunt manifesta secundum sensum, tamen minus sufficiens videtur quam Platonis positio.'

Index of Names

Abelard 219–20
Ackrill, J. L. 256, 257
Adam, K. 187
Aertsen, J. 109
al-Ghazali 75, 76
Alberigo, Giuseppe 51
Albert the Great 50, 217
Anscombe, G. E. M. 35, 38, 147
Anselm 219
Aristotle (*see also* subject index) 167, 241
Aubenque, Pierre 277
Aubert, J.-M. 197
Audet, Th.-André 52

Bakker, P. 119
Baltes, Matthias 273
Barnes, Michel René 32, 33
Barth, Karl 31, 38, 211–12
Baudrillard, Jean 175
Baur, J. 186
Beierwaltes, Werner 248, 273, 277
Berg, D. 199
Berger, D. 189, 193, 199, 216
Bernard of Clairvaux 219–20
Beyschlag, K. 214
Biggar, Nigel 171
Billot, Louis 29
Black, Rufus 171
Blanchette, Oliva 150
Bockenforde, W. 197
Bockle, F. 197
Boff, Clodovis 207
Boland, Vivian 248, 255, 271
Bonaventure 221, 229, 245
Bonino, Serge-Thomas 30
Booth, Edward 248

Bouëssé, Humbert 224
Bouquillon, Thomas 163–4
Boyle, Joseph M. 176
Boyle, Leonard E. 43, 47, 50, 51
Brinkhuis, M. 119
Burrell, David B. 34–5, 76, 77, 79, 80, 108, 109, 118, 147
Butler, Judith 168

Cahill, Lisa Sowle 175–6
Cajetan, Thomas de Vio 196, 222
Callus 51
Cano, Melchior 203, 222
Capreolus, John 49
Caprile, Giovanni 193
Caputo, John D. 39, 86–90
Carabine, Deidre 78
Catão, Bernard 224–5, 237
Cessario, Romanus 225
Chauvet, L.-M. 220
Chenu, Marie-Dominique 29, 51, 66, 108, 112, 154, 187, 188, 191, 192, 217
Chesterton, G. K. 151
Clark, Mary T. 270
Clarke, W. Norris 248, 250, 264, 266–7, 268, 269
Collingwood, R. G. 154
Congar, Yves 191, 192
Corbin, Michel 108, 109, 110, 112, 133, 154, 218
Costa, Cristina D'Ancona 75
Crombie, I. M. 257
Crotty, Nicholas 224
Curran, Charles E. 170–1

Davidson, Arnold 83

Index of Subjects